The Cogniti of Vision

Martha J. Farah

University of Pennsylvania

Blackwell
Publishing

First published 2000
Transferred to digital print 2002

2 4 6 8 10 9 7 5 3 1

Blackwell Publishers Inc.
350 Main Street
Malden, Massachusetts 02148
USA

Blackwell Publishers Ltd
108 Cowley Road
Oxford OX4 1JF
UK

Library of Congress Cataloging-in-Publication Data
Farah, Martha J.
    The cognitive neuroscience of vision / Martha J. Farah.
        p.   cm. — (Fundamentals of cognitive neuroscience)
    Includes bibliographical references and index.
    ISBN 0–631–21402–X (hbk : alk. paper). — ISBN 0–631–21403–8 (pbk. : alk. paper)
    1. Vision.   2. Cognitive neuroscience.   3. Visual perception.
I. Title.   II. Series.
    [DNLM: 1. Visual Cortex—physiology.   2. Visual Perception.   WL 307   bF219c   2000]
    QP475.F27   2000
    612.8'4—dc21
    DNLM/DLC
    for Library of Congress   99–38076
                                                                          CIP

British Library Cataloguing in Publication Data
A CIP catalogue record for this book is available from the British Library.

Commissioning Editor: Martin Davies
Development Editor: Alison Dunnett

Typeset in $10\frac{1}{2}$ on 13 pt Palatino
by Graphicraft Limited, Hong Kong

Printed and bound in Great Britain by
Marston Lindsay Ros International Ltd,
Oxfordshire

For Teddy

Contents

Illustrations

Series Editors' Preface

Science often seems to proceed in an excruciatingly slow and incremental manner. Between initial grant submissions and renewals, between first-year projects and doctoral defenses, it is rare to see significant change in our theories or methods. For researchers in cognitive psychology and behavioral neuroscience, the 1970s and early 1980s were periods of this type of steady but not terribly exciting progress.

By the mid-eighties, however, something decidedly non-incremental happened: a new field, called cognitive neuroscience, was born. Those of us lucky enough to have been working in the parent disciplines of cognitive science and neuroscience at this time experienced a major change in our thinking about mind and brain. Before, they had seemed related in principle, but not in any way that was tractable in research practice. Now the relation between mind and brain seemed not only tractable, but essential for further progress in understanding mind and brain. By the end of the decade, cognitive scientists were using data from brain-damaged patients and functional neuroimaging to test theories of normal cognition, and neuroscientists were using cognitive theories and methods, including computational modeling, to interpret brain anatomy and physiology. A host of new meetings, societies, journals, and funding initiatives signaled that a new field had been established.

From the perspective of the late 1990s, cognitive neuroscience continues to flourish, and to attract new researchers from the ranks of graduate students and senior scientists alike. Unfortunately, these individuals face a problem: the dearth of general, introductory reading in cognitive neuroscience. It was with this problem in mind that we undertook to edit the *Fundamentals of Cognitive Neuroscience* series. The books in this series are primers on the essential topics of cognitive neuroscience. Each volume provides a theory-oriented overview of the current state of the art in its area, drawing upon the results of multiple research techniques. In addition to the present volume, other volumes currently in press or in preparation will cover Attention, Language, Memory, Motor Control, and Vision. Additional volumes are likely to be commissioned in the near future.

Humans are visual creatures, and much of our brain is devoted to the processing of visual input. The cognitive neuroscience of vision is therefore central to our understanding of mind and brain. It is also one of the most successful areas within cognitive neuroscience, drawing on a number of highly developed component disciplines such as visual psychophysics, machine vision, and visual neurophysiology, and forging an integration among them. This book surveys the state of our knowledge, highlighting the impressive degree of integration that has been achieved, as well as the major issues still unresolved.

Martha J. Farah
Mark H. Johnson

Preface

Writing this book has been an education for me, and not just because I had to learn most of the contents of the first chapter in order to write it! What really came as news to me was the profound change that has taken place in vision research over the past fifteen years, in the direction of truly integrative cognitive neuroscience. The last time I attempted to learn about the anatomy and physiology of vision, or about visual psychophysics, they were fields unto themselves, with relatively little mutual contact and even less contact with the fields of machine vision, cognitive psychology, and neuropsychology. These latter fields themselves grew in a fairly independent fashion throughout the sixties and seventies, with similarly sparse connections between them. As someone working on vision and making use of ideas from many of these disciplines, I was of course aware that the cognitive neuroscience of vision was a going concern. Yet until I stepped back and attempted to review the whole field of vision research, I did not fully appreciate the sea change that has occurred. Not that vision is solved or the synthesis is anywhere near complete! But the best single-unit physiologists are now thinking about the function that their cells of interest subserve, drawing on the concepts and methods of cognitive psychology and neuropsychology, and about how those cells might function within larger populations, drawing insights from computational vision systems. Reciprocally, the molar-level work of cognitive psychology and neuropsychology is making use of ideas and constraints from the known anatomy and physiology of vision and from the nature of computation in neural networks. Certain yawning gaps aside (e.g., binding within the ubiquitous distributed representations of the visual system, the achievement of orientation and other constancies), the major tasks of our visual system are being characterized and increasingly constrained by a broad base of different empirical approaches. If you squint, you can see one big picture.

Oddly enough, the one division that remains virtually unbridged is not a disciplinary boundary but simply the division between the study of early visual processing and later or so-called high-level vision. Any of the recent books you can find on vision will almost exclusively cover one end or the other, despite their more general titles. Because my modest little goal for this book was to cover it all, from the retina to consciousness, I made a special effort to include early vision here. My strategy was to start with basic textbooks, follow their references to review articles, and from there wade into the primary literature. I hope this long and painful writing process does not make for long and painful reading!

I am indebted to several colleagues for their help and advice while I was writing this book. In alphabetical order, they are John Duncan, Charlie Gross, Steve Hillyard, Mark Johnson, Jack Nachmias, Larry Palmer, and Bob Rafal. Larry Palmer, in particular, saved me from publishing dozens of embarrassing mistakes in the first two chapters, and always straightened me out with patience and diplomacy. Some of the research described in the later chapters was carried out by me in collaboration with others, and I'd like to take this opportunity to thank them again for their colleagueship. Collaborators whose insights and guidance are most directly apparent in the pages that follow include Geoff Aguirre, Laurel Buxbaum, Dave Plaut, Thad Polk, and Jim Tanaka. I would also like to acknowledge the excellent editorial work of Martin Davies at Blackwell's, and the sources of funding that supported the writing of this book: NINDS, NIA, and the Guggenheim Foundation. Finally, I would like to thank Irene Kan, who never balked at handling the piles of references, permissions, and other book-related work for which she was sorely overqualified, and whose good ideas and good cheer in all realms of work continue to be appreciated.

Acknowledgments

The author and publishers are grateful to the following for permission to reproduce or adapt material:

The MIT Press, Cambridge, for M. J. Farah, "Are there orthography-specific brain regions? Neuropsychological and computational investigation," in R. M. Klein and P. A. McMullen (eds), *Converging Methods for Understanding Reading and Dyslexia*, in press; M. J. Farah, "Visual perception and visual awareness after brain damage: A tutorial review," in M. Moscovitch and C. Umilta (eds), *Conscious and Unconscious Information Processing: Attention and Performance XV*, 1994.

Archives of Neurology and the authors, for an extract from D. F. Benson and J. P. Greenberg, "Visual form agnosia," *Archives of Neurology*, 20, 1969.

Where illustrations have been reproduced from previously published sources, full copyright acknowledgment is included in the relevant caption.

chapter one

Early Vision

1.1 Light, eye and brain

At this moment, light reflected from the page you are reading is being focused by the lens in the front of your eye to form an image on the retina in back. The image illuminates a mosaic of retinal cells that contain light-sensitive molecules. The light energy changes the shape of these molecules, which in turn changes the electrical states of the cells. In this way a light image, no different from what shines on the screen of a movie theater, is transformed into a neural image.

What happens next is the subject of this book. It is a story that can be told from start to finish only if one is willing to accept educated guesses at some junctures and frank declarations of ignorance at others. Nevertheless, if we allow ourselves the use of placeholders in our explanations of visual processing at any one stage, to be filled in by future research, I believe it is possible to tell a continuous narrative. With the retina as the starting point, and conscious awareness as the final destination, I do not feel too apologetic about using some placeholders! On the contrary, I am heartened by the amount of the understanding that has accumulated about each of the intervening levels of visual processing, and by the potential for integrating these different levels into a coherent whole.

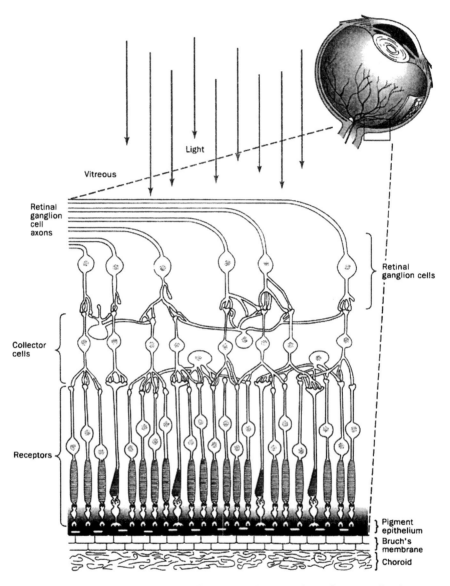

Figure 1.1   Cross-section through the retina, showing three functionally distinct layers of cells: receptor cells, collector cells, and ganglion cells.

From R. Sekuler and R. Blake, Perception, New York, McGraw-Hill, 1994.

1.2 The retina

Figure 1.1 is a cross section of the retina showing its three layers of cells, beginning with the photoreceptors. Notice that the photoreceptors come in two different shapes, rods and cones, from which they get their names. Rods and cones differ functionally from one another because of the different photosensitive chemicals they contain and the locations of those chemicals within them, as well as their different patterns of connectivity to cells in subsequent layers. Together they provide the first example of a general design strategy that is found throughout the visual system.

The duplex retina: the first instance of a general principle

Vision involves a surprising degree of division of labor, by which a seemingly unitary function is carried out by multiple specialized systems that operate in parallel. Among researchers in early vision, it tends to be called "partitioning," "multiplexing," or "parallelism," whereas "modularity" is the usual terminology in high-level vision and visual cognition. We can only guess at the teleological reason for such division of labor in any particular case, but often it appears to be a fairly straightforward solution to the problem of tradeoffs between two important processing requirements. In this case, at the very first layer of neurons in the visual system, there is a tradeoff between sensitivity to light and spatial resolution.

If the output from many receptor cells is pooled, lower levels of light can be detected. But this gain in sensitivity comes at the cost of lower spatial resolution. That is because once the outputs from different points on the retina are pooled, the information has been lost concerning which of those points were stimulated and which were not. Good resolution can be maintained by limiting the number of photoreceptor outputs that converge on later cells, but this results in poor sensitivity to low levels of light. Rather than choose one tradeoff or the other, the visual system partitions the image into two: one that favors sensitivity and one that favors resolution. The duplex retina therefore has a system of rods, with their greater individual sensitivity and their extensive convergence onto bipolar collector cells and

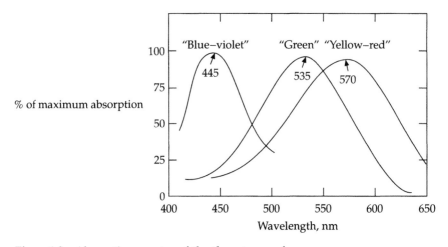

Figure 1.2   Absorption spectra of the three types of cones.
From H. R. Schiffman, Sensation and Perception: An Integrated Approach *(3rd ed.), New York, John Wiley and Sons, 1990. Copyright 1990. Reprinted by permission of John Wiley & Sons, Inc.*

ganglion cells, to give us a low resolution image of the world that persists under conditions of low illumination. It also has a system of cones, with their much more limited convergence, to give us a high resolution image of the world provided there is ample light (see Dowling, 1987, for further discussion of photoreceptors).

In addition to this difference between rods and cones, there are also differences among the cones. Cones can have one of three different photopigments, which absorb different wavelengths of light to different degrees. The strength of a cone's response is proportional to the amount of light energy absorbed by its pigment. Figure 1.2 shows the functions relating wavelength and absorption for the three different types of cone. The perceptual quality of color corresponds roughly to the physical property of wavelength (what is "rough" about this correspondence will be explained in the next chapter), so color or wavelength is represented in our nervous systems initially as the profile of responses across the three types of cone. For example, red is represented by activity in the long wavelength cones with relatively little response in the short and medium wavelength cones; progressively shorter wavelengths would each have a unique representation in terms of progressively more activity in the medium and short

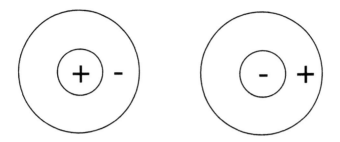

Figure 1.3 Schematic depiction of on-center/off-surround (left) and off-center/on-surround (right) receptive field structures.

wavelength cones and less activity in the long wavelength cones. The representation of a large set of entities, such as the set of discriminably different wavelengths, in terms of a profile of activity across a smaller number of basic features or dimensions, such as the three cone types, is an example of distributed representation. We will encounter distributed representation repeatedly at later stages of visual processing, and its benefits and drawbacks will be discussed in chapters 3 and 6, respectively.

A consequence of color vision's reliance on cones is that we are effectively color blind in low illumination. Recall that cones traded resolution for sensitivity, and are consequently inactive in the near-dark. This has more than once caused problems for a dinner guest trying to find my house: They remember the bright purple door that distinguishes my row house from the rest of the Philadelphia-Quaker-plain exteriors on the block, but on a winter evening they can see only shades of grey.

Retinal ganglion cells

Before the image has even left the eye, it has undergone extensive additional processing. One major result of this processing is that absolute levels of illumination have been all but laundered out of the image, replaced by a retinotopic map of *differences*: points in the visual field where a light region abuts a dark one. At the level of the individual retinal ganglion cell, this is reflected in the center–surround organization of their receptive fields, shown in figure 1.3. The so-called "on-center" cells are excited by light in a small patch of locations in the visual field ("on-center") and inhibited by light in the immediately adjacent regions ("off-surround"), and the "off-center" cells show the opposite reactions to light in center and surround (Dowling, 1987). This retinal processing is useful groundwork for the eventual perception of objects, because objects are not associated with any particular level of brightness, but rather with differences in brightness between themselves and their background. By passing only the difference values on to later levels, the differences can be amplified without having to represent the enormous range of values that would result from the amplification of the absolute levels. Similarly, the groundwork for color perception is laid by an "on–off" organization contrasting the outputs from different cone types.

Yet another major partitioning of the image occurs before it leaves the eye. This is the splitting of the image into the M and P channels, named for the magnocellular and parvocellular layers of the lateral geniculate nucleus (LGN) to which they project. (The M and P retinal ganglion cells are also sometimes referred to as parasol and midget cells, respectively; labels which bear a helpful mnemonic relation to the shapes and sizes of the two cell types, but an unfortunate alphabetic relation to their target LGN layers.) These two channels, which begin to diverge at the very first synapse of the visual system, between photoreceptors and collector cells (Shapley, 1995), have complementary strengths and weaknesses from the point of view of later perception. The M ganglion cells receive input from a relatively large number of photoreceptors, giving them good light sensitivity, or equivalently, good temporal resolution, in that the larger number of inputs allows them to sample for a shorter time. As already remarked, however, the good temporal resolution comes at the price of spatial resolution. The P cells receive input from a relatively small number of photoreceptors, giving them relatively good spatial resolution but correspondingly poor temporal resolution. Once again, mother nature chose to multiplex the image into two channels rather than accept the compromise of any single point on the tradeoff function, as represented in figure 1.4.

The M and P ganglion cells differ in ways other than their sheer number of inputs (see Reid, 1999, for a review). Among these differences, M cells are larger, with broader axons and consequently faster

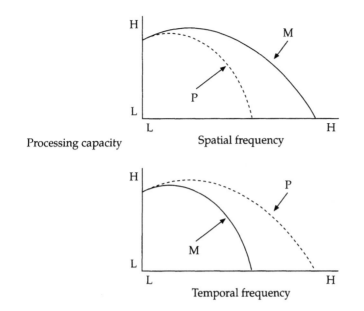

Figure 1.4 Schematic depiction of the complementarity of M and P channels for spatial and temporal information.

From P. H. Schiller, "Parallel pathways in the visual system," in B. Gulyas, D. Ottoson, and P. E. Roland (eds), Functional Organisation of the Human Visual Cortex, *Oxford, Pergamon Press, 1993.*

nerve conduction velocities, and their responses are more transient that those of P cells. Another important difference is that P cells show color selectivity whereas M cells do not. These differences are all consistent with a proposed division of labor between the M and P channels more generally, which will be discussed in the next section on the LGN. Briefly, the temporal resolution of the M cells equips them well for the perception of motion, as well as the detection of sudden stimulus onsets for purposes of redirecting spatial attention. The spatial resolution and color sensitivity of the P cells equips them for a major role in object recognition, for which pattern, color, and texture are important.

The bundle of axons leaving the eye, known as the optic nerve, splits into a number of pathways, two of which play the predominant roles in visual perception. (The remainder are involved in various visual reflexes and circadian rhythms.) The largest pathway, and the one most important for human vision, is called the geniculostriate pathway, because it includes the lateral geniculate nucleus and striate (or primary visual) cortex. The other important perceptual pathway out of the eye is the collicular pathway, which includes the superior colliculus and the pulvinar, converging with the geniculostriate pathway only in visual association cortex. The collicular pathway will not be discussed further in this chapter except to say that it is the phylogenetically older visual pathway, and in higher primates is involved mainly in spatial orienting and eye movement control. The collicular visual system will be discussed again in the last chapter, in connection with the syndrome of "blindsight."

1.3   The lateral geniculate nucleus (LGN)

The LGN is made up of the aforementioned magnocellular and parvocellular layers, and depicted in virtually every existing book on vision because this layered structure is so pleasingly distinct. There are two magnocellular layers, visible at the bottom of figure 1.5, and four parvocellular layers, visible at the top. The size difference for which the two cell types were named is easily visible. There is one LGN in each cerebral hemisphere, and each receives input from both eyes, although each eye's input remains segregated in different layers of the LGN, with each eye's "on" and "off" P cells also projecting to separate layers. Thus, the contralateral eye sends input to layers 1, 4, and 6, and the ipsilateral eye sends input to layers 2, 3, and 5.

The functional characteristics of neurons in the magnocellular and parvocellular layers of the LGN are much like those of the M and P cells of the retina, from which they receive input (Reid, 1999). As already mentioned, the receptive fields are monocular. Neurons in all layers show a center–surround organization. Magnocellular layers possess the best temporal resolution and parvocellular layers possess the best spatial resolution. Wavelength sensitivity is seen in most cells of the parvocellular layer, but not in the magnocellular layer. Although there are some differences between the responses of retinal ganglion cells and cells in the LGN – for example the LGN cells may have more powerful inhibitory surrounds than retinal ganglion cells

Figure 1.5 Section through the LGN of one hemisphere showing its two magnocellular layers (with their visibly larger cell bodies) on the bottom and four parvocellular layers on top. The dashed line shows the location of cells in each layer representing a single location in the visual field, demonstrating the precision of registration among each layer's retinotopic map.
From D. H. Hubel, Eye, Brain, and Vision, *New York, Scientific American Library, 1988.*

(Maffei and Fiorentini, 1972) – there does not appear to be any major transformation of the visual image going from retina to LGN.

This raises the question: What is the LGN for? At present, any answer to this question remains purely speculative. Most current speculations center on a possible modulatory role for the LGN, suggested by its connectivity with other brain areas. The LGN receives a major projection from the reticular activating system (Burke and Cole, 1978), which controls general level of arousal. It also receives a massive efferent, or feedback, input from visual cortex. Thus, the LGN is well situated to gate or amplify visual input to cortex as a function of both level of arousal and current cortical state. It is also possible that the LGN serves a developmental purpose, facilitating the wiring of the eye with the physically distant cortex in early life by providing a waystation.

Retinotopy in the LGN and beyond

The segregation of optic fibers into the six layers of the LGN is accomplished without disrupting the retinotopic organization of the image. Furthermore, the six retinotopic maps in each LGN are in register, so that a single point in the visual field is represented by cells directly above and below each other through the different layers. An indication of the precision of retinotopy and registration can be seen in figure 1.5. The superimposed line indicates the locations of cells in each layer corresponding to a single location in the visual field.

Retinotopy is common throughout the brain's visual representations, even in systems as remote from the retina as visual working memory representations in prefrontal cortex (Goldman-Rakic, 1987). In this sense, it is not at all metaphorical to refer to many visual representations as "images." When fixating the "C" in the word "CAT," for example, the neural representation of the A is physically located between the neural representations of C and T in many different parts of the brain. An appropriately graphic demonstration of this principle in the monkey brain can be glimpsed by looking ahead to figure 1.7.

Retinotopy has many advantages, including the "if it ain't broke" advantage of being the original format of visual information. In addition, the conservation of retinotopy allows easy communication between neurons representing neighboring parts of the visual field, and such local interactions are crucial to a huge number of visual functions, from replacing absolute levels of illumination with intensity differences as already discussed, to the computation of stereoscopic depth. Retinotopy also provides a common framework within which the representation of an object at one location can be co-indexed among disparate brain areas, which may be important for attentional processes discussed in chapter 7, and undoubtedly facilitates the wiring up of visual areas during development.

Division of labor between M and P channels

The properties of individual M and P cells in the retina, and magnocellular and parvocellular cells in the LGN, suggest that these two highly segregated systems serve different visual functions. What direct evidence do we have? One source of evidence comes from experiments in which sections of layers in the LGN of monkeys have been lesioned with small injections of ibotenic acid (Merigan and Maunsell, 1993; Schiller and Logothetis, 1990), thus disabling one of the two systems' representation of one sector of the visual field. The monkeys in these experiments can then be tested in psychophysical experiments to map out their impaired and preserved perceptual abilities. Although the results do not support total independence between the functions of the two systems, the overall pattern is more consistent than not with the predictions based on properties of individual cells: parvocellular damage has the most pronounced effect on color perception, and also affects form and depth perception at high spatial frequencies and low temporal frequencies; and magnocellular damage has the most pronounced effect on motion perception, and also affects form and depth perception at high temporal frequencies.

A surprising claim that has been made about the magnocellular layer of the LGN is that it is the locus of impairment in developmental dyslexia (Livingstone, Rosen, Drislane, and Galaburda, 1991). Given that reading is the paradigm case of static pattern recognition requiring good resolution of high spatial frequencies, this claim has been met with considerable skepticism. Nevertheless, its proponents point to psychophysical and physiological evidence from dyslexics showing sluggish responses to visual transients and autopsy findings of magnocellular layer abnormalities. As with most other proposals concerning the underlying problem in dyslexia, the final evaluation of this idea awaits further research (see Lovett, 1997, for further discussion).

The different characteristics of the M and P channels are an early manifestation of a division of labor found throughout the visual system. Phrased in the most general terms, the division is between systems specialized for objects' *appearances*, and systems specialized for objects' *spatio-temporal properties*. We will return to this dichotomy at the end of chapter 2, as an organizing scheme for the topics to follow. For the time being we need only note that, as a rough cut through the complexity of visual neurophysiology, it captures a certain thematic similarity in the way visual information is partitioned at different stages of visual processing. We have already seen the relation of the M and P cells of the retina, and the magnocellular and parvocellular layers of the LGN, to an "appearance" versus "temporal" dichotomy. In fact, the perception of location in space (as opposed to fine spatial acuity for pattern perception) seems to cluster with the functions of temporal resolution and motion perception in higher level visual areas, and hence the more general dichotomy can be signified as "appearance" versus "spatio-temporal" properties. In the remainder of this chapter we shall see how this segregation of anatomical connections and functional properties continues into primary visual cortex.

1.4   The primary visual cortex

The major cortical projection of visual information from the LGN is to primary visual cortex, also known as area 17 (in Brodmann's numbering scheme), striate cortex (for its stripe, visible to the naked eye), and V1 (first cortical visual area). The fibers linking LGN and primary visual cortex, which are called the optic radiation, preserve retinotopy while splaying out on their way to cortex such that the upper regions of the visual field are represented by fibers coursing ventrally (lower) and the lower regions by fibers coursing dorsally (higher).

In the days before CT scanning, the anatomy of the optic radiations and primary visual cortex allowed lesions to be roughly localized by mapping patients' visual fields, as shown in figure 1.6. Homonymous visual field defects, that is, areas of blindness that affect both eyes equally, imply that the lesion is posterior to the optic chiasm, as input from the two eyes is separate more anteriorly. Because the left optic radiation projecting to left visual cortex represent only the right visual field, and vice versa, visual field defects also reveal the side of the lesion. The altitude of the visual field defect is also informative, with lower quadrant blindess suggesting a parietal lesion because of the dorsal course of the optic radiation, and upper quadrant blindness

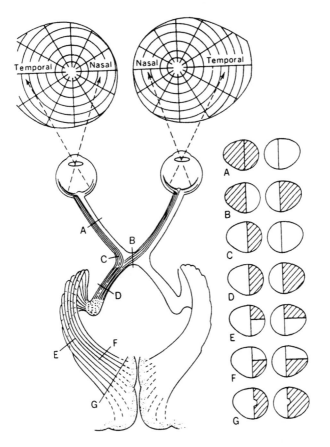

Figure 1.6 Correspondences between location of lesion within the visual system and pattern of visual field defects.
From J. Homans, A Textbook of Surgery, Springfield, IL, Charles C. Thomas, 1945.

suggesting a temporal lesion because of the ventral course. An early and classic generalization about the anatomy of face recognition was based on this type of analysis. J. C. Meadows (1974) reviewed the visual field charts of a large number of cases of prosopagnosia, or face recognition impairment, and found a preponderance of left upper quadrant defects, often with defects in the upper right as well. From this he was able to infer that the critical substrates for face recognition are in the right temporal cortex or bilateral temporal cortices in most people, a conclusion that has only been confirmed and fine-tuned with the advent of structural and functional brain imaging in recent years.

Within primary visual cortex the image continues to have a strong retinotopic organization. The allocation of relatively more neurons to the representation of the central few degrees of the visual field, where objects of interest are generally located through eye and head movements, results in a distortion of the image that has been termed "cortical magnification." The retinotopy and cortical magnification of primary visual cortex are known to us through a variety of methods. In the early decades of this century, neurologists correlated the locations and sizes of patients' regions of blindness with the locations and sizes of their cortical lesions measured post mortem. Of course, single unit recording in animals and functional neuroimaging in humans have also now confirmed these two properties. The most photogenic evidence for retinotopy and cortical magnification in primary visual cortex comes from the deoxyglucose radioactive labeling method. In Tootell, Silverman, Switkes, and Valois' (1982) classic study, a monkey fixated a polar grid stimulus shown on the left of figure 1.7 while radioactive tracer accumulated in metabolically active brain cells. The pattern of radioactivity in this monkey's primary visual cortex is shown on the right. It is a strikingly literal image of the stimulus, distorted only by cortical magnification.

Simple and complex cells

A major change in the image representation going from LGN to cortex is seen in the new variety of receptive field structures in primary visual cortex. Although center–surround cells are still found, one can discern at least two new and qualitatively distinct categories of receptive field structures (see von der Heydt, 1995, for a more complete review). David Hubel and Torsten Weisel were awarded a Nobel Prize for the discovery of these cells' function and anatomical organization, and for pioneering the technique of single cell recording in cortex, which soon became the predominant neurophysiological research method. Here is Hubel's description of the historic moment in 1958, in which the pair of researchers obtained their first recording from primary visual cortex, and discovered how different the receptive fields of these cells were from the retinal and LGN cells they knew:

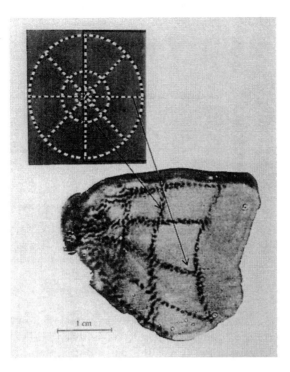

Figure 1.7 Pattern of metabolically active cells in the primary visual cortex of one hemisphere in a monkey who fixated the radial pattern shown above, demonstrating both retinotopy and cortical magnification of the fovea.

From R. Tootell et al., "Deoxyglucose analysis of retinotopic organization in primate striate cortex," Science, 218, 1982. Copyright 1982 American Association for the Advancement of Science.

The position of the microelectrode tip ... was unusually stable, so that we were able to listen in on one cell for about nine hours. We tried everything short of standing on our heads to get it to fire ... After some hours we began to have a vague feeling that shining light in one particular part of the retina was evoking some response, so we tried concentrating our efforts there. To stimulate, we used mostly white circular spots and black spots. For black spots, we would take a 1 by 2 inch glass laboratory slide, onto which we had glued a black spot, and shove it into a slot in an optical instrument ... to project onto the retina. For white spots, we used a slide of the same size made of brass with a hole drilled in it ... After about five hours of struggle, we suddenly had the

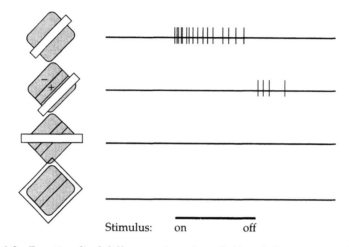

Stimulus: on   off

Figure 1.8   Bar stimuli of different orientations (left) and the responses they evoke from a simple cell in primary visual cortex (right).
From D. H. Hubel, Eye, Brain, and Vision, *New York, Scientific American Library, 1988.*

impression that the glass with the dot was occasionally producing a response, but the response seemed to have little to do with the dot. Eventually we caught on: It was the sharp but faint shadow cast by the glass as we slid it into the slot that was doing the trick . . . Most amazing was the contrast between the machine-gun discharge when orientation of the stimulus was just right, and the utter lack of a response if we changed the orientation or simply shined a bright flashlight into the cat's eyes. (Hubel, 1988).

Hubel and Weisel (1962) classified the cells they discovered into three categories. "Simple cells" respond to edges at particular locations and orientations within the visual field, as shown in figure 1.8. They are like center–surround cells in that particular regions of the visual field excite and inhibit them. They differ from center–surround cells in that the excitatory and inhibitory regions are elongated, and thus mere spots of light, or edges at the wrong orientation, will have little effect on their response level.

"Complex cells" are aptly named in that the relation between light and dark regions of the visual field, on the one hand, and the cells' responses, on the other, is much more complex than for the previous two cell types. Indeed, it is impossible to represent a receptive field for these cells in any way analogous to figures 1.3 and 1.8. Complex cells represent a more abstract type of visual information, at least partially independent of location within the visual field. Some complex cells are selective for a certain length of contour, and for this reason were initially classified as a separate category of cells, known as "hypercomplex" or "end-stopped."

It is difficult to read about center–surround, simple, and complex cells and not conclude that they represent a feedforward sequence or hierarchy of visual processing. The cells' responses become increasingly specific with respect to the form of the stimulus (from any light discontinuity to an oriented edge or bar) and increasingly general with respect to viewing conditions (from just one location to a range of locations relative to fixation). These dual trends in form specificity and viewing-condition generality are the essence of visual object recognition. Extrapolated, they would culminate in cells that respond to as specific a form as can be recognized (e.g., your grandmother's face) generalized over changes in size and orientation as well as location (e.g., front view or profile). Furthermore, it is easy to imagine how a fairly simple pattern of excitatory connections, funneling input from each level to the one above, could account for increasing stimulus specificity and viewpoint generality. Figure 1.9 illustrates the relation between center–surround cells and simple cells, which could themselves converge on a complex cell, according to this idea. In principle the process could be continued all the way to "grandmother cells," and this would certainly constitute a solution to the problem of object recognition. However, it is not the only possible solution and there are reasons to believe it is not really a feasible solution. In the next chapter we will discuss the pros and cons of "grandmother cells" and the alternatives in more detail. But quite apart from the question of extrapolating beyond primary visual cortex, can we even assume that center–surround, simple, and complex cells constitute a hierarchical progression? And if so, a progression towards what?

Hubel and Weisel (1962) originally conjectured that there was a hierarchical relation among center–surround, simple, and complex cells, as shown in figure 1.9. In more recent years, a variety of alternative conceptions have been entertained for the wiring up of these three cell types. Horizontal connections within primary visual cortex have received more attention, and ways in which such connections

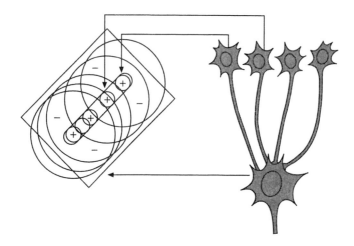

Figure 1.9   Illustration of the idea that simple cells result form the feedforward convergence of a set of center–surround cells.
Adapted from D. H. Hubel and T. N. Wiesel, "Receptive fields, binocular interaction and functional architecture in the cat's visual cortex," Journal of Physiology, 160, 1962.

could create simple cell receptive fields by lateral interaction, as opposed to the purely afferent vertical convergences hypothesized by Hubel and Weisel, have been explored (e.g., Gilbert, 1992).

Not only have the relations among the different cell types, and the genesis of simple and complex receptive fields, been subject to much discussion and reconsideration; so have the interpretations of those receptive field structures, in the sense of their perceptual function or purpose. In Hubel and Weisel's original experiments, the stimuli that evoked the strongest responses from simple and complex cells were oriented edges and bars. However, there are two problems with inferring from these data that simple and complex cells are edge and line detectors. First, it is difficult to exclude the possibility that some as yet untried stimulus would evoke an even better response (although it is possible to search a stimulus space for an optimal stimulus automatically, if one grants certain assumptions about the functions relating stimulus changes to cells' responses). Second, even if one could be certain of having mapped the true receptive field, interpreting that receptive field relative to its function in perception involves a very different kind of scientific inference. Unlike a simple question of fact concerning receptive field structure, which could be disconfirmed by a single observation, questions of function are harder to answer definitively, and depend on broad considerations encompassing one's psychological theory of perception and one's knowledge of the properties of cells up and downstream.

An interesting illustration of the ambiguity of receptive field structures, relative to their perceptual function, comes from a neural network simulation developed by Lehky and Sejnowksi (1988). The goal of their network was to represent the shape of a surface explicitly in terms of the orientations and curvatures of the axes of curvature, given a greyscale image. This is a nontrivial problem because the pattern of light intensity values over the surface depends jointly on the surface shape, angle of illumination with respect to the surface, reflectance of the surface, and orientation of the surface with respect to the viewer. The input image had been filtered through the equivalent of center–surround receptive fields, and the network was trained with a set of correct pairings of input images with surface curvature descriptions using the backpropagation learning rule. Learning by backpropagation involves a two-step mapping first between the input patterns and patterns in a layer of so-called hidden units interposed between input and output units, and then between the patterns in the hidden units and the desired output patterns. When the learning process was complete, Lehky and Sejnowski analyzed how the network was performing the task, and in particular, what the hidden units were doing. Expressed in terms of receptive fields, the hidden units had developed oriented receptive fields that could be activated maximally by bars of a particular orientation at a particular location. In other words, their receptive fields were just like those of simple cells. But in this case it seems wrong to say that the function of these units is to represent line segments or edges. We know what their function is because we know the one and only purpose for which they developed, to help extract the principle curvature from images of surfaces! The relevance of this simulation to the study of real simple cells is that it raises the question: How can we know if they, too, have some purpose other than representing edges and lines? The short answer is we cannot.

This brief excursion into the realm of alternative interpretations for the functions of simple and complex cells should remind us of how much we can know about the anatomy and physiology of the brain while remaining essentially clueless about the functionality of this anatomy and physiology. The "bottom-up" research approach of strict reductionists – understand all the components and you'll understand the whole – is unlikely to work for a system as complex as the brain. Hubel and Weisel's research yielded an exquisitely detailed picture of the organization and function, at the neuronal level, of primary visual cortex, and this picture has been revised and elaborated by a number of other groups. Yet we still know relatively little about how this part of the brain subserves perception, in the sense of identifying functional perceptual mechanisms with the machinery described by neuroscientists. In the remainder of this chapter we will encounter this type of disappointment again. The organization of the early visual cortices has been subject to intensive study in neuroscience, resulting in some hard-won and, in their own way, beautiful descriptions of visual anatomy and physiology. However, in many cases it has been impossible to assign any functional role to this organization, and when such attributions have been made they have been controversial.

Organization of orientation-selective cells in primary visual cortex

In addition to describing the receptive field properties of cells in primary visual cortex, Hubel and Weisel also documented a highly systematic anatomical organization for these cells, and subsequent work by them and others has revealed other intricacies of organization as well. A brief summary of these anatomical discoveries is presented here, along with the familiar question, "What is the functional significance?", and some attempts at an answer.

As already mentioned, simple and complex cells have preferred orientations. An electrode penetration that is exactly perpendicular to the cortical sheet will encounter cells with the same orientation preference. For this reason, Hubel and Weisel coined the term "columns" to describe the organization of orientation selectivity in visual cortex. Moving over a bit and penetrating again, one finds a column with a different orientation preference. The preferences of neighboring columns are not random; they vary in a smooth and systematic way, with greater displacements on the cortical surface corresponding to

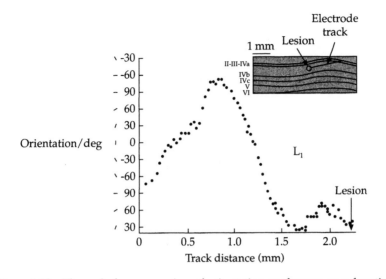

Figure 1.10 The orderly progression of orientation preference as a function of electrode position during an oblique penetration of primary visual cortex.
From R. C. Reid, "Vision," in M. J. Zigmond, F. E. Bloom, S. C. Landis, J. L. Roberts, and L. R. Squire (eds), Fundamental Neuroscience, *San Diego, Academic Press, 1999.*

greater angular disparities between the preferred orientations of the columns. As shown in figure 1.10, a penetration that is oblique with respect to the cortex will pass through multiple columns, revealing the gradual change in orientation preference from column to column.

Superimposed upon the varying orientation preference is another dimension of variation: eye preference, or "ocular dominance." Although information from the two eyes converges in primary visual cortex, it is nevertheless true that most neurons respond more to one eye's inputs than to the other's. These groupings by ocular dominance are also called columns. It takes about eighteen to twenty columns to represent all orientations for both eyes, and such an aggregate is called a "hypercolumn." Each hypercolumn encodes information about one small sector of the retina, and neighboring hypercolumns represent neighboring sectors of the retina. Figure 1.11 shows an idealized rendering of the combined orientation and ocular dominance organization. These are not really so straight and orthogonal, as can be seen in figure 1.12, where grey lines show orientation columns with the same orientation preference and black lines show same-eye

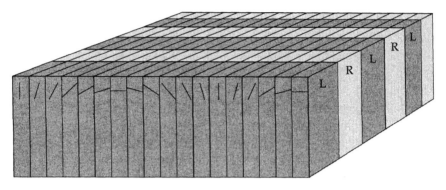

Figure 1.11   Idealized depiction of the organization of orientation selectivity and ocular dominance in primary visual cortex.

Adapted from D. H. Hubel and T. N. Wiesel, "Receptive fields, binocular interaction and functional architecture in the cat's visual cortex," Journal of Physiology, *160, 1962.*

Figure 1.12   Reconstruction of the actual relations between orientation columns (gray) and ocular dominance columns (black) in primary visual cortex.

From K. Obermayer and G. G. Blasdel, "Geometry of orientation and ocular dominance columns in monkey striate cortex," Journal of Neuroscience, *13, 1993.*

ocular dominance columns. Given the tendency for neighboring columns to share orientation preference and ocular dominance, "walls" would have been a better architectural word than "columns" to describe these groupings. Ocular dominance columns, in particular, may run for many millimeters through cortex, while being just a fraction of a millimeter wide.

What is the purpose or the advantage of the columnar organization just described? In effect, it is a reasonably efficient spatial arrangement for minimizing the distance between neurons representing similar stimulus properties along three different stimulus dimensions simultaneously (eye of origin, orientation, and retinotopic location), and there may be computational advantages to this. For example, it allows for the pooling of information from columns representing similar properties, to improve signal discriminability: If a single column whose preference is vertical edges seen from one eye at one location is responding, there might indeed be a vertical bar out there, or there might be some random noise in that part of the system. The latter possibility is less likely if vertically tuned neurons in a different ocular dominance column also respond, or if neurons tuned to 15-degree edges at the same location also respond to some extent, or if neurons tuned to vertical edges at an adjacent location also respond. Alas, this is pure conjecture.

A different, but not mutually exclusive, kind of answer to the question of "why this organization" concerns the processes by which the cells in primary visual cortex acquire their stimulus preferences, which may produce the organization as a kind of side effect. A cell's receptive field is determined by its pattern of connections to other cells and their receptive fields. Such connections can be modified, particularly during certain developmental "critical periods" by the patterns of activity among the cells. The Hebb rule, which can be summarized metaphorically as "neurons that fire together wire together," tells us that neurons in primary visual cortex will acquire receptive field characteristics depending on the correlations among their activations and the activations of other neurons to which they are connected. The statistics of visual experience and early visual pathway activity contain many correlations that are relevant to setting up or preserving connections between neurons in cortex that represent similar

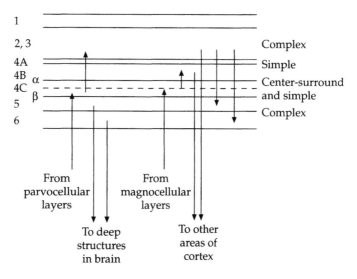

Figure 1.13   Layers of primary visual cortex, with distribution of cell types and afferent and efferent connections shown.

From D. H. Hubel, Eye, Brain, and Vision, *New York, Scientific American Library, 1988.*

orientations at similar locations and to neurons that represent input to the same eye (e.g., Miller, Keller, and Stryker, 1989).

There is one final dimension of organization that should be mentioned here, a histological organization which has important correspondences with the response properties of individual neurons and with the connectivity of primary visual cortex to up and downstream areas. This is the layered structure of cortex, which runs orthogonal to the orientation and ocular dominance columns. Figure 1.13 shows a simplified schematic illustration of this organization, with inputs from the LGN arriving in layer 4C (alpha and beta, for magnocellular and parvocellular inputs, respectively), output to other cortical areas leaving from layers 2, 3, and 4B, and different distributions of center–surround, simple, and complex cells among layers 2 through 6.

Cytochrome oxidase-rich patches

Cytochrome oxidase is an enzyme that is found in certain portions of visual cortex. Its role in visual perception, if any, is not known, but it has functioned as a marker for another type of organization within

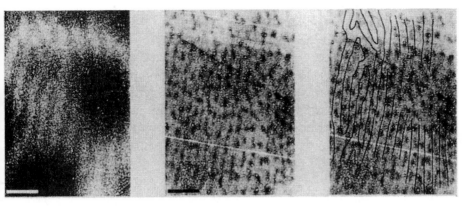

Figure 1.14 Ocular dominance columns (left) and cytochrome oxidase blobs (middle) and their relation to one another (right).
From J. C. Horton and D. H. Hubel, "A regular patchy distribution of cytochrome-oxitdase staining in primary visual cortex of the macaque monkey," Nature, 292, 1981. Reprinted with permission; copyright 1981 Macmillan Magazines Ltd.

primary visual cortex. Wong-Riley (1979) stained primary visual cortex for cytochrome oxidase, and in layers 2 and 3 she saw what she described as "puffs": scattered spots of stained tissue. In subsquent years Hubel and Livingstone related these structures, which they term "blobs," to a large-scale theory of visual perception linking the earlier retinal and geniculate M and P channels with later anatomical and physiological systems in association cortex, and with perceptual functions including color, shape, and motion perception.

Before discussing the connections of blobs and so-called interblob tissue to up and downstream areas, let us relate them to the organization so far discussed for primary visual cortex. As already mentioned, they are found in layers 2 and 3. Their relation to ocular dominance columns is shown in figure 1.14, with ocular dominance columns revealed by radioactive tracer, and blobs revealed by staining for cytochrome oxidase. Using blood vessels as anchorpoints for alignment, the two images were superimposed, showing that blobs are located in the centers of ocular dominance columns. The relation of blobs to orientation columns was investigated by Hubel and Livingstone (1987), who made tangential electrode penetrations of the kind that originally revealed the existence of orientation columns, and found periodic interruptions of the orderly progression through different orientations, where cells responded to all orientations equally. These points corresponded to the locations of blobs.

Physiologically, blobs are distinguished from interblob regions of layers 2 and 3 not only by their insensitivity to orientation, but also be being monocular, indifferent to direction of motion, and primarily responsive to low spatial frequencies (Livingstone and Hubel, 1984). So what are these one-eyed, orientation- and direction-blind, fuzzy-sighted blobs good at? Color perception, or more specifically, wavelength discrimination. Many blob cells respond to light in the center of their receptive field only within a narrow band of wavelengths, and are inhibited by complementary colors; in some cells the surround region of their receptive field shows the opposite preferences. In contrast, cells in the interblob regions of the same cortical layers show relatively less wavelength discrimination, but good tuning for high spatial frequencies, binocularity, and orientation selectivity. These contrasted with yet a third class of cells, in layer 4B, that are sensitive to binocular disparity, selective for orientation but not wavelength, and highly selective for direction of motion.

Livingstone and Hubel (1988) suggested that these three classes of cells constituted an elaboration of the earlier M and P divisions. According to their original hypothesis, layer 4B was the continuation of the magnocellular stream (via layer 4C alpha) and was specialized for motion perception and stereoscopic depth perception. Both blobs and interblobs were continuations of the parvocellular processing stream (via layer 4C beta) and were specialized for color perception and shape perception, respectively. Layer 4B, blobs, and interblobs project to different parts of V2, which can also be discerned by staining for cytochrome oxidase concentrations (dark-staining thick and thin stripes, separated by pale stripes respectively). The response properties of cells in V2 seem broadly consistent with the further continuation of specialized processing streams, and Livingstone and Hubel have further sketched out possible projections for these two streams beyond V2, into higher level association cortices. Figure 1.15 shows the patterns of connectivity and segregation among systems, along with hypothesized visual functions of each.

Livingstone and Hubel's sweeping hypothesis provided a much-needed "big picture" for the often detail-oriented world of visual neurophysiology. Unfortunately, only parts of their idea currently

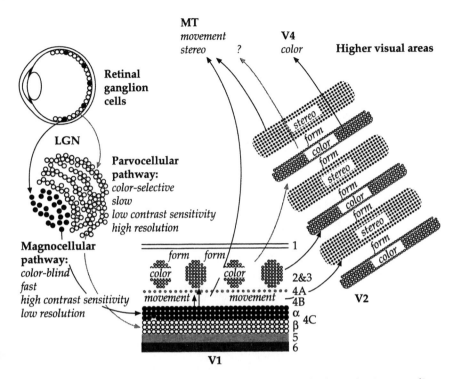

Figure 1.15   Original version of Livingstone and Hubel's hypothesis, according to which anatomically and physiologically defined subdivisions of the visual system formed independent streams of processing from the retina through extrastriate cortex, with each stream responsible for distinct perceptual functions.

From M. S. Livingstone and D. H. Hubel, "Segregation of form, color, movement, and depth: anatomy, physiology, and perception," Science, 240, 1988. Copyright 1988 American Association for the Advancement of Science.

remain plausible. As they and others continued to study the connectivity among early visual areas, it became clear that the hypothesized segregation into streams breaks down at many points. Although there is considerable segregation at each level of the visual system, and distinctions between color, fine or detailed form, motion, and depth seem to capture some of the relevant functional specializations within each level, no area's function can be fully characterized by a single-word label. Furthermore, the notion of "streams" – the carrying forward of segregation across levels of processing – is only sometimes true. For example, both blobs and interblobs are now known to receive both magnocellular and parvocellular inputs (Nealey and Maunsell, 1994) and area V4, which is believed to be of special importance for color perception, receives input from both parvocellular and magnocellular layers of the LGN (Ferrera *et al.*, 1992, 1994). The effects of LGN lesions on psychophysical judgments, described earlier, also argue against a complete segregation. On the other hand, the vast majority of input to area MT in remote extrastriate cortex, an area crucial for motion perception, is magnocellular (Maunsell *et al.*, 1990), consistent with a high degree of segregation in this case.

In the next chapter we will return to the issue of specialization and segregation at higher levels of visual cortex in the context of the "two cortical visual systems" hypothesis. Segregation is also manifest, implicitly, in the remainder of the book: the chapters on object, face, and word recognition are exclusively concerned with "appearance" processing by ventral visual areas; and the chapters on attention and neglect are primarily concerned with "spatio-temporal" processing by dorsal visual areas.

chapter two

From Local to Global Image Representation

2.1 Stuff versus things

Early vision has been characterized as representing "stuff" rather than "things" (Adelson and Bergen, 1991). This is apt in that the retina, LGN, and primary visual cortex produce a representation of the visual field that is rich in information about each local point, yet relatively lacking in large scale structure. Orientation, wavelength, motion, binocular disparity, and a variety of other visual properties at each point of the light array are well represented by the time the image reaches primary visual cortex. But properties of coherent objects, such as their shape, color, motion, and location in the world, have not yet been represented. In the broadest terms, the goal of vision is to take the array of light that hits the retina and derive a representation of the *things* that gave rise to it. From the stage of primary visual cortex, with its predominantly local representation of the image, we have a long way to go towards that goal.

The most immediate task is to begin to represent more global aspects of the image: to determine which bits of contour and surface "go together," in the sense of belonging to the same object, to assess the overall pattern of motion across the visual field for consistency with coherent object motion or viewer motion in a particular direction, and to infer the true color of an object's surface by taking into account the wavelengths present throughout the image. Much of this processing takes place in extrastriate cortex, the belt of visual association cortex surrounding primary visual cortex.

We begin our discussion of global image processing with color and motion perception. In addition to being perceptual problems that are solved by the strategy of *combining* information from neighboring image locations, color and motion perception have also been held up as examples of highly *segregated*, independent processing streams or "modules." The contradiction is only superficial, in that the hypothesized segregation and independence for each of these dimensions of vision is relative to other dimensions of vision, not relative to the same visual dimension at other image locations. That is, color perception would be considered to be modular if it was functionally independent of the perception of motion and other visual dimensions, such that it could be compromised only by lesions that have no effect on other perceptual abilities. For both color and motion perception, we will consider below the degree to which their brain implementation is modular.

2.2   Color perception

Before discussing the sense in which color perception requires a transition from local to global image processing, let us review color processing in early vision. Color perception begins with the partitioning of the light signal into three wavelength ranges, corresponding to the retina's three cone types. Within the retina, color contrast is enhanced by P cells, whose center–surround receptive field structures respond to discontinuities between colors. Contrast, sometimes called "opponency," continues in the parvocellular layers of the LGN to an even greater degree, that is, with even more pronounced effects of the surround portion of the receptive field. In primary visual cortex, cells in layers 2 and 3 carry color information in both blob and interblob regions, with blob cells being particularly tuned to color. Contrast effects are further boosted at this level by double opponent responses in some cells, that is, a center–surround organization in which complementary colors have opposite excitatory and inhibitory effects in a given region of the visual field. The blobs project to the thin stripes of V2, which also has color-selective responses, and which in turn projects to V4.

Up to this point, the responses of color-selective neurons correspond fairly directly to the wavelengths present in the immediate vicinity of their relatively small central receptive fields. In this sense it is more accurate to speak of them as wavelength-selective than color-selective. This is not a coy reluctance to use a psychological term when only physical parameters can be measured. Rather, it is a real distinction between the context dependence of color perception, and the context independence with which local wavelengths are signaled by neurons in the retina through V2.

Color constancy

To understand the role of global image context in color perception, recall a little high school physics: Light is composed of a spectrum of different wavelengths, and when it interacts with an opaque surface some wavelengths will be absorbed and the rest will be reflected. The color of an object is determined by the wavelengths that it absorbs, a property of the material's electronic structure. Our perception of object color is based on reflected light, but of course the spectral composition of reflected light depends on both the spectral reflectance or true color of the surface and the spectral composition of the incident light. Thus the likely composition of the incident light must be taken into account if the color of a surface is to be inferred from the wavelengths it reflects. Our ability to do this is termed "color constancy."

Because the same light that illuminates one object in a scene generally illuminates much if not all of the rest of the scene, context is useful for disentangling the ambient light from the spectral reflectance of individual objects. Thus the wavelengths present throughout the image can be used to infer the nature of the ambient light and hence achieve color constancy. Land (1977) demonstrated the importance of context in the perception of color using large fields of colored patches, which he termed "Mondrians" after the artist who painted canvases with squarish patches of color. The perceived color of a particular patch appears constant with varying illumination, so long as the illumination is homogeneous. However, if the patch is illuminated by one light and its context by another, color constancy breaks down.

Zeki (1983) has recorded from wavelength-sensitive cells in visual cortex while Mondrians were presented to them and while varying the spectral composition of the ambient light. In early visual areas, neuronal activity is a function of the wavelengths reflected from whichever patch of color is in the cell's receptive field. Remarkably, this is not the case in area V4. Instead, many V4 neurons respond to the color of the Mondrian patch and are not influenced by changes of illumination. Their responses agree with the color percepts of a human observer rather than with the wavelengths that a telephotometer would detect. Schein and Desimone (1990) report that the receptive fields of V4 neurons often have large inhibitory surrounds, in some cases extending into the opposite visual hemifield, and that the surrounds are tuned to the same wavelength as the excitatory central receptive field. This would have the effect of discounting any wavelength present in the center of the receptive field if it were also present in the broad context of the surround, and thus suggests a general candidate mechanism for the color constancy shown by V4 neurons. The role of long-range cortical interactions in the computation of color constancy is supported by the finding of color constancy failure for stimuli separated by the visual midline in a split-brain patient, whose hemispheres had been surgically disconnected to control epilepsy (Land *et al.*, 1983).

Is V4 "the color center"?

There is no doubt that V4 plays a role in color perception, although the exact nature of that role has been the subject of some debate. Is color perception modular, in the sense described earlier of depending only on certain neural mechanisms or brain areas that are not also needed for other visual abilities? Zeki appears to endorse the modularity of color perception, and in particular the idea that V4 is the "color center," although this stance has been controversial. Oddly enough, Zeki's writings (e.g., 1983, 1990, 1993) do not include an explicit statement of what it would mean for V4 to be the color center. In discussing the history of the idea of a color center, he contrasts it with extreme holist views of visual perception, which deny any division of labor within the visual system. Thus the color center hypothesis may only amount to the very moderate and reasonable hypothesis that V4 is more involved in the perception of colors than other areas, rather than the stronger hypothesis that, of the visual association areas, V4 is both necessary and sufficient for color perception, or that V4 plays no role other than color perception.

Moving beyond hermeneutics, empirical research on V4 has garnered a fascinating if not altogether consistent body of information about the role of this area in color perception. It promises insights not only about color perception, but about the more general issue of specialization and division of labor among higher cortical processes. Let us review this research and then attempt to synthesize it.

Cerebral achromotopsia

The earliest evidence for a color center comes from human neuropsychology. Since the nineteenth century, neurologists have described patients whose main visual disturbance, following a stroke, was a loss of color perception (see Zeki, 1990, for a review). Such "achromotopsic" patients may show good acuity, motion and depth perception, and object recognition. Not infrequently, object, face, and word recognition are transiently affected, and in some cases recognition disorders permanently accompany the color blindness, presumably because the critical lesion sites for cerebral color blindness are near the critical lesion sites for pattern recognition. One particularly fascinating case of achromotopsia was reported at length in the *New York Review of Books* by Sacks and Wasserman (1987), who begin their article with a letter they received from the patient:

> "I am a rather successful artist just past 65 years of age. On January 2nd of this year I was driving my car and was hit by a small truck on the passenger side of the vehicle.
> When visiting the emergency room of the hospital, I was told that I had a concussion. While taking an eye examination, it was discovered that I was unable to distinguish letters or colors. The letters appeared to be Greek letters. My vision was such that everything appeared to me as viewing a black and white television screen.
> Within days, I could distinguish letters and my vision became that of an eagle – I can see a worm wiggling a block away. The sharpness of focus is incredible.
> BUT – I AM ABSOLUTELY COLOR BLIND.
> . . . My brown dog is dark grey. Tomato juice is black. Color TV is a hodge-podge. Etc. Etc."

The artist was given several objective tests of color perception such as the Ishihara plates, consisting of numerals defined solely by color contrast with the backgrounds, and the Farnsworth–Munsell test, in which equiluminant disks must be arranged by color, and his performance on these tests confirmed that he had no color perception whatsoever. Other aspects of his vision, including his reading, appeared normal.

Achromotopsia affected the artist's life in a number of ways. At a practical level, he was forced to rely on his wife for help in selecting each day's clothes, and required that foods be set out in fixed positions so that he could discriminate mustard from mayonnaise and ketchup from jam. After being stopped by the police for running two red lights, he realized that he must also rely on the position of traffic lights. Disgusted by the changed appearance of most foods, he began to prefer food that is naturally black or white: rice, olives, black coffee and yogurt. Even in his imagination he could no longer experience color; all aspects of his self-generated visual imagery remained clear and vivid except for color, a parallelism between imagery and perception that will be discussed further in chapter 9. The inability to either see or imagine color was distressing for the artist, who had previously used color extensively in his work. Figure 2.1 shows one painting from a series done by this patient after his injury, intended to convey the grimness of a world seen in shades of grey.

In many cases, a unilateral lesion will result in color loss in just one hemifield, consistent with retinotopic mapping of the human color center, and this condition is known as "hemiachromotopsia." A particularly selective and well-studied case of hemiachromotopsia was described by Damasio, Yamada, Damasio, Corbett, and McKee (1980). Although acuity, depth perception, motion perception, and object recognition were normal in both hemifields, they differed strikingly for color perception: "He was unable to name any color in any portion of the left field of either eye, including bright reds, blues, greens and yellows. As soon as any portion of a colored object crossed the vertical meridian, he was able instantly to recognize and accurately name its color. When an object such as a red flashlight was held so that it bisected the vertical meridian, he reported that the hue of the right half appeared normal while the left half was gray."

Achromotopsia should be distinguished from three other color-related disorders that sometimes follow brain damage in humans.

Figure 2.1 Still life painted by an artist with acquired cerebral achromatopsia, intended to convey his visual experience to others.

"Color anomia" refers to an impairment in producing the names of colors. It is sometimes seen in isolation from anomia for other types of words (Goodglass, Wingfield, Hyde, and Theurkauf, 1986) but it is not a disorder of color perception. There is no difficulty performing the types of color perception tests that the achromotopsic artist failed and no subjective loss of color perception.

"Color agnosia" is a less clearly defined entity, which like color anomia does not involve impaired color perception. It is said to involve a loss of knowledge about colors. I have never understood what is meant by this, and indeed almost every author seems to have a different interpretation in mind (Tranel, 1997; Kinsbourne and Warrington, 1964; Luzzatti and Davidoff, 1994; DeVreese, 1988). At least some of the data on color agnosia seem to require an explanation that is neither perceptual nor linguistic *per se*: Kinsbourne and Warrington showed that their patient could learn arbitrary associations between pairs of objects, noncolor names, and numbers, but could not learn associations between colors and noncolor names or numbers, nor between color names and other things. Furthermore, in these and other tasks, both the "colors" black, white, and grey, and the names "black," "white," and "grey," were spared.

Moving right along, to a third and more comprehensible type of color-related disorder, we come to impaired color–object association. With this disorder, the patient sees colors normally and knows how to use color names in the context of overlearned or abstract associations ("lemon yellow" or "green is the color of envy"). But knowledge of the typical colors of objects in the absence of a verbal association is impaired. This could be one specific result of a more general impairment in visual image generation, to be discussed further in chapter 9.

The lesions in achromotopsia are usually on the inferior surface of the temporo-occipital region, in the lingual and fusiform gyri. In full achromotopsia they are bilateral, and in hemiachromotopsia they are confined to the hemisphere contralateral to the color vision defect.

Evidence from neuroimaging

Positron emission tomography (PET) and event-related potentials (ERPs) provide largely consistent results with the human lesion literature. In an early study comparing passive viewing of colored Mondrians with passive viewing of greyscale Mondrians that were matched for luminance, a single area showed a significant difference in blood flow as measured by PET. It was located in lingual and fusiform gyri bilaterally, in perfect accord with the evidence from achromotopsia (Lueck, Zeki, Friston, Deiber, Cope, Cunningam, Lammertsma, Kennard, and Frackowiak, 1989). A later paper by the same group (Zeki, Watson, Lueck, Friston, Kennard, and Frackowiak, 1991) replicated this result with a larger number of subjects. In a PET study contrasting attention to the color of elements in a display with passive viewing of the same display, or with attention divided among multiple stimulus attributes, Corbetta, Miezin, Dobmeyer, Shulman, and Petersen (1991) found color-related activity localized to two regions: the collateral sulcus (which runs between the fusiform and lingual gyri; hence another finding consistent with the human lesion literature) and dorsolateral occipital cortex, an area not previously associated with color perception.

Gulyas and Roland (1994) also used PET to identify color-specific processing areas, and found activation in the previously mentioned areas as well as a host of others in occipital, temporal, parietal, and frontal cortices bilaterally. The involvement of such widespread areas may be due to the less well-controlled nature of their comparison. In the color condition, subjects viewed random noise patterns made of yellow, green, blue, and red, and judged whether reds predominated. In the comparison condition, subjects viewed black and white random noise patterns and judged whether white predominated. In the comparison task, stimuli were either balanced between black and white or white predominated (one target, one foil), whereas in the color task, stimuli were either balanced or any of the colors could predominate (one target, four foils). In addition, the displays in the two conditions were not matched for luminance contrast. Hence, it is reassuring that this PET comparison did show activation in the same areas that have been identified previously, as it did involve color perception, but it is not terribly troubling that so many other, previously unnoticed, areas became active, as the conditions being compared differed in ways other than the presence of color.

A different method was used to localize cortical color processing in the human brain by Allison, McCarthy, Nobre, Puce, and Belger (1994). They studied epileptic patients who, for diagnostic purposes, had electrodes temporarily implanted in their brains. ERPs recorded with such electrodes allow precise localization of their sources. Subjects passively viewed blue or red checkerboard patterns, to which ERPs were recorded, and before each pattern they were shown an adaptation stimulus with either the same color or the other color. The authors reasoned that only color-sensitive regions would show a difference in response to checkerboard preceded by same versus different color adapting stimuli. Such areas were identified in the fusiform and lingual gyri, and in the same general region of dorsolateral occipital cortex that was activated in Corbetta *et al.*'s PET study. Using the same electrodes to stimulate the patients' cortices with a weak current, they found that just these areas tended to produce alterations in color perception when stimulated.

Conflicting evidence and unresolved issues

Single unit recording in monkeys shows V4 to have a large number of wavelength-selective cells, many of which modulate their responses according to the wavelengths present in broad areas of the image, thus accomplishing color constancy. Humans can lose color perception

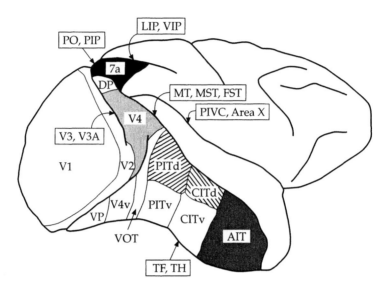

Figure 2.2   Location of V4 in the monkey brain.
Drawn according to figures published in J. H. R. Maunsell and W. T. Newsome, "Visual processing in monkey extrastriate cortex," Annual Review of Neuroscience, *130, 1987, copyright 1987 by Annual Reviews; and D. C. Van Essen, "Functional organization of primate visual cortex," from A. Peters and E. D. Jones (eds),* The Cerebral Cortex, *vol. 3,* Visual Cortex, *New York, Plenum Publishing, 1985.*

after focal lesions of visual association cortex, and the critical lesion site in these cases is the one location that is consistently activated by color in neuroimaging experiments. What a beautiful convergence of evidence for a color center in monkey and man! Alas, there is other evidence that requires, at the least, a modification of these ideas on localized color processing, and possibly a reconsideration of the most essential parts of the claim.

One reason for caution when interpreting the single unit data and the human lesion and neuroimaging data in terms of the same hypothesized color center is the patently different locations of the relevant areas in monkey and man. As shown in figure 2.2, monkey area V4 is fairly high up on the lateral surface of the hemisphere. As shown in figure 2.3, the human color center, as identified by lesions and neuroimaging, is on the inferior surface of the brain, and if anything, more medial than lateral. Of course, the evolutionary changes by which monkey and human brains differ might be expected

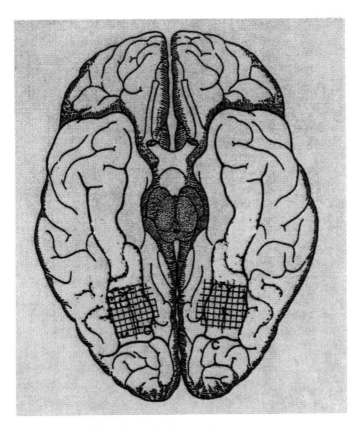

Figure 2.3 Location of the "color center" of the human brain, identified by ERPs recorded from the cortical surface (grid) and two PET studies (labeled C and L).

From T. Allison, G. McCarthy, A. C. Nobre, A. Puce, and A. Belger, "Human extrastriate visual cortex and the perception of faces, words, numbers and colors," Cerebral Cortex, 5, 1994. Reprinted by permission of Oxford Unviersity Press.

to rearrange the gross anatomy somewhat, and so it is possible that homologous areas would be found in different places. Indeed Clarke and Miklossy (1990) examined the cytoarchitecture, patterns of myelinization, and callosal connections of the posterior brain areas in monkey and man, and concluded that the human homologue of monkey V4 is likely to be in an inferior position, on the posterior fusiform gyrus. Thus the different positions of the putative color centers of the two species is not reason to conclude that they are not equivalent;

nevertheless, it deprives us of what could have been a reassuring sign of their equivalence, had they been located in areas that were obvious homologues.

Another qualification that must be added to the statement that V4 is "the color center" is that V4 is also a crucial area for form-related processing. It is the major source of input to temporal lobe areas that house object representations. Accordingly, most of its cells are selective for simple aspects of form, such as certain aspect ratios and spatial frequencies (Desimone and Schein, 1987). Of course, this does not imply that V4 is not an essential, or even *the* essential, area for color perception. It simply means that V4 is not a "dedicated" color module, with no other visual functions.

The most stubbornly inconsistent data concerning the existance of a color center come from Heywood and Cowey's (1987, 1992) studies of color perception in monkeys with lesions of V4. These investigators reasoned that, if monkey V4 and the critical lesion site for achromotopsia in humans are homologues, then bilateral lesions of V4 should create achromotopsic monkeys. The results could not have been more opposite to the predictions. Unlike human achromotopsics, who are utterly color blind but have normal object recognition and pattern vision, Heywood and Cowey's operated monkeys relearned the color discrimination tasks used to assess color perception, and eventually showed only the most subtle impairment, but had profound and enduring deficits in form discrimination! To verify that their tasks were not somehow inadequate, they tested a human achromotopsic with the same tasks and he performed appropriately poorly (Heywood and Cowey, 1993). Thus Heywood and Cowey were led to question the equation of the human color center with area V4, saying that such an equation "implies its lengthy migration from the lateral surface, ventrally to the fusiform gyrus, a migration which fails to maintain topological relations and therefore seems highly unlikely" (1993, p. 202).

In sum, there is strong evidence in favor of a specialized color center in the human brain, coming from both functional neuroimaging and studies of achromatopsia, and the latter source of evidence also implies that this area is necessary for color perception. The differences between lesion effects in monkey and human brains are puzzling. Do they result from a qualitative difference between monkey and human brains? Or from a nonhomology between the ventral areas implicated in studies of the human brain and the lateral areas that have been studied in monkeys? These issues will probably not be resolved until the human functional neuroimaging studies can be replicated with monkeys.

2.3 Motion perception

Just as local measurement of wavelength provides ambiguous information about object color, so local measurement of motion in early visual areas provides ambiguous information about object motion. And just as the solution for color perception was to go from local to global, using wavelengths present in the surrounding image to disambiguate each local measurement, so too motion perception requires global processing, in the sense of using information from multiple local measurements. Before examining what is known about the more global motion representation of higher visual areas, let us review the main facts about local motion representation in early visual areas.

Most visually responsive neurons respond better to a moving stimulus than to a stationary one. This is not necessarily the mark of a system devoted to motion perception, however. In most cases the response to motion is not direction-selective, and is presumably the result of reduced fatigue or habituation in afferent pathways. It seems more sensible to speak of direction-selective neurons, and their upstream inputs, as comprising a system for motion perception. By this criterion, we can identify the M cells of the retina and the magnocellular layer of the LGN as part of a visual motion system, for although they are not direction-selective, they are optimized for detecting moving stimuli (as discussed in the previous chapter) and they provide input to the earliest direction-selective cells to be found in the primate brain, in primary visual cortex. (Lower species have direction-selective cells in more peripheral parts of their visual systems, for example the retinal flying bug detectors of Lettvin, Maturan, McCulloch, and Pitts', 1959, famous report, "What the Frog's Eye Tells the Frog's Brain.") The direction-selective cells of V1 are found in layer 4B; some of these project directly to area MT (for "middle temporal"), shown in figure 2.4, and some project to the thick

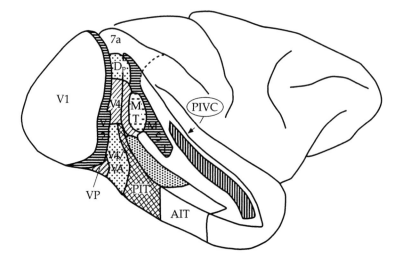

Figure 2.4   Location of MT in the monkey brain.
Modified from J. H. R. Maunsell and W. T. Newsome, "Visual processing in monkey extrastriate cortex," Annual Review of Neuroscience, *130, 1987; copyright 1987 Annual Reviews.*

cytochrome-oxidase stripes of V2, and from there to area MT. Both areas V2 and MT have direction-selective neurons, and indeed most all of the neurons in MT are direction selective. Although the magnocellular layers of the LGN project fairly widely, providing input to blobs and interblobs, and ultimately contributing to activity in area V4, the inputs to area MT are almost exclusively magnocellular (Maunsell, Nealey, and DePriest, 1990). In other words, although extreme views of M and P system segregation are contradicted by evidence of divergence as these pathways project into cortex, it nevertheless appears that area MT receives relatively pure magnocellular input.

The aperture problem

Imagine you are a simple cell in layer 4B of primary visual cortex, tuned to vertical edges, and such an edge passes from left to right (let us say "eastward") through your receptive field at a slow speed, causing you to fire. Now imagine the edge with a different motion: moving quickly and "northeastward." And for a third variant, at an

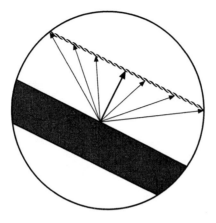

Figure 2.5   The aperture problem: With just this local view of the moving line, we cannot tell if it is moving at one speed in a direction perpendicular to itself, or at a faster speed in a direction more aligned with itself.

From T. J. Sejnowski and S. J. Nowlan, "A model of visual motion processing in area MT of primates," in M. S. Gazzaniga (ed.), The Cognitive Neurosciences, *Cambridge, MA, MIT Press, 1995.*

intermediate speed and "east by southeastward." Although you are called a direction-selective cell, you would fire equally to all three events; they would look the same to you. As is illustrated schematically in figure 2.5, through the small "aperture" of your receptive field, you can only perceive the component of motion that is perpendicular to your orientation selectivity. Solving the aperture problem requires combining information from different apertures, and in this sense arriving at a more global view of the scene.

The contrast between the measurement of component motion and the perception of real stimulus motion has been studied using patterns composed of differently oriented stripes, like that shown in figure 2.6. When the pattern as a whole moves from left to right, the motion components measurable though local apertures move in two different directions. Of course, if we combine the information available about neighboring one-dimensional component motions, we can reconstruct the real two-dimensional motion of the pattern. When shown moving patterns like figure 2.6, V1 neurons invariably respond to the component motions, whereas a sizeable fraction of the cells in area MT respond to pattern motion (Movshon *et al.*, 1985). These

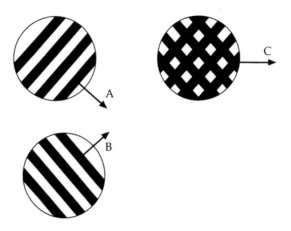

Figure 2.6　Example of stimuli used in experiments distinguishing component and pattern motion perception. The plaid pattern on the right is perceived by us, and responded to by our pattern-selective neurons, as moving to the right, but component-selective neurons respond to the diagonal motions of the component stripes.
From R. J. Snowden, "The perception of visual motion," Current Opinion in Neurobiology, 2, 1992.

cells, which have considerably larger receptive fields than their V1 inputs, have combined information about neighboring local component motions.

The component-selective cells of V1 and MT thus represent a local type of motion information, and the pattern-selective cells of MT represent a more global type of motion information that is derived from the combined responses of multiple local responses, and which corresponds to the true two-dimensional motion of patterns in the visual field. A further step towards even more global processing of motion information takes place in area MST (for "medial superior temporal"), to which area MT projects. MST cells have yet larger receptive fields, and are selective for complex motions that involve broad sectors of the visual field, such as shrinking, enlargement, rotation, and translation. These properties of the "flow field" presumably play an important role in visuo-motor behavior, including orienting with eyes and head movements, and locomotion, as they convey information about looming objects' time to contact, and the viewer's heading.

Is MT the "motion center"?

The same questions that were asked about area V4 and color perception can be asked about MT and motion perception. They can be answered with more confidence in this case, because of the essentially perfect agreement among all sources of evidence. Just about every method in the cognitive neuroscience arsenal has been deployed in testing the relation between MT and motion perception, and the results suggest that MT is the crucial brain area in monkeys and humans, being both necessary and sufficient (among the higher visual areas) for the perception of motion. A very brief summary of this work will be given here.

Psychophysics with single neurons and whole brains

One way to assess the relation between the activity of a particular set of neurons and the perceptual ability of the whole brain is to compare their psychophysical functions. If they show similar functions relating the accuracy of a given perceptual discrimination to the relevant physical stimulus parameters, then there is no reason to assume that other brain mechanisms are involved, and hence there is reason to infer that the neurons under study exclusively mediate the perceptual ability. Britten, Shadlen, Newsome, and Movshon (1992) did this with MT and a direction discrimination task.

The task was to decide which of two possible directions of motion predominated in a large set of moving dots, like that shown in figure 2.7. On any given trial, a subset of the dots moved in one of the two directions to be discriminated (left versus right, or up versus down) and the rest moved in random directions. The larger the proportion of dots moving in a correlated way, the easier the task. Britten *et al.* trained the monkeys to make a behavioral response indicating the perceived direction of coherent motion, and also recorded the activity of neurons selective for the direction to be discriminated. Although a small number of cells outperformed or underperformed the whole monkey, the vast majority showed the exact same ability to discriminate direction of motion, as measured by the amount of correlation needed in the display to enable reliable discrimination.

No Correlation   50% Correlation   100% Correlation

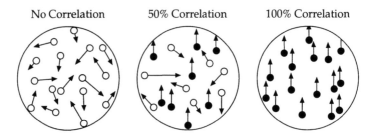

Figure 2.7   Example of stimuli used in experiments measuring direction discrimination. The smaller the proportion of coherently moving dots, the harder the discrimination.
From W. T. Newsome and E. B. Pare, "A selective impairment of motion perception following lesions of the middle temporal visual area (MT)," Journal of Neuroscience, 8, 1988.

Further evidence that the perceptual judgments of the whole animal are based solely on activity in MT comes from an analysis of behavioral and neural responses on trials in which the proportion of correlated motion was too low to allow reliable responding. On such trials, MT neurons selective for the direction to be discriminated will fire sometimes and produce no response at others. Remarkably, the animal's behavioral responses correlate highly with these neuronal responses. The monkey's errors on such trials are caused by the MT neurons' errors! (It might seem strange that behavior would correlate so well with single neuron responses when there are so many neurons in MT contributing to perception. Apparently activity among MT neurons is correlated, at least as regards this stimulus discrimination, and thus little additional information is obtained when the whole population is pooled; Newsome, Shadlen, Zohary, Britten, and Movshon, 1995.)

Yet further evidence of the crucial role of MT activity in motion perception is provided by microstimulation studies, in which neurons with known direction preferences are stimulated by a weak current and the animal's perceptual judgments are studied by behavioral means. Salzman, Murasugi, Britten, and Newsome (1992) took advantage of the fact that direction-selective neurons in MT tend to cluster in groups with similar direction preferences, so that stimulating with a microelectrode will tend to activate many cells with similar direction preferences, and the preferences can be known without recording from a huge number of cells. They compared the monkey's behavioral responses in the direction discrimination task when cells with relevant direction preferences had been stimulated and when they had not, and found a systematic biasing of the monkey's responses (and thus presumably the monkey's perceptions) toward the direction preferred by the stimulated cells. Thus, Newsome and his colleagues have overcome a significant limitation on the kinds of inferences that can be drawn on the basis of simply measuring brain activity, whether in single unit recording experiments or in functional neuroimaging of whole brains. They have shown that activity in MT is not only correlated with motion perception, but is actually causal of motion perception. They have thus ruled out the (admittedly pretty implausible) alternative hypothesis that MT activity is just a spillover or side-effect of activity elsewhere, and that it is the activity elsewhere that actually enables motion perception.

Lesions in monkey and man

Another method for establishing that a particular brain area is causally related to a perceptual process is the time-honored lesion method, which can be applied with some modifications to both animal and human subjects. Newsome and Pare (1988) used the motion discrimination task just described with monkeys who had undergone unilateral lesioning of area MT by injection of ibotenic acid. Consistent with the idea that MT is specialized for motion perception (i.e., needed for motion perception and not needed for other visual processes), these monkeys suffered large impairments for motion discrimination in the contralateral hemifield (analogous to hemiachromatopsia, and consistent with the retinotopic mapping of MT) and no impairments in color perception, acuity, or stereoscopic depth perception. One slightly puzzling aspect of Newsome and Pare's results is that motion discrimination in their task gradually recovered in the operated animals. It is currently unknown what new pathways have been recruited in these animals to solve the task. However, in a similar task Cowey and Marcar (1992) found that complete removal of area MT caused an enduring impairment, and in a speed discrimination task, Schiller (1993) likewise found long-term effects of MT lesions.

Turning to the human brain, there have been a small number of cases described of humans who have lost the ability to see motion following brain damage (see Zeki, 1993 for a review). By far the best-studied case is that of Zihl, Von Cramon, and Mai (1983). This was the case of L.M., a 43-year-old woman who, following bilateral strokes in the posterior parieto-temporal and occipital regions, was left with a few mild neuropsychological impairments and a major visual impairment, namely the complete inability to perceive visual motion. In addition to an elegant series of experimental investigations, the authors elicited the following information from L.M. herself (p. 315):

> The visual disorder complained of by the patient was a loss of movement vision in all three dimensions. She had difficulty, for example, in pouring tea or coffee because the fluid appeared to be frozen, like a glacier. In addition, she could not stop pouring at the right time, since she was unable to perceive the movement in the cup (or a pot) when the fluid rose. Furthermore, the patient complained of difficulty following a dialogue because she could not see the movement of the face and especially the mouth of the speaker. In a room where more than two people were walking she felt very unwell and insecure, and usually left the room immediately because "people were suddenly here or there but I have not seen them moving." The patient experienced the same problem, but to an even more marked extent in crowded streets or places, which she therefore avoided as much as possible. She could not cross the street because of her inability to judge the speed of a car, but she could identify the car itself without difficulty. "When I see the car at first, it seems far away. But then, when I want to cross the road, suddenly the car is very near." She gradually learned to estimate the distance of moving vehicles by means of the sound becoming louder.

Zihl *et al.* (1983) tested L.M.'s visual perception in a variety of simple experimental tasks and compared her performance with that of normal subjects. In her color and depth perception, object and word recognition, and a variety of other visual abilities tested by these authors, L.M. did not differ significantly from normal subjects. In addition, her ability to judge the motion of a tactile stimulus (wooden stick moved up or down her arm) and an auditory stimulus (tone-emitting loudspeaker moved through space) was also normal.

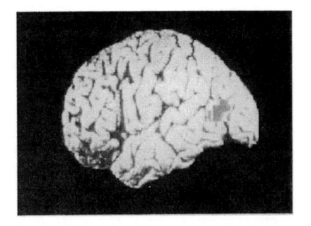

Figure 2.8 Reconstruction of presumed critical lesion for producing motion blindness in a human.
From S. Zeki, A Vision of the Brain, Oxford, Blackwell Scientific Publications, 1993.

In contrast, her perception of direction and speed of visual motion in horizontal and vertical directions within the picture plane and in depth was grossly impaired. In a follow-up study, Zihl, Von Cramon, Mai, and Schmid (1991) found L.M.'s condition essentially unchanged.

Overall there is an impressively good correspondence between the monkey and human lesion literatures. Both species show a sparing of all visual functions other than motion perception. Both species show a profound and, with bilateral lesions, permanent, impairment in a variety of visual motion tasks. And in both species the critical brain area is similarly situated. Figure 2.8 shows a reconstruction of what Zihl and colleagues take to be the relevant area of damage in their case L.M., projected onto a lateral view of the brain. Making allowances for the overall differences between human and monkey brains, this part of L.M.'s lesion looks a lot like the location of MT shown in figure 2.2.

Functional neuroimaging in humans

Converging evidence for a motion center in the human brain comes from imaging the brains of normal humans performing tasks involving motion perception. Zeki *et al.* (1991) compared patterns of regional cerebral activity during passive viewing of sets of black squares against a white background, when the squares moved and when they were stationary. Many visual areas were activated in both of these conditions, but only a small region at the junction of areas 19 and 37 on the lateral surface of the brain, corresponding well with the lesion shown in figure 2.8, was significantly more active in moving condition relative to the stationary condition. A similar localization is suggested by the visual attention experiment of Corbetta *et al.* (1991): Attention to the motion of a moving display results in more neural activity in this area than attention to other visual aspects of the same display.

   In sum, there is evidence from functional neuroimaging and from patient studies that visual motion perception is carried out in a localized brain region, and that this region is necessary for motion perception. A similar conclusion follows from a number of ingenious studies of monkey neurophysiology. The cerebral basis of motion perception seems to be similar in monkeys and humans, with a common localization in posterior lateral temporal cortex.

2.4   Image segmentation: from local to global form perception

The trend from local to global image properties is also very much apparent in the processing of form information. The receptive field sizes of neurons in primary visual cortex constitute very small windows through which to view the world. Somehow the visual system must determine that a tiny glimpse of table top and a tiny glimpse of table leg are related in a way that a tiny glimpse of chair back or teapot are not, even if they are separated by the same or even less distance. This task has been referred to as *image segmentation*, because it involves segmenting the regions corresponding to the table apart from other regions of the image, and as *perceptual grouping*, because just the regions corresponding to the table must be grouped together. It is also sometimes known as *binding*, because those same regions must be bound together, but this term also has a more general use, as when the redness and roundness of an apple are bound together.

Although image segmentation does not seem an especially pressing issue for a visual system that is processing gratings and bars, or even Snodgrass and Vanderwart pictures that appear in the center of an otherwise blank computer screen, it is an important and difficult task with real world visual scenes. Look up from this book and you will see many objects, some touching and some partially occluded or occluding. Segmenting that image into regions corresponding to objects, or at least a set of regions that are rough candidates for objects, is a prerequisite for object recognition. Otherwise, we would be trying in vain to recognize countless non-objects composed of random sectors of adjacent objects, such as lower-half-of-coffee-mug-plus-central-third-of-napkin-plus-overhanging-ivy-leaf. Image segmentation appears to be an interactive process, in that both bottom-up and top-down mechanisms contribute (Vecera and Farah, 1997). The neural bases of image segmentation have been studied experimentally for little more than a decade, although there are some much older clinical case studies that also appear relevant.

Context and the single cell

One overly simple but handy measure of the increase in global processing in the visual system is the steady increase in receptive field size going from earlier to later visual areas. Figure 2.9 provides a graphical representation of this progression. There are more qualitative signs as well of a transformation from purely local to more global form perception, whereby neurons representing one small part of an image become increasingly sensitive to the overall structure of the image. The most dramatic example of this is the finding that some cells respond to illusory contours, such as those forming the triangle in figure 2.10. Von der Heydt, Peterhans, and Baumgartner (1984) first demonstrated that when inducing stimuli (such as the pacmen in figure 2.10) are arranged so as to induce an illusory contour in the receptive fields of cells in the visual cortex of monkeys, some cells in V2 respond as if there were a real contour present. Modifications of the stimulus display that weakened the perception of the illusory contours for human observers, such as occluding one of the pacmen, also weakened the cells' responses. More recent studies have discovered illusory contour-responsive cells in V1, albeit a smaller proportion (e.g.,

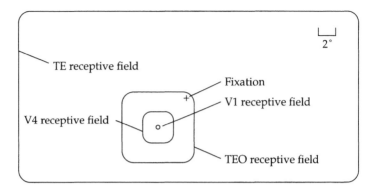

Figure 2.9   Relative sizes of receptive fields for neurons in different parts of the visual system.

Based on data from D. Boussaoud et al., "Visual topography of area TEO in the macaque," Journal of Comparative Neurology, *306, 1991; and R. Desimone and S. J. Schein, "Visual properties of neurons in area V4 of the macaque: sensitivity to stimulus form,"* Journal of Neurosphysiology, *57, 1987.*

Figure 2.10   An example of illusory contours form in a ghostly triangle.
From S. Zeki, A Vision of the Brain, *Oxford, Blackwell Scientific Publications, 1993.*

Sheth, Sharma, Rao, and Sur, 1996). These findings demonstrate an increasing effect of global form perception going from the neurons of V1 to V2, insofar as illusory contours can only be seen as part of a global form.

Little is known about the mechanisms by which the large-scale structure of objects in the visual field influences representation in these relatively early, retinotopically mapped areas. In a recent review article on long-range interactions in vision, Spillman and Werner (1996) lay out the array of possibilities that are currently under consideration. These include purely bottom-up mechanisms that bring together information from disparate locations in the visual field by simple feedforward convergence, lateral interactions among cells with disparate receptive fields at a given level of processing, and top-down mechanisms whereby higher-level areas that have received feedforward convergence then feed back to earlier areas. Clearly it is too early in the history of this issue to rule any class of ideas out!

One specific mechanism bears describing in some additional detail because of the attention it has received, both favorable and disapproving. This is the mechanism of synchronized oscillations in neuronal activity. Von der Malsburg (1985) is credited with first proposing that, in principle, different parts of a distributed representation could be flexibly bound together and distinguished from other representations by the temporal characteristics of their activity. More specifically, reciprocal interactions among the participating neurons could bring their patterns of firing into synchrony. This synchrony could bind together information within a single brain region through lateral interactions, or across regions and levels of processing. A number of different predictions follow from this general hypothesis, which are in the process of being tested (see Singer, 1999, for a review).

One of the earliest tests was reported by Gray, Konig, Engel, and Singer (1989), who found evidence of synchronization between cells in the same visual area when they were responding to different parts of a single object, but not when they were responding to different objects. Anaesthetized cats were shown one of three types of display, as illustrated in figure 2.11: A single long line moving in one direction, two separate but collinear line segments moving coherently in one direction, and the same two separate line segments moving in opposite directions. Cells whose receptive fields included the upper and lower parts of the line were most synchronized when stimulated by a single long line, less so for the two coherently moving lines, and least for the two differently moving lines, an ordering that reflects the

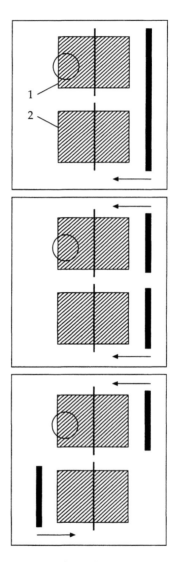

Figure 2.11   A single line passing through two cells' receptive fields (top) results in more synchrony between the cells activity than a broken line (middle), which in turn produces more synchrony than two separately moving line segments (bottom), demonstrating a relation between degree of "objecthood" and amount of synchrony.

From A. K. Engel et al., "Temporal coding in the visual cortex: new vistas on integration in the nervous system," reprinted from Trends in Neurosciences, 15, 1992, *with permission from Elsevier Science.*

decreasing "objecthood" of the displays. Subsequent studies have demonstrated synchronization across different visual areas, in awake as well as anaesthetized animals, and in monkeys as well as cats.

Despite this encouraging body of support, the role of synchronization in binding is far from established. One reason for skepticism is that synchronized oscillations are not always observed, under conditions in which binding must presumably occur (e.g., Tovee and Rolls, 1992). Another reason is the generic problem of inferring causality from correlation. Even if synchrony were always observed when binding occurs, we would not know whether it contributes causally to binding, or whether it is merely a side-effect of binding or of other processes that cause or result from binding. In the absence of experimental manipulations of synchrony, it is hard to see how this issue will be settled.

Human vision without perceptual grouping: apperceptive agnosia

A very different source of insight into the neural bases of grouping can be found in the visual abilities and deficits of people who do not perceive the large-scale organization of the visual field. For reasons yet unknown, these cases are almost always the result of carbon monoxide poisoning or anoxia, and though the structural brain damage is diffuse, the functional loss is impressively focal. Benson and Greenberg (1969) reported the case of a 24-year-old soldier who was overcome by fumes from a faulty heater while in the shower. To quote from their classic case description of apperceptive agnosia:

> Visual acuity could not be measured with a Snellen eye chart, as he could neither identify letters of the alphabet nor describe their configuration. He was able to indicate the orientation of a letter "E," however, and could detect movement of a small object at standard distance. He could identify some familiar numbers if they were slowly drawn in small size on a screen. He could readily maintain optic fixation during fundoscopic examination, and optokinetic nystagmus was elicited bilaterally with fine, 1/8 inch marks on a tape . . . Visual fields were normal to 10 mm and 3 mm white objects, and showed only minimal inferior constriction bilaterally to 3 mm red and green objects. . . .

The patient was able to distinguish small differences in the luminance (0.1 log unit) and wavelength (7–10 mu) of a test aperture subtending a visual angle of approximately 2 degrees. While he could detect these differences in luminance, wavelength, and area, and could respond to small movements of objects before him, he was unable to distinguish between two objects of the same luminance, wavelength, and area when the only difference between them was shape.

Recent and remote memory, spontaneous speech, comprehension of spoken language, and repetition were intact. He could name colors, but was unable to name objects, pictures of objects, body parts, letters, numbers, or geometrical figures on visual confrontation. Yet he could readily identify and name objects from tactile, olfactory, or auditory cues. Confabulatory responses in visual identification utilized color and size cues (a safety pin was "silver and shiny like a watch or a nail clipper" and a rubber eraser was "a small ball"). He identified a photograph of a white typewritten letter on a blue background as "a beach scene," pointing to the blue background as "the ocean," the stationery as "the beach," and the small typewriter print as "people seen on the beach from an airplane." He consistently failed to identify or to match block letters; occasionally he "read" straight line numbers, but never those with curved parts. He could clumsily write only a few letters (X, L) and numbers (1, 4, 7), but often inverted or reversed these. Although he could consistently identify Os and Xs as they were slowly drawn, or if the paper containing them was moved slowly before him, he was unable to identify the very same letters afterwards on the motionless page. He was totally unable to copy letters or simple figures, and he could neither describe nor trace the outline of common objects. . . .

He was unable to select his doctor or family members from a group until they spoke and was unable to identify family members from photographs. At one time he identified his own face in a mirror as his doctor's face. He did identify his own photograph, but only by the color of his military uniform. After closely inspecting a scantily attired magazine "cover girl," he surmised that she was a woman because "there is no hair on her arms." That this surmise was based on flesh color identification was evident when he failed to identify any body parts. For example, when asked to locate her eyes he pointed to her breasts. . . . (pp. 83–5)

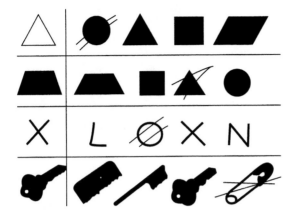

Figure 2.12 Shape matching task, in which the leftmost shape must be matched to the identical shape in the row to the right. The scratch marks indicate the responses of an apperceptive agnosic.
From M. Farah, Visual Agnosia: Disorders of Object Recognition and What They Tell Us About Normal Vision, *Cambridge, MA, MIT Press, 1990.*

In sum, the patient was able to perceive local features of the visual field such as brightness, color, motion, and line orientation, but could not recognize shapes, be they letters, objects, or faces. Indeed, his guesses at object and person identity were based on color, rather than shape. Even the simplest tests of shape perception were beyond this young man. For example, figure 2.12 shows a shape matching task that he was given, with his answers indicated by the score marks.

I have proposed that the underlying cause of the shape perception impairment in such cases is a failure to group the accurately perceived local features (Farah, 1990). Several observations are consistent with this interpretation. The spontaneous use of tracing strategies by many of these patients provides one clue (Adler, 1944; Efron, 1968; Gelb and Goldstein, 1918; Landis, Graves, Benson, and Hebben, 1982). Patients will trace letters and shapes with their fingers, and if prevented from using this strategy will sometimes substitute head movements tracking the contour of the stimulus to be recognized. This strategy uses two intact abilities to circumvent the visual impairment. The first is the ability to perceive very local visual contour information, which enables the patient to move their finger or their gaze and head posture from its current position on a line or edge to a closely neighboring position in the same line or edge. The second is the ability to recognize global shapes kinesthetically, for example, to recognize that one's finger has just moved through an M-shaped trajectory. Tracing is therefore consistent with preserved local perception with impaired grouping of the local elements into more global forms.

The conditions under which the tracing strategy fails also support the grouping deficit hypothesis. Slashes superimposed on a figure, gaps in the figure, or even a pristine shape for which a single contour forks into two, all foil the tracing strategy. In these respects the commonalities across cases are striking. For example, Gelb and Goldstein (1918; translated by Ellis, 1938, pp. 317–18) describe one early case thus:

> If prevented from moving his head or body, the patient could read nothing whatever . . . His movements led to reading only if they corresponded to normal writing movements. If required to trace a letter the "wrong" way, he was quite at a loss to say what letter it was . . . If a few cross-hatching marks were drawn across the word, he followed these when he reached them and consequently lost all sense of what the word was . . . the scratches "derailed" him and he was unable to rediscover the correct path . . . If the scratches were made with a different colored pencil, no difficulty was encountered; the same held for very thick letters and very thin scratches . . . It may be said that his tracing was quite "planless," if by plan we mean guidance based on an antecedent grasp of the structure of the object to be traced. If the drawing given him to be traced were, like a circle, of such a character that he had one route to follow, the result was always successful. Not so, however, with drawings where several lines led away from a single point. (Ellis, 1938, pp. 317–18)

Many years later, similar observations were made by Landis *et al.* (1982, p. 522):

> When allowed to trace, X could recognize simple geometric figures if the point of departure for tracing was unimportant (e.g., circle, triangle). With more complex figures he was misled by unimportant lines. He would give different answers for the same drawing,

Figure 2.13 An apperceptive agnosic read this pattern as 7415, demonstrating his extremely local perception of form.
From T. Landis et al., "Visual recognition through kinaesthetic mediation," Physiological Medicine, 12, 1982.

dependent upon the point of starting to trace, and often described incidental background features as meaningful . . . Reading aloud was performed slowly but accurately. This "reading" was accomplished by rapid tracing of letters, parts of letters or words with his left hand alone or with both hands . . . [When] movement of the fingers could be prevented . . . this abolished reading.

As a demonstration of the slavishly local tracing strategy used by their patient, Landis *et al.* (1982) designed the stimulus pattern shown in figure 2.13. The patient consistently read the figure as "7415."

In sum, both the use of a tracing strategy and the conditions under which it loses effectiveness are informative about the perceptual abilities of apperceptive agnosics. They are consistent with extremely local visual perception, and an impairment in the process of grouping the local elements of the visual field into more global objects or patterns.

Motion may enable apperceptive agnosics to group stimuli. Recall from the case report of the soldier that he could recognize some shapes when slowly drawn or when the paper they were drawn on was moved. The same has been observed in other cases as well. For example, Landis *et al.* (1982) report that their patient was as good at recognizing letters "written in the air" as the hospital staff members present. This suggests that grouping by motion may be accomplished by separate mechanisms from grouping by static stimulus properties. In a sense, the success demonstrated by these patients with moving stimuli is further evidence that their impairment lies in the grouping process *per se*, as their knowledge of more global visual forms can be accessed by motion cues and must therefore be preserved.

2.5 The two cortical visual systems: an overview of what's to come

The processes discussed in this chapter represent major steps away from the local nature of visual representation at the periphery of our visual systems. But merely knowing the color of an object, or its motion, or being able to segregate it from other objects and from the background, still leaves much to be desired in the way of useful vision. Specifically, at this stage of vision we have yet to accomplish the recognition of objects, and their spatial localization in a framework other than retinal coordinates. Also left out of the discussion so far is the attentional selection of some objects or locations for further perceptual processing or for action, and the reinstatement of perceptual representations during visual imagery. The remainder of this book is devoted to these topics, which are sometimes collectively referred to as high-level vision. Before plunging in, let us take a bird's-eye view of the overall design of the high-level visual system.

The idea of "two cortical visual systems" is that the visual processes underlying object recognition on the one hand, and object localization and attention on the other, are implemented in functionally independent processing streams, localized in the ventral and dorsal visual association cortices, respectively (Ungerleider and Mishkin, 1982). The terminology associated with this idea is based on an analogy with the subcortical and cortical visual systems mentioned in chapter 1, which branch apart after leaving the retina. These "two visual systems" have complementary functional specializations, with the cortical system being more important for object identification and the subcortical system being more important for spatial localization (Schneider, 1969). The terms "what" and "where" have sometimes been used as shorthand for the two systems' functions. When Ungerleider and Mishkin coined the term "two cortical visual systems," they were calling our attention to a similar division of labor within the cortex, which has also been summarized as "what" versus "where."

The earliest evidence for this division of labor came from neurological case reports in which patients were selectively impaired at either object recognition or spatial vision (Lange, 1936; Potzl, 1928). Given the subjectively seamless experience of knowing what and where an object is when we look at it, these dissociations are striking. Patients with bilateral posterior parietal damage may quickly and easily recognize an object (at least, once they have found it), but cannot point to it or describe its location relative to other objects in the scene (Holmes, 1918). Conversely, patients with bilateral inferior occipitotemporal damage may perform well on these simple localization tests as well as more complex tests of spatial cognition, while failing to recognize simple drawings of familiar objects, short printed words, or the most familiar of faces (Farah, 1990). These dissociations can be extreme, with poor or even chance performance in one domain and perfectly normal performance in the other. In testing one agnosic patient on a complex spatial task, three-dimensional mental rotation, I found I could not keep up with him, and had to simply record his answers for later scoring. His performance on this difficult task proved perfect (Farah, Hammond, Levine, and Calvanio, 1988). In other visual spatial abilities as well, such as describing routes from memory, this man leaves me in the dust, despite his devastated visual recognition abilities.

The same dissociation, in a weaker form, is found after unilateral right hemisphere brain damage. Newcombe and Russell (1969) tested Second World War veterans with penetrating head wounds on two kinds of task, shown in figure 2.14. In the "closure" task, designed to tax visual recognition, patients had to judge the age and gender of faces rendered as fragmentary regions of light and shadow. In the maze task, designed to tax spatial processing, patients had to learn, by trial and error, the correct path through a matrix. Two subgroups of patients were defined, corresponding to the lowest 20 percent of scores on each of the two tests. The resulting subgroups were non-overlapping, and indeed each group performed on a par with the remaining subjects on the other test, supporting the idea that "what" and "where" are processed independently. Furthermore, the men with poor closure performance all had posterior temporal lesions, whereas the men with poor maze performance all had posterior parietal lesions, supporting the localization of "what" and "where" processing proposed by Ungerleider and Mishkin (1972).

Experimental studies of lesions in animals have confirmed the general distinction between "what" and "where" processing, and the localizations in ventral and dorsal visual association cortex for each.

(a) *Visula "closure" task: examples of materials.*

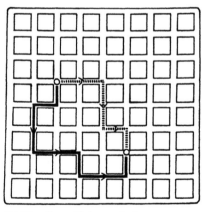

(b) *Visually-guided maze task:*
schematic representation of paths.
⋯⋯➤ = path one.   *➡ = path two.*

Figure 2.14   Examples of stimuli designed to tax visual recognition and spatial learning in a study of unilateral right-hemisphere damaged patients.

From F. Newcombe and W. R. Russell, "Dissociated visual perceptual and spatial deficits in focal lesions of the right hemisphere," Journal of Neurology, Neurosurgery, and Psychiatry, 32, *1969, with permission from BMJ Publishing Group.*

(a)   (b)

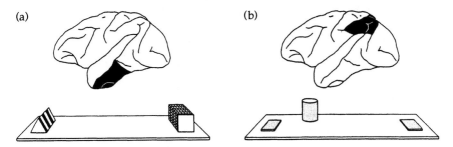

Figure 2.15   (a) Typical pair of patterns to be discriminated, impaired after inferotemporal lesions in monkeys. (b) Typical arrangement of a spatial landmark and food wells in a spatial learning experiment, impaired after posterior parietal lesions in monkeys.
From M. Mishkin et al., "Object vision and spatial vision: two cortical pathways," Trends in Neurosciences, *6, 1983, with permission of Elsevier Science.*

In one classic study, for example, monkeys were taught two different kinds of associations (Pohl, 1973). In the object version, shown in figure 2.15a, the monkey was rewarded when he chose the novel object in a pair, rather than the object that he was just shown. In the spatial version, shown in figure 2.15b, the reward was hidden in the food well nearest a single landmark. Removal of inferotemporal cortex impaired the monkeys' performance on just the object association, whereas removal of posterior parietal cortex impaired their performance on just the spatial association. Many other studies of inferotemporal and parietal lesions, to be reviewed in chapters 4, 7, and 8, provide further support for these conclusions.

Recordings of brain activity in normal monkeys and humans also support the general idea of the two cortical visual systems. Many experiments have analyzed the stimulus properties that determine the activity of cells in inferotemporal cortex and posterior parietal cortex of monkeys. As will be described in more detail in chapters 4 and 7, inferotemporal cells are sensitive to object identity and not location, whereas posterior parietal cells seem generally selective for location rather than stimulus identity. When normal humans are required to recognize objects while their regional cerebral blood flow is measured, the most consistent increases are ventral, as will be described in more detail in chapter 4. When the task is changed to one of spatial attention, posterior parietal cortex shows the most consistent increases, also to be described in more detail in chapter 7.

As broad-based as the evidence is for "what" and "where" systems in the ventral and dorsal visual pathways, the distinction is not universally accepted. One criticism concerns the absolute and categorical nature of the distinction, with the implication that areas in the "what" pathway would never contribute to spatial functions and vice versa (Zeki, 1983). At least some information about both "what" and "where" is represented in both systems. Despite the emphasis on location-invariance in inferotemporal shape representations, for example, neurons in these areas do show some location selectivity (Desimone, Schein, Moran, and Ungerleider, 1985). Similarly, selectivity for shape attributes has been observed in the responses of some neurons in the supposed "where" system (Sereno and Maunsell, 1998). But anyone tempted to discard the whole idea of specialized spatial and object vision systems on the basis of such data should remember the highly selective impairments in these abilities that follow the loss of neurons in the dorsal and ventral visual systems, respectively. Whatever those inferotemporal neurons know about location, and whatever their parietal counterparts know about object shape, falls far short of what is needed for functional vision.

Other criticisms of the two cortical visual systems hypothesis concern the function attributed to the dorsal pathway. Lawler and Cowey (1987) have argued that spatial attention, not spatial perception, is what is impaired after posterior parietal damage. Milner and Goodale (1995) suggest that the dorsal route is concerned not with spatial perception but with visuomotor control, in effect not "where" but "how." Each round of criticisms sharpens our understanding of the organization of high-level vision by introducing new data that redefine the boundaries between the functions of the dorsal and ventral visual systems.

With the wisdom of hindsight, it would be quite surprising if the visual system happened to conform to the precise meanings of English-language words like "what," "where," or for that matter "how." The search for the perfect everyday word to label these neural systems, or the worry that not all features of these words' meanings are appropriate to describing these systems' functions, may distract us from the important points: the insight that there is extensive, if not total, division of labor between these two systems, and the growing body of empirical evidence helping to characterize that division.

chapter three

The Problem of Visual Recognition

3.1 From image to object: a hard problem

Three-dimensional objects can cast radically different images on the retina under different viewing conditions. The position of the viewer with respect to the object determines not only the position and size of the object's image in the picture plane, but also which of its surfaces are visible, foreshortened, or occluded. Different lighting conditions will also reveal surfaces or hide them in shadow, and may introduce spurious edges where an illuminated surface ends and shadow begins. Thus, whereas an object's identity is quite directly related to its three-dimensional shape, it bears a far more complex relation to its projected images.

The problem of visual recognition is the problem of identifying a distal object using only the proximal two-dimensional image that arrives at the retina. That proximal image is only partly determined by the shape of the distal object; various aspects of the viewing conditions such as the spatial relation between the viewer and the object are also determinants.

We have a choice of two solutions to this problem. We can either tackle the dismally underdetermined geometry of inferring the true three-dimensional shape of the object from the image, with few if any clues about the spatial disposition of the object. Or we can take on the cumbersome task of learning a separate association between each

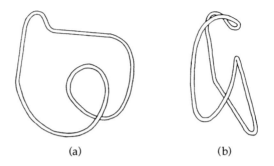

(a)   (b)

Figure 3.1   Two views of a novel object used in experiments demonstrating viewpoint dependence in object recognition.
From I. Rock et al., *"The effect on form perception of change of orientation in the third dimension,"* Journal of Experimental Psychology: Human Perception and Performance, 7, *1981; copyright 1981 by the American Psychological Association; reprinted with permission.*

view of the object and its identity, and always running the risk of encountering a novel view (e.g., of a hungry tiger).

3.2   Psychophysical studies of object recognition in normal humans

The way in which we infer object identity from object image has been a central issue for cognitive psychologists, who have proposed a range of models. At one extreme is the hypothesis that we associate images directly with object identities, without ever inferring the three-dimensional shape of the object. Irvin Rock first suggested that human shape perception is tightly bound to viewing conditions, and that we get along with rather limited access to the true, three-dimenional shapes of objects (e.g., Rock, Di Vita, and Barbeito, 1981; Rock and Di Vita, 1987). Subjects in his studies were shown bent wire forms, like those in figure 3.1, in an incidental learning task. After viewing these forms from one perspective, subjects were later shown the same forms from both the same and different perspectives, along with new forms, and asked to recognize which were seen previously. Subjects performed dramatically worse with new than with old perspectives, and in some cases were no more likely to recognize a form from a new perspective than they were to falsely recognize an entirely new form. Logothetis, Pauls, Bulthoff, and Poggio (1994) report similar findings with normal monkeys, using computer-generated images of both wire forms and irregular blob-shaped forms called amoeba.

The generality of these findings was called into question by Farah, Rochlin, and Klein (1994), who replicated the finding of extreme viewpoint dependence when using wire forms, but found reasonably robust generalization to new orientations when the same shapes previously constructed from wires had clay surfaces interpolated within the frames. Although wire forms were originally chosen for these studies to minimize self-occlusion (because the inability to recognize previously occluded sides of a novel shape would be a trivial finding), they may constitute a special case that is not representative of the stimuli we normally recognize. Wires provide poorer depth cues than surfaces, and normal viewpoint invariance may be particularly demanding of the quality of information available about the locations of each part of a shape in depth, as this information must be entered into the computations that factor out, or correct for, the particular viewing perspective. For this reason, irregular surfaces (which provide less redundant depth information) and stimuli presented on computer screens or viewed monocularly (which lack binocular depth information) may also lead researchers to underestimate the normal capacity for orientation-invariant shape perception. Indeed, when Logothetis *et al.* (1994) substituted common objects such as teapots and spaceships for their wire frame or amoeba stimuli, their monkeys showed good orientation-invariance (despite the fact that objects such as teapots and spaceships would be novel objects to laboratory monkeys).

At the other extreme is the view that shape is not only perceivable independent of viewing conditions, but that it is equally easy to recognize a shape from a familiar or a novel perspective. Michael Corballis has presented the most persuasive arguments for this view (e.g., 1988). He has shown that subjects are equally fast and accurate to name letters and numbers at any orientation (Corballis, Zbrodoff, Shetzer, and Butler, 1978). Pierre Jolicoeur has pointed out that such performance may be dependent on practice, and that when subjects first encounter a stimulus in a novel orientation they do require more time to recognize it (Jolicoeur, 1985). Of course, both Corballis' and Jolicoeur's findings apply to changes of orientation within the picture plane, which involve no foreshortening and may therefore pose a very different problem to the visual system than the changes in depth orientation used by Rock and followers.

Tarr and Pinker have documented the ability of normal subjects to recognize abstract shapes that have been rotated in the picture plane and in depth. In their early studies (Tarr and Pinker, 1989), they taught subjects to recognize novel geometric forms and then tested their ability to identify the forms at different orientations in the picture plane. They found that subjects could perform this task with high levels of accuracy. They also found that the time it took to recognize a rotated form was proportional to the angular disparity between the stimulus and the most similar previous view, the hallmark of mental rotation. More recently, they have generalized this finding to changes of depth perspective (Tarr, 1995). Their interpretation of these results is that our stored representations combine shape and viewpoint information, in agreement with Rock and colleagues, but that we are able to transform these representations to match shapes across changes in viewpoint, in contrast to the extreme viewpoint-dependent position. An interesting exception is the case of symmetrical shapes, which can be recognized equally quickly regardless of orientation, whether they be abstract shapes (Tarr and Pinker, 1990) or drawings of real objects (McMullen and Farah, 1991). Tarr and Pinker suggest that the reduced spatial complexity of symmetrical patterns, whose features need be ordered in one dimension only, allows them to be recognized in an entirely viewpoint independent fashion.

The only general conclusion that can be drawn from the results surveyed here is that the ability to discern the identity of a familiar object from a novel image may depend strongly on the type, complexity, and familiarity of the object. Under at least some circumstances we can get past the specifics of the image, either by transforming the image until it corresponds to a familiar one or by factoring the image into the separate contributions of true object shape and viewing conditions. Possible mechanisms for carrying out these solutions to the problem of visual recognition, and their computational costs and benefits, are discussed in the next section.

3.3 Shape representation: a computational framework

Certain information about objects is explicit in image representations, such as those registered by a digital camera or those found on the retina and in early visual areas: the set of locations in the visual field taken up by the objects, the distance from the viewer of various points on the objects' surfaces, and so on. In contrast, information that is more immediately relevant to visual recognition is only implicit in those representations. That is, with some further processing of the image, it may be possible to make explicit the three-dimensional shape of the distal object that could potentially project such an image, or the transformation that would align the current image with one already stored in memory. This way of looking at the process of visual object recognition, as a process of explicitly representing information that is initially only implicit, highlights the crucial role of representation in visual recognition.

Machine vision is a field in which researchers are forced to confront, head-on, issues of shape representation for visual recognition. The choice of a representation for shape is arguably the most fundamental design decision that goes into a recognition system. David Marr was an early and influential theorist in the field of machine vision, who also had a taste for metatheory. Of his many contributions, one was a framework for describing and evaluating shape representations. That framework will be summarized here, and used to guide discussion in the following chapter.

Desiderata for a system of shape representation

Marr and Nishihara (1978) enumerated five types of criteria on which shape representations can be evaluated for their usefulness in object recognition.

Accessibility refers to the feasibility of deriving the shape description from an image. It must of course be possible, in principle, to derive the representation from the image, that is, the image must at least implicitly contain the relevant information. In addition, it is desirable that the shape representation be recoverable without placing huge demands on resources such as time and hardware.

Scope refers to the range of stimuli for which the representation is effective. Many successful machine vision systems achieve their success by sacrificing scope, for example, specializing in machine parts, handwriting, or views of aerial terrain. Clearly, a system specialized for handwriting would not be able to recognize three-dimensional objects. Even systems that are not explicitly special-purpose, but are designed to teach us something about the problem of vision, may have severely limited scope. For example, Waltz's (1975) vision system, a classic of early artificial intelligence, could interpret the three-dimensional structure of a scene made up of blocks that were partly occluded and foreshortened. It did so by using the mutual constraints among the ways that different types of corner images could combine, which of course limits the system to objects composed exclusively of planar side, straight edges, and corners! Marr and Nishihara took it as a given that human object recognition was accomplished by one general-purpose system of wide scope, and that such scope was therefore in principle attainable. Whether or not this is true will be taken up in some detail in the next chapter.

Uniqueness refers to the desirable property that a given image of an object will always be assigned the same shape description. As an example of how a representation could fail to have uniqueness, Marr and Nishihara offer polynomial surface representations. Depending on the choice of coordinate system, the equation representing the surface shape will look quite different. Unless there is some way of constraining the choice of coordinate system, the same image could be assigned different shape descriptions on different occasions.

Stability refers to the tendency for images of the same or similar objects, viewed under different conditions, to be assigned the same or similar shape representation. Stable shape representations capture the commonality of the intrinsic shape of an object despite the radical changes in appearance possible when perspective, illumination, or the positions of movable parts change, and they also capture the similarity relations that exist among images of similar objects. There is an inherent tension between the need for stability of representations and the need for sensitivity of representations, the last desideratum to be described.

Sensitivity refers to the ability of a system of representation to distinguish subtle differences between similar shapes and between different images of the same shape. Face recognition, for example, requires representations with a truly impressive degree of sensitivity, to recognize differences among individuals that amount to very small differences in the geometry of their faces, while still possessing enough stability to recognize them under different viewing conditions and with different facial expressions.

Although stability is the first desideratum we tend to think about when considering the problem of object recognition, and it is a tall order on its own, the mere listing of these other criteria reminds us of the full extent of what our visual system is accomplishing during object recognition. We don't just see that a chair is a chair when approached from different angles, we also see this quickly and effortlessly (accessibility), we can do the same for other carpentered objects, noncarpentered objects, faces, and printed words (scope), we never fail to interpret the chair image the same way (uniqueness), and we can nevertheless discern slightly different chairs (sensitivity).

Dimensions of shape representation

Marr and Nishihara (1978) also laid out a framework for classifying different possible systems of shape representation. They distinguish such systems according to their coordinate systems, shape primitives, and organization. David Plaut and I (Plaut and Farah, 1990) used this framework as a way of organizing the literature on the functions of inferotemporal cortex, and added one additional dimension of classification, which we called implementation. Here I will review these four dimensions, which create a space of possible systems of shape representation, so that we can then review the available data and ask: Where is our shape representation system located on each dimension of this space?

Coordinate system

Notwithstanding the "what"/"where" distinction discussed in chapter 2, shape is really nothing more than a set of locations occupied by an object. The representation of these locations must be relative to some coordinate system, and the choice of coordinate system is therefore a fundamental aspect of any system of shape representation.

In viewer-centered coordinate systems, locations are specified relative to the viewer. Initially, visual stimuli are represented in our nervous systems in retinotopic coordinates, that is, in two dimensions of space with an origin fixed with respect to the retina. If either the object or our eyes move with respect to one another, the retinotopic representation changes. The retinotopic coordinate system is one type of viewer-centered coordinate system. As viewers have a number of movable parts, there are multiple viewer-centered coordinate systems that can be decoupled from one another. For example, head-centered, trunk-centered, and even hand-centered coordinates might in principle be used to represent spatial locations. Viewer-centered representations, especially retinotopic representations, have the advantage of being highly accessible and unique. However, they suffer from poor stability: Every time the object or viewer moves relative to one another, the representation changes.

Environment-centered coordinate systems are those in which locations are specified relative to the environment. As such, they are stable over movements of the viewer. If the object itself moves, however, the environment-centered representation changes. Deriving an environment-centered representation requires that the viewer be able to compute and continually update the spatial relation of the environment to himself. In principle this can be done using visual cues (e.g. horizon line if outdoors, architectural features such as floors if indoors, or the outer frame of a computer screen for experimental tasks at near range), and proprioceptive cues. Thus, the improved stablity of an environment-centered system requires additional computation, that is, it is gained at the cost of decreased accessibility.

Object-centered coordinate systems are those in which the locations occupied by the different parts of the object are represented in a coordinate system intrinsic to, or fixed relative to, the object. A description such as "the receiver is on the top of a telephone, and the dial is in front" makes use of a kind of object-centered coordinate system, in the sense that the phone's top and front (specifically, the places where the receiver and dial are found) stay the same whether the phone is right-side up from our viewing perspective, upside-down, or sideways. Object-centered representations are position- and orientation invariant, because as the object moves relative to the viewer, so does the coordinate system being used to represent the object. This results in object-centered representations having perfect stability. Alas, there is no free lunch to be had here; the perfect stability has a high pricetag in terms of accessibility and uniqueness. How do you assign an object-centered coordinate system before you have recognized the object? Certain geometric properties that can be derived prior to recognition might help, for example, elongation and symmetry can be used to assign axes to a shape. Whether such an approach is feasible in general has yet to be shown.

For many years it was assumed that object recognition must involve the representation of object shape in object-centered coordinates, because of the inherent stability of these representations (e.g., Marr, 1982; Pentland, 1986). However, their poor accessibility and uniqueness have led some computational vision researchers to explore the possibility of using viewer-centered representations. For example, in Ullman's (1989) system, a viewer-centered representation of object shape is used, with a spatial transformation that normalizes the image relative to the stored viewer-centered model. This is accomplished by means of "alignment keys," three orientation-invariant features present in the image and the stored model, which Ullman has shown are sufficient to determine the necessary spatial transformation for alignment.

It is also possible to envision a form of representation that is partly viewer-centered and partly object-centered. A three-dimensional coordinate system is specified by seven degrees of freedom: three for its location in the three dimensions of space, three for its orientation relative to the three axes, and one for scale. One way to compromise on the tradeoff between stability on the one hand, and accessibility and uniqueness on the other, is to use a coordinate system that is object-centered in some degrees of freedom and viewer-centered in others. A concrete example of such a representation has been used by Koenderink and van Doorn (1979), who showed that three-dimensional objects can be represented with a relatively small set of what they call "characteristic views." As shown in figure 3.2, the different views correspond to different depth rotations of the object, and his system is therefore viewer-centered for the degrees of freedom corresponding to rotation about the x and y axes. The views are related to one another by a graph structure that encodes the spatial relations among them. The representation of the individual views makes use of a kind of object-centered representation such that variation in size, position,

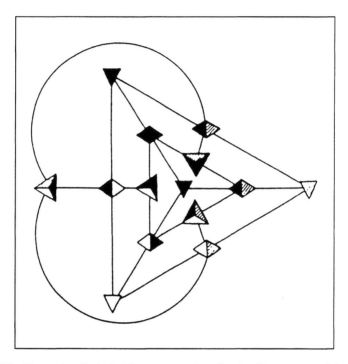

Figure 3.2   Example of a hybrid representation that is object-centered for size, position, and picture-plane orientation, and viewer-centered for depth orientation, with relations among different views encoded as a graph.
From *J. J. Koenderink and A. J. Van Doom, "The internal representation of solid shape with respect to vision,"* Biological Cybernetics, *32, 1979.*

and picture plane orientation among images corresponding to each of these generic views will not affect their match to the relevant view.

Primitives

In most current theories of object representation, what is localized within a coordinate system is not simply points in space, or pixels, but some element of shape: either contour, surface, or three-dimensional shape. Contour-based primitives are relatively accessible, and indeed we saw in chapter 1 that contours appear to be extracted from the visual image early in cortical visual processing. The best known

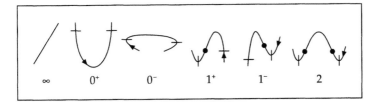

Figure 3.3 "Codons," a type of contour-based primitive proposed by Hoffman and Richards.
From W. Richards and D. D. Hoffman, "Codon constraints on closed 2D shapes," Computer Vision, Graphics and Image Processing, *31, 1985.*

contour-based object recognition system is Hoffman and Richards' "codon" system, shown in figure 3.3, in which shape is built up out of a set of primitive contour types defined by curvature extrema. A shortcoming of this system is its limited scope, specifically, just those objects that can be recognized on the basis of their silhouette shapes. In general, contour-based primitives pose problems for the stability of object representation across different viewing conditions: Depth rotations can drastically change the outline shape of curved surfaces (e.g., a potato chip), and lighting can create spurious internal contours.

Surface-based primitives and volume-based primitives allow for broader scope and better stability. An example of a surface-based representation is Marr's "$2\frac{1}{2}$-D sketch", shown in figure 3.4, which specifies the orientation of an object's surface at each location. The accessibility of surface-based primitives may be roughly as good as for contour-based primitives, given the results of Lehky and Sejnowski described in chapter 1.

Among computer vision systems that aim for broad scope, volume-based primitives are common. These include Marr's (1982) generalized cylinders as well as geons (Biederman, 1987), and superquadrix (Pentland, 1986). Examples of these are shown in figure 3.5. Volume-based primitives seem ideal for object recognition, as they can in principle represent the full geometry of the object; however, deriving them from an image is a computational challenge, which has yet to be solved in the general case. Thus for primitives, as for coordinate systems, we face a tradeoff between stability and accessibility.

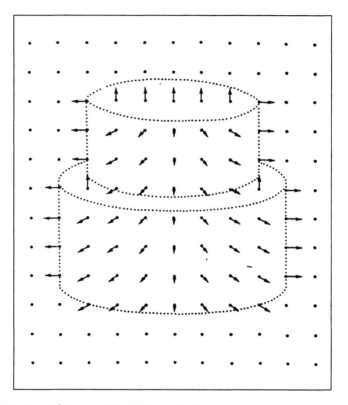

Figure 3.4   The "2½D sketch" of Marr, which uses surface-based primitives.
From D. Marr and H. K. Nishihara, "Representation and recognition of the spatial organization of three-dimensional shapes," Proceedings of the Royal Society of London, B, 200, 1978.

Figure 3.5   (*opposite*) Examples of three well-known sets of volume-based primitives. (a) Pentland's "superquadrix." (b) Marr's "generalized cylinders" and complex shapes composed thereof. (c) Biederman's "geons" and complex shapes composed thereof.
From D. Marr and H. K. Nishihara, "Representation and recognition of the spatial organization of three-dimensional shapes," Proceedings of the Royal Society of London, B, 200, 1978; I. Biederman, "Matching image edges to object memory," Proceedings of the First International Conference on Computer Vision, London, IEEE Computer Society; R. Bajcsy and F. Solina, "Three-dimensional object representation revisited," Proceedings of the First International Conference on Computer Vision, London, IEEE Computer Society.

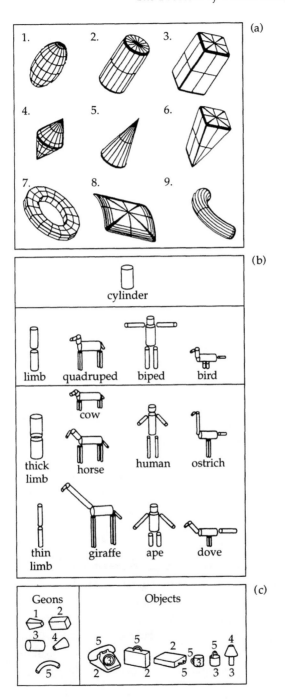

(a)

(b)

(c)

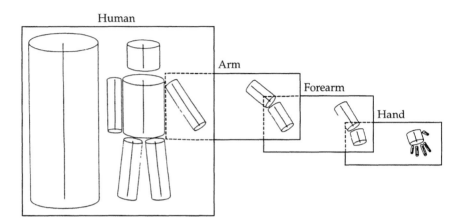

Figure 3.6   A hierarchically organized representation of the human body.
From D. Marr and H. K. Nishihara, "Representation and recognition of the spatial organization of three-dimensional shapes," Proceedings of the Royal Society of London, B, 200, 1978.

Organization

The final dimension of shape representation discussed by Marr and Nishihara concerns the degree and type of organization among the elements of a shape representation. They contrast the representation shown in figure 3.5, in which all elements have the same status with respect to one another, to a representation in which groups of spatially adjacent elements of roughly the same scale are organized together into a higher-order part. Figure 3.6 illustrates such an organization in which groups of primitives make up parts at one level, and groups of those parts can form a yet higher-order part at the next level.

Implementation

The fourth dimension of shape representation to be reviewed here was not included by Marr in his discussion of object representation, but was added by myself and David Plaut in the review article cited earlier (Plaut and Farah, 1989). Marr carefully distinguished between system properties such as coordinate system, primitive, and organization, which he termed "algorithmic," and implementational properties, which he regarded as a different level of description from algorithm. In contrast to symbolic computational architectures, neural network computation blurs the distinction between the algorithmic and implementational level. In any case, it is of interest to characterize the design of the human object recognition system in terms of its implementation as well as its more classically computational characteristics. Two aspects of implementation will be considered here: the nature of the computations underlying memory search, and the local versus distributed nature of representation.

Visual recognition requires that memory be searched for a representation that resembles the current stimulus input. In a conventional computer, an input is recognized by comparing a symbolic representation of that input to symbolic representations stored in memory, using an explicit comparison process which is itself part of a stored program in the computer. The process is analogous to taking the title of a book that you have written on a piece of paper, and searching the library shelves to find the same title written on the spine of a book. It is possible that visual recognition also works in this way, with a processor comparing a high-level representation of the appearance of the stimulus to stored representations. When a match is found, the associated semantic knowledge of the object is then available, just as the contents of the book become available once the title has been located on the shelf.

A very different way of implementing search is by the use of neural networks. Representations correspond to activation of certain neuron-like units, which are interconnected in a network. The extent to which the activation of one unit causes an increase or decrease in the activation of a neighboring unit depends on the "weight" of the connection between them; positive weights cause units to excite each other and negative weights cause units to inhibit each other. Upon presentation of the input pattern to the input units, all of the units connected with those input units will begin to change their activation under the influence of two kinds of constraints: the activation value of the units to which they are connected and the weights on the connections. These units might in turn connect to others, and influence their activation levels in the same way. In recurrent, or attractor, networks the units downstream will also begin to influence the activation levels of the earlier units. Eventually, these shifting activation levels across the units of the network settle into a stable pattern of activation, which is the representation that corresponds to the recognized object. That pattern is determined jointly by the input activation (the stimulus input) and the weights of the network (the system's knowledge of all objects).

The two ways of implementing search are so different it is difficult to compare them except at a very abstract level. For instance, one can say that the system's knowledge in a symbolic implementation of memory search consists of separate stored representations of the stimulus and the comparison procedure, whereas in a neural network it consists just of the connection weights, which store knowledge of object appearance and carry out the search process. Although in both types of system there is a distinction between the early representations of the stimulus closer to the input level and the high-level object representations that underlie object recognition, there are two tokens of the high-level representation involved in symbolic search, the "perceptual" representation derived from the stimulus and the stored "memory" representation, whereas there is only one token in neural network search. Distinctions such as "structure versus process" and "perception versus memory," which seem almost logically necessary when one is thinking in terms of symbol manipulation, dissolve when one considers the neural network implementation of memory search.

The issue of local versus distributed representations concerns the way in which objects are represented by physical units. Local representations are like "grandmother cells," in that there is a one-to-one mapping of things represented onto things doing the representing. For example, your grandmother and only your grandmother would be represented by activation of one particular unit. In contrast, with distributed representations there is a many-to-many mapping of things represented onto things doing the representing. For example, a distributed representation of your grandmother would be a pattern of activation over a number of units. Those same units, when entertaining different patterns of activation, would also represent other things. Let us make the example concrete: Your grandmother could be represented by activity in units representing such features as grey hair, blue eyes, and a wrinkly smile. Another elderly acquaintance could be represented by activity in the grey hair and wrinkly smile units, but be distinguishable from your grandmother because the brown eye unit would be active and the blue eye unit inactive. Of course, the features that underlie a distributed representation need not correspond to intuitive, nameable features.

The concept of distributed representation is relative in two ways. First, representations can be said to be distributed or local only relative to a given domain of represented things. In the example just given, the representations are distributed with respect to people, and local with respect to attributes of people such as hair and eye color. Second, there can be degrees of distributedness. A given representation can involve activity in a large or small proportion of the total number of units, making it very distributed or less distributed (sometimes called sparse), as well as the extreme local alternative of just one unit per representation.

Distributed representation is an efficient way to represent and retrieve information in a network of highly interconnected representational units like the brain. In addition to allowing a larger number of entities to be represented with a given number of units, distributed representation has two other major advantages over local representation: First, systems of distributed representations degrade "gracefully" when damaged. Instead of losing knowledge of entire entities when damaged, the system maintains knowledge of all entities, albeit in degraded form, because no unit of representation is crucial to the representation of any entity. Second, systems of distributed representation tend automatically to generalize knowledge about one entity to other similar entities. This is because similar entities have attributes in common, and are therefore represented by activation of partly overlapping sets of units. Any learning that associates activation of those units with others representing other information will do so for any entity whose representation includes activation of those units (see Hinton, McClelland, and Rumelhart, 1986, for a full discussion of distributed representation). Of course, in some circumstances "generalization" amounts to interference: If we are trying to represent the meanings of words, for example, generalization will tend to make the knowledge that "cup" is something to drink from interfere with learning that "pup" is a young dog and has nothing to do with drinking. Thus, different degrees of distributedness may be appropriate for different perceptual and cognitive systems.

chapter four

Object Recognition

4.1 Object representation in inferior temporal cortex: a miracle occurs

The visual representations of the retina, LGN, and the occipital lobe are all retinotopic images. Retinotopy is a ubiquitous organizing principle for the representations of early and intermediate vision. But as we saw in the last chapter, the information that is explicitly available in such representations is not particularly useful for object recognition. Images bundle together the true shape of an object and the perspective from which it is viewed, whereas the identity of the object is of course related only to the former.

Accordingly, the neural substrates of visual recognition are not among the retinotopic areas just mentioned. Instead, they are located in inferior temporal areas in both monkey and man. Lesions to this area have devastating effects on animals' performance in tasks testing object perception, and on human object recognition after neurological disease or injury. The results of single unit recordings in IT are consistent with this. Compared to V4 and the visual areas preceding it, neurons in inferotemporal cortex show considerable constancy over changes in viewing conditions, and virtually no retinotopy.

How can visual representation change so radically going from V4 to IT, just one synapse away? This transformation, from image to object, is reminiscent of the famous cartoon shown in figure 4.1. In

"I think you should be more explicit here in step two."

Figure 4.1 Sidney Harris's classic cartoon, which about sums up our understanding of the neural information processing performed between V4 and IT.
From Harris, "I think you should be more..." in Chalk Up Another One: The Best of Sidney Harris, *New Brunswick, NJ, Rutgers University Press, 1992; copyright Sidney Harris.*

this chapter I will try to better characterize the miracle, if not fully explain it, calling upon lesion and single unit recording studies in monkeys, and lesion and neuroimaging studies in humans.

4.2 The neural bases of shape recognition in monkeys

Lesion studies in monkeys

The experimental study of temporal cortex and visual object recognition dates back to the research of Kluver and Bucy (1937), on what is

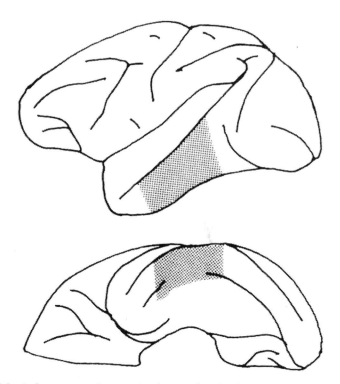

Figure 4.2   Inferotemporal cortex in the monkey brain.
From P. Dean, *"Visual behaviour in monkeys with inferotemporal lesions,"* in D. J. Ingle
et al. *(eds),* Analysis of Visual Behavior, *Cambridge, MA, MIT Press, 1982.*

now known as the Kluver–Bucy syndrome. These researchers removed
the entire temporal lobes of monkeys bilaterally, and found complex
changes in social, sexual, and eating behavior of the animals. Later
research attempted to fractionate the syndrome and relate specifically
visual impairments to specific cortical regions within the temporal
lobe. The inferior temporal gyrus, also known as inferotemporal cortex or von Bonin and Bailey area TE, was eventually shown to be the
critical area for producing the visual deficits (Mishkin, 1954, 1966;
Mishkin and Pribram, 1954). Figure 4.2 shows the location of this area
in the macaque brain.

    The functional role of inferotemporal cortex in vision was initially
conceptualized in terms of visual learning, rather than visual object
recognition as discussed so far in this chapter. However, this difference

has more to do with terminology and with the particulars of the experimental tasks used in these early laboratories than with any substantive distinction between the visual abilities impaired in the monkeys and what we would call visual object recognition.

In the typical experimental paradigm, monkeys were trained to respond differentially to one stimulus, the target stimulus, presented in advance of or alongside other "choice" stimuli. The animal would be required to press a response button under the choice stimulus that matched the target in order to obtain a reward, and performance was typically measured in terms of number of learning trials to reach a criterion. Compared to normal monkeys and operated control monkeys, monkeys with inferotemporal lesions showed severe impairments in these tasks (e.g., Blum *et al.*, 1950; Mishkin, 1966; Pribram, 1954). Assessment of the visual fields, acuity, and visual thresholds of these monkeys showed that the impairments could not be attributed to elementary visual sensory impairments. Assessment of discrimination learning in modalities other than vision confirmed the specificity of the impairments for visual discrimination learning (see Plaut and Farah, 1990, for a more detailed review).

Two other early findings suggest that the impairment of IT-lesioned monkeys is not in visual learning *per se*, but in object representation. First, IT lesions cause a loss of previously acquired visual discriminations (e.g., Pribram, 1954). This finding is more clearly analogous to an impairment of visual object recognition, in that the monkeys have lost knowledge of familiar objects. Second, IT-lesioned monkeys show qualitative as well as quantitative abnormalities in their visual discrimination learning, and these qualitative abnormalities are suggestive of an inability to represent visual objects *per se*, as opposed to position, size, brightness, or local features. For example, they may generalize their responses on the basis of just one dimension or feature of the target stimulus (e.g., Butter, Mishkin and Rosvold, 1965; Butter, 1968; Iwai, 1985), and have been noted to ignore shape altogether in favor of brightness (Iverson and Weiskrantz, 1967).

Iwai (1985) showed that even when IT-lesioned monkeys had succeeded in learning to discriminate between the target stimulus of a triangle and the wrong choice of a circle, they were not doing so on the basis of shape *per se*. Instead, they seemed to be responding to the parallelism between the base of the triangle and the edge of the board

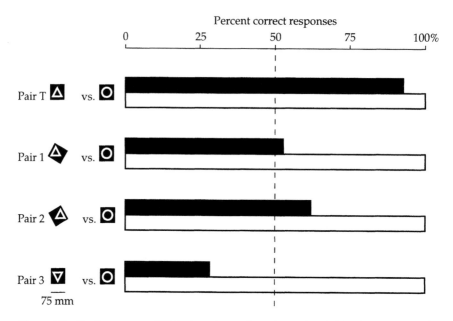

Figure 4.3   Performance of IT-lesioned monkeys in a visual discrimination task, showing their inability to transfer a learned discrimination to displays of the same shapes when the local spatial characteristics of the stimuli were changed. *From E. Iwai, "Neuropsychological basis of pattern vision in macaque monkeys,"* Vision Research, 25, 1985, with permission from Elsevier Science.

on which the stimuli were presented. When the board was rotated, but the stimuli remained in the same orientation, the monkeys could no longer perform the discrimination. Furthermore, as shown in figure 4.3, Iwai found that these monkeys showed transfer of learning to new discriminations when the spatial location of some of the earlier patterns' features is maintained, but not when the same features were shifted in space. This suggests that, to the extent that the IT-lesioned monkeys could learn a discrimination, they were treating it as a spatial discrimination rather than a shape discrimination.

Once the general hypothesis of defective object representation after IT lesions was accepted, inquiry moved on to the next stage: What is the nature of stimulus representation in IT? Much research in the 1970s and subsequently has been aimed at answering this question. The general approach has been to infer which stimulus properties are normally encoded (or not encoded) in IT representations by showing which stimulus properties IT-lesioned monkeys are impaired at using (or not impaired at using) as a basis for discrimination. On the basis of our current knowledge, a reasonable short answer might be: IT represents aspects of the intrinsic shape of a stimulus that are useful for recognition, and omits most aspects of stimulus appearance that depend on viewing conditions. Only a few representative studies will be reviewed here. More detail can be found in Plaut and Farah (1990).

Position is one visual property that is clearly a red herring for purposes of object recognition, and normal monkeys will easily generalize a visual discrimination learned in one hemifield to the other. Monkeys with bilateral IT lesions are impaired at this generalization, however (Gross and Mishkin, 1977; Seacord, Gross, and Mishkin, 1979). This implies that they have lost representations in which position is not represented, in other words, representations that are general across positions. The retinal image size of the stimulus is another visual property that depends on viewing conditions and not just intrinsic object geometry, and this is another property that IT-lesioned monkeys have trouble ignoring. For example, Humphrey and Weiskrantz (1969) trained monkeys to discriminate disks of two absolute sizes, varying their distance and hence their retinal image size. IT-lesioned monkeys were unable to relearn the discrimination, instead responding on the basis of retinal size or distance. This implies that IT representations normally encode the absolute size of an object, an intrinsic object property useful for recognition, rather than its distance *per se* or its retinal image size.

IT-lesioned monkeys are also impaired at generalizing across views of the same stimulus in a different orientation (Weiskrantz and Saunders, 1984), implying that orientation is yet another of the incidental image properties that has been laundered out of IT representations. A discrepant finding was reported by Holmes and Gross (1984), who found no impairment in discriminating size- and orientation-transformed stimuli, but this may have to do with the relatively simple nature of the discriminations (J vs. π, or P vs. T, pairs which can be distinguished on the basis of a local feature such as a hook or a closed loop) and the fact that only a single positive stimulus (hence feature) had to be learned by the monkeys. Finally, variations in illumination prevent IT-lesioned monkeys from seeing the equivalence of objects (Weiskrantz and Saunders, 1984), implying that IT representations are unaffected by patterns of shadow and light falling on object surfaces. IT-lesioned monkeys show little or no impairment in tasks that require discriminating between (as opposed to generalizing between) patterns and their mirror images (Gross, 1978), suggesting that handedness is yet another dimension over which the normal observer tends to generalize on the basis of object representations in IT.

4.3   Single unit studies in monkeys

The technique of single cell recording was applied to inferotemporal cortex by Charles Gross and collaborators beginning in the late 1960s. Early recordings from anaesthetized animals showed large bilateral receptive fields responsive to visual stimuli (e.g., Gross, Schiller, Wells, and Gerstein, 1967). Although some cells responded well to virtually any visual stimulus, others responded with some degree of selectivity to shape, color, or texture (see Desimone, Schein, Moran, and Ungerleider, 1985, for a review). Unlike cells in V4, the main source of input to IT, cells in inferotemporal cortex are not retinotopically organized (Desimone and Gross, 1979), but tend to cluster in groups with similar response properties (Fuster and Jervey, 1982). Recordings from awake animals have shown the ways in which neuronal activity is dependent on task demands. The responses of IT cells are enhanced during visual discrimination, compared to when the monkey need not perform any actions contingent on the stimulus (Richmond and Sato, 1987), and become larger and more selective as the difficulty of the discrimination increases (Spitzer, Desimone, and Moran, 1988). However, IT cells do not carry motivational information *per se*; they are not sensitive to the association of a stimulus with reward (Rolls, Judge, and Sanghera, 1977). Most striking was the observation that some cells in IT are tuned to highly specific aspects of stimulus shape. For example, Gross, Rocha-Miranda and Bender (1972) recorded from a cell that responded vigorously to a monkey hand, with diminished responses to increasingly different-shaped stimuli, as shown in figure 4.4.

Although the finding of a hand-selective cell was met with surprise and outright skepticism at the time, many different laboratories have

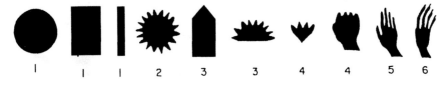

| I | I | I | 2 | 3 | 3 | 4 | 4 | 5 | 6 |

Figure 4.4 The range of stimuli used to test the selectivity of a "hand cell" in monkey IT cortex. The more different the stimulus shape from a monkey hand, the smaller the cell's response.
From C. G. Gross et al., *"Visual properties of neurons in inferotemporal cortex of the macaque,"* Journal of Neurophysiology, *35, 1972.*

subsequently observed IT cells with highly selective responses for particular patterns and objects (e.g., Baylis, Rolls, and Leonard, 1985; Desimone, 1991; Miyashita, Date, and Okuno, 1993; Perrett, Mistlin, and Chitty, 1987; Tanaka, Saito, Fukada, and Moriya, 1991; Yamane, Kaji, and Kawano, 1988). Figure 4.5 shows examples of the shapes for which neurons in IT show selectivity.

In many ways, these neurons appear to be representing objects. One manifestation of this is their general preference for real objects: they respond more vigorously to three-dimensional objects or models of objects than to their outline silhouettes (Desimone, Albright, Gross, and Bruce, 1984). Indeed, they are selective for objects and may be relatively nonselective for Adelson and Bergen's (1991) "stuff": Sary, Vogel, and Orban (1993) identified neurons that were selectively responsive to a particular shape defined by luminosity differences (e.g., a white star on a black background) and found that they were also responsive to the same shape defined by texture cues and motion cues (e.g. a star-shaped region of speckles with the same average luminosity as its background, defined by larger, sparser speckles or speckles moving in a different direction).

Many IT cells are selective for faces, some even showing selectivity for one face over another (Baylis, Rolls, and Leonard, 1985). "Face cells" cease to respond if the features of the face are present but scrambled (Desimone *et al.*, 1984), suggesting that the overall structure of the face is important, and not simply the presence of local features. This conclusion was strengthened by a quantitative study in which neuronal responses were best predicted by combinations of various inter-feature distances within the face (Yamane, Kaji, and

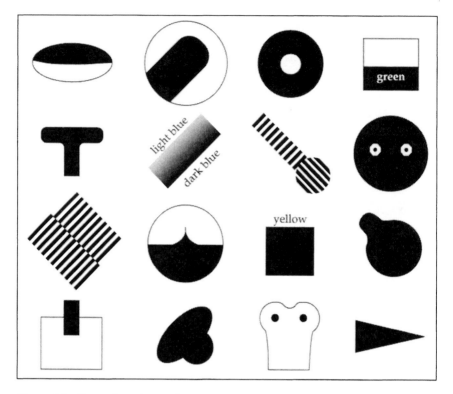

Figure 4.5   Examples of stimulus patterns for which cells in IT cortex show selectivity.

From K. Tanaka, "Inferotemporal cortex and object vision," Annual Review of Neuroscience, 19, copyright 1996 by Annual Reviews.

Kawano, 1988). Further discussion of face cells will be deferred until the next chapter.

A fuller characterization of the information represented by cells in IT comes from experiments in which specific properties of a stimulus are varied while recording from a cell responsive to that stimulus (see Tanaka, 1996, for a comprehensive review). The results of these experiments are generally consonant with the conclusions of the lesion studies reviewed earlier, and with the general view that IT represents objects *per se* as opposed to incidental image features. For example, the position (e.g., Desimone, Albright, Gross, and Bruce, 1984), retinal image size (e.g., Sato, Kawamura, and Iwai, 1980), and picture plane

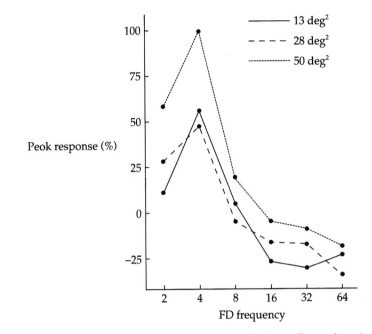

Figure 4.6 The response strength of a shape selective cell as a function of shape similarity (represented on the x-axis as Fourier Descriptor Frequency) and as a function of stimulus size (dotted, dashed, and solid lines). Note that there is shape selectivity, in that the functions are peaked, but the selectivity is not absolute; there is a generalization gradient to other similar shapes. Similarly, the selectivity shows size invariance, in that all functions are peaked for the same FD frequency, but the size invariance is not absolute; the cell responds more vigorously to one size than to the others.

From R. Desimone et al., *"Contour, color and shape analysis beyond the striate cortex,"* Vision Research, 25, 1985, *with permission of Elsevier Science.*

orientation (e.g., Desimone *et al.*, 1984) have relatively small effects on cells' responses to an optimal shape, as illustrated by the data in figure 4.6.

Changes in depth orientation create more complex changes in the retinal image than changes in picture plane orientation, and the effect on IT cells, responses are less consistent. Perrett, Smith, Potter, Mistlin, Head, Milner, and Jeeves (1985) report face cells that respond preferentially to profile or frontal views of faces, as well as cells that generalize to some degree over depth rotations. Hasselmo, Rolls,

Baylis and Nalwa (1989) report similar findings, and note that some orientation-independent cells maintain a preference for one face over another across rotations in depth. The effects of picture plane and depth rotations on cells' responses to nonface objects have been systematically investigated by Logothetis, Pauls and Poggio (1995) using complex wire frame and amoeba stimuli. They report some generalization, better for picture plane than depth rotations, but in no case was orientation-invariance complete.

4.4   Disorders of shape recognition in humans

The earliest clues about the neural bases of object recognition came not from the laboratory but from the neurology clinic, specifically from study of patients with visual agnosia. Visual agnosia is a blanket term for a wide array of visual disorders affecting object recognition, in which elementary visual functions such as acuity and visual fields are grossly intact, or at least adequate to allow for recognition (see my 1990 book on agnosia for a taxonomy and detailed review). Agnosias are commonly divided into the "apperceptive" and "associative" varieties, a distinction introduced by Lissauer (1890). According to Lissauer, object recognition could be impaired because the object is not adequately perceived, or because the percept fails to be associated with relevant knowledge in memory. Agnosic patients whose perception is obviously impaired, despite intact or at least adequate visual sensory function, were classified as apperceptive agnosics on the assumption that their impairment lay in the stage of "apperception." Agnosic patients whose perception seemed grossly intact were classified as associative agnosics on the assumption that their impairment lay in the stage of "association" of percept and memory. In the words of Teuber (1968), these patients experience "a normal percept, stripped of its meaning."

The apperceptive/associative distinction is valid in the sense that there are agnosic patients with and without blatant perceptual impairments, and their underlying problems do appear to be different. In other words, there is reason to draw a line between two general types of patients, on purely empirical grounds. However, the interpretation suggested by Lissauer's terms "apperceptive" and "associative" is probably wrong. The underlying problem in associative agnosia is likely to be perceptual too, and not one of "association." In fact, of the two types of visual agnosia most relevant to the issue of shape perception, one of them is associative visual agnosia; the other is a disorder that is usually grouped with the apperceptive agnosias, termed "perceptual categorization deficit."

4.5 Associative visual agnosia

Although the term "associative visual agnosia" has itself been used to cover a range of disorders (see Farah, 1990), in its narrow sense it refers to an impairment in visual object recognition that is not attributable to defective semantic knowledge of the objects nor to clinically apparent perceptual difficulty. To be considered an associative agnosic, a patient must demonstrate the following features: First, he or she must have difficulty recognizing visually presented objects. This must be evident in ways other than just naming, such as sorting objects by category (e.g., putting kitchen utensils together, separate from sports equipment) or pantomiming the objects' functions. If the trouble is confined to naming objects, and is not manifest in nonverbal tests of recognition, then the problem is either anomia or, if confined to the naming of visual stimuli, optic aphasia (see chapter 9). Second, the patient must demonstrate that knowledge of the objects is available through modalities other than vision, for example by tactile or auditory recognition, or by verbal questioning (e.g., what is an egg beater?). Some dementias may result in a loss of knowledge about objects regardless of the modality of access, and this is distinct from a visual agnosia (e.g., Hodges, Patterson, Oxbury, and Funnell, 1992; Martin and Fedio, 1983; Warrington, 1995). Third, the patient must be able to see the object clearly enough to describe its appearance, draw it, or answer whether it is the same or different in appearance compared with a second stimulus.

An interesting illustrative case of associative visual agnosia was reported by Rubens and Benson (1971). Their subject was a middle-aged physician who became agnosic following an acute hypotensive episode. His mental status and language abilities were normal, his visual acuity was 20/30, and although he had a right homonymous hemianopia (blindness in his right visual field) his visual fields were certainly larger than those of many non-agnosic individuals. They report that:

> For the first three weeks in the hospital, the patient could not identify common objects presented visually, and did not know what was on his plate until he tasted it. He identified objects immediately on touching them. When shown a stethoscope, he described it as "a long cord with a round thing at the end," and asked if it could be a watch . . . He was never able to describe or demonstrate the use of an object if he could not name it. . . . He could match identical objects, but not group objects by category (clothing, food) . . . He was unable to recognize members of his family, the hospital staff, or even his own face in the mirror . . . Remarkably, he could make excellent copies of line drawings and still fail to name the subject . . . He easily matched drawings of objects he could not identify, and had no difficulty discriminating between complex nonrepresentational patterns differing from each other only subtly. He occasionally failed because he included imperfections in the paper or printer's ink." (pp. 308–9)

In this classic case we see all the elements of associative agnosia: Impaired recognition of visually presented objects, demonstrated verbally and nonverbally, in a patient with normal intellect and apparently adequate visual perception. Recognition of objects through other modalities is intact, and copying and matching ability appear remarkably preserved. Figure 4.7 shows four drawings that this patient was unable to recognize, along with his excellent copies. Figure 4.8 shows the copies of four other agnosic patients, demonstrating the generality of the striking dissociation between perception (as measured by copying ability, at least) and recognition.

Evidence for a shape perception impairment

How can someone be of sound mind, see pictures clearly enough to produce the copies shown in figures 4.7 and 4.8, and yet not recognize the pictures? This constellation of abilities and impairments seems almost paradoxical, and perhaps for this reason the very existence of visual agnosia has been doubted (e.g., Bay, 1953; Bender and Feldman,

Figure 4.7   Copies of pictures made by an associative visual agnosic who could not recognize the pictures, either before or after copying them.
From A. B. Rubens and D. F. Benson, "Associative visual agnosia," Archives of Neurology, 24, 1971, with permission of the American Medical Association.

1972). The good drawings and preserved matching ability of such patients also invites the conclusion that perception is intact, and that the fault lies in the process of associating a normal percept with memory knowledge.

Although a failure of association is one possible explanation, it is also possible that perception itself is at fault despite appearances to the contrary. Several considerations suggest that a perceptual impairment underlies associative agnosia. First, although the final products of these patients' copying efforts are often normal, the process by which they produce the copies is generally reported to be abnormal. The words "slavish" and "line-by-line" are often used in describing the manner of copying in these cases (e.g., Ratcliff and Newcombe, 1982; Wapner, Judd, and Gardner, 1978), including the patient of

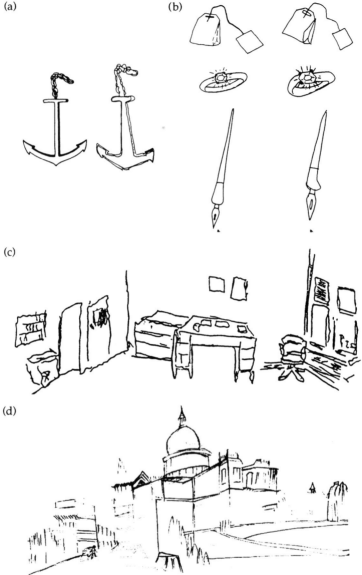

Figure 4.8 More examples of the good-quality copies made by associative visual agnosics who do not recognize their subject matter. (a) an anchor; (b) a teabag, ring, and pen; (c) the office in which the patient was sitting; (d) St. Paul's Cathedral.

From G. W. Humphreys and M. J. Riddoch, To See But Not to See: A Case Study of Visual Agnosia, Hillsdale, NJ, Lawrence Erlbaum Associates, 1987, reprinted by permission of Psychology Press Limited; M. J. Farah, Visual Agnosia: Disorders of Object Recognition and What They Tell Us About Normal Vision, Cambridge, MA, MIT Press, 1990; W. Wapner et al., "Visual agnosia in an artist," Cortex, 14, 1978.

Rubens and Benson, who was observed copying by Brown (1972). My own observations of L.H., an agnosic to be described in more detail in the following chapter, is that his drawings are executed abnormally slowly, with many pauses to check the correspondence of each line of the copy and the original. The impressive rendition of St. Paul's Cathedral by Humphreys and Riddoch's (1987) case H.J.A. impresses us in a different way when we learn that he spent 6 hours on it!

In evaluating the copying techniques of associative visual agnosics as evidence for a visual perceptual impairment, we should consider the alternative possibility that decreased availability of semantic knowledge might interfere with copying. A normal person's semantic grasp of what an object is might be expected to help a person keep the object's elements in working memory while it is being copied. However, it does seem unlikely that an absence of top-down semantic support for perception or perceptual working memory would be responsible for a 6-hour copying session! Nor does it seem able to explain the slavish line-by-line approach reported in so many cases, as normal subjects do not copy meaningless patterns in this way.

Several other observations are consistent with an impairment in visual perception, although these vary in their decisiveness. Associative visual agnosic patients are also abnormally sensitive to the visual quality of stimuli, performing best with real objects, next best with photographs, and worst with line drawings, an ordering reflecting increasing impoverishment of the stimulus (e.g., Levine and Calvanio, 1989; Ratcliff and Newcombe, 1982; Riddoch and Humphreys, 1987; Rubens and Benson, 1971). Tachistoscopic presentation, which also reduces visual stimulus quality, also impairs associative agnosic performance dramatically. Although this would seem to be *prima facie* evidence for a visual impairment, an absence of top-down semantic support can also account for an increase in sensitivity to visual factors (Tippett and Farah, 1994).

Potentially more decisive evidence comes from the nature of the recognition errors made by associative agnosics. The vast majority of errors are visual in nature, that is, they correspond to an object of similar shape (e.g., Levine, 1978; Ratcliff and Newcombe, 1982). For example, on four different occasions when I asked case L. H. to name a picture of a baseball bat, he made four different errors, all reflecting shape similarity: paddle, knife, baster, thermometer. The subject of

Davidoff and Wilson (1985) made some semantic as well as visual errors, but she was able to correct her semantic errors later when offered a forced choice between her initial answer and the correct one, whereas her visual errors were less tractable. Although visual errors can be accounted for by impaired access to semantic knowledge (Hinton and Shallice, 1991), such accounts predict accompanying semantic errors. Therefore, for those cases in which visual shape errors are found in the absence of semantic errors, it is likely that visual shape perception is at fault.

The matching of unfamiliar faces and complex meaningless designs, in which semantics would not play a role, also provides decisive evidence for a visual perceptual impairment. Changing the angle or lighting in the photograph of a face impairs agnosics' ability to match unfamiliar faces (Shuttleworth, Syring, and Allen, 1982). The matching of abstract geometric forms is even less likely to depend on semantic knowledge than the matching of unfamiliar faces. Recall that Rubens and Benson's patient occasionally mistook flaws in the paper or printer's ink for a part of the design, reminiscent of IT-lesioned monkey's use of local, idiosyncratic features in visual discrimination learning. Levine (1978) administered a visual discrimination learning task to an associative agnosic, and found her unable to learn a subtle discrimination between two patterns after 30 trials.

In sum, associative visual agnosics appear to be the human analog of the IT-lesioned monkeys described earlier. A variety of evidence suggests that they fail to recognize objects because they fail to represent their shape in a normal way. The extremely slow and slavish copying technique, the sometimes isolated occurrence of visual shape errors, and abnormalities in performance at matching abstract designs, all point fairly directly to a shape perception impairment. The analogy holds anatomically as well. Although the human lesions tend to be somewhat more posterior than in the monkey brain, they are inferior and generally include temporal as well as occipital cortex.

4.6   Perceptual categorization deficit

Warrington and her colleagues have described another type of visual recognition impairment, which they term "apperceptive agnosia," and which they characterize as an impairment of perceptual categorization. Because the term "apperceptive agnosia" has been used in a variety of different ways by different authors, and because it has been used most consistently to label the disorder of grouping discussed in chapter 3, I have referred to the present disorder as "perceptual categorization deficit" (see Farah, 1990, for a detailed review of the literature on this form of agnosia). The cardinal feature of perceptual categorization deficit, first documented by Warrington and Taylor (1973), is an inability to recognize objects viewed from unusual perspectives, or to match pairs of objects depicted in one usual and one unusual perspective. Warrington (1985) has cited unpublished data showing that the same type of patient also has difficulty recognizing objects photographed under conditions of uneven or unusual illumination. Figure 4.9 shows examples of the kinds of stimuli used in this research.

On the face of things, perceptual categorization deficit appears to be the loss of just those "miraculous" representations discussed at the outset of this chapter. Indeed, Warrington's research on perceptual categorization deficit was the only neuropsychological evidence cited by David Marr in his landmark (1982) book on vision, and he presented it as bearing on the representations underlying object recognition. In this context, he interpreted the disorder as an inability to transform the image representation to an object-centered representation of shape, from which perspective and other aspects of the viewing conditions had been eliminated.

Although perceptual categorization deficit has attracted the attention of many leading researchers since Marr as a source of clues to the mechanisms of orientation invariance, there are reasons to doubt its direct relevance. First, these patients are not impaired in everyday life. Their deficit is manifest only on specially designed tests. This is in sharp contrast to associative visual agnosics just described, who are significantly handicapped by their visual disorder. Perhaps more to the point, it is also in contrast to the predicted effects of derailing vision at a retinotopic or image-based stage of representation.

A second and related point is that these patients have not been demonstrated to have an impairment in matching objects across different views. What, you say? Although readers may remember learning that perceptual categorization deficit involves a problem in matching different views of objects, all that has been demonstrated is

Figure 4.9   Examples of photographs used to test for a perceptual categorization deficit. (a) unusual view (b) unusual lighting.
From M. J. Farah, Visual Agnosia: Disorders of Object Recognition and What They Tell Us About Normal Vision, *Cambridge, MA, MIT Press, 1990.*

a problem matching a usual to an *unusual* view. Although one could construct a test in which different usual views of objects must be matched, the tests used so far have always included an unusual view. In my experience normal subjects often require a few seconds to identify these unusual views, and published data show that their performance is not without error (e.g., Warrington and Taylor, 1973). This raises the possibility that the recognition or matching of unusual views requires a kind of effortful processing above and beyond object perception proper. Such processing might more aptly be called visual problem solving than visual recognition.

A third reason for questioning whether perceptual categorization deficit results from a loss of the visual shape representations normally used in object recognition comes from its associated neuropathology. Everything we know about the localization of visual shape representation in nonhuman primates implicates the ventral visual system bilaterally. Perceptual categorization deficit in humans generally follows unilateral right hemisphere lesions, and is particularly associated with parietal damage (Warrington and Taylor, 1973).

In sum, despite the initial impression that perceptual categorization deficit represents a selective impairment of viewpoint-invariant object recognition, a closer look at both behavior and anatomy casts doubt on this idea. Indeed, although Warrington (e.g., 1985) once viewed perceptual categorization as the first of two main stages of object recognition (the second being the access of semantic knowledge), in more recent writings she has stated that "we would now wish to argue that perceptual categorization systems may be an optional resource rather than an obligatory stage of visual analysis" (Warrington and James, 1988).

4.7 Neuroimaging studies of object recognition in humans

The recently developed techniques of PET and fMRI have the potential to localize object recognition processes in the human brain with greater precision than is possible with naturally occurring lesions. Functional neuroimaging can also be used to answer certain questions about functional characteristics of object recognition, through inferences based on localization information. Geoffrey Aguirre and I recently surveyed the neuroimaging literature on object recognition (Farah and Aguirre, 1999). From a large set of published studies that involved viewing or making judgments about visually presented stimuli, we found 17 whose design made it possible to at least roughly isolate visual recognition *per se.*

The 17 relevant studies are listed in table 4.1. Beyond a shared affinity for Snodgrass and Vanderwart pictures, they are a heterogeneous collection of designs. Some simply contrasted passive viewing of visual stimuli (e.g., line drawings of objects, printed words or pseudowords, photographs of faces) with passive viewing of control stimuli (e.g., fixation points, scrambled pictures, textures). Others

Table 4.1   Studies which roughly isolate visual recognition *per se.*
(From M. J. Farah and G. K. Aguirre, 1999.)

Study	Task
Words	
Petersen *et al.*, 1988	*Passive* viewing of words vs. fixation
Petersen *et al.*, 1990	*Passive* viewing of words and pseudo-words vs. passive viewing of false fonts
Howard *et al.*, 1992	Read aloud visually presented words vs. view false fonts and say "crime"
Price *et al.*, 1994, exp. 1	Read aloud visually presented words vs. perform feature decision on false fonts
Price *et al.*, 1994, exp. 2	*Passive* viewing of words vs. passive viewing of false fonts
Menard *et al.*, 1996	*Passive* viewing of words vs. fixation
Puce *et al.*, 1996	*Passive* viewing of letter strings (nonwords) vs. passive viewing of textures
Polk *et al.*, 1998	*Passive* viewing of AltErNAtIng case words vs. passive viewing of consonant strings
Objects	
Sergent *et al.*, 1992a	Living/nonliving judgment regarding Snodgrass and Vanderwart (S&V) pictures vs. fixation
Sergent *et al.*, 1992b	Living/nonliving judgment regarding S&V pictures vs. judge gratings as vertical or horizontal
Kosslyn *et al.*, 1994	Matching S&V pictures with their names vs. viewing random patterns of lines
Kosslyn *et al.*, 1995	Picture verification performed upon S&V-style line drawings of objects and auditorily presented "entry level" words vs. scrambled lines and words
Malach *et al.*, 1995	*Passive* viewing of objects vs. passive viewing of phase randomized pictures
Menard *et al.*, 1996	*Passive* viewing of S&V pictures vs. fixation
Kanwisher *et al.*, 1997	*Passive* viewing of S&V pictures (and novel S&V-style objects) vs. passive viewing of scrambled lines

Table 4.1   (cont'd)

Study	Task
Faces	
Sergent *et al.*, 1992b	Gender categorization of faces vs. judge gratings as vertical or horizontal
Haxby *et al.*, 1994	Matching faces across shifts of gaze vs. alternating button presses to scrambled faces
Haxby *et al.*, 1996	Encoding (viewing) faces vs. alternating button presses to scrambled faces
Puce *et al.*, 1996	*Passive* viewing of faces vs. passive viewing of textures
McCarthy *et al.*, 1997	*Passive* viewing of faces amongst phase randomized objects vs. viewing of phase randomized objects

contrasted active experimental tasks with control tasks intended to match at least some of the processing demands of the experimental task other than the need for object recognition. The experimental tasks included judgments such as living versus nonliving, name verification (e.g., is this a *tree*?), and for faces, verification of male versus female. The control tasks in these studies used stimuli such as scrambled pictures or gratings that were either passively viewed or the object of different judgments, such as horizontal versus vertical.

An optimist might view the heterogeneity in the designs of these studies as an opportunity to identify the cortical areas that participate in visual recognition independent of the particulars of task and stimulus. A pessimist might expect the variability in designs, especially the imperfect ways in which control tasks are matched to experimental tasks, to obscure the true neural locus of visual recognition. Figure 4.10, showing the 84 activation maxima from the 17 studies, suggests that the pessimist's prediction may be closer to the truth. The only generalization that one can make, on the basis of these data, is that visual recognition is a function of the posterior half of the brain!

Before giving the pessimist the last word, let us explore this data set a bit further to see if there are clusters of maxima, within the overall scatter, corresponding to particular aspects of task design or

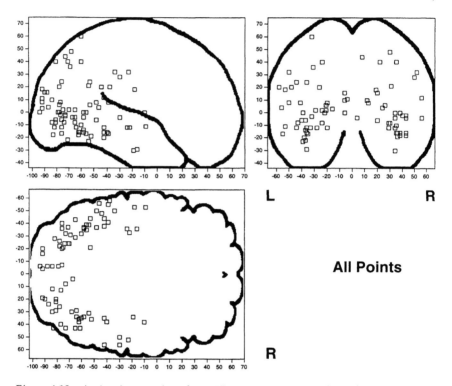

Figure 4.10 Activation maxima from 17 neuroimaging studies of visual recognition.

From M. J. Farah and G. K. Aguirre, "Imaging visual recognition: PET and fMRI studies of the functional anatomy of human visual recognition," Trends in Cognitive Sciences, 3, 1999.

stimuli. The first distinction to look at, if task variability and imperfect control conditions are a concern, is the active versus passive nature of the experimental task. Active tasks, because they involve more processing beyond simply seeing and recognizing the stimulus, are prone to spurious maxima if the control condition fails to match perfectly the nonrecognition processing. Figure 4.11 shows the maxima associated with the contrasts between experimental and control conditions for active and passive tasks separately. The active tasks cover a slightly broader range of brain than the passive, but the difference hardly accounts for the overall scatter. Both active and passive tasks produce widely distributed maxima.

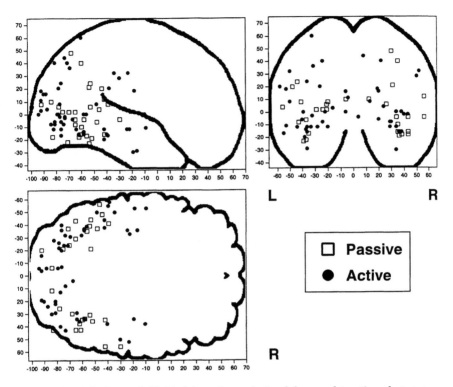

Figure 4.11 Maxima subdivided into those derived from subtractions between passive object viewing and passive baseline tasks, and those derived from subtractions between active object recognition tasks (e.g., living/nonliving classification) and corresponding active baseline tasks.

From M. J. Farah and G. K. Aguirre, "Imaging visual recognition: PET and fMRI studies of the functional anatomy of human visual recognition," Trends in Cognitive Sciences, 3, 1999.

The possibility that different categories of stimuli may be recognized using different neural systems is a question that will be taken up in more detail in the following two chapters. It is an example of an issue concerning the functional organization of visual recognition, rather than its anatomical localization *per se*, that can be addressed using neuroimaging data. If the regions activated by object, face, and word recognition are segregated into different parts of visual cortex, this would support a category-specific organization. For present purposes, the possibility of category-specific recognition systems is of

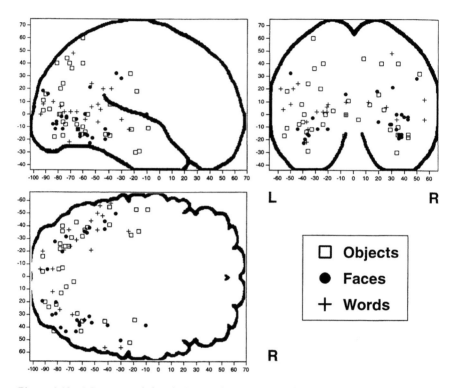

Figure 4.12   Maxima subdivided into those derived from visual recognition of objects, faces, and printed words.

From M. J. Farah and G. K. Aguirre, "Imaging visual recognition: PET and fMRI studies of the functional anatomy of human visual recognition," Trends in Cognitive Sciences, 3, 1999.

interest as a way of explaining the seemingly nonfocal nature of activation maxima associated with visual recognition. Perhaps the scatter apparent in figures 4.10 and 4.11 can actually be subdivided into some number of more compact non-overlapping clusters. Figure 4.12 shows that subdividing the studies by category of stimulus does not greatly reduce the scatter.

On the basis of the findings summarized so far, it would be fair to say that functional neuroimaging has not taught us much regarding the neural bases of object recognition in humans. Different studies produce different results, and the source of the variability is unclear. It does not appear to result from the different categories of stimuli used in these studies, nor does it appear to result from the variability in the tasks used to study recognition. What could be wrong?

What neuroimaging studies localize is the psychological process, or processes, by which an experimental task and a control task differ. With this in mind, look again at the designs summarized in table 4.1. The experimental tasks generally do require more visual recognition than the control tasks. The problem is that this is not the only difference between the experimental and control tasks. In the passive viewing tasks, the experimental and control stimuli often differ dramatically, by such gross measures as luminance flux, size, and complexity. In the active tasks, both stimuli and task instructions differ dramatically. There is little wonder that the results of these studies do not superimpose.

There is no reason why functional neuroimaging studies cannot be designed to better isolate the processes of interest, and indeed a few good examples already exist. Most of these specifically address the issue of specialization for different categories of stimuli, and were designed using experimental and control tasks that differ minimally. Because they do not isolate object recognition *per se*, but instead isolate specific subtypes of object recognition relative to one another, they will be described in the two chapters that follow, on the question of specialized recognition systems for faces and printed words.

4.8 Neural representations underlying object recognition: a computational interpretation

Having reviewed a broad array of empirical findings on visual object processing in the brains of humans and their primate cousins, we are now in a position to try to deduce some constraints on the nature of the underlying representations.

Coordinate system: empirical evidence

The evidence from single unit recordings and lesions in monkeys rules out the simplest versions of a viewer-centered or an environment-centered coordinate system. The relatively invariant responses of at least some IT cells to a given shape over changes in position, size, and picture plane orientation relative to viewer and environment are not consistent with a coordinate system anchored to either. The impairment of IT-lesioned monkeys in generalizing learned visual object discriminations to new views of the objects, and their normality at learning to discriminate different views of a single object, also suggest that IT neurons possess some degree of viewpoint-invariance. Finally, the ability of IT-lesioned monkeys to generalize a learned discrimination to new patterns when some of the features of the earlier patterns stay in the same position relative to the monkey and/or the environment, but not when the same features are shifted to a new position (see figure 4.3), is further evidence for an abnormal reliance on viewer-centered or environment-centered representation and hence a loss of more abstract representations of shape.

Although these data clearly rule out the use of a plain viewer-centered or environment-centered coordinate system, they do not definitively implicate an object-centered coordinate system in IT. Recall that when a viewer-centered system is augmented with associative learning and normalization processes, it too will enable viewpoint-invariant object recognition. In the terms used to describe the problem at the outset of this chapter, there are two ways to deal with the bundling together of shape and perspective in retinotopic representations. One is to undo the bundle, and this is equivalent to computing an object-centered representation. The other, less aesthetic but easier to accomplish, is simply to sort the bundles according to the objects that gave rise to them. They can be sorted according to their intertransformability (e.g., this viewpoint-dependent representation can be rotated and enlarged to match that one) or through explicit learning (e.g., this viewpoint-dependent representation is my grandmother and so is that one) or a combination (as proposed by Tarr and Pinker, 1989).

In short, it is possible that IT does not house object-centered representations *per se*, but rather the ability to associate multiple viewer-centered representations and/or transform one viewer-centered representation to another. Two empirical observations lend some degree of support to the latter alternative, although the issue is far from resolved. First, the invariances for position, size, and orientation that we see in the responses of IT neurons are always imperfect (see figure 4.6). Indeed some studies, with wire and amoeba-like stimuli, find rather limited orientation invariance (Logothetis, Pauls, and Poggio, 1995). This is not what would be expected if objects' shapes were being represented in an object-centered coordinate system, which does not contain perspective information. In contrast, it is easier to see how perspective could have residual effects on the processing of a system that never eliminated perspective information in the first place. Unusual views might be less well-learned or require additional normalization with consequent additional likelihood of error. A second observation that lends credence to the viewer-centered alternative is the demonstrated ability of IT neurons to learn associations between patterns (Miyashita, Date, and Okuno, 1993). These cells have been shown to acquire selectivity for arbitrary pairs of stimuli that have been repeatedly associated, a necessary ability for deriving invariances from viewer-centered representations through learning.

Foldiak (1991) has proposed a simple computational mechanism by which viewpoint-independent representations could emerge from seeing a given object from different perspectives. He combined the idea that different views of an object are often clustered in time, with the idea that cells' activity takes some time to decay. The consequence of these two ideas is the following: An active cell in a higher visual area such as IT might remain active throughout the time that a moving object activates first one set of cells then another in earlier retinotopic areas, and by correlation-driven learning this will associate both of the retinotopic representations with the same higher-level representation. Wallis and Rolls (1997) have developed similar ideas in the context of the physiology of the different visual areas, going from V1 to IT.

Primitives: empirical evidence

Surprisingly, no research has directly addressed the nature of the geometric primitives used in primate, including human, object recognition. Nevertheless, there are clues available from a number of sources that show a reassuringly high degree of agreement in pointing to either surface-based or volumetric primitives for the shape representations underlying object recognition in IT. Discriminating between surface-based and volumetric primitives is not possible at present, but at least contour-based primitives can be tentatively ruled out.

Two indications of noncontour-based representation are available in the literature on IT lesions in monkeys. First, these animals are impaired at perceiving shape equivalence over changes in the pattern of shadow and light falling on the object. Such changes do not affect the depth information needed to derive surface and volumetric representations, but they do affect the pattern of spurious contours. This suggests that the object perception of IT-lesioned monkeys is abnormally reliant on contour information, and hence that they differ from normal monkeys by an inability to derive noncontour-based representations. The finding that IT lesions also impair monkeys' ability to perceive shapes in random dot stereograms, which have no contours, provides additional evidence that the function of IT includes noncontour-based representation. Recordings from IT neurons are also consistent with this interpretation. The preference of these neurons for three-dimensional objects, or models of objects, over flat outline shapes suggests the importance of surface properties such as texture, shadow, and disparity, which provide cues to the surface or volumetric shape. Perhaps most compelling is the finding that IT neurons respond selectively to shape whether defined by luminosity differences, which form the basis for static contour, or by texture or motion differences, which do not give rise to contours in the sense of elongated zones of transition from light to dark. Research on the face perception of agnosic patients also suggests that they may be more dependent on contours than a normal human, in that they have difficulty seeing the equivalence of faces photographed from the same angle but with a different play of light and shadow. Their heightened sensitivity to the differences between drawings, photographs, and real objects may also reflect an impaired ability to extract or infer surface and/or volume information.

The evidence that IT represents shape in terms of surface-based or volumetric primitives contrasts with at least one common interpretation of the response properties of cells in earlier occipital areas, reviewed in chapter 1, according to which they represent edges and contours. Thus, one way in which the representation of the stimulus appears to be transformed in going from early occipital to inferotemporal representations is that the building blocks of shape representation go from contours to some higher-order geometric primitive, either surfaces or volumes.

Organization: empirical evidence

Studies of object vision in monkeys have relatively little to tell us concerning the degree and type of organization imposed on object shape by the primate visual system. The one source of direct evidence is the finding that face cells show greatly diminished responses to scrambled faces. If face parts were explicitly represented as units of shape in their own right in a hierarchy of shape representation, then the representation of the scrambled face would still be partially equivalent to the representation of the intact face at the part level of the hierarchy. The lack of response to scrambled faces suggests that face cells do not embody a hierarchically organized representation of shape. However, as will be argued in the next chapter, this particular aspect of face cell function may well be unrepresentative of the cells involved in representing nonface objects.

Turning to the human evidence, the behavior of some agnosic patients seems very relevant to the issue of hierarchical shape representation. When shown an object or picture that they cannot recognize, agnosics frequently guess its identity on the basis of its local parts or features. For example, an animal with a long tapered tail might engender "rat" or "mouse" as a guess. A baby carriage whose wheels have metal spokes might be called a "bicycle." This behavior invites interpretation in terms of a hierarchical system of shape representation, whose lower level part representations are relatively intact but whose higher level integration of the parts is damaged or unavailable. Riddoch and Humphreys (1987) have explicitly suggested that such an impairment in the integration of local parts into higher and more global levels of a shape hierarchy may underlie certain cases of agnosia. They introduced the term "integrative agnosia" for such cases.

In addition to the use of local parts for guessing the identity of objects, they point to several other aspects of agnosic performance that seem consistent with this interpretation, specifically: Impaired recognition of briefly presented stimuli (because, they argue, if parts are serially encoded more time will be required), impaired recognition of overlapping drawings (because impaired part integration will be further taxed by the possibility of misconjoining the parts of different objects), impaired discrimination of real objects from pseudo-objects composed of mismatched parts of real objects, and greater impairment relative to normal subjects at recognizing more complex depictions (because these contain more parts).

Because the idea of integrative agnosia has important implications for the issue of the organization of visual object representations, let us scrutinize it further. Although there is no doubt that an impairment in integrating shape parts into global wholes is consistent with the findings just listed, such an impairment is not the only way to account for these findings.

First, consider the basic finding that agnosics may guess the identity of objects based on a single correctly perceived part. While consistent with an impairment in integration of parts, it is also consistent with almost any type of impairment in shape processing capacity, as the shape of a part will always be simpler than the shape of a whole object. Above and beyond this, in any system for which there is a fixed probability of recognizing a given shape (part or whole), there will be more successes with just parts than with just wholes, simply because parts are more numerous.

The other features of integrative agnosia are similarly ambiguous with respect to the underlying impairment in shape representation. The slower speed of agnosic object recognition is hardly a unique prediction of impaired part integration, nor is the detrimental effect of overlapping pictures, as almost any impairment of shape perception one can think of would be expected to slow the process and make it less robust to interfering contours. Similarly, object decision would be expected to be impaired whenever shape perception is defective in any way. The difference in performance between silhouettes and detailed drawings after unspecified perceptual impairment could take the form of better performance the more information is available (hence drawings better than silhouettes) or better performance the simpler that shape to be perceived (hence silhouttes better than drawings), but certainly the latter prediction is not unique to a specific impairment of part integration.

In sum, we know little at this point about the organization of object shape representations. There is no evidence from monkeys or humans that specifically implicates a hierarchical organization for the object representations of IT.

Implementation: empirical evidence

With respect to the type of search process that underlies visual object recognition, the question can be posed thus: Are there two tokens of a high-level object representation, one derived from the stimulus and one waiting in memory against which the stimulus representation is matched? Or does the stimulus get encoded and recoded, starting in early visual areas in which the representation is determined largely by the innate structure of the visual system, and ending with still just one token representation in higher-level areas, in which the representation is determined by a structure that results from learning? In the former case, one can point to distinct perceptual and mnemonic representations of the object, within high-level visual areas. In the latter case, there is no distinction between perception and memory; if one's memory is changed or disrupted, so is one's high-level perception. High-level visual representations are perceptual, in the sense that they are derived from stimulus input, and they are mnemonic in the sense that the pattern of weights responsible for their derivation is determined by experience (in contrast to the smaller role of experience in setting the weights at earlier stages of visual processing).

If object search is implemented in the first way, in common with search in symbol-manipulating computers, then it should in principle be possible to destroy the memory representation but retain the high-level perceptual representation of the object. If object search is implemented in the second way, in common with neural network computation, then impaired performance on tests of object recognition (memory) will always be accompanied by impaired performance on tests of object perception. Although no direct tests of this prediction have been made in either the monkey or the human literature, the apparent universality of impaired object perception in associative agnosia, discussed earlier, is more consistent with a neural network implementation of search.

The degree of distributedness of object representation has been addressed most directly in the single unit recording literature. The striking specificity of IT neurons for particular shapes, even for one face over another, might seem to suggest the kind of one stimulus–one neuron system of representation that is equivalent to a localist implementation. However, even these highly selective neurons show some degree of generalization, responding in varying degrees to different faces. Thus, for a given object or face, a number of neurons will be active to varying degrees, equivalent to a distributed representation (Young and Yamane, 1992).

The spatial scale of functional neuroimaging, and the necessity of combining data from multiple trials, makes comparable evidence impossible to obtain from humans. However, one of the neuroimaging studies cited earlier is nevertheless relevant to the issue of distributed representation. Kanwisher, Woods, Iacoboni, and Mazziotta (1997) compared patterns of brain activity while their subjects viewed line drawings of real objects, line drawings of made-up objects, and scrambled line drawings that had no three-dimensional interpretation as an object. As expected, they found inferotemporal activation associated with viewing the objects, relative to the scrambled displays. They also found equivalent activation associated with viewing the made-up objects. This is consistent with a distributed system of representation, in which a made-up object can be represented by a novel ensemble of the same parts used to represent familiar objects.

The graded way in which object recognition breaks down after IT lesions is also indicative of a system of distributed representation. IT-lesioned monkeys and human agnosics do not lose the ability to recognize arbitrary subsets of all objects, such as tall things with corners. Agnosias may be more or less severe, consistent with more or less of a distributed representation having been damaged, but by and large they affect all objects equally. There are two well-established exceptions to this generalization, to which we now turn. Both face recognition and printed word recognition may make use of cortical representations that are to some extent segregated from each other and from object representation.

chapter five

Face Recognition

5.1 Are faces "special"?

Everything that was said in chapter 3 about the problem of object recognition would seem to apply equally well to the problem of face recognition. Aside from finding certain exemplars of this category particularly endearing, it is hard to see the difference between faces and other objects. As illustrated in figure 5.1, faces present us with highly variable images depending upon the angle from which we view them and the positions of their moveable parts. Whether the content of the image is a common object or a face, our visual system must create a representation that is invariant over at least a range of such viewing conditions, yet discriminates among exemplars.

This very reasonable sounding argument for common mechanisms underlying face and object recognition is contradicted by an array of empirical findings in developmental psychology, psychophysics, and neuropsychology. The neuropsychological evidence, from brain-damaged humans and from neuroimaging studies of normal humans, is arguably the strongest evidence and will be the focus of this chapter. Just two examples of evidence from outside of neuropsychology will be described here.

Developmental psychologists have shown that we come into the world predisposed to treat faces differently from other objects. For example, human infants only 30 minutes of age will track a moving

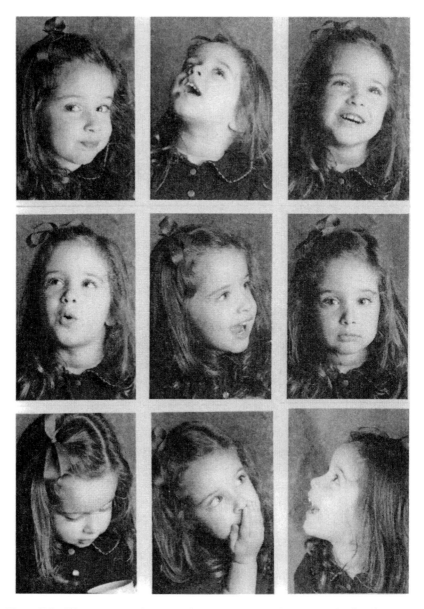

Figure 5.1   We are so proficient at face recognition that it may be hard to appreciate what radically different images fall on our retinas when a single face changes its expression or orientation.

Photographer: Tommy Leonardi

face farther than other moving patterns of comparable contrast, complexity, symmetry, and so on (Johnson, Dziurawiec, Ellis, and Morton, 1991). This and other studies of infant face perception are reviewed by Johnson (1997).

Psychophysical studies of orientation effects on pattern perception show a marked and robust difference between faces and other complex objects with canonical upright orientations (e.g. a piano or a house). Whereas most objects are a bit harder to recognize upsidedown than rightside up, inversion makes faces dramatically harder for normal adult subjects to recognize (see Valentine, 1988, for a review). To appreciate this first hand, try recognizing each of the well-known faces in figure 5.2 before turning the book upside-down. The inversion effect and other differences in the visual information processing of faces and nonface objects are reviewed by Farah, Wilson, Drain, and Tanaka (1998).

These findings indicate that face recognition and the recognition of other objects are not functionally identical: Face recognition has earlier developmental precursors and is more orientation-sensitive than the recognition of other types of object. Strictly speaking, however, this does not imply that face recognition is accomplished using a different system from object recognition. Perhaps faces are simply the first type of shape that a general-purpose recognition system is programmed to process. Likewise, faces might simply require more of an orientation-sensitive type of processing than other objects, accomplished by a single, general-purpose system.

To decide the issue of whether there is just one recognition system or two separate systems for faces and nonface objects, we need some criteria for individuating recognition systems. I propose three criteria by which face and nonface object recognition can be said to be functions of different systems. The first criterion is anatomical. If face and nonface object recognition depend on different parts of the brain, they are functions of different systems by an anatomical criterion. Another criterion is functional independence, by which I mean the ability of each system to operate without the other. Finally, systems can be individuated according to their information processing functions. By this criterion, different systems should not be mere physical and functional duplicates of one another, but should process information in different ways. In the remainder of this chapter, I will

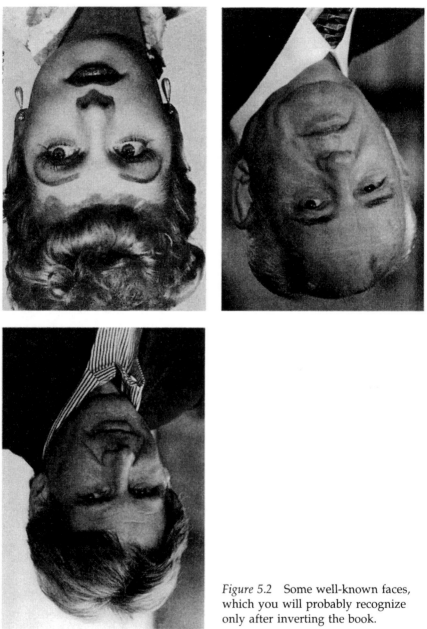

Figure 5.2   Some well-known faces, which you will probably recognize only after inverting the book.

review neuropsychological and neurophysiological evidence that face and object recognition are different systems by all of these criteria.

5.2   Neural systems underlying face and object recognition

Face cells

Single unit recording would seem to offer excellent prospects for comparing brain mechanisms of face and object recognition. The anatomical localization could not be better, and the ability to systematically vary stimulus attributes while recording should permit the testing of hypotheses concerning functional properties of face and object representations. However, of the many interesting things we have learned about face perception from the study of face cells, the relationship between face and object recognition is not among the issues so far illuminated. Following a brief description of the general properties of these cells, I will consider what few clues they might offer as to whether face recognition is "special."

Face cells respond vigorously to faces yet show little response to nonface objects or scrambled arrays of face parts. Figure 5.3 shows typical responses of a face cell to a variety of different stimulus patterns. Face cells have been found throughout the inferotemporal cortex of monkeys, although they cluster in certain functional subdivisions near the superior temporal sulcus (STS), where they comprise up to 20 percent of the cells of the anterior STS (Baylis, Rolls, and Leonard, 1987). Like other pattern-selective cells discussed in the previous chapter, face cells display invariance over position, size, and in some cases orientation. Conversely, their selectivity is related to various aspects of facial appearance, including facial identity (e.g., Baylis, Rolls, and Leonard, 1985), emotional expression (Hasselmo, Rolls, and Baylis, 1989), and direction of gaze (Perrett, Oram, Harries, Bevan, Hietanen, Benson, and Thomas, 1991). Analyses of the aspects of facial appearance that drive the cells suggest that configuational relations among multiple facial features are critical (Yamane, Kaji, and Kawano, 1988). Although many face cells respond differentially to different faces, it is not the case that any given cell is representing just one face. Rather, each cell has a gradient of responsiveness to a range of faces, and any

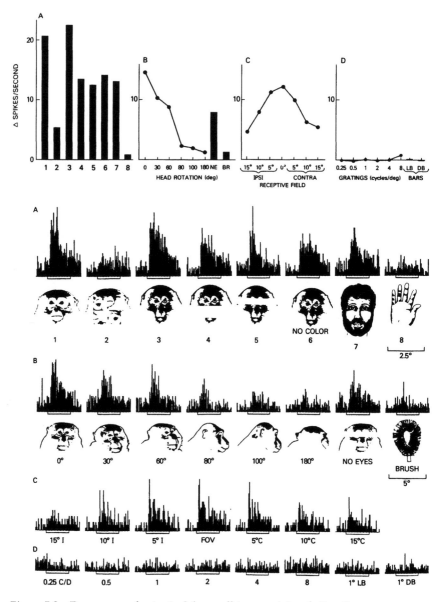

Figure 5.3   Responses of a typical face cell to a variety of stimuli.
From R. Desimone, T. D. Allbright, C. G. Gross, and C. Bruce, "Stimulus-selective properties of inferior temporal neurons in the macacque," Journal of Neuroscience, 4, 1984.

given face will evoke activity at different levels over a subset of the face cell population. Face cells thus comprise a system of distributed representation.

Some authors have emphasized the commonalities between face cells and other object-selective cells in IT. Gross and Sergent (1992) point to several such commonalities, including: the lack of segregation (with face and nonface pattern-selective cells found together in all regions of IT), the apparent use of distributed representation for both faces and nonface patterns, the similar spatial invariances of both face and object-selective cells, and the modifiability of both types of cell's responses as a function of experience.

On the other hand, the sheer number of face cells in certain areas seems distinctive. Monkeys also recognize food, cages, other laboratory apparatus, and so on, yet no area has been found with 20 percent of the cells responding selectively to any of these objects. A second, and possibly related difference, concerns the optimal stimuli for driving face and nonface cells. Although complexity and similarity are notoriously difficult concepts to measure, the optimal stimuli for nonface cells seem less complex and less specific than for face cells (for example, see figure 4.5). This might suggest that individual IT neurons represent the relatively simpler component parts of objects, with the objects themselves coded as ensembles of such parts. The idea that objects are represented in terms of their component parts to a greater degree than faces will arise again later in the chapter.

In any case, the issue of commonalities and differences between face cells and other pattern-selective cells may be moot, from the perspective of face recognition research, if face cells are not actually needed for face recognition. Heywood and Cowey (1992) tested the functional role of STS, the region of IT in which face cells are most concentrated, by ablating it bilaterally in monkeys and assessing their postoperative face recognition abilities. Surprisingly, the monkeys had no lasting impairment of face recognition. Instead, they had a severe impairment in discriminating gaze direction, an impairment that has also been observed in humans with face recognition impairments (Campbell, Heywood, Cowey, Regard, and Landis, 1990). It is possible that face cells elsewhere in IT are involved in face recognition *per se*. Perhaps the critical region in monkeys is more ventral and medial regions of temporal cortex, homologous to the regions of the human brain implicated in face recognition by neuroimaging and

, of face recognition impairments. At present, these ideas re-
pure speculation.

Prosopagnosia

Associative visual agnosia, discussed in the previous chapter, does
not always affect the recognition of all types of stimuli equally. Patients with prosopagnosia have particular difficulty recognizing faces.
To the extent that they can recognize familiar people, they rely on
nonfacial cues such as voice, distinctive clothing, or hairstyle. The
disorder can be so severe that even close friends and family members
will not be recognized. Indeed, even the patient's own face cannot be
recognized. The prosopagnosic, L.H., related the following story to
me. He was attending a conference held at a busy hotel and attended
by many of his colleagues. He rounded a corner and found himself
walking towards someone he took to be an acquaintance. He found
the man's behavior bizarre, however, staring at him without returning his greeting. A few seconds later he realized he was facing a
mirror. Although many prosopagnosics have some degree of difficulty recognizing objects other than faces, in many cases the deficit
appears strikingly disproportionate for faces. L.H., for example, rarely
experiences recognition difficulties with objects in his everyday life.

The most straightforward interpretation of prosopagnosia is consistent with anatomically separate recognition systems for faces and
objects. More precisely, prosopagnosia suggests that there is some
system that is necessary for face recognition, and either unnecessary
or less important for object recognition.

There is an alternative explanation for prosopagnosia, however,
according to which faces and other types of object are recognized
using a single recognition system. One need only suppose, quite plau-
sibly, that faces are the most difficult type of object for the recognition
system. Prosopagnosia can then be explained as a mild form of agnosia,
in which the impairment is detectable only on the most taxing form
of recognition task. This account has the appeal of parsimony, in that
it requires only one visual recognition system, and perhaps for this
reason has gained adherents.

To determine whether prosopagnosia is truly selective for faces,
and hence whether the human brain has specialized mechanisms for

recognizing faces, we must therefore assess the prosopagnosic performance on faces and nonface objects *relative to* the difficulty of these stimuli for normal subjects. One technical difficulty encountered in such a project is that normal subjects will invariably perform nearly perfectly on both face and nonface recognition tasks. The resultant ceiling effect will mask any differences in difficulty that might exist between tasks, making it pointless to test normal subjects in the kinds of recognition tasks that have traditionally been administered to patients. With this problem in mind, researchers have devised visual recognition tasks that test learning of novel face and nonface objects. By having subjects learn to recognize specific new exemplars of faces and other types of object, it is possible to titrate normal subjects' level of recognition performance so that it falls between ceiling and floor.

The first researchers to address this issue directly were McNeil and Warrington (1993). They studied case W.J., a middle-aged professional man who became prosopagnosic following a series of strokes. After becoming prosopagnosic, W.J. made a career change and went into sheep farming. He eventually came to recognize many of his sheep, although he remained unable to recognize most humans. The authors noted the potential implications of such a dissociation for the question of whether human face recognition is "special," and designed an ingenious experiment exploiting W.J.'s newfound career. They assembled three groups of photographs: human faces, sheep faces of the same breed kept by W.J., and sheep faces of a different breed, and attempted to teach subjects names for each face. Normal subjects performed at intermediate levels between ceiling and floor in all conditions. They performed better with the human faces than with sheep faces, even those who, like W.J., worked with sheep. In contrast, W.J. performed poorly with the human faces, and performed normally with the sheep faces. These data suggest that W.J.'s recognition impairment does not affect the recognition of all groups of visually similar patterns, but is selective for human faces.

My colleagues and I took a similar approach, but used common objects rather than faces of another species to compare with human face recognition (Farah, Levinson, and Klein, 1995). Our subject was L.H., a well-educated professional man who has been prosopagnosic since an automobile accident in college. L.H. is profoundly prosopagnosic, unable to recognize reliably his wife, children, or even

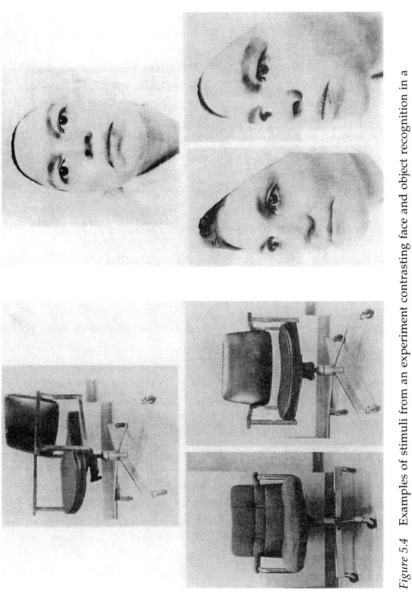

Figure 5.4 Examples of stimuli from an experiment contrasting face and object recognition in a prosopagnosic.

From M. J. Farah et al., "Face perception and within-category discrimination in prosopagnosia," Neuropsychologia, 33, 1995, with permission of Elsevier Science.

himself in a group photograph. Yet he is highly intelligent, and seems to have little or no difficulty recognizing other types of visual patterns such as printed words or objects. Although he has a degree of recognition impairment with drawings of objects, this is still less severe than his impairment with faces.

We employed a recognition memory paradigm, in which L.H. and control subjects first studied a set of photographs of faces and nonface objects, such as forks, chairs, and eyeglasses. Subjects were then given a larger set of photographs, and asked to make "old"/"new" judgments on them. This larger set was designed so that for each face and nonface object in the "old" set there was a highly similar item in the "new" set. Figure 5.4 shows examples of stimuli from this experiment. For example, one of the study items was an upholstered swiveling desk chair with arms. Among the larger set of test photos, there were two upholstered swiveling desk chairs with arms, one of the "old" chair and one of a "new" chair. Whereas normal subjects performed equally well with the faces and nonface objects, L.H. showed a significant performance disparity, performing worse with faces than with objects.

One could still maintain that prosopagnosia is not face-specific, and instead attribute the poor performance with faces to the need for within-category discrimination. According to this alternative hypothesis, the underlying impairment in prosopagnosia is in recognizing individual exemplars of any large and visually homogeneous category. To test this hypothesis directly, we carried out a second experiment in which subjects learned exemplars of the category "face" and an equivalent number of highly similar exemplars all drawn from a single nonface category, namely eyeglass frames. As before, L.H. was disproportionately impaired at face recognition relative to nonface recognition, when his performance is considered relative to normal subjects. This implies that prosopagnosia is not a problem with recognizing specific exemplars from any visually homogeneous category, but is specific to faces.

In essence, the design of the previous experiments amounts to a comparison between a prosopagnosic's performance with faces and his performance with stimuli that are like faces (in their recognition difficulty, in their membership in a visually homogeneous category) without being faces or, more precisely, without being processed by the hypothesized face-specific recognition mechanism. Stating the experimental design in this way suggests the ideal nonface comparison stimulus: upside-down faces. As mentioned earlier, inverting a face makes it much harder for normal subjects to recognize. On the basis of the face inversion effect, it is generally assumed that if a specialized face recognition mechanism exists, it is specialized for the processing of upright faces. Inverted faces therefore constitute ideal comparison stimuli: They are equivalent to upright faces in virtually all physical stimulus parameters, including complexity and inter-item similarity, but do not engage (or engage to a lesser extent) the hypothesized face-specific processing mechanisms.

My colleagues and I (Farah, Wilson, Drain, and Tanaka, 1995) reasoned that if L.H.'s underlying impairment was not face-specific, then he would show a normal face inversion effect. In other words, he would perform normally with upright faces relative to his performance on inverted faces. In contrast, if he had suffered damage to neural tissue implementing a specialized face recognition system, he would show an absent or attenuated face inversion effect. That is, he would be disproportionately impaired with upright faces, relative to his performance on the comparison stimuli, inverted faces.

L.H. and normal subjects were tested in a sequential matching task, in which an unfamiliar face was presented, followed by a brief interstimulus interval, followed by a second face, to which the subject responded "same" or "different." The first and second faces of a trial were always in the same orientation, and upright and inverted trials were randomly intermixed. As expected, normal subjects performed better with the upright than with the inverted faces, replicating the usual face inversion effect.

In contrast, L.H. was significantly more accurate with inverted faces – he showed an inverted inversion effect! This outcome was not even among the alternatives we had considered. We had assumed that if he had an impaired face processor, it would simply not be used in this task, leading to the prediction of an absent or attenuated face inversion effect. Instead, it appears he has an impaired face-specific processor, which is engaged by the upright but not the inverted faces, and used despite being disadvantageous. This result was confirmed in additional studies, which invariably showed either statistically significant or nonsignificant trends in the same direction.

The inverted inversion effect found in this prosopagnosic subject has two main theoretical implications. One concerns the "control structure" of visual recognition. L.H.'s specialized face perception system was apparently contributing to his performance even though it was impaired and clearly maladaptive. This suggests that the specialized face system operates mandatorily, reminiscent of Fodor's (1983) characterization of special-purpose perceptual "modules" as engaged mandatorily by their inputs. The idea that the face system cannot be prevented from processing faces, even when damaged, may also explain why W.J. was able to learn to recognize individual sheep after his strokes but could not learn to recognize human faces. The second implication concerns the selectivity of prosopagnosia. L.H.'s disproportionate impairment on upright relative to inverted faces implies that an impairment of face-specific processing mechanisms underlies his prosopagnosia.

The general conclusion of these studies of W.J. and L.H. is that prosopagnosia represents the selective loss of visual mechanisms necessary for face recognition, and not necessary (or less necessary) for other types of object recognition. In terms of the criteria discussed earlier, this implies that the face recognition system is separately lesionable and hence anatomically distinct from the object recognition system.

Prosopamnesia: a selective impairment of new face learning

Individuals such as W.J. and L.H. are impaired at both new face learning and recognition of previously familiar faces, as would be expected if the substrates of face representation were damaged. My colleagues and I recently encountered someone with an even more selective impairment: Case C.T. is impaired at learning new faces, but is relatively preserved in his recognition of previously familiar faces and in his learning of other nonface visual objects (Tippett, Miller, and Farah, in press). This pattern of performance is consistent with a disconnection between intact face representations and an intact medial temporal memory system. As such, it provides additional evidence that the anatomical substrates of face representation are distinct from the representation of other objects, as they can be selectively disconnected from the substrates of new learning.

C.T.'s face perception was normal as measured by the Benton and Van Allen face matching task (Benton, Hamsher, Varney, and Spreen, 1983). He also performed normally on the face inversion task used with L.H., in terms of overall level of performance and the presence of an inversion effect. His learning of verbal material and even visual material other than faces is also normal. However, when given the face and eyeglass learning task, he performed similarly to L.H. Additional evidence of his inability to learn faces comes from his identification of famous faces. For people who were famous prior to C.T.'s head injury, he performed within the range of age-matched control subjects on a forced choice "famous/not famous" task, whereas for more recently famous individuals his performance was many standard deviations below normal.

One celebrity allows for an especially well-controlled comparison between premorbid and current face recognition: In the case of Michael Jackson, the singer's dramatic change in appearance following C.T.'s injury provides us with a "between-face, within-celebrity" comparison. C.T. quickly and confidently recognized photographs of Jackson taken at about the time of C.T.'s injury. However, he did not recognize a later photograph, taken the year we tested C.T., despite the singer's high visibility in the media at that time, due to a lawsuit.

Anatomical localization of face recognition: evidence from brain-damaged patients

The fact that brain lesions can selectively impair face recognition relative to object recognition, as in prosopagnosia, and selectively disconnect face recognition from brain regions necessary for new learning, as in prosopamnesia, implies that its neural substrates are anatomically separate from the substrates of nonface object recognition. Thus face recognition meets the first criterion proposed above for being a different system from object recognition. However, if we are interested in knowing precisely where, in the human brain, face recognition is localized, these cases are relatively uninformative. L.H. and C.T. both sustained head injuries followed by surgery. In both cases widespread brain areas were affected. W.J.'s brain damage was the result of at least three strokes, and was also widespread.

Surveys of the lesions in larger groups of prosopagnosics are more helpful for localization, as the regions of overlap among different patients can be identified. Damasio, Damasio, and Van Hoesen (1982) studied three of their own patients with prosopagnosia, as well as consulting the literature for lesion localizations in ten other autopsied cases. They concluded that the critical lesion site is in ventral visual association cortex bilaterally.

DeRenzi, Perani, Carlesimo, Silveri, and Fazio (1994) reviewed much of the same case material, along with more recent cases and data from living patients whose brain damage was mapped using both structural MRI and PET. Their findings supported the ventral localization of face recognition, but called for a revision of the idea that bilateral lesions are necessary. Some patients became prosopagnosic after unilateral right hemisphere damage. The possibility of hidden left hemisphere dysfunction in these cases was reduced by the finding of normal metabolic activity in the left hemisphere by PET scan. De Renzi *et al.* conclude that there is a spectrum of hemispheric specialization for face recognition in normal right-handed adults. Although the right hemisphere may be relatively better at face recognition than the left, most people have a degree of face recognition ability in both hemispheres. Nevertheless, in a minority of cases, face recognition is so focally represented in the right hemisphere that a unilateral lesion will lead to prosopagnosia.

The intrahemispheric localization of face recognition has been elaborated most recently by Clarke, Lindemann, Maeder, Borruat, and Assal (1997), who again confirmed that ventral visual association cortex was crucial, but also showed that virtually non-overlapping lesions within this broad zone can result in prosopagnosia. This finding is consistent with the idea that face recognition mechanisms are distributed within much of ventral temporal and occipital cortex, such that a lesion of sufficient size affecting either the anterior or posterior part of this broad zone can disrupt face recognition.

The lesion sites associated with prosopagnosia are, as a group, clearly different from the lesions associated with object agnosia in the absence of prosopagnosia. The latter syndrome is almost invariably the result of a unilateral left hemisphere lesion, although confined to roughly the same intrahemispheric region (Farah, 1991; Feinberg, Schindler, Ochoa, Kwan, and Farah, 1994).

Anatomical localization of face recognition: evidence from functional neuroimaging

When we study the lesions of prosopagnosics, we are not just localizing the neural systems needed for face recognition; we are localizing the systems needed for face recognition and not for object recognition. It is for this reason that prosopagnosia is relevant to the question of whether face recognition and object recognition are unitary or rely on different systems. A similar contrast can be made with functional neuroimaging, by directly comparing regional brain activity while recognizing faces to regional brain activity while recognizing objects. Relatively few neuroimaging studies of visual recognition have included this comparison. As we saw in the previous chapter, most used either face stimuli or object stimuli. For present purposes, however, only those studies using both types of stimuli within the same experimental design are relevant.

Kanwisher, Chun, McDermott, and Ledden (1996) used fMRI to compare regional brain activity while subjects viewed photographs of faces and of objects. An objects-minus-faces subtraction revealed areas more responsive to objects than faces and the reverse subtraction revealed an area more responsive to faces than objects. Both types of stimuli activated inferior temporo-occipital regions, with face-specific activation confined to part of the right fusiform gyrus. A follow-up study identified the same fusiform face area and systematically verified its specificity for faces by comparing its response to faces and to scrambled faces, houses, and hands (Kanwisher, McDermott, and Chun, 1997). Similar conclusions were reached by McCarthy, Puce, Gore, and Allison (1997), who found right fusiform activation unique to passive viewing of faces relative to objects or scrambled objects, and left fusiform activation unique to flowers relative to scrambled objects.

5.3   Functional properties of face and object recognition

The anatomical differences between face and object recognition satisfy one basic criterion for attributing these two recognition functions to different underlying systems. Other criteria, based on the functional properties of face and object recognition, can also be addressed using neuropsychological data. In this section I will review research relevant to the two functional criteria mentioned earlier: mutual independence and information processing differences.

Mutual independence of face and object recognition: evidence from preserved face recognition in visual agnosia

Some associative visual agnosics show the opposite pattern from prosopagnosia. They appear to have more difficulty with object recognition than with face recognition (Farah, 1991; Feinberg, Schindler, Ochoa, Kwan, and Farah, 1994; Moscovitch, Winocur, and Behrmann, 1997). This pattern of impairment is interesting for two reasons. First, it offers further disconfirmation of the hypothesis that prosopagnosia is just a mild disorder of a general-purpose object recognition system, with faces simply being harder to recognize than other objects. If this were true, how could it be possible for a person to do better with faces than with other objects? Second, taken in conjunction with prosopagnosia, it shows that face and object recognition are functionally independent, in that either one can continue to work without other.

On the basis of prosopagnosia alone, we can infer that face recognition depends on a specialized recognition system that is either unnecessary or less necessary for the recognition of other objects. But this generalization is compatible with two very different hypotheses concerning the functional relations between face and object recognition. Figure 5.5a shows a cognitive architecture in which all stimuli are first processed by one general system, and then faces receive further processing by the system that is specialized for faces. Figure 5.5b shows a more radical alternative, in which the face and object systems process their respective stimulus types independently and in parallel.

Given the intuition that face recognition requires processing that is somehow more elaborate or demanding than object recognition, which presumably motivated the alternative accounts of prosopagnosia described in the last section, one might expect the first type of arrangement to hold. According to this view there is a specialized face

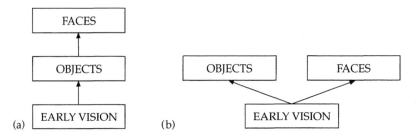

Figure 5.5 Two types of relations between a specialized face recognition
system and an object recognition system.
From M. J. Farah, "Is face recognition 'special'? Evidence from neuropsychology," Behavioral
Brain Research, 76, 1996, with permission of Elsevier Science.

system, but it is not functionally independent from the object system;
it requires input from the object system and performs further processing on that input. This arrangement contrasts with the second, according to which earlier visual processes deliver their products to two
parallel, independent systems, one of which is required to recognize
faces and the other of which is required to recognize other objects.

The existence of associative visual agnosics with relatively spared
face recognition implies that the systems subserving object and face
recognition must be functionally independent. In figure 5.5b, prosopagnosia and object agnosia sparing faces correspond to lesioning
the "face" box and the "object" box, respectively. There is no part of
figure 5.5a that can be lesioned to produce object agnosia sparing
faces.

The most detailed study of object agnosia with preserved face
recognition comes from Moscovitch, Winocur, and Behrmann (1997).
Their patient, C.K., suffered a closed head injury resulting in severe
agnosia. The authors relate some telling examples of C.K.'s real life
difficulties with object recognition. For example, after noticing that he
had not touched a cup of coffee he had requested during a testing
session, the experimenters asked whether he no longer wanted it. He
replied that he did, but was not certain which of the containers on the
desk was a cup of coffee.

Despite his profound object agnosia, C.K. is entirely normal in his
ability to recognize faces. In a test with 140 famous faces, he performed

well within the range of control subjects, and even held his own with a more challenging test of famous faces photographed at different ages (e.g., Winston Churchill as a child). In one particularly enjoyable demonstration of the object–face dissociation, the experimenters showed him paintings by the seventeenth-century Italian artist Arcimbaldo, in which collections of objects were arranged to make faces, as shown in figure 5.6. Whereas normal viewers quickly see both objects and faces in these pictures, C.K. saw only faces initially, and for most of the paintings never even noticed that there were nonface objects present!

Functional differences between face and object recognition

Given that face and object recognition are mutually independent systems localized in different brain regions, it stands to reason that they are doing something different. How does the nature of visual information processing within the face and object recognition systems differ? Most answers to this question emphasize the greater importance of overall shape in face recognition, often couched in terms of words like "gestalt" or "holistic" (see Farah, Wilson, Drain, and Tanaka, 1998, for a review).

In order to test the hypothesis of holistic face representation, the first order of business is to define this word, so favored by new-age gurus and health-food fanciers, in terms of objective information-processing concepts. An early and influential attempt to say how face recognition might be holistic was made by Diamond and Carey (1986) in an article on the determinants of the face inversion effect. They distinguished between what they called *first order relational information*, which is sufficient to recognize most objects, and *second order relational information*, which is needed for face recognition. First order relational information consists of the spatial relations of the parts of an object with respect to one another. In contrast, second order relational information exists only for objects whose parts share an overall spatial configuration, and consists of the spatial relations of the parts relative to the prototypical arrangement of the parts. For a face, the first order relational information would include the spatial relations among the eyes, nose, and mouth, for example. The second order relational information would include the spatial locations of these

Figure 5.6   An agnosic patient with preserved face recognition saw this painting by Archimbaldo as a face, pure and simple.

From M. Moscovitch et al., "What is special about face recognition? Nineteen experiments on a person with visual object agnosia and dyslexia but normal face recognition," Journal of Cognitive Neuroscience, 9, 1997.

parts relative to the overall arrangement of eyes, nose, and mouth in a prototypical or average face.

Jim Tanaka and I conducted a direct test of the hypothesis that second order relational information is particularly sensitive to inversion, and that this sensitivity underlies the face inversion effect (Tanaka and Farah, 1991). We reasoned that the strongest and most direct test of such a hypothesis would involve nonface stimuli, and would consist of varying the relative importance of first and second order relational information for stimulus recognition while holding other aspects of the stimuli and task constant. To this end, we taught subjects to identify dot patterns that either shared a common configuration, each pattern having been generated from a prototype by small changes in dot position, or that did not. In two experiments, we obtained a moderate inversion effect for the dot patterns, but no difference between the two types of patterns. We concluded that relatively greater reliance on second order relational information does not necessarily result in greater sensitivity to pattern inversion.

More recently, Rhodes, Carey, Byatt, and Proffitt (1998) conducted an even more direct test of the hypothesis that face recognition is holistic in the sense of using second order spatial relations. Rather than measure the inversion effect, they measured accuracy of recognition *per se*. By manipulating the similarity relations among computer-generated faces, they could determine whether or not subjects were basing their recognition decisions on a comparison with a stored prototype. Contrary to the hypothesis, faces were recognized without reference to prototypes, and in this respect were processed no differently from the simple geometric shapes that the researchers had included as a potentially contrasting stimulus set.

A different sense in which face recognition could be said to be "holistic" is based on concepts of shape representation introduced in chapter 3. Recall that computational systems for object recognition often represent object shape with some degree of hierarchical decomposition, such that the shape of the whole object is represented in terms of the explicitly represented shapes of parts of the object (see figure 3.6). Tanaka and I proposed that face recognition is an exception to this generalization. Whole faces undergo little or no decomposition into explicitly represented parts for purposes of recognition. Most of the evidence supporting a less part-based, more holistic form of representation for faces comes from psychophysical work with normal subjects. Because the physiological and neuropsychological evidence is based on the concepts and methods of the psychophysical research, a brief summary of that research will be presented here.

One way of measuring the relative contribution of part and whole information in face recognition is based on the finding that when a portion of a pattern corresponds to a part, in the natural parse of the pattern by the visual system, it will be better remembered. Recognition of an isolated portion thus provides an assay for the degree to which a portion of a pattern is treated as a psychologically real part by the viewer. Tanaka and Farah (1993) taught subjects to identify faces and various contrasting classes of nonface stimuli, and then assessed the degree to which the parts of these stimuli were explicitly represented in subjects' memories. For example, in one experiment illustrated in figure 5.7, subjects learned to name a set of faces (e.g., Joe, Larry, etc.), as well as a set of houses (Bill's house, Tom's house, etc.). Subjects were then given two-alternative forced choice tests of the identity of isolated parts (e.g., "Which is Joe's nose?", "Which is Bill's door?") or whole patterns in which the correct and incorrect choices differ only by a single part (e.g. "Which is Joe?", when confronted with Joe and a version of Joe with the alternative nose from the isolated part test pair; "Which is Bill's house?", when confronted with Bill's house and a version of Bill's house with the alternative door from the isolated test pair). We found that, relative to their ability to recognize the whole faces and houses, subjects were impaired at recognizing parts of faces compared to parts of houses. Could the difference be caused by the nature of the parts themselves? No, because the same pattern of results were obtained when faces were compared to scrambled faces and inverted faces, whose parts are identical.

Tanaka and Sengco (1997) showed that these results should not be interpreted simply in terms of a part-based representation in which, for faces, the configuration of parts is particularly important. If this were the case, changes in configuration would affect overall face recognition, but so long as individual parts are explicitly represented, this manipulation should not affect the recognition of the individual parts *per se*. Testing this prediction by comparing upright faces to inverted faces and houses, they again found evidence of holistic

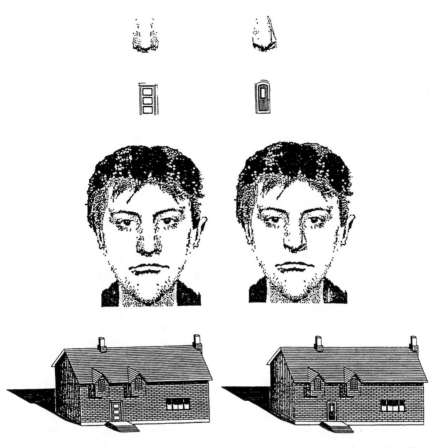

Figure 5.7   Examples of stimuli from an experiment contrasting the availability of part information for face and house recognition.

From M. J. Farah, "Is face recognition 'special'? Evidence from neuropsychology," Behavioral Brain Research, *76, 1996, with permission of Elsevier Science.*

coding of upright faces. The results of these experiments are consistent with the following hypothesis: during the learning and subsequent recognition of the houses, scrambled faces, and inverted faces, subjects explicitly represented their parts, whereas during the learning and subsequent recognition of the intact upright faces they did not, or they did so to a lesser extent.

Another way in which we have tested the holistic representation hypothesis is by seeing whether it could explain the face inversion effect (Farah, Tanaka, and Drain, 1995). If face recognition differs from other forms of object recognition by the use of relatively undecomposed or holistic representations, then perhaps the face inversion effect results from the use of holistic, or nonpart-based, representation. In the first experiment we taught subjects to identify random dot patterns and later tested their recognition of the patterns either upright or inverted. Half of the patterns learned by subjects were presented in a way that encouraged parsing the pattern into parts: Each portion of the pattern corresponding to a part was made from a distinctive color, so that grouping by color defined parts. The other half of the patterns learned were presented in all black, and the test stimuli for all patterns were presented in black. When subjects had been induced to see the patterns in terms of parts during learning, their later performance at identifying the patterns showed no effect of orientation. In contrast, when they were not induced to encode the patterns in terms of parts, they showed an inversion effect in later recognition.

In a second experiment on the inversion effect, we manipulated subjects' encoding of faces and then tested their ability to recognize the faces upright and inverted. Subjects were induced to learn half of the faces in a part-wise manner, by presenting them in the "exploded" format described earlier, whereas the other half of the faces to be learned were presented in a normal format. All faces were tested in a normal format. For the faces that were initially encoded in terms of parts, there was no inversion effect. In contrast, faces encoded normally showed a normal inversion effect. These results suggest that what is special about face recognition, by virtue of which it is so sensitive to orientation, is that it involves representations with relatively little or no part decomposition.

In another series of experiments we assessed the degree of part decomposition online during the perception of faces, using two types of experimental paradigm (Farah, Wilson, Drain, and Tanaka, 1998). In the first, we measured the relative availability of part and whole representations by requiring subjects to compare single features of simultaneously presented pairs of faces, and observed the influence of irrelevant features on their ability to judge the similarity or difference of the probed feature. For example, they might be asked whether two faces have the same or different noses. To the extent that subjects have explicit representations of the separate features of a face, then they should be able to compare them with one another. To the extent that they do not have explicit representations of these features, but only a holistic representation of the entire face, then they should suffer cross-talk from irrelevant features when judging the probed feature. The amount of cross-talk with upright faces was significantly more than with inverted faces, suggesting that the relative availability of parts and wholes differed for the two orientations, with parts less available in upright faces.

In three additional experiments we explored the effect on face perception of masks composed of face parts or whole faces. As Johnston and McClelland (1980) reasoned in their experiments on word perception, to the extent that masks contain similar shape elements to those used in representing the stimulus, the mask will interfere with perception of the stimulus. The effects of part and whole masks on the perception of upright faces were compared to their effects on the perception of words, inverted faces, and houses. In all cases, part masks were relatively less disruptive than whole masks for upright face perception, when compared to the effects of part and whole masks on the perception of words, inverted faces, and houses.

Although the single unit recording literature has not been very informative on the question of separate versus unitary systems for face and object recognition, it does provide clues to the role of parts in face perception. The holistic hypothesis predicts that face cells should function essentially as templates relative to a normalized stimulus pattern. That is, scrambling the features of a face should not just reduce a cell's response but should abolish it, even though there remains partial similarity between the intact and the scrambled face at the level of features. In contrast, deleting a feature should not have a dramatic effect on the cell's response, as only one region of the pattern has been changed. Both of these predictions are borne out by recordings from face cells, as illustrated in figure 5.3 (Desimone, Albright, Gross, and Bruce, 1984).

Seemingly contradictory evidence has been discussed by Perrett, Mistlin, and Chitty (1987), who point out that temporal cortex contains cells responsive to eyes and mouths as well as faces. They have suggested that these facial feature cells may provide the input to face cells, so that face representations are built up from representations of face parts. Although it is indeed tempting to conjecture that the part cells provide input to the face cells, two considerations weigh in favor of caution before accepting this interpretation of the part cells. First, Desimone (1991) has pointed out that the selectivity of the part cells for face parts *per se* has been less well established than the selectivity of face cells for faces. That is, the possibility remains that these cells may be representing more elementary visual attributes such as dark spots surrounded by bits of white rather than eyes. Second, only eye and mouth cells have been reported, and these parts of the face convey expressions that are important social cues for primates. In the absence of nose cells, chin cells, etc., it seems more likely that the eye and mouth cells form part of a system for nonverbal communication rather than facial identity recognition. The hypothesis that the part cells are the input to the face cells could be tested by analysis of response latencies. Although the finding that the earliest part responses were earlier than the earlier face responses would be ambiguous, the reverse finding would decisively rule out the hierarchical hypothesis.

A comparison between the optimal stimuli for face cells and nonface cells also suggests that object representation in IT may be more part-based than face representation. The typical nonface shapes that evoke the best response are considerably simpler in shape than many of the real objects that we (and presumably monkeys) recognize (see e.g. figure 4.6). This is consistent with a distributed representation of objects in which the individual elements of the representation correspond to parts.

The ideal evidence for different face and object recognition systems would not simply demonstrate functional differences between face and object recognition, as in the case of the psychophysical evidence from normal humans, nor would it simply demonstrate that face-selective neurons represent shape information in one way, without a contrast for object-selective neurons. The ideal evidence would provide a functional contrast (missing from the single unit data) indexed directly to neural systems (not possible with the psychophysical data). There is a small body of research that meets these criteria, carried out with the prosopagnosic and object agnosic patients already discussed, L.H. and C.K.

Recall that L.H. and C.K. are in many ways mirror images of each other. L.H. can read and recognize most objects except faces; C.K. is alexic and agnosic for everything except faces. The symmetry extends to more detailed investigations of their abilities as well. For example, when C.K. was given our test of face and eyeglass recognition, on which L.H. showed a face recognition impairment, he showed selective sparing for faces (unpublished data collected with Marlene Behrmann). L.H.'s inverted inversion effect (better performance with inverted than upright faces) is mirrored in C.K.'s abnormally large inversion effect (a greater-than-normal decrement in face recognition going from upright to inverted faces). The link established earlier between the inversion effect and holistic or nonpart-based shape representation (Farah *et al.*, 1995) is consistent with the idea that the face recognition system, damaged in L.H., relies on holistic representation and the object recognition system, damaged in C.K., relies on part-based representation. Phrased differently, L.H. now looks at the world in terms of its parts, and C.K. looks at the world holistically.

Direct evidence for this conjecture comes from studies with L.H. and C.K. in which the availability of part and whole information has been manipulated. Farah, Tanaka, and Drain (described in Farah, 1996) tested L.H. on short-term memory for faces presented either in a normal format or "exploded," so that the parts of the face were presented separately. Whereas normal subjects performed better with the normal faces, presumably because they could encode them as wholes, L.H. performed roughly equivalently, whether given the opportunity to encode the faces as wholes or forced to encode them as parts. This result is consistent with the hypothesis that the face recognition ability that has been lost in prosopagnosia involves the representation of faces as wholes. Among the studies reported by Moscovitch *et al.* (1997) is one in which photographs of faces were cut into parts and exploded on a single page. Although normal subjects found the exploded famous faces only slightly harder to recognize, C.K.'s performance dropped precipitously. The results of this and numerous other experiments with this patient led the authors to conclude that face and object recognition differ in their reliance on part representations. (Not all of Moscovitch *et al.*'s results with C.K. accord so perfectly with the version of the holistic face perception hypothesis offered here, but their results with normal subjects also differ from Tanaka's and mine, raising questions about the comparability of our experimental paradigms. Another point of divergence between the two research programs is in their operationalization of "part," which for Moscovitch *et al.* appears to include arbitrary fragments as well as structural components in a shape hierarchy: e.g., see experiments 13 and 14).

Expertise, subordinate classification, and face-specificity

Another difference between the visual information processing of face recognition and common object recognition is the level of expertise typically involved. People are face experts. We see a large number of faces almost every day, and have a prodigious memory capacity for them. In addition, there is a difference in the level of categorization typically required for face and object recognition. For most purposes, simply knowing the "basic object level" category (Rosch, Mervis, Gray, Johnson, and Boyes-Braem, 1976) of an object suffices; we can get by in life knowing that this is a toothbrush and that is a lamp. In contrast, face recognition requires a finer grained, or subordinate-level, classification; we recognize that this is not just a face, but John's face. Perhaps not coincidentally, a characteristic of visual expertise is that subordinate classification is carried out as quickly and easily as basic object level categorization, at least for dog show judges and bird watchers (Tanaka and Taylor, 1991).

In the light of these differences between face and object recognition, Isabel Gauthier and collaborators have suggested that what is "special" about face recognition is the expertise used to recognize faces at the subordinate level of categorization (Gauthier, Anderson, Tarr, Skudlarski, and Gore, 1997; Gauthier and Tarr, 1997; Gauthier, Williams, Tarr, and Tanaka, 1998). Or, in terms less friendly to the thesis of this chapter, face recognition is not special, but simply the most commonly encountered case of expert subordinate object recognition. They have carried out a series of studies using behavioral measures and neuroimaging to test the hypothesis that face recognition is special only insofar as it requires subordinate classification and is dependent on expertise. The results have provided partial, but not complete, support for their idea.

The possible relevance of level of categorization to the "specialness" of face recognition was demonstrated in an fMRI study of basic and subordinate level categorization of objects (Gauthier *et al.*, 1997). Subjects were shown picture–word pairs and had to decide whether the picture illustrated the word. Words were either basic object labels (e.g., "bird") or subordinate (e.g., "pelican"), enabling the researchers to isolate the parts of the visual system that were significantly more active during subordinate than basic level categorization. Among the areas of significant difference was a region in the fusiform gyrus, looking roughly like the region activated by face recognition in previous studies by other investigators. However, Gauthier and colleagues were careful to point out that the face–object dissociations seen in other imaging studies as well as patients cannot be explained simply in terms of a confound with level of categorization. Their claim is simply that level of categorization must be carefully controlled. Of course, this has been done in some of the imaging studies, such as Kanwisher *et al.*'s (1997) comparisons of face recognition with hand and house recognition, as well as in Farah *et al.*'s (1995) comparison of prosopagnosic recognition of faces and eyeglass frames. On the basis of these studies, we can conclude that face recognition is distinct from object recognition, even at the subordinate level.

The combination of subordinate classification and expertise is a more plausible contender for the explanation of face–object dissociations. Gauthier and colleagues have tested this hypothesis by training normal subjects to become experts at recognizing novel nonface objects called "greebles." As can be seen in figure 5.8, greebles share a common part structure in the same way that faces do, with two "boges," a "quiff," and a "dunth." Subjects in these experiments learned names for each individual greeble. In addition, they also learned to classify the greebles by "gender" and by "family." The examples shown in figure 5.9 help to clarify what these terms mean in the context of greebles. After many hours of training, subjects became greeble experts, with fast, accurate greeble recognition and equivalent performance with subordinate (individual greeble) and basic level (gender and family) recognition.

Gauthier and Tarr (1997) sought to replicate, with greebles, the effects of facial context on face part discrimination that Tanaka and I found. Recall that we taught subjects new faces, and then asked them to identify a given face's eyes, nose, or mouth from a pair. With intact upright faces, but not other stimuli, subjects performed better when the pair was presented in the context of a whole face. Although greeble parts were discriminated more effectively in the context of a whole

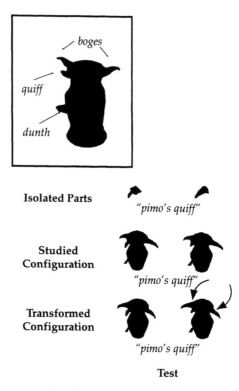

Figure 5.8   The anatomy of a Greeble.
From I. Gauthier and M. J. Tarr, "Becoming a 'Greeble' expert," Vision Research, 37, 1997.
Copyright 1997, with permission from Elsevier Science.

greeble, the effect was not influenced by expertise. They did find an effect of expertise on the sensitivity of the context effects on configuration, analogous to Tanaka and Sengco's finding. In a later study, Gauthier *et al.* (1998) attempted to replicate a number of findings from the face recognition literature with greebles, and again found mixed results. The earlier finding of a whole greeble advantage for parts recognition was not replicated, and no greeble inversion effect was found. However, other purportedly face-specific effects were found with greebles, specifically the brightness inversion effect (reversing black and white makes faces and greebles hard to recognize) and the composite effect (top and bottom halves of different faces and greebles are difficult to recognize when aligned to make a whole).

GREEBLES

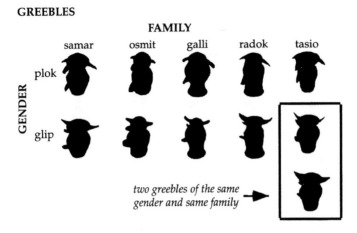

Figure 5.9 Examples of Greebles and their family, gender, and individual differences.
From I. Gauthier and M. J. Tarr, "Becoming a 'Greeble' expert," Vision Research, 37, 1997. Copyright 1997, with permission from Elsevier Science.

The available data are simply inconclusive at this point, with some purportedly face-specific effects obtained with greebles, and others not. Box scores may not tell the whole story in any case. Perhaps the most important contribution of the greeble work is that it forces us to think more deeply about the meaning of the claim "faces are special." If face recognition were no different from expert subordinate level recognition, would we conclude that faces are not special? Or would we conclude that faces are special in that, for 99 percent of the human race (excluding dog show judges, bird watchers, and undergraduates in certain psychology experiments at Yale), they are the objects for which we carry out expert subordinate recognition?

Or should we question the assumption that faces are the only commonly encountered object for which we are expert at subordinate recognition? Printed word recognition also requires visual expertise, and arguably requires subordinate classification as well. It is as unhelpful to know that a word is a word, without knowing which word, as it is to know that a face is a face, without knowing which face. If we grant that word recognition is another common case of expert subordinate recognition, then we disconfirm the hypothesis of Gauthier and colleagues. There is already abundant evidence, to be reviewed in the next chapter, that word recognition depends on a distinct neural system from face and object recognition.

Is there some other difference between faces and greebles, on the one hand, and printed words, on the other? Gauthier describes one when she notes that, like faces, "all greebles share similar parts in a common spatial configuration" (1998, p. 2402). This is different from words, which have different numbers of parts with no constraint on their locations: an A can go in any position, whereas a nose is always in the middle position. Thus, the expert/subordinate hypothesis could be saved by making it the expert/subordinate/common-parts-in-common-layout hypothesis. But now we are awfully close to describing a set of task and stimulus properties that simply amount to face recognition! And indeed, it seems to me that the more one gets to know individual greebles, the more facelike they seem.

chapter six

Word Recognition

6.1 Visual word recognition: another special-purpose system?

Visual word recognition raises many of the same issues as face recognition concerning division of labor in high-level vision and the existence of specialized visual recognition systems. Visual word recognition can appear to be selectively impaired after brain damage, in a syndrome known as "pure alexia." But just as the selectivity of prosopagnosia can be questioned, on the grounds that faces might just be the hardest type of object to recognize, or require the finest within-category discriminations, so can the selectivity of pure alexia be questioned. Word recognition makes heavy demands on certain visual processes that are less critical for everyday object recognition; perhaps the impairment of pure alexia lies here, rather than in a truly orthography-specific recognition system.

Whatever wariness we might have felt about hypothesizing a face-specific recognition system came from our preference for theoretical parsimony. Unless absolutely forced by the data to posit multiple special-purpose systems, we will try to get by with a single recognition system. Likewise, the idea of an orthography-specific recognition system is less parsimonious than a general-purpose system that recognizes words as well as faces, cars, and kitchen sinks, and has therefore been met with skepticism. However, the lack of parsimony is only one of the problems with this idea, and not the most serious.

The worst problem with the idea of an orthography-specific recognition system has to do with the nature of the category "orthography." This category is entirely arbitrary and culturally transmitted. Arab or Japanese readers, for example, would not be able to distinguish the letters of our writing system from other small shapes made from line segments, including digits, because there is no set of visual features that mark letterhood. Furthermore, the ability to read does not go far enough back in the evolutionary history of our species to have influenced our genes. How could the brain develop a localized, dedicated system for such an arbitrary and evolutionarily recent category of stimuli?

6.2   Categories and levels of processing in hypothesized "category-specific" brain systems

Before attempting to resolve this issue, let me clarify the relation between purported orthography-specific visual recognition impairments and other category-specific recognition impairments, some of which have been widely discussed in the neuropsychological literature in recent years. These include some other strong contenders for the "most implausible dedicated brain system" award.

Elizabeth Warrington and Tim Shallice caused a stir in 1984 by publishing a paper in which they described three postencephalitic patients with disproportionate loss of knowledge of living things (plants and animals). They were careful to note that the impairment might not be linked to aliveness *per se*. Nevertheless, the living/nonliving dichotomy captured most of the patients' behavior quite well. In the years that followed a large number of patients with so-called "category-specific deficit for living things" were described after encephalitis, head injury, and stroke, suggesting that some factor other than extreme rarity had prevented this disorder from being reported earlier. I suspect that the operative factor was the implausibility of a "living things center" in the brain, which would have led many researchers to ignore or discount the trends in patients' behavior that were indicative of such a center. Indeed, some researchers remain skeptical, and a number of critiques have also been published in recent years (see Kurbat and Farah, 1998, for a review). Fuller discussions of this interesting area of research can be found in Saffran and Schwartz (1994) and Farah and Grossman (1997).

For present purposes, just two points concerning living things impairments will be made. First, there is good reason to believe that the underlying loss in these cases is in knowledge of visual appearance, not knowledge of living things *per se*, and that visual appearance is so central to the representation of living things that retrieval of any knowledge of living things is impaired by the visual knowledge loss (Farah and McClelland, 1991; Thompson-Schill, Aguirre, D'Esposito, and Farah, 1999; Warrington and Shallice, 1984). Second, the impairment seems to be in "semantic memory," or general world knowledge, not in visual recognition, as it affects the ability to answer verbal questions about living things as well as recognize them when presented visually (Farah, Hammond, Mehta, and Ratcliff, 1989). Although it is common for patients with this so-called category-specific knowledge impairment to have a visual agnosia as well, this is likely to result from neighboring critical lesion sites, and the impairment can be found without concomitant visual agnosia (DeRenzi and Lucchelli, 1993). In sum, this type of impairment has very different implications from pure alexia for the architecture of the normal mind and brain. It is consistent with specialized brain systems individuated by perceptual modality (in this case visual information) rather than arbitrary categorical distinctions, and it relates to the architecture of semantic memory rather than visual recognition.

Perhaps the most notorious example of a category-specific impairment is the "fruit and vegetable" impairment first reported by Hart, Berndt, and Caramazza (1985). Their patient did poorly naming fruits and vegetables, but was only mildly impaired at naming other types of objects, including other foods! The level of processing impaired in this case seemed to be word retrieval, as the patient performed well on most other tasks involving fruits and vegetables.

I had the opportunity to study a similar case with Marcie Wallace, and we verified that our patient's impairment was not attributable to the differences in the difficulty of naming fruits and vegetables (measured by factors like familiarity, lexical frequency, and age of acquisition) and that the impairment was limited to name retrieval. Our patient was able to circumlocute and describe the fruits and vegetables he could not name, including typical dishes in which they were served, growing season, and so on. This implies that his impairment was not in semantic memory. His naming was impaired whether he was trying to name pictures of fruits and vegetables, whether he was trying to name them from verbal descriptions, or whether he was trying to name them from their taste. This implies that his impairment was not in visual recognition. In sum, the fruit and vegetable impairment appears to be a category-specific anomia, and its implications for the architecture of the normal mind and brain therefore relate to language and not vision. It is consistent with a relatively local form of representation, allowing relatively narrow losses of knowledge, involved in mapping semantics onto names, for which there is some independent computational rationale (see Farah and Wallace, 1992).

In this chapter I will review what we know about the neural substrates of reading with the goal of answering the questions: Is there a specialized visual word recognition system in the human brain? And, what implications do cerebral specialization for reading have for the nature and origins of cerebral specialization more generally?

6.3   Pure alexia: a brief description

Patients with pure alexia are impaired at visual word recognition, despite intact auditory word comprehension, intact ability to produce written language, and apparently intact recognition of visual patterns other than printed words. Its defining characteristics are thus largely exclusionary: It is an impairment of visual word recognition that is not secondary to other problems with language or vision, and is in this sense "pure." The "purity" of the condition seems especially striking when one sees a patient write a complete sentence with accuracy and ease, and then struggle without success to read it!

Most pure alexic patients are not absolutely incapable of reading. More often, they read abnormally slowly, and with errors, but often succeed in the end at recognizing words. Their attempts at reading usually consist of recognizing one letter at a time, a strategy known as

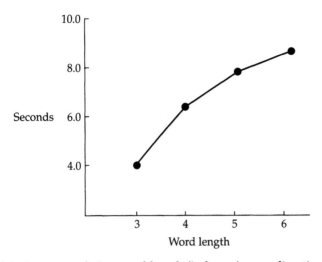

Figure 6.1 Function relating word length (in letters) to reading time (in seconds) for a pure alexic patient.
From D. N. Bub et al., "Word recognition and orthographic context effects in a lettery-by-letter reader," Brain and Language, 36, 1989.

"letter-by-letter" reading. Letter-by-letter reading is often very obvious, as the reader will say the letters aloud, but even when reading silently, pure alexics take proportionately longer to read words with more letters, consistent with a letter-by-letter strategy. Figure 6.1 shows the average single word reading latencies of one pure alexic as a function of the number of letters in the word. Three-letter words take, on average for this patient, four seconds to read, and latency increases steeply with additional letters. Not surprisingly, the slope levels off somewhat for the longest words, as their identities can usually be guessed before the very last letter is recognized. More severe pure alexics may require 10 or 20 seconds to recognize even three-letter words, and if pushed to read longer words may spend literally minutes at the task.

There have been three general types of hypothesis put forth in neuropsychology to explain pure alexia, each with clear implications for the question: Does the human brain contain a dedicated reading area? I will review these three hypotheses here and add a fourth new hypothesis.

6.4 The visual–verbal disconnection hypothesis

The first attempt to explain pure alexia was originally proposed by Déjerine (1892), and more recently championed by Geschwind (1965). According to this account, reading consists of associating visual information in occipital cortex with language representations in posterior language areas. This is done by way of the left angular gyrus, adjacent to the Wernicke's area, which is hypothesized to contain stored multimodal associations linking the visual and sound patterns of printed words. Thus, pure alexia results from any lesion that disconnects the visual cortex from the left angular gyrus. The neuropathology of pure alexia is generally consistent with this hypothesis (e.g. Damasio and Damasio, 1983; Greenblatt, 1983), often involving a left occipital lesion (causing blindness in the right visual field) and damage to the adjacent splenium (disconnecting left visual field information from the left hemisphere). Despite the anatomical support for this interpretation of pure alexia, it is not an altogether satisfying explanation. For one thing, although it is not in any way *inconsistent* with the letter-by-letter reading strategy of pure alexic patients, it is also not *explanatory* of this highly characteristic feature of the syndrome.

It is, of course, possible that disconnection may contribute to some particularly severe cases of pure alexia. I recall one patient who was virtually unable to read at all, and whose letter-by-letter reading often involved letters that bore no relation to the word he was looking at. His oral verbal responses seemed to be running free, independent of orthographic input, with a tendency towards perseveration, and his picture naming had the same unrelated and often perseverative qualities. The total impression was of exactly a disconnection in the pathways that normally link visual input and verbal output. Yamadori (1980) reported two relatively severe cases of pure alexia with what he called "unilateral dyscopia," the inability to copy written characters with one hand. In both cases the right-hand copies were worse than the left, consistent with the inability of visual information to reach the left hemisphere. The more severe case, who was entirely unable to read written characters, showed the more complete dissociation in copying between the left and right hands.

The disconnection account, as described by Geshwind, does not involve any reading-specific components. General-purpose visual mechanisms are hypothesized to be disconnected from a language center, which is not itself specialized for visual language. Indeed, disconnection accounts in neuropsychology are usually marked by their extreme parsimony, invoking only the most elementary faculties, and explaining apparently complex higher level impairments by particular disconnections among these simpler elements. In light of this, it is interesting to note that Déjerine's version of the disconnection account differed from Geshwind's on the issue of reading-specific brain regions. Déjerine proposed that the brain's visual areas do contain reading-specific substrates, and that the relevant disconnection was between these and the auditory language areas (Bub, Arguin, and LeCours, 1993).

6.5 The visual impairment hypothesis

According to a second type of hypothesis, pure alexia results from an impairment of visual perception, which is not limited to the perception of printed words during reading but is merely most obvious in this context. Many authors have noted that pure alexic subjects who are not at all agnosic for real objects may nevertheless misidentify line drawings, particularly if complex (e.g., Friedman and Alexander, 1984). Pure alexic subjects may even be impaired at simple letter-matching tasks, in which briefly presented pairs of letters must be judged same or different (Behrmann and Shallice, 1995; Bub, Black, and Howell, 1989; Kay and Hanley, 1991; Reuter-Lorenz and Brunn, 1990). When naming letters presented in isolation or identifying them in the context of word reading, pure alexics tend to confuse similar-looking letters (e.g., Patterson and Kay, 1982) and show increased interference in single letter naming from similar-looking letters (Arguin and Bub, 1993). The role of visual similarity in these errors suggests that the breakdown occurs at a visual stage of processing.

What is the specific nature of the visual impairment? One version of the hypothesis focuses on problems with visual-spatial attention (Rapp and Caramazza, 1991), although attentional problems do not appear to be characteristic of pure alexia in general (e.g., Behrmann and Shallice, 1995). Another version, according to which basic shape perception is impaired, was rejected by Arguin and Bub (1993) on the basis of a patient's normal performance in a visual feature conjunction task. This is a task in which subjects must search for a target stimulus distinguished from nontarget stimuli by a conjunction of two visual features, in this case black (as opposed to white) and X (as opposed to O). This may not have been the best test of the shape perception impairment hypothesis, because the conjunction was not between shape features, but between a shape feature (straightness) with a color or intensity feature. In contrast, the task they used to assess postperceptual processing required searching for a target letter among other letters and therefore did involve shape–feature conjunction.

Simultanagnosia

Marcie Wallace and I attempted to revive interest in a specific hypothesis concerning the perceptual impairment in pure alexia that was first put forth by Kinsbourne and Warrington in 1962, according to which early shape perception is at fault (Farah and Wallace, 1991). The initial support for the hypothesis came from a series of elegant tachistoscopic experiments by Kinsbourne and Warrington (1962) in which the speed of processing single and multiple visual shapes, both orthographic and non-orthographic, could be assessed. These experiments showed that alexics' tachistoscopic recognition thresholds for single forms (letters of simple pictures) were within normal limits, but that their thresholds departed dramatically from those of normals when more than one form had to be recognized. In an ingenious series of experiments, they found that the visual processing "bottleneck" in these patients was determined solely by the number of separate forms to be recognized. Spatial factors such as size, position, and separation of the stimuli had no effect. They therefore concluded that these patients had a disorder of simultaneous form perception, or "simultanagnosia," and that this disorder was the cause of their alexia: because they could recognize only one letter at a time, they were forced to read letter by letter.

Levine and Calvanio (1978) replicated and extended the findings of Kinsbourne and Warrington with three new cases of what they termed "alexia-simultanagnosia." Among the novel results of their study were three findings that helped to pinpoint the locus of processing impairment more precisely than the original Kinsbourne and Warrington studies. First, Levine and Calvanio demonstrated that the difficulty with multiple stimuli is present even when the task does not involve naming the stimuli but merely judging whether any two of the stimuli in an array are identical or not. This implies that the limitation is truly affecting perception *per se*, and not the process of labeling the percept. Second, subjects made more errors in this matching task when the letters in the display were visually similar (e.g. OCO, as opposed to OXO), again suggesting a visual locus for the processing breakdown. Finally Levine and Calvanio contrasted the effects of position cues presented just before and just after the stimulus array on subjects' performance. If shape recognition *per se* is limited to just one item, then the pre-cue should improve performance because it allows the subject to recognize the one item that has been cued, but the post-cue should not, because it comes after the stimulus array has disappeared and thus cannot guide selective perception. In contrast, if the bottleneck is occurring after shape recognition, in some short-term memory buffer or labeling process, then the post-cues should also help. Levine and Calvanio found that subjects were helped by the pre-cues: if they knew in advance *which* letter (indicated by the position of a pre-cue) from a multiletter array they were to report, they could do so accurately, even with the other letters present. However, if the cue came after perceptual processing has been completed it did not help, again implicating visual recognition *per se* as the locus of impairment.

Wallace and I found evidence for a limitation of the rapid encoding of multiple visual shapes in nontachistoscopic tasks as well. Ekstrom, French, and Harmon (1976) developed a large set of factor-analyzed paper and pencil tasks testing a range of cognitive and perceptual abilities. Three of these tasks loaded on a factor that came to be labeled "Perceptual Speed," and required the rapid recognition of multiple shapes. One of the three tests involved searching for occurrences of the letter "e" in printed words, and is therefore not ideal for testing the hypothesis that pure alexics have an impairment beyond their inability to read (although the task does not require reading the words *per se*). The other two were more informative, in that they did not involve verbal materials at all. In one, subjects must determine whether pairs of number strings are identical or differ by one digit. In the other, subjects view rows of small pictures and for each row must find a target picture. We tested a pure alexic subject with these tests, and found him to be impaired on all three (Farah and Wallace, 1991). We have subsequently tested three other pure alexic patients, all of whom were impaired.

Sekuler and Behrmann (1997) have also replicated these findings with three additional subjects. In addition, they assessed pure alexics' abilities to make use of grouping processes in perceptual judgments in multi-element displays, as a further test of the hypothesis. They report that when gestalt factors do not facilitate the grouping of elements in these tasks (the grouping of distractors in a visual search task, or the grouping of object parts in a object-based attention task), pure alexics' performance deviates disproportionately from that of control subjects. These results are consistent with the multiple-parts or simultanagnosia hypothesis. Although Sekuler and Behrmann failed to find a monotonically increasing effect of number of parts for the patients, which they interpreted as inconsistent with the specifics of our hypothesis, normal subjects also failed to show this effect, raising the possibility that the visual system's parse of the stimuli differed from the experimenters' intended parse.

The foregoing studies of visual perception in pure alexia are all studies of associations. They are therefore all vulnerable to a particular type of alternative explanation, involving two separate abilities that depend upon neighboring brain regions and hence are destroyed by the same lesion. Perhaps the perceptual impairment is a separate consequence of the lesion that causes pure alexia, rather than being causal of the alexia. The ambiguity of associational data provided the motivation for us to manipulate the difficulty of visual perception and assess its effect on the reading of a pure alexic (Farah and Wallace, 1991). We used additive factors logic to identify the stage of reading that gives rise to the abnormal word-length effect (i.e., the stage of reading at which the process is forced to proceed letter by letter), and specifically to test whether it is a visual stage of processing. According to additive factors logic, if two experimental manipulations affect the same stage of processing, their effects will be interactive, whereas if they affect separate stages their effects will be additive (Sternberg,

point

moral

until

Figure 6.2   Examples of clear (unmasked) and degraded (masked) word stimuli used to assess the causal role of visual impairment in pure alexia.
From M. J. Farah and M. A. Wallace, "Pure alexia as a visual impairment: a reconsideration," Cognitive Neuropsychology, 8, 1991; reprinted by permission of Psychology Press Ltd.

1969). We presented our subject with words of varying length to read, printed either clearly or with visual noise superimposed, as shown in figure 6.2. The visual quality of a stimulus is a factor known to affect the stage of visual perception. We found that word length and visual quality interacted in determining reading latency. Specifically, the word-length effect was exacerbated by visual noise, as shown in figure 6.3. This finding is consistent with a perceptual locus for the word-length effect in this experiment, and with the more general hypothesis that an impairment in the rapid perception of multiple objects or multipart objects underlies pure alexia.

A computational interpretation of simultanagnosia

Why might the brain recognize multiple shapes with a distinct and separately lesionable system? Computationally, the recognition of multiple shapes poses a special problem, distinct from the problem of recognizing complex shapes or unfamiliar shapes (to mention two other ways in which shape perception can be made difficult). The special problem for multishape recognition is cross-talk or interference among the representation of separate shapes, which will be more severe the more distributed the representation.

Although distributed representation has many computational benefits and is used in a number of brain systems including the visual object recognition system, it is not well-suited to representing a number

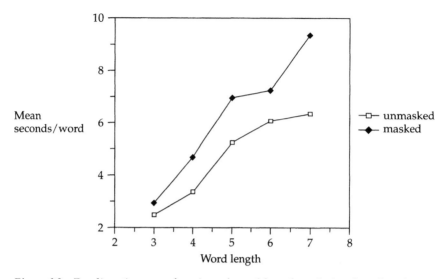

Figure 6.3 Reading time as a function of word length and visual quality for a pure alexic. Masking has a bigger effect the longer the word, implying a common locus for the effects of visual quality and word length.

From M. J. Farah and M. A. Wallace, "Pure alexia as a visual impairment: a reconsideration," Cognitive Neuropsychology, 8, 1991; reprinted by permission of Psychology Press Ltd.

of items simultaneously. This is because once two distributed representations have been superimposed, it is difficult to know which parts of each of the two distributed representations go together. This problem is illustrated in the top part of figure 6.4. The bottom part of figure 6.4 shows that one way around this problem is to develop more localist representations. A tentative interpretation of the perceptual impairment of pure alexics is that they have lost a region of cortex in which shape information is represented in a relatively more local manner. This allows for the possibility that word and object recognition differ in degree rather than in kind: Both make use of a common type of visual ability, namely the localist representation of shape that enables multiple shapes to be encoded without cross-talk, although word recognition is relatively more dependent on that ability than object recognition. This conclusion contrasts with the next type of explanation that has been offered for pure alexia, according to which it is caused by an impairment specific to orthography.

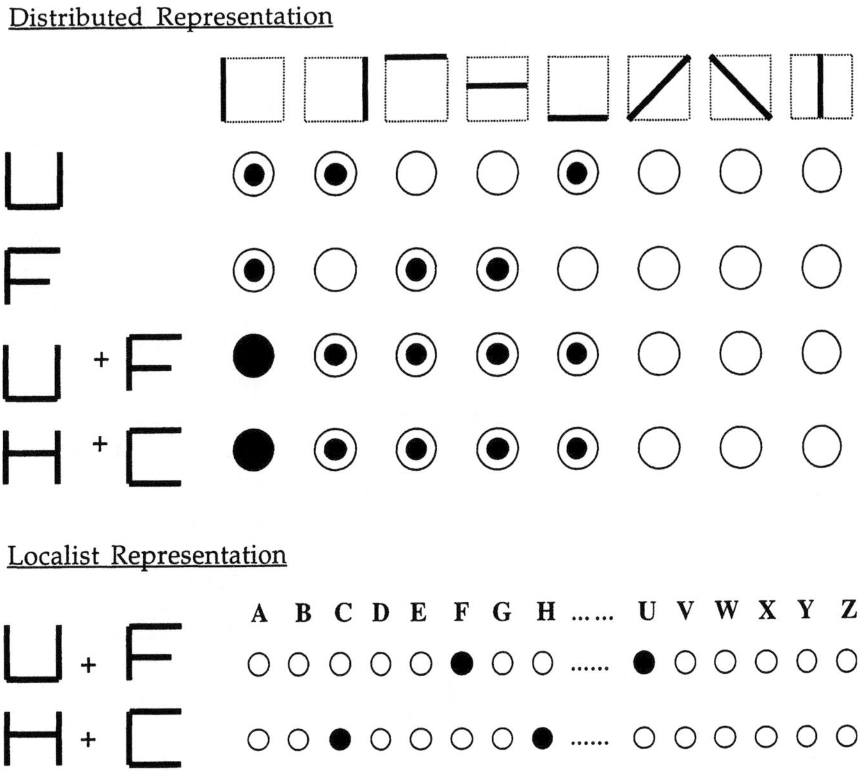

Distributed Representation

Localist Representation

		A	B	C	D	E	F	G	H	......	U	V	W	X	Y	Z
⊔ + F		○	○	○	○	○	●	○	○	......	●	○	○	○	○	○
H + ⊏		○	○	●	○	○	○	○	●	......	○	○	○	○	○	○

Figure 6.4 Illustration of the problem of interference when multiple shapes are represented in a distributed manner (above) and the avoidance of this problem by adopting local representation (bottom).

6.6   The orthography-specific impairment hypothesis

There are a number of levels of orthographic representation that could be impaired in pure alexia, including individual letters and whole word representations. In 1980 Warrington and Shallice proposed that pure alexia was the result of damage to relatively high-level orthographic representations of words and morphemes. They call these representations "word forms" and pointed out that a loss of word forms can explain the characteristic letter-by-letter reading of pure alexics, as their visual word recognition cannot make use of word forms and must therefore proceed via individual letter recognition and knowledge of spelling.

The evidence presented by Warrington and Shallice in favor of their hypothesis was of two kinds. First, they assessed various visual capabilities in an attempt to rule out visual perception as the locus of impairment. By a process of elimination, this would strengthen the case for a word form impairment. However, despite having used a number of different perceptual tasks, many of which involved displays of multiple items, none of the tasks specifically taxed the process of rapid perception of multiple shapes, which is the leading alternative hypothesis. For example, some of the tasks were not speeded, some involved foreknowledge of target locations (eliminating the need to recognize all but the target stimuli), and so on (see Farah and Wallace, 1991, for a detailed review of these tasks).

Second, Warrington and Shallice manipulated reading difficulty in two ways that they believed would render subjects relatively more dependent on visual wordforms. In one experiment they compared the reading of print to the reading of script, and found performance with script to be worse. In a second experiment they compared reading words that had been presented tachistoscopically, for a half second, to reading nontachistoscopic word presentations, and found a marked decrement in reading performance with tachistoscopic presentations.

Patterson and Kay (1982) proposed a modification of the word form hypothesis, according to which the word form system is intact, whereas its input from letter recognition systems is limited to one letter at a time. This hypothesis can account for all of Warrington and Shallice's data. In fact, both versions of the word form hypothesis are compatible with all of the data collected by Warrington and Shallice and Patterson and Kay, and both groups acknowledge this (Patterson and Kay, 1982; Shallice, 1984, ch. 4). Patterson and Kay's reasons for preferring their alternative include several indirect and, in their words, "intuitive" considerations. One of the most compelling is their observation (1982, p. 433) that for some patients "enormous effort was required to identify letters; but, once that had been achieved, moving from letters to the word was virtually automatic." This is the opposite of what one would expect if the word forms themselves were damaged. In terms of the commonality versus specificity of reading and other forms of visual recognition, however, Patterson and Kay's modification of Warrington and Shallice's hypothesis maintains the idea of a visual word form system specific to orthography.

The word superiority effect and word forms in pure alexia

Word form hypotheses have not fared well in the face of more recent demonstrations that at least some pure alexic subjects show a "word superiority effect." The word superiority effect refers to the facilitation of letter perception when letters occur in the context of a word or pseudo-word, relative to a nonword or, in some cases, no flanking letters at all (Reicher, 1969; Wheeler, 1970). The facilitation of letter perception by word or word-like contexts is not simply the result of a bias to guess letters that would make a word, because it is observed even in forced-choice tasks when both choices make a word: for example, when the stimulus is ROAD and subjects are asked whether the second character was an O or an E.

The word superiority effect might seem paradoxical at first, for one usually thinks of letters being perceived before words, yet here words are influencing letter perception. Nevertheless, it can be explained using the framework of connectionism. Letters are indeed perceived before words, in the sense that their representations begin to be activated before word representations begin to be activated (Johnston and McClelland, 1980). However, if we assume that letter activation is not complete by the point at which word representations begin to be activated, and if we also assume that activated words both compete with one another in a winner-take-all manner *and* feed activation back down to their component letter representations, the facilitating influence of words on letter perception no longer seems mysterious. McClelland and Rumelhart (1981) present a computational model that accounts in a simple and parsimonious way for most of the findings concerning word superiority in letter perception. Figure 6.5 shows a schematic depiction of part of their model. Because of the importance of this issue to the interpretation of pure alexia, a brief overview of the model will be offered here.

Letter units are initially activated by an amount proportional to the input they receive from the units representing their constituent

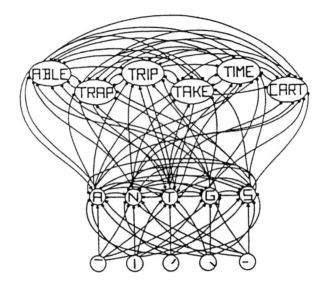

Figure 6.5   Part of the letter and word representation network of the Interactive Activation and Competition model, which explains the word superiority effect in terms of bi-directional excitation of letters and the words that contain them, and inhibition among competing word representations.
From J. McClelland and D. E. Rumelhart, "An interactive activation model of context effects in letter perception: part 1. An account of basic findings," Psychological Review, *88, 1981; copyright 1981 by the American Psychological Association; reprinted with permission.*

features. The letter units then pass activation on to the words with which they are consistent. For example, if there appears to be a "t" in the first position, that will cause the words "trap," "trip," "take," and "time" to gain activation. In addition, word units are inhibited by the activation of units that are inconsistent with the word. For example, "able" will be inhibited by the unit representing an initial "t," as activation in these units represents incompatible hypotheses, and "able" will also be inhibited by activation in other word units for the same reason. So far, this model would seem to account for word recognition, but it is not yet clear how it accounts for the word superiority effect, nor is it clear how it accounts for phenomena involving pseudo-words, that is, statistical approximations to real words. The word superiority effect is explained by postulating feedback from the word level to the letter level. Switching to a different set of examples from those shown in figure 6.5, if the word shown is "read," and perception of the letter in the second position is just barely adequate, so that the "e" unit is ever so slightly more activated than the "o" unit, then this will give the edge to the word "read" over the word "road." Inter-word inhibition will then drive the activation of the "road" unit down, and feedback from the word level to the letter level will therefore consist of greater "top-down" support for "e" than for "o." Thus, people will be more accurate at discriminating "e" from "o" in the context of "read" than in a nonword context or alone. Why should pseudo-words also give rise to superior letter perception, given that there are no units corresponding to them at the word level? Because pseudo-words are sufficiently similar to real words that their constituent letters will at least partially activate some real word units: "yead," for example, will activate "year," "bead," "read," and so on. Once these word units have become activated, they will inhibit other word units that are less consistent with the activated letter-level units, and will provide top-down support for the letters that do occur in the words similar to "yead," including, for example, the "e" in the second position.

The word form hypothesis would seem to predict an absent or at least attenuated word superiority effect in pure alexic subjects. In contrast, the perceptual impairment hypothesis predicts a normal word superiority effect, because however degraded the visual representation of letters, they will to some degree activate word representations and thus receive top-down support. In two cases pure alexic subjects have shown word superiority effects, calling into question at least the strongest form of the word form hypothesis according to which they are lacking a visual word form system (Bub, Black, and Howell, 1989; Reuter-Lorenz and Brunn, 1990). Bub *et al.* compared their subject's performance with that of an age-matched non-alexic subject who had a similar visual field defect, and found that relative to this control subject, their pure alexic showed a normal word superiority effect. This suggests that the word form system was intact in this pure alexic subject.

In contrast, two pure alexics have not shown word superiority effects (Behrmann, Black, and Bub, 1990; Kay and Hanley, 1991), which might imply that the word form hypothesis is the correct interpretation of some cases of pure alexia but not others. Before we resort to subtyping, however, it is worth considering the ways in which a single underlying condition can manifest itself differently in combination with some other factor that varies from case to case. It is possible that a visual shape encoding impairment, rather than a word form impairment, underlies all cases of pure alexia. We know from research with normal readers that the word superiority effect is greatly diminished or abolished when subjects attempt to read a letter in a particular position, rather than distributing their attention more normally, across several letter positions (Johnston and McClelland, 1981). Of course, letter-by-letter reading consists of just this strategy: first reading the letter in the first position, then reading the letter in the second, and so on.

In the two cases that showed a word superiority effect, analysis of their accuracy as a function of letter position indicated that they had abandoned the letter-by-letter strategy in the context of the experiment. Although they required much longer exposure durations than normal subjects to attain the same overall level of performance, consistent with diminished visual recognition capacity, the *profile* of performance over letter positions was similar to that of normal control subjects: accuracy was highest in the first and last letter positions, and lower in the middle letter positions, consistent with a normal strategy of distributing attention over all letter positions, and the normal advantage for end letters. The two cases who did not show a word superiority effect did not abandon their letter-by-letter reading strategy in the experiment: Berhmann *et al.*'s case and Kay and Hanley's case both showed a gradient of performance across letter positions, with best performance in the first position, next best in the second, and so on. Even within one case, there is a correlation between the profile of performance across letter positions and the word superiority effect: in one variant of the experiment, Bub *et al.*'s case failed to show the word superiority effect, and also showed the left-to-right gradient in accuracy over letter positions. Thus, the available evidence suggests that it may be the presence versus absence of the letter-by-letter strategy while performing the experimental task, rather than the presence versus absence of word form knowledge, that determines whether pure alexics will show a word superiority effect.

In sum, evidence for the word form hypothesis is, at present, weak. The finding that pure alexics have difficulty reading tachistoscopically presented words, or words written in script, is no more diagnostic of a wordform impairment than of an impairment of visual shape encoding more generally. The variable findings concerning the word superiority effect are also ambiguous. Preservation of the word superiority effect suggests a locus of impairment other than the word form system, and is consistent with a prelexical perceptual impairment. Even when the word superiority effect is not found, independent evidence concerning perceptual strategy in these cases supports an explanation consistent with general (as opposed to orthography-specific) perceptual impairment.

The possibility of an orthography-specific impairment in letter representation, as opposed to wordform representation, has received less systematic study. As early as Déjerine's (1892) study of pure alexia, clinicians have noted that some pure alexics seem to have more trouble recognizing single letters than other types of shapes, including single digits. Unfortunately, there has yet to be a well-controlled experimental demonstration of this, and there are many possible confoundings between the letter/nonletter distinction and other factors predictive of recognition difficulty. For example, letter recognition might be worse than digit recognition simply because there are more letters than digits, and hence more possible confusions for any one item. Intermixing letters and digits circumvents this problem, and Thad Polk and I have seen one patient who maintained her advantage of digits over letters under mixed conditions. It is surprising that so little attention has been paid to discrepancies between letter and number recognition in pure alexia, given its relevance to the issue of orthography-specificity.

Neuroimaging evidence for a wordform area

The earliest PET studies to address cognitive issues in a systematic way involved reading (see Posner and Raichle, 1998, for an overview), and there is now a large body of evidence from PET and fMRI concerning the brain localization of reading and related perceptual and language processes. Consistent with the wordform hypothesis, this evidence suggests that there is a region of extrastriate visual cortex that is specialized for orthography. A variety of experimental designs have been used (see table 4.1) to isolate the process of visual word recognition, and although there is some variability from study to study in the resulting localization, the studies unanimously support the existence of cortex specialized processing for words and orthographically legal pseudo-words, relative to strings of nonletter shapes (Howard, Patterson, Wise, Brown, Friston, Weiller, and Frackowiak, 1992; Petersen, Fox, Snyder, and Raichle, 1990; Price, Wise, Watson, Patterson, Howard, and Frackowiak, 1994). Indeed, even when pseudo-words are presented in AlTeRnAtInG cAsE, which renders them far less familiar as general visual patterns than a consonant string in ALL UPPER or all lower case, they evoke more activation in the wordform area (Polk and Farah, 1998), implying that this area is truly responding to orthographic regularities *per se* and not general visual pattern familiarity.

6.7 A fourth hypothesis: general visual impairment most severe for orthography

It seems sensible to divide the space of alternative hypotheses for explaining pure alexia into those that are orthography-specific and those that hypothesize a visual impairment for orthographic and non-orthographic stimuli alike. Indeed, I originally took this to be the basic decision that should sit at the base of our Baconian decision tree for understanding pure alexia (e.g., Farah and Wallace, 1991). But it is possible that mother nature did not design the brain with neat, binary alternatives in mind. There is another, hybrid possibility, which I now believe bears scrutiny. It is the hypothesis that pure alexia is the result of a general visual impairment, which affects the rapid perception of multiple shapes from any category, but which is most severe for letters. There are both empirical and theoretical reasons to take this hybrid hypothesis seriously. As we have already seen, the neuroimaging data showing orthography-specific activations, and the patient data showing preserved number recognition, suggests that the human brain may contain a dedicated word recognition system. On the theoretical side, recent research with artificial neural networks provides a mechanism whereby a generalized impairment with particular severity for orthographic material could arise naturally, and without hypothesizing two separate lesions.

Self-organization of a "letter area"

Thad Polk and I have explored some of the ways in which self-organizing systems can respond to statistical regularities in our visual environment, particularly orthographic regularities. By "self-organizing system" I refer to a class of neural network models that learn without a teacher, or external source of information conveying "right" or "wrong." Indeed, in such systems there is no "right" or "wrong" because there is no target pattern to be learned. Rather, the strength of connections among the neuron-like units of such a network is changed simply as a function of the correlations among the activity levels of the units in the network. The best-known learning rule for self-organizing systems is the Hebbian rule, that "Neurons that fire together wire together." In other words, when the activity levels of two units are positively correlated, the connection strength between them increases. This increases the likelihood that their activations will be correlated in the future, as activation of one will cause the other to become active by virtue of the strengthened connection. In this way, the network develops a repetoire of stable patterns of activation, in the sense that activation patterns that are close to the learned pattern (e.g., contain part of it) will be transformed into the learned pattern and tend to remain active. These stable patterns can be viewed as representations of whatever inputs to the network evoke the patterns.

If it is assumed that prior to learning, neighboring neurons have excitatory connections among them, such that activating one neuron tends to activate its neighbors, then it is possible to account for a number of aspects of cortical representation by the simple mechanism of Hebbian learning. For example, topographic maps such as the somatasensory homunculus arise because neighboring locations in the input to be represented (locations on the body surface, in the case of the homunculus) tend to be activated at the same time. Because of the short-range excitatory connections, this biases neighboring units of the network to represent neighboring regions of the input (e.g., Merzenich, 1987). The emergence of ocular dominance in cortex (e.g., Miller, Keller, and Stryker, 1989), and location-invariant shape representations (Foldiak, 1991) are two other aspects of the organization of the visual system that we have already seen explained with self-organizing systems (see chapters 1 and 4).

In the foregoing examples, statistical regularities in the environment interact with correlation-driven learning to give rise to organized cortical representations. For example, the statistical regularity of correlated activity at neighboring locations of the input space leads to topographic mapping of that space. Polk and I reasoned that orthographic statistical regularities in the visual environment would also interact with the correlation-driven learning of self-organizing systems in much the same way. The most obvious aspect of the statistics of orthography is the co-occurrence among letters. If you are looking at one letter, you are probably seeing many other letters, and you are unlikely to be seeing a digit. In contrast, if you are looking at a digit, there is a good chance that you are seeing other digits at the same time, rather than letters.

We found that, across a number of variations in simple Hebbian-type learning rules and network architectures, the co-occurrence of letters with letters and digits with digits led the network to segregate its letter and digit representations (Polk and Farah, 1995a). In other words, the network developed specialized letter and digit areas. This is because once a unit in the network has begun to represent one letter, spreading activation will cause its neighbors to become active when that letter is presented. Other items that are presented along with that letter will therefore be biased to come to be represented by the neighbors of the original letter's representing unit, because those neighbors will be active during the presentation of the other item. The fact that the co-occurring items will usually be other letters means that other letters' representations will cluster around that first one.

If the statistics of the input are adjusted to take into account the greater co-occurrence of letters with letters than of numbers with numbers, the simulation then tends to organize with letter areas only. Digits and other shapes remain intermixed. This accounts for the observation that letter perception may be worse than digit perception in some pure alexic subjects.

The idea that co-occurrence drives the organization of visual shape representations toward a segregated letter area was tested with a group of subjects whose visual experience with letters and digits conforms to very different statistics. Thad Polk and I tested postal workers who spend eight hours on alternate days sorting Canadian mail by postal code. These codes consist of alternating letters and numbers, for example M5M 2W9. As a measure of the segregation of letter representations from number representations, we used the degree to which letters pop out, in a visual search task, against a background of numbers. If letter representations are indeed segregated from number representations, then the presence of a letter can be detected by the presence of activity in the letter area, without the need to individually recognize the characters in a display. Letters are indeed detected among numbers faster than among letters (e.g., Jonides and Gleitman, 1972), consistent with the existence of segregated letter representations in normal subjects. As predicted, Canadian mail sorters showed less of a difference between these two conditions than postal worker control subjects (Polk and Farah, 1995b).

Self-organization of abstract letter identities

A variation on the same type of mechanisms that create segregation of letter areas in self-organizing systems can also create case-invariant letter representations, sometimes referred to as abstract letter identities. Just as correlation-driven learning tends to drive together representations of stimuli that occur at the same time in the previous model, because the network is in a similar state when the co-occurring stimuli are presented, it will also drive together the representations of stimuli that occur in similar contexts, because the similar contexts will evoke similar network states. For a visual network, "similar" naturally means similar-looking. Note that a number of letters do look similar in their upper and lower case forms, for example C and c, P and p. Thus, if the network sees *CAP* and *cap*, the similar contexts for A and a will tend to drive the representations of those shapes together. A variety of simulations bear this out (Polk and Farah, 1997); a representative outcome of this learning process is shown in figure 6.6. These simulations demonstrate the computational feasibility of the hypothesis that certain aspects of the statistics of the orthographic environment could not only form a letter area in visual cortex, but could form an area representing abstract letter identities. In light of this, it is interesting to note pure alexic subjects are generally disproportionately impaired in visual matching tasks requiring cross-case matching (Behrmann and Shallice, 1995; Bub, Black, and Howell, 1989; Kay and Hanley, 1991; Reuter-Lorenz and Brunn, 1990).

A   D   E

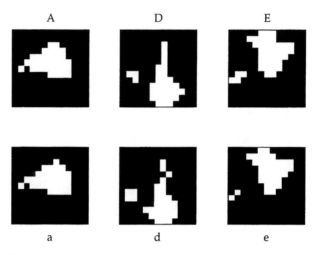

a   d   e

Figure 6.6   Representations of the upper- and lower-case forms of three letters, which developed spontaneously in a Hebbian network exposed to upper- and lower-case words. Different looking forms of the same letters came to be represented by roughly the same distributed patterns of activity.

From T. A. Polk and M. J. Farah, "A simple common contexts explanation for the development of abstract letter identities," Neural Computation, 9, 1997.

If letter representations are segregated within the visual system, by the type of mechanism proposed here, then our visual system does contain orthography-specific components and pure alexia could follow from damage to such a component. However, because this component segregates out within an area that is already specialized for representing multiple shapes simultaneously, most lesions would be expected to result in some degree of general impairment in the recognition of multiple shapes as well as a more severe impairment for the recognition of orthography and an especially severe impairment for tasks requiring the representation of abstract letter identity, such as cross-case matching.

6.8   Conclusions

Does the human brain contain tissue that is dedicated to reading, that is, required for reading and not required for any other tasks? The answer to this question has implications for the interpretation of pure alexia, as well as the genesis of functional brain architecture in general.

The nature of pure alexia

Much of the research on pure alexia in the past ten years has focused on a binary decision: Is it a visual impairment affecting all types of stimuli, or is it orthography-specific? Reluctantly, I have come to the conclusion that the truth is probably more complex than either of these two alternatives. Although I was initially impressed with the evidence for a visual impairment that extends beyond orthography, an accumulation of clinical observations suggests that visual letter perception, if not word perception, may be disproportionately impaired in some pure alexics. Both observations can be accommodated by an hypothesis of "specialization within specialization." The more general visual impairments are caused by damage to a brain region specialized for rapid encoding of multiple shapes, which may involve a computational strategy of localist representation. Among the shapes most frequently processed in this area are letters, seen mainly in the context of words, and by the mechanisms proposed by Polk and myself (Polk and Farah, 1995a; 1997) these will segregate out within this multiple shape encoding area, forming an even more specialized sub-area, and possibly coming to represent abstract letter identities. Depending upon the exact location of the lesion relative to these areas, pure alexics would be expected to have a visual impairment for rapid encoding of multiple visual shapes, with varying degrees of orthography-specificity.

Dedicated neural systems: how do they arise?

Consider some uncontroversial examples of functions known to make use of dedicated brain tissue: Color vision, face perception, motor control, spoken language. Localized brain damage can render a person color blind, prosopagnosic, paralyzed or apraxic, or aphasic. In contrast, evidence has yet to be presented for a localized brain system dedicated to chess playing or ballet. That is, brain damage has never been found to impair chess ability while sparing general intellect, perception, memory, as well as poker and canasta playing. It cannot

impair ballet while sparing ballroom and belly dance. The following generalization seems to fit these observations, as well as most
people's intuitions on the issue: Brain tissue becomes dedicated to a
particular psychological function through genetic mechanisms. Only
abilities that evolved can be carried out by specialized brain regions.
Setting aside the example of reading, it seems a plausible empirical
generalization that learning within an individual's lifetime cannot
create new brain areas.

Of course, learning modifies the brain, in the sense that it alters
connections between individual neurons. Learning and other forms
of experience can even alter the organization of a brain area. The
work of Merzenich (e.g., 1987) in the somatasensory system is probably the best known example of this. After finger amputation, stimulation of the adjacent fingers results in their neural representations
taking over the brain tissue that once represented the lost digit.
But even this more molar type of experience-driven change in brain
organization falls well short of the genesis of a new functionally-
defined area. Unless one adopts a rather unnatural parse of brain
architecture, according to which the representation of each digit in
the somatasensory system and each visual field location in the visual
system is a separate "area" or "system," no new areas or systems
have been created or destroyed as a result of experience in these
experiments on plasticity. In contrast, if learning to read leads to the
creation of an area specialized for visual word recognition, then
experience as well as genetics can play a major role in determining
the existence and nature of specialized brain systems.

Perhaps because of their implications for the genesis of functional
brain architecture, other acquired dyslexias involving post-visual impairment have recently been scrutinized for evidence of true reading
specificity. Surface dyslexia, in which the reading of irregular words
(e.g., leopard, yacht) is impaired, was traditionally interpreted as a
loss of whole-word representations, leaving the reader dependent
on the use of grapheme-to-phoneme rules which work poorly with
irregular words (Coltheart, 1985). More recently, however, it has
been suggested that surface dyslexia may result from a loss of semantic representations, a nonreading-specific impairment (Patterson and
Hodges, 1992). According to this new view, irregular words are particularly dependent on word recognition, including recognition of the

words' semantics, for pronunciation. Phonological dyslexia, in which the reading of nonwords is impaired, was traditionally interpreted as a loss of the grapheme-to-phoneme route to word recognition, leaving the reader dependent on whole word representations, which do not exist for nonwords. However, this form of dyslexia may also be secondary to a more general linguistic problem, namely impaired phonological representation (e.g., Farah, Stowe, and Levinson, 1996; Coltheart, 1985). In sum, acquired disorders of reading provide important clues to the genesis of functionally specialized brain areas. Although more research is needed to address the issue with certainty, it appears that pure alexia may provide the clearest evidence so far available for localization of a category of knowledge that is fundamentally arbitrary, lacks an evolutionary history, and is learned relatively late in life.

chapter seven

Visual Attention

7.1   A functional characterization of attention

From image construction on the retina to the segmentation and identification of objects in extrastriate occipital and temporal regions, the
previous chapters have described a cascade of remarkably efficient
and powerful visual information processing. Do all of the stimuli
impinging on our retinas get swept along in this cascade equally, or
does the flow of visual information processing terminate differently
or earlier for some stimuli than for others? The answer is that stimuli
do receive differential processing. The mechanisms whereby some
stimuli are selected for processing over others are collectively known
as "attention."

Computational pressures for attention

The first question that one can ask about attention is why it exists at
all. Why not represent all stimuli to an equal degree? The classic
answer to this question given in introductory psychology texts is that
the brain has limited processing capacity, and that the rational way of
adapting to this limitation is to process only the most relevant stimuli
fully. This answer is probably correct, but it does leave open the
equally basic questions of why, and in what sense, our processing
capacity is limited.

One place to look for an understanding of our processing limitations is at the level of our response systems (e.g. Allport, 1989). A computational reason for selecting one or a small number of stimuli for processing, rather than the dozens of distinct objects found in most visual scenes, is patent in the hardware limitations of having just two hands with which to reach for visual stimuli, and one fovea (or more precisely, two yoked foveas) toward which to direct stimuli with eye movements. However, a response bottleneck does not perforce imply limited processing of stimuli within the visual system. Indeed, one of the ways that so-called "late" attentional selection (i.e., just prior to response execution) has been demonstrated is to show that more information about the visual properties of unattended stimuli exist in the system than are manifest in overt responses (e.g. Driver and Tipper, 1989). Stimulus information is apparently winnowed out at multiple loci in the brain, and the question of why it must be winnowed within the visual system is not directly addressed by the need for selection within response systems. The most that can be said is that, without the capacity to respond simultaneously to large numbers of stimuli, there is less pressure to fully process large numbers of stimuli simultaneously within the visual system.

Another type of processing limitation, affecting the visual system directly, results from the use of distributed representations. Recall from chapter 4 that distributed representations involve the use of a common set of hardware units (in the brain, presumably neurons) to represent a variety of different stimuli. This has several advantages, including economy of hardware, automatic generalization, and graceful degradation. However, it also has a major disadvantage, which has already been discussed in the context of letter representation for word perception in the previous chapter: When more than one stimulus is represented simultaneously, the two patterns are superimposed in the same set of units, resulting in mutual interference or cross-talk (see figure 6.4).

There are several ways of coping with the problem of interference and cross-talk. One is to reduce the degree of distributedness of the representation, and thereby strike a compromise between the loss of some of the economy, automatic generalization, etc. of fully distributed representations and the reduced interference of a local code. Rather than involving every unit in the representation of every item, different fractions of the units would participate for different items. There is some evidence that the brain does implement such a compromise, at higher levels of visual representation at least: Moderately distributed representations, also known as sparse population codes, have been demonstrated for inferotemporal face representations (Young and Yamane, 1992). Another solution to the problem of interference is to bind the attributes of a single stimulus by synchrony of neural firing. The idea of synchronized oscillations as a basis for binding was discussed in chapter 2.

Another very general solution to the problem of interference or cross-talk in distributed representations, which is closest to what we normally think of as "attention" in psychology, is to limit the processing of stimuli to one portion of the scene at a time. Much of the history of attention research in cognitive psychology has been devoted to understanding just what the nature of the "portions" are. This will be determined by the type of stimulus representation that serves as the locus of attentional selection. Stimuli could be selected in relatively early map format representations, on the basis of their location within the map, with one location at a time attended. Alternatively, stimuli could be selected at the level of object representations, one object at a time. These alternatives are not simple to discriminate because there is usually a one-to-one correspondence between objects and the locations they occupy. Even representations of stimulus attributes such as color or motion could presumably serve as a locus for selection, allowing stimuli of just a certain color or just a certain type of motion to receive full processing at a given moment. Whatever the locus of selection within the visual system, the processing of selected stimuli downstream from that locus will be relieved of interference from nonselected stimuli. By switching among stimuli over time, all stimuli can eventually receive full processing.

Forms of visual attention

Historically, cognitive psychologists have focused on spatial selection, sometimes invoking the metaphor of an attentional "spotlight" that can be swept across the visual field to facilitate perception of illuminated stimuli (e.g., Eriksen and Hoffman, 1973; Posner, 1980). The spotlight metaphor fits well with many findings within cognitive psychology. For example, Posner and colleagues have shown that normal subjects are faster in responding to the onset of a stimulus (the "target") when an earlier stimulus (the attentional "cue") occurs in the same spatial location (e.g., Posner, 1980). Two other striking examples of evidence that attention is fundamentally spatial come from Shulman, Remington, and McLean (1979) and Hoffman and Nelson (1981). The first group showed that when attention was cued from one location to another, perception of stimuli at irrelevant intermediate positions were fleetingly facilitated, as if a spotlight were being swept across the visual field. The second group showed that when normal subjects correctly named letters appearing at multiple locations in the visual field, they were more likely to succeed at an orientation discrimination task when the oriented forms occurred near the location of the letters, suggesting that we cannot attend to a stimulus without attending to its location.

Location seems a particularly likely basis for attentional selection from the vantage point of neuroscience as well. Most of the brain's representations of visual stimuli take the form of spatially formatted maps, predominantly retinotopic maps. Location is thus widely available as a stimulus attribute on which to select, and has the further advantage of providing a common index to bind the representations of a given stimulus across different areas within the visual system. The existence of salient attentional impairments following damage to the human and animal dorsal visual system, also known as the "where" system, provides further plausability for the hypothesis that attention selects among competing stimulus locations. Indeed, the plainly spatial nature of hemispatial neglect, the attentional limitation that typically follows damage to the dorsal visual system, and which will be discussed at length in the next chapter, implies strongly that visual attention selects among stimuli on the basis of their location.

Of course, there is no reason to think that attention selects among stimuli at only one locus in the visual system. Although spatial attention has received the most study, there is also evidence for selection from representations of nonspatial dimensions. For example, color provides an efficient basis for the attentional filtering of stimuli, particularly when there is a large difference in hue between the attended and unattended stimuli (Wolfe, 1998).

Attentional selection can also occur from object representations. Duncan (1984) devised an experiment in which the normal confound between a single location and a single object was eliminated, by presenting pairs of superimposed objects at a single location. Subjects were asked to report properties of the objects after a brief presentation of the object pairs. They were just as good at reporting two properties of a single object as one, but there was a performance decrement when one property from each of two objects had to be reported, consistent with their perceiving an object at a time rather than a property at a time or a location at a time. Vecera and Farah (1994) showed that this form of selection was truly nonspatial by including a condition in which the two objects were spatially separated along with Duncan's superimposed condition. Spatial separation did not increase the performance decrement in reporting properties from two objects relative to a single object, implying that the object representations being operated on by attention were devoid of location information.

The delineation of different forms of attention and their functional characteristics is a central issue in cognitive psychology. The small fraction of that literature cited here is merely an indication of the variety of types of representation likely to serve as loci for attentional selection within the visual system. An excellent review of the psychology of attention can be found in a book by that name, written by Hal Pashler (1998).

7.2   The neural bases of attention

Two empirical issues

In this chapter we will address two general sets of questions about the neural bases of attention. First, how does attention affect visual information processing at different stages? Specifically, at what levels of the visual system does attention exert its effects, and by what mechanisms? Second, what neural systems control the allocation of attention? What is the division of labor among the different components of the attentional network? These questions can be addressed using evidence from a variety of sources, including lesion studies of animals, single unit recordings, studies of brain-damaged humans, and functional neuroimaging of normal humans. Although each empirical approach has emphasized different forms of attention and issues concerning attention, such that the results obtained by different methods do not always dovetail as perfectly as one might wish, there is sufficient overlap of subject matter and findings that it seems worth attempting an overall synthesis. Finally, because of the wealth of information about one particular impairment of attention in humans, the neglect syndrome, a separate chapter will be devoted to reviewing what the neglect syndrome has taught us about visual attention and visual space representation in the human brain.

7.3 Levels and mechanisms of selection in cortical visual areas

Cognitive psychologists debated the "early" (or relatively peripheral) versus "late" (or relatively central) selection issue for many years. One reason for the longevity of this issue is that the methods of cognitive psychology are very indirect with respect to the physiological locus and real-time effects of attention on perception. For example, evidence of spatial selection has been taken by some to favor the relatively early retinotopically mapped visual areas of the brain as the locus of attentional selection. However, many representations that one might well call "late" also have a spatial format, for example the spatial working memory areas of the prefrontal cortex (Goldman-Rakic, 1988). Only when researchers began to localize attentional effects to specific brain areas could we obtain decisive evidence concerning the loci of attentional selection in vision.

The earliest available evidence on attention and the brain comes from clinical observations of patients with attentional impairments after brain damage. These data are not particularly helpful, however, for answering the question of the locus or loci of attentional selection in the brain, because lesions occurring at different levels of the visual system proper will not only affect attentional selection but perception itself. It is not very interesting to learn that a cortically blind patient cannot selectively attend to visual stimuli! Evidence from brain-damaged humans will be mentioned briefly in the second part of this chapter, in discussing the attention network beyond visual sensory areas, and an in-depth discussion of the human visual attentional impairment known as visual neglect will be the topic of the next chapter.

Evidence from event-related potentials

Among the earliest findings to address the issue of early versus late attentional selection were the event-related potential (ERP) findings of Hillyard and colleagues. They began this work in the auditory system, showing enhancement of early components of the ERP to auditory stimuli occurring at attended, relative to unattended, locations (Hillyard and Picton, 1978). More recently, work from this lab and others has applied the excellent temporal resolution and increasingly good anatomical localization of ERPs to address the anatomical locus of visual spatial selection.

Mangun, Hillyard, and Luck (1993) presented visual stimuli at four possible locations while subjects maintained attention at one location, and compared the ERPs elicited by these stimuli when occurring at attended and unattended locations. As shown in figure 7.1, attention enhanced stimulus processing, relative to the unattended condition, as early as the P1 component of the visual ERP, which peaked in this experiment at about 100 ms after stimulus onset. Analyses of the gradient of this ERP effect over the scalp suggest an anatomical locus of occipital association cortex for early visual selection by location. No evidence of attentional selection within primary visual cortex was observed. These findings agree with other ERP studies of attention to visual location in which the attended location was cued from trial to trial (Mangun and Hillyard, 1995) and guided by the subject in a visual search task (Luck, Fan, and Hillyard, 1993). Other studies have found ERP markers for nonspatial visual attention, which differ from the spatial form of attention. For example, the effects of attention to stimulus dimensions such as color and shape are not manifest in the visual ERP until 250–300 ms after stimulus presentation (e.g., Eimer, 1997; Aine and Harter, 1984; Hillyard and Anllo-Vento, 1998). This time course is consistent with the general idea that location is explicitly represented at the earliest stages of visual processing, whereas color and form are explicitly represented only in higher extrastriate visual areas.

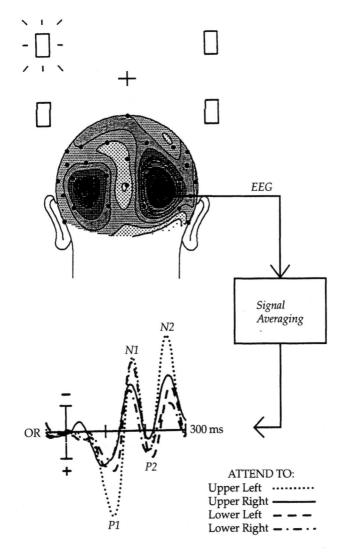

Figure 7.1 ERP evidence concerning the timecourse and location of attentional effects in vision. From top to bottom: Experimental display, current density on scalp at latency of P1 attentional effect, and ERP waveforms for upper left stimulus under different attentional conditions, showing enhancement of P1, N1, and N2 components.

From I. Schindler and G. Kerkhoff, "Head and trunk orientation modulate visual neglect," in NeuroReport, 8, 1997.

Taken as a whole, the ERP findings suggest that visual attention operates at multiple loci. There is ERP evidence of selection from representations in which location is explicitly represented as well as representations in which dimensions such as color and shape are explicitly represented. Not surprisingly, this evidence also shows that selection at these different loci have correspondingly different timecourses. Analysis of the scalp distribution of the ERP effects suggest that spatial selection occurs in extrastriate visual cortex rather than primary visual cortex (Clark and Hillyard, 1996; Hillyard, Vogel, and Luck, 1998).

What do ERP results tell us about the mechanisms by which information is selected at these different levels of processing? More specifically, do the attentional effects on ERPs to visual stimuli reflect facilitation of the attended stimuli or inhibition of the unattended stimuli? Most of the studies just reviewed cannot answer this question, because they involved direct comparisons between ERPs to attended and unattended stimuli, rather than comparisons between ERPs in these conditions and a neutral, "no attention" control condition. One study that did include such a condition was carried out by Luck, Hillyard, Mouloua, Woldorf, Clark, and Hawkins (1994). They presented stimuli in one of four positions, and either cued subjects' attention to one position at the outset of a trial, by an arrow pointing to that position, or gave a "neutral" cue, consisiting of arrows pointing to all four positions. They found evidence of both facilitation and inhibition, associated with different ERP components at different latencies. The early P1 component (80–120 ms) showed inhibition of unattended stimuli relative to the same stimuli in the neutral condition, but no attentional facilitation. The slightly later N1 component (140–80 ms) showed facilitation of attended stimuli relative to the neutral condition, but no inhibition of unattended stimuli.

Evidence from PET

Bloodflow-based functional neuroimaging studies in normal humans provide some additional clues to the locus of attentional selection, with more direct anatomical localization than is afforded with scalp-recorded ERPs. Early studies, carried out mainly with PET, failed to show selective enhancement of processing in the earliest cortical visual

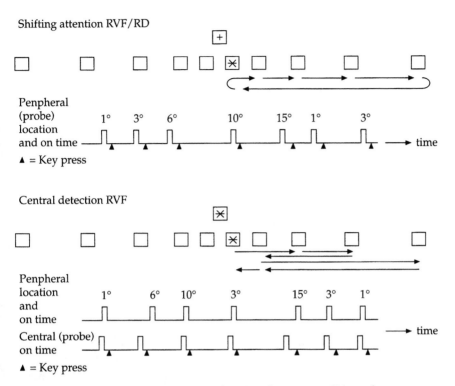

Figure 7.2 An early PET experiment, showing the two conditions that were subtracted with the intention of isolating spatial attention effects in vision.
From M. Corbetta et al., "A PET study of visuospatial atention," Journal of Neuroscience, 13, 1993.

areas with spatial attention. However, the designs of many of these studies were not optimized for finding differences between attended and unattended processing in early visual areas. For example, in a classic early PET study of attention, Corbetta, Miezin, Shulman, and Petersen (1993) compared the two conditions diagrammed in figure 7.2. In one condition subjects attended to stimuli in the center of the visual field while stimuli occurred in an unpredictable sequence of locations to one side. In the other, there were no central stimuli and subjects attended to the more peripheral stimuli which followed a predictable sequence of locations. Corbetta and colleagues compared these two conditions and failed to find greater occipital activation in the second relative to the first. However, in both of these conditions subjects were attending to stimuli. Furthermore, the unpredictable nature of stimuli in the first condition may have attracted some degree of attention to the peripheral locations.

Compared to the ERP studies just reviewed, which built fairly directly on work in cognitive psychology, PET researchers tended to operationalize attention with novel tasks, partly because of the need for blocking of experimental conditions. For example, the two conditions of Corbetta *et al.* (1993) just described do not closely resemble previously published attentional paradigms in the cognitive psychology literature. Vandenberghe, Dupont, De Bruyn, Bormans, Michiels, Mortelmans, and Orban (1996) manipulated a number of task components in their PET study of attention, including the following: The need to merely detect versus discriminate an attended stimulus; the position of the stimulus in the visual field; and the presence or absence of distractor stimuli. They found dramatic effects on the patterns of brain activity associated with attention.

In view of the strong influence of seemingly minor task variations, the study of Heinze, Mangun, Burchert, Hinrichs, Scholz, Munte, Gos, Scherg, Johannes, Hundeshagen, Gazzaniga, and Hillyard (1994) is of particular interest. They used the same experimental paradigm with both PET and ERP. Recall that, of all the approaches reviewed here, research ERPs gives the clearest evidence of early spatial selection, although anatomical localization with this method is the most indirect and fraught with difficulty. By comparing PET and ERP evidence on the effects of attention in the exact same paradigm, we can begin to separate out such factors as task differences, the potential for faulty localizations with ERP, and the potential for false negative outcomes with PET. The Heinze *et al.* ERP study replicated earlier work consistent with attentional modulation in occipital visual areas, and their PET study produced clear evidence of occipital enhancement with a spatial attention manipulation.

Another PET study with clear and interpretable results concerns attention to dimensions other than spatial location (Corbetta *et al.*, 1990). Figure 7.3 shows the types of display used. A number of small shapes at scattered locations have a particular color, shape, and speed of motion, and the purpose of the study was to map the brain areas involved in attention to each of these three dimensions. Halfway

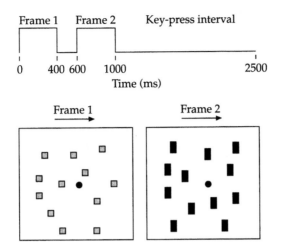

Figure 7.3 Example of a trial from a PET experiment on attention to different dimensions of vision, in which subjects judged whether the sequentially presented frames were the same or different in their colors, shapes, or speeds of motion.

From M. Corbetta et al., "Attentional modulation of neural processing of shape, color and velocity in humans," Science, 248, 1990; copyright 1990 the American Association for the Advancement of Science.

through each trial the display is replaced, and the color, shape, or speed may change or remain the same. Subjects are told in advance of a block of trials whether to compare the two displays with reference to their color, shape, or speed, and to respond "same" or "different." Recall from chapters 2 and 4 that areas V4 and MT play specialized roles in color and motion perception, and that IT is crucial for shape perception. These areas become activated during attention to their specialized dimensions: Attention to color is associated with activation of V4, motion with MT, and shape with IT.

Evidence from fMRI

A new generation of imaging studies, conducted with fMRI, have produced results that show much greater consistency with each other and with results from other methodologies. This consistency is at least partly due to the trend towards more conventional experimental designs, adapted from the cognitive psychology literature. Recent fMRI studies have found clear effects of spatial attention in extrastriate visual cortex when subjects were instructed to monitor changing stimulus arrays for target pictures or symbols and attention was varied between fixation and the target position (Kastner, De Weerd, Desimone, and Ungerleider, 1998) or between one side of fixation and the other (Mangun, Buonocore, Girelli, and Jha, 1998).

Even more recently, fMRI has detected attentional changes in primary visual cortex. Martinez, Anllo-Vento, Sereno, Frank, Buxton, Dubowitz, Wong, Hinrichs, Heinze, and Hillyard (1999) presented subjects with two clusters of stimuli, located to the left and right of fixation, each of which contained a center T surrounded by plus signs. Their subjects' task was to attend to one side or the other, as cued by an arrow which changed direction every 20 seconds, and monitor for an upside-down T at the attended location. With this straightforward visual discrimination task, made challenging by the presence of distractors (plus signs), and straightforward instructions to attend to one side or the other, attention-related increases in bloodflow were found in many occipital visual areas, including primary visual cortex. Martinez and colleagues also recorded ERPs while subjects performed the task, and replicated the usual finding of no attentional modulation of ERP components generated in primary visual cortex, in seeming contradiction of their fMRI findings.

Ghandi, Heeger, and Boynton (1998) also cued spatial attention to one side or the other of fixation, in a speed discrimination task, and compared these conditions with the passive viewing of the same moving stimuli. Consistent with the PET findings of Corbetta and colleagues, attention to motion activated area MT (see also Watanabe, Sasaki, Miyauchi, Putz, Fujimaki, Neilsen, Takino, and Miyakawa, 1998). In addition, like Martinez and colleagues, they found attention-related changes in primary visual cortex. Several other groups have found attentional effects in primary visual cortex in tasks involving different manipulations of attention, including foveal versus surrounding locations (Somers, Dale, Seiffert, and Tootell, 1999) and less specific comparisons of attention versus passive viewing (Shulman, Corbetta, Buckner, Raichle, Fiez, Miezin, and Petersen, 1997; Watanabe *et al.*, 1998).

Evidence from single unit recordings

Single unit recordings in monkeys offer excellent temporal resolution, and anatomical localization superior even to bloodflow methods, albeit limited to one site at a time. Starting in the mid-1980s, researchers undertook the near-heroic task of training monkeys to perform visual attention tasks and recorded the responses of cells within different visual areas to attended and unattended visual stimuli. One of the first studies to use this approach was reported by Moran and Desimone (1985). They trained monkeys to perform a sequential same/different matching task on stimuli at various locations within the visual field while the monkeys fixated centrally. In addition, the monkeys were trained to perform this task only at a location that had been cued by the experimenters at the start of a block of trials, and ignore stimuli presented at other locations. While the monkeys performed this task, Moran and Desimone recorded from cells in V1, V4, and IT that were selectively responsive to one of the two possible stimuli.

Moran and Desimone's findings for V4 cells are illustrated in figure 7.4. When the monkey attended to the location of a stimulus to which the cell was responsive, in a location encompassed by the cell's receptive field, the cell responded normally. However, when the monkey ignored the same stimulus in the same location, the cell responded less. Spatial attention inhibited the processing of unattended stimuli, in effect changing the spatial extent of the cell's receptive field to exclude unattended locations. In contrast, when the attended location was outside a cell's receptive field, unattended stimuli falling within that receptive field were not inhibited. Moran and Desimone found the same effects of spatial attention when they recorded from cells in IT, but not when they recorded from cells in V1. In the latter case, receptive fields were too small to encompass both attended and unattended stimuli, so that V1 inhibition would have had to affect stimuli outside of the attended receptive field, which was not observed in V4.

More recent studies of the effects of spatial attention on neuronal responses in the monkey visual system have confirmed some aspects of these results as well as suggesting some extensions and revisions.

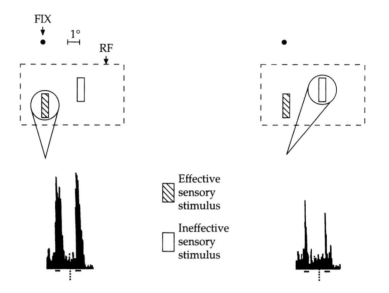

Figure 7.4   Typical displays, showing location to which attention was cued, and resultant neural activity in a classic study of attentional effects on individual neurons in monkey area V4.

Adapted from J. Moran and R. Desimone, "Selective attention gates visual processing in extrastriate cortex," Science, 229, 1985; copyright 1985 the American Association for the Advancement of Science.

In some studies, attention has been found to modulate cells' responses even when the unattended stimuli fall outside the cells' receptive fields. Using a spatially cued visual discrimination task, Motter (1993) found evidence of selection when unattended stimuli fell outside the recorded cell's receptive field. Similar results were obtained by Connor, Preddie, Gallant, and Van Essen (1997) and Luck, Chelazzi, Hillyard, and Desimone (1997). Some studies have found attentional modulation of cells in V1 in difficult visual discrimination tasks (Motter, 1993; Vidyasagar, 1998).

The question of whether attention consists of facilitation of attended stimuli or inhibition of unattended stimuli has also received varied answers from different studies. Of the studies that included the baseline condition necessary to partition attentional effects into facilitation and inhibition, Moran and Desimone found only inhibition, whereas Motter and Luck *et al.* found facilitation of attended stimuli as well.

As with the imaging studies, the variability in findings here is presumably attributable to the many differences in tasks and stimulus displays used. In general, attentional effects in primary visual cortex are found when animals are performing difficult visual discriminations and stimuli are presented in a cluttered field. This is consistent with the idea that attention will be deployed maximally only when distractors threaten to impose cross-talk on perceptual representations, and the quality of those representations is critical. The role of such task variables is supported by Motter's (1993) observation that the amount of visual clutter was related to the size of the attention effects.

So far this review of attentional effects has focused on the differential processing of attended and unattended stimuli. Can single unit recordings tell us anything about the state of attention *per se*, prior to and independent of the effects on processing the attended stimulus? Specifically, how does attention affect cells' spontaneous firing rates, prior to stimulus presentation? Luck *et al.*'s (1997) results speak directly to this question. In both areas V2 and V4, there was a 30–40 percent increase in the baseline activity of cells associated with the state of attention. Similar increases in baseline activity have been observed in tasks presumed to involve nonspatial forms of attention (Chelazzi, Miller, Duncan, and Desimone, 1993; Fuster and Jervey, 1982). The natural interpretation for this activity is as top-down activation from higher areas involved in directing attention.

There are also preliminary findings on the effects of attention in cortical visual areas other than V1–V4, and cued by features other than spatial location, although here too the agreement among studies is less than perfect. Recording in dorsal stream areas, Treue and Maunsell (1996) found effects of spatial attention on the motion responses of cells in MT and MST. However, Groh, Seidemann, and Newsome (1996) recorded in the same areas during a different motion perception task and failed to observe attentional modulation.

Attention to objects, or more strictly speaking object properties, has also been studied using single unit recording. Chelazzi, Miller, Duncan, and Desimone (1993) trained monkeys to attend to a complex picture, regardless of its location, and recorded the activity of neurons in IT. At the outset of each trial, a picture was shown at fixation. This served as a cue, directing the monkeys' attention to this particular pattern in a subsequent array. Following a delay, a small set of pictures were

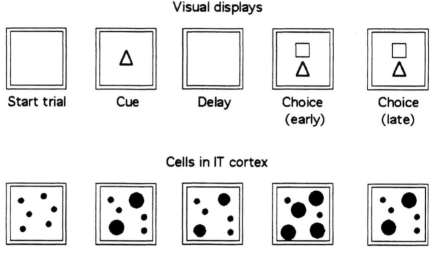

Figure 7.5   Typical sequence of stimuli, and schematic representation of neural activity, in an experiment on attention to object properties, showing eventual inhibition of activity representing unattended stimuli.

shown at locations arrayed around fixation, and the monkeys' task was to refixate the cued picture. Like attention to location, attention to a complex pattern was found to inhibit neuronal responses to unattended stimuli.

Figure 7.5 is a schematic diagram of the stimulus events and consequent neural activity in this task. Neurons that are normally responsive to a stimulus showed an initial response upon presentation of the stimulus, which was quickly inhibited when the stimulus was to be ignored. Neurons responsive to the cued picture maintained an intermediate level of activity during the delay and upon the return of the cued picture resumed and maintained their full activity, in some cases showing enhanced responses.

Attentional effects on visual representation in human and monkey cortex: an integration

Let us emerge from the swarm of methodological details and discrepant findings in these four literatures and look for some general principles.

To begin with, spatial visual attention modulates early processing in modality-specific visual cortex. All methods reviewed here provide converging evidence for selection in extrastriate visual cortex. There is less agreement concerning the involvement of primary visual cortex. ERPs seem to draw a line between extrastriate visual areas and striate or primary visual cortex, suggesting that attention operates only above the level of primary visual cortex. Functional neuroimaging and single unit recording studies suggest that the nature of the task demands may determine whether attentional effects are manifest in primary visual cortex, with more difficult visual discriminations and more potentially distracting stimuli yielding earlier and more pronounced attentional effects. However, task differences alone will not get us off the hook in explaining the absence of V1 effects in ERP studies. Recall that Martinez and colleagues (1999) found attentional effects in V1 in their fMRI experiment and not in their ERP experiment, despite using the exact same task.

In confronting this discrepancy, Martinez and colleagues were led to propose an interesting hypothesis concerning the role of V1 representations in attention. They suggest that V1 is indeed a locus of attentional selection, under the influence of higher visual areas, but only after it has done some initial processing of stimuli in a manner unaffected by attentional state. They point out that their ERP recordings may reflect only the initial processing of the stimulus in V1, and not the later top-down modulation. In contrast, the relatively long time constant of fMRI bloodflow measurement would capture these later effects. This idea is partially supported by Vidyasagar's study of single cells in V1, in which he found two latency ranges of V1 attention effects.

In sum, it seems likely that spatial attention causes differential processing of attended stimuli in areas as early as primary visual cortex. It also appears that such extremely early selection occurs mainly when tasks demand a high degree of attention, and possibly only in processing that is subsequent to the initial registration of the stimulus.

All four methods provide converging evidence for nonspatial forms of attention at higher loci within the visual system, including selection by color, shape, and motion. Attention to each of these stimulus characteristics appears to operate in the same cortical areas that mediate their perception: area V4 for color, IT for shape, and MT for motion.

The mechanisms of selection within visual areas, both early and late, are poorly understood. There is evidence of facilitation of attended stimuli as well as inhibition of unattended stimuli. We have only the scantiest of clues as to how these modulations of neuronal activity are achieved. The single unit data suggest that in some, but not all, cases there is a sustained rise in baseline activity for neurons representing the attended stimulus. Both single unit and ERP data provide evidence of increased neuronal gain, that is, a larger difference in activity between the presence and absence of a stimulus, when it is attended. These alternatives, and their possible implications for neuroimaging experiments, are discussed in detail by Hillyard and colleagues (Hillyard, Vogel, and Luck, 1998).

In attempting a more conceptual integration, I can think of no more useful framework than that of Duncan and Desimone (e.g., Duncan, 1996; Desimone and Duncan, 1995). They have proposed a way of thinking about visual attention based on some very general qualitative characteristics of neural networks, which accommodates a number of the findings reviewed above and which also provides a good general view of the relation between these relatively early visual areas and the higher order areas involved in attention, to which we will next turn.

Duncan and Desimone suggest that selection is the result of competition among stimuli to be represented within relatively early visual areas. Competition will result in fewer or just one stimulus being actively represented at one time, accomplishing the goal of preventing cross-talk in distributed representations. Competition is ubiquitous in neural networks (e.g., lateral inhibition) and is consistent with the observation that the strongest attentional effects found in single unit recording experiments came from closely spaced stimuli. Another ubiquitous property of neural networks, pattern completion, will tend to enforce the active representation of a single stimulus across different visual areas and domains of representation (e.g., color, motion, etc.). Hence, attending to, say, a certain color will result in preferential processing of all aspects of the stimulus having that color, and thereby solve the binding problem or, in slightly different terminology, accomplish "feature integration" (e.g., Treisman and Gelade, 1980).

According to Duncan and Desimone, the winner of the competition is determined by both bottom-up and top-down factors. Sheer intensity of a stimulus is one bottom-up factor that will tend to win neural competitions and hence grab attention. Novelty is another, for similar reasons: Compared to an habituated stimulus, the neural representation of a novel stimulus is stronger. Competition may also be biased in favor of a particular stimulus by top-down or efferent activation of the relevant representations from higher order brain areas. It is to these areas and their contribution to attention that I now turn.

7.4 Controlling attention

At the heart of the concept of attention is intentionality. The man on the street's ideas about attention emphasize its voluntary nature ("Please pay attention"; "I will attend to this later"), and within cognitive psychology the study of attentional control has been right up there with the early versus late selection issue as a major focus of attention research (e.g., Schneider and Shiffrin, 1977; Posner and Presti, 1987). Within cognitive neuroscience, we have learned that other brain areas are involved in normal attentional functioning, beyond the extrastriate areas mentioned in the previous section. A natural interpretation is that these other areas subserve attentional control.

Of course, the distinction between attentional control mechanisms and the representations within which attention operates is a bit artificial in the context of the kind of distributed competitive system described by Duncan and Desimone. According to their view, competition among representations operates at all levels of the visual system, and either top-down or bottom-up factors can tip the competitive balance in favor of one stimulus' representation over others. Nevertheless, to the extent that the activity in early visual cortical representations can be biased by activation from other areas, one could describe the role of those other areas as "control."

Subcortical structures

The superior colliculus and the pulvinar are among the brain areas involved in visual attention. The superior colliculus has been associated most closely with the control of eye movements, which comprise an external but very important means of biasing processing in favor of particular stimuli. When monkeys are trained to maintain fixation and shift their covert spatial attention to peripheral locations in the visual field, no attentional effects are seen (Wurtz and Goldberg, 1972).

The role of the pulvinar in attention has been a subject of debate, with some researchers proposing a specific role for this structure in the attentional gating or filtering of stimulus representations prior to cortical processing (e.g., Crick, 1984; LaBerge and Buchsbaum, 1990) and others disagreeing. Duncan (1996) cites a number of studies in which different parts of the pulvinar were either permanently lesioned or reversibly deactivated in monkeys without specific impairments in attention. Instead, these manipulations had the effect of degrading or slowing perceptual processing in general, whether attention was required or not. Unilateral lesions caused an extinction-like pattern of performance, whereby stimuli on the affected side were further disadvantaged in the presence of stimuli on the unaffected side. These observations are consistent with a role for the pulvinar in attention just insofar as it contributes to the strength or competitiveness of stimulus representations.

The superior colliculus and the pulvinar form part of an interconnected network with the two main cortical regions subserving attentional control, in the parietal and frontal cortices. These cortical areas will be the focus of the rest of this chapter.

Prefrontal and parietal cortices and the control of attention

Given the general characterization of prefrontal cortex as the "executive" system of the brain, essential for the regulation of complex task performance, it would not be surprising to learn that the control of visual attention is partly a function of prefrontal cortex. In the light of modern working memory research, which has associated prefrontal cortex with the active maintenance of stimulus representations in the absence of stimuli (e.g., Goldman-Rakic, 1988), it makes sense that this brain region would be the source of Duncan's (1996) top-down activation that biases the competition among stimulus representations in early visual areas. There is, in fact, evidence that prefrontal cortex plays an important role in the control of visual attention.

Although the frontal eye fields are similar to the colliculus in showing attentional effects only in conjunction with eye movements, the dorsolateral prefrontal cortex shows enhanced processing of attended stimuli even in the absence of eye movements (di Pellegrino and Wise, 1993a). Cells in this area also maintain their activity during working memory tasks and during active attention to particular locations in space in advance of a stimulus (e.g., Fuster, 1973; di Pelligreno and Wise, 1993b), and their pre-stimulus activity is related to the level of attention demanded by the task (Lecas, 1995). Thus it seems likely that they are a source of biasing activation to earlier visual areas.

At present the best evidence for prefrontal control of attention in humans comes from bloodflow-based neuroimaging techniques. The existence of visual–spatial neglect after frontal damage is not particularly informative on the subject of attentional control. As we will see in the next chapter, the attentional problems of neglect patients do not seem to correspond to an impairment of just the volitional control of attention. It is just as hard to summon the attention of a neglect patient by bottom-up means (e.g., the onset of a salient contralesional stimulus) as by top-down means (e.g., the instruction to direct attention contralesionally). Neither are ERP studies very useful in this regard. Obtaining an ERP requires time-locking on the "event" of interest, which in studies of visual attention has been the target stimulus. Unless the recording epochs were time-locked to the presentation of the attentional cue, one would not expect to measure the brain activity underlying the control of attention.

Early PET studies of attention almost invariably found prefrontal activations, but suffered the same problem of experimental designs that were not appropriate for isolating attentional control *per se*. For example in the study of Corbetta *et al.* (1993), the subtraction between the condition in which subjects shift their attention through a predictable sequence of locations and the condition in which subjects passively view stimuli occurring at the same locations reveals dorsolateral prefrontal activation. The authors suggest that this prefrontal activation may be associated with the need to both attend and make overt responses. However, the two conditions also differ in terms of the need for top-down attentional control. These findings are therefore consistent with the hypothesis that top-down attentional control is generated in prefrontal cortex. Corbetta (1998) briefly describes a more recent study in which subjects made no overt responses, and reports similar prefrontal activation, lending further support to the attentional control interpretation of the prefrontal activity. We can also look to the subtraction of the central attention condition from the shifting attention condition for evidence, as there is arguably more controlling of attention to do when the to-be-attended location shifts moment by moment than when it remains constant throughout a block of trials. Despite the equivalence in the response components of the two conditions, this subtraction again produces significant prefrontal activation.

Other studies allow comparisons between spatial attention conditions and control conditions consisting of passive viewing (Heinze *et al.*, 1994; Woldorff *et al.*, 1997) or simple detection (Vandenberghe *et al.*, 1996), and all reveal prefrontal activation. Unfortunately, the interpretation of these subtractions is ambiguous, as the two conditions differed in a number of ways beyond the requirement for top-down attention. For example, in Heinze *et al.*'s attention condition, subjects performed a pattern matching task, whereas in the passive viewing condition they did not.

The first PET study specifically intended to isolate attentional control systems was carried out by Nobre, Sebestyen, Gitelman, Mesulam, Frackowiak, and Frith (1997). They compared brain activity when subjects were given two kinds of location cues for directing their attention. One kind of cue was simply the brightening of a box at the to-be-attended location, the "same side" condition, which should have the effect of summoning attention to the correct location by bottom-up means. The other kind of cue was the brightening of the box opposite the to-be-attended location, the "opposite side" condition, which requires that the subject direct attention to the correct location by top-down means. Although both conditions produced prefrontal activation when compared with an appropriate control condition, there was not significantly more prefrontal activation when subjects were cued with the opposite box. This null result may not be so surprising, in view of the design of this experiment. Both conditions seem likely to evoke both bottom-up and top-down control of attention. Although bottom-up attention will facilitate stimulus processing only in the "same side" condition, it will occur to an equal degree in both conditions. Furthermore, subjects would have been just as likely to use top-down attentional processes in the "same side" as in the "opposite side" condition, given that the cues were equally predictive in the two conditions. The absence of prefrontal activation in the critical subtraction may be explicable in this way.

The recent fMRI study of Rosen, Rao, Caffarra, Scaglioni, Bobholz, Woodley, Hammeke, Cunningham, Prieto, and Binder (1999) overcomes these problems with a design that controls the sensory and response requirements of two conditions that nevertheless differ in the control of attention. In the "exogenous" condition attention is summoned bottom-up by a nonpredictive cue in a possible stimulus location, whereas in the "endogenous" condition attention is directed top-down by a predictive arrow cue located at fixation. They found activation of many of the same areas as previous studies in both attention conditions, including bilateral parietal and frontal areas, but found one area of activation distinctive to the endogenous condition: right dorsolateral prefrontal cortex. These findings fit perfectly with the view that spatial working memory provides the biasing activation to lower areas when spatial attention is under volitional control, and that attentional selection itself proceeds in the same way whether the biasing activation enters the system top-down or bottom-up.

We have the clearest evidence linking a brain region to visual attention in the case of the posterior parietal lobe, which figure 7.6 locates on diagrams of both the human and monkey brains along with key anatomical divisions within posterior parietal cortex. Neurons in monkey area LIP (lateral intraparietal) have larger responses to attended stimuli (Bushnell, Goldberg, and Robinson, 1981), and maintain tonically increased responses for attended locations in the absence of a stimulus (Gnadt and Andersen, 1988). Almost every PET experiment ever conducted in which humans have attended to specific locations in space has shown superior parietal activation (e.g., Corbetta *et al.*, 1993; Corbetta, Shulman, Meizin, and Petersen, 1995; Heinze *et al.*, 1994; Nobre *et al.*, 1997; Rosen *et al.*, 1999; Vandenberghe *et al.*, 1996; for an exception see Heinze *et al.*, 1994). Abundant evidence from brain-damaged humans also implies that the posterior parietal lobe, more than any other brain structure, is critical for visual attention. In the immediate aftermath of posterior parietal damage, particularly in the right hemisphere, patients almost invariably present with some degree of visual neglect or extinction, both conditions involving attentional dysfunction on the contralesional side of space.

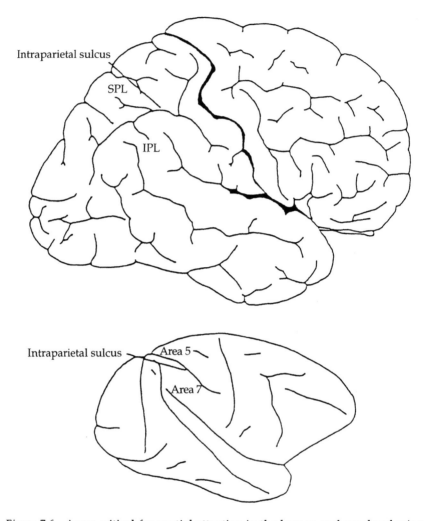

Figure 7.6   Areas critical for spatial attention in the human and monkey brains.
From A. D. Milner, "Neglect, extinction and the cortical streams of visual processing," in
P. Their and H. O. Karnath (eds), Parietal Lobe Contributions to Orientation in 3D Space,
Heidelberg, Springer-Verlag, 1997.

What is less clear is the specific role or roles subserved by parietal
cortex in visual attention. For example, various studies have attemped
to tease apart such normally interrelated factors as the shifting of
attention to a location (e.g., on the left) versus in a direction (e.g.,

towards the left; see Corbetta *et al.*, 1993; Baynes, Holtzman, and Volpe, 1986; Posner, Walker, Friedrich, and Rafal, 1987), or the spatial reference frames used to define left versus right (Behrmann and Moscovitch, 1994; Farah, Brunn, Wong, Wallace, and Carpenter, 1990) without achieving a unanimous answer. Perhaps the most gapingly open question concerning the parietal contribution to attention is this: Given the likely role of prefrontal cortex in generating top-down attentional effects in extrastriate cortex, and given the evidence of attentional enhancement of neuronal processing in extrastriate cortex, why do we need a parietal lobe?

A raison d'être *for the parietal cortex in attention*

If our conception of attention is one of bottom-up competition among extrastriate stimulus representations, with the possibility of biasing those competitions using activity generated in prefrontal cortex, this does seem to lead to an awkward conclusion: That the cortical visual attention network should be functionally complete with prefrontal cortex as a source of top-down attentional biases and the various extrastriate visual areas in which competitive phenomena have been observed. But this leaves out the cortical area that has traditionally been most closely associated with attention on purely empirical grounds! Is the posterior parietal lobe merely a waystation linking anterior and posterior areas, needed because the physical distance from prefrontal cortex to occipital cortex is too great to cover with just one axon and synapse?

My answer to this facetious question concerns the computational issues involved in mediating between two very different kinds of representation: the relatively high-level representations of objects in space that we use to guide our top-down allocation of attention, and the retinotopically mapped, modality-specific representations of visual stimuli that are subject to the competitive interactions underlying attentional effects. When we allocate attention to an object at a partic-ular location, we do not want our attention to jump to a different object the instant we move our eyes, nor presumably do we want to limit our attention to the visual aspects of the object while denying attentional facilitation to the processing of its auditory or tactile properties. I suggest that the role of parietal cortex is to avoid these problems.

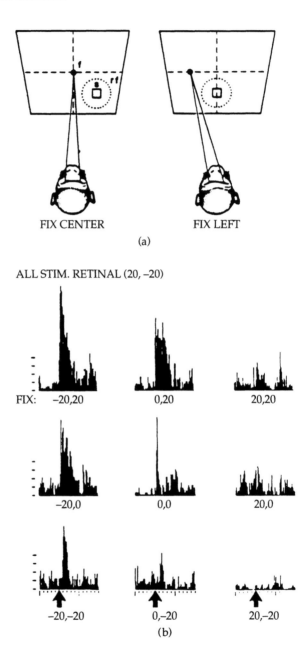

FIX CENTER   FIX LEFT

(a)

ALL STIM. RETINAL (20, −20)

FIX: −20,20   0,20   20,20

−20,0   0,0   20,0

−20,−20   0,−20   20,−20

(b)

In real life, unlike attention experiments, we do not maintain a constant fixation. This means that the correspondence between the retinotopic coordinates of a stimulus and its location in the world will be continually shifting, and creates the need for a translation process between coordinate systems. There is evidence that neurons in parietal cortex accomplish just this translation.

Andersen, Essick, and Siegel (1985) recorded from neurons in area 7a of monkey parietal cortex while varying not only the position of stimuli in the visual field but also the position of the monkey's fixation, as shown in figure 7.7a. They found that cells' responses depended on both factors. Specifically, they found that the response of a cell to a stimulus at the same retinotopic location was modulated by the animal's angle of gaze. Figure 7.7b shows the drop-off in response to stimuli presented at the same location in retinotopic coordinates as the position of fixation departs in both vertical and horizontal directions from the optimal position. A simple neural network simulation suggests that these eye-position-gated representations are indeed serving to create a representation of space that is stable over eye movements. Zipser and Andersen (1988) trained a network to associate pairings of retinotopic location and eye position with locations in space, and found that the network solved this problem by developing units whose "receptive fields" were retinotopic but modulated by eye position.

Of course, a single cell whose retinotopic location coding is modulated by eye position does not give unambiguous information about the location of a stimulus in head-centered space. Referring to figure 7.7b, for example, the cell's response for fixation $(0, -20)$ and $(20, 0)$ are indistinguishable. A population of such cells, however, will

---

Figure 7.7 (*opposite*) Examples of procedure and results from a classic study of space representation in Area 7a of the parietal lobe. (a) The locations in external space of a cell's receptive field when the monkey fixates center and left. (b) The cell's responses to stimuli at nine different real-world locations, presented so that they fell in the same retinotopic receptive field. Each histogram is labeled with the monkey's fixation location. The modulation of activity as a function of fixation location provides information about the real-world location of stimuli.

From R. A. Andersen et al., "Encoding of spatial location by posterior parietal neurons," Science, 230, 1985; copyright 1985 the American Association for the Advancement of Science.

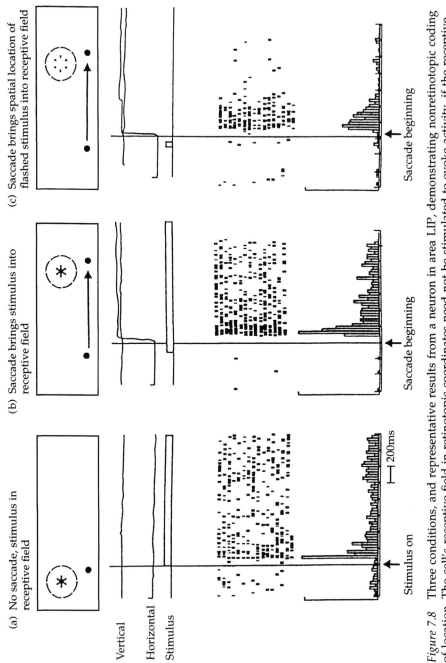

Figure 7.8 Three conditions, and representative results from a neuron in area LIP, demonstrating nonretinotopic coding of location. The cell's receptive field in retinotopic coordinates need not be stimulated to evoke activity, if the receptive field is shifted by an eye movement to a location in space previously occupied by a stimulus.

From J. R. Duhamel et al., "The updating of the representation of visual space in parietal cortex by intended eye movement," *Science* 225, 1992.

narrow the possible interpretations down to one location in space. This is a form of distributed representation. As such, it is subject to cross-talk when more than one stimulus must be located. Perhaps not coincidentally, the location of these representations downstream in visual processing from the competitive interactions underlying attentional effects in extrastriate visual cortex solves this problem by limiting parietal representations to just the attentional "winners."

More recently, cells with truly nonretinotopic receptive fields have been described in area LIP (lateral intraparietal). Duhamel, Colby, and Goldberg (1992) trained monkeys to fixate and then move their eyes to the location of a flashed visual stimulus. As diagrammed in figure 7.8, these cells encode the immediate memory trace of a location in space, shifting their retinotopically-defined receptive fields in correspondence with saccades.

Another difference between attention experiments and real life concerns the number of perceptual modalities that are relevant at any given moment. Asterisks on video screens do not make noises or brush by one's body as they appear, but our perception of real objects is not limited to a single modality at a time. Just as attention can be more usefully allocated to a representation of the world that is stable with respect to eye movements, it can also be more usefully allocated to a supramodal representation in which the visual, auditory, and tactile qualities of objects are properly co-indexed with respect to one another. For example, if a sound or a touch draws one's attention to a certain part of the scene, it would be adaptive to have the visual properties of that part of the scene also receive preferential processing.

Posterior parietal cortex is a good candidate, anatomically, for the integration of multiple sensory and motor representations of the world, with connections to visual, somatasensory, auditory, and motor brain areas (Andersen, 1989). Indeed, cells have been recorded whose receptive fields cross modalities. An impressive example of this comes from the work of Duhamel, Colby, and Goldberg (1992), who recorded from area VIP (ventral intraparietal) while presenting a monkey with visual and tactile stimulation. In order for such cells to provide a useful supramodal representation for attention, they must not only respond to stimuli in both modalities, they must also respond similarly in both modalities as a function of the stimulus location. Figure 7.9 shows that the visual and somatasensory receptive

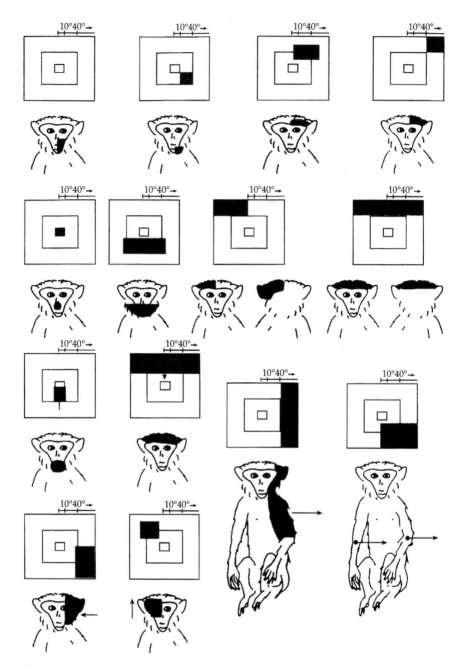

Figure 7.9   Demonstration of the spatially coincident visual and tactile receptive fields of neurons in LIP.

From J. R. Duhamel et al., *"Congruent representations of visual and somatosensory space in single neurons of monkey ventral intraparietal cortex (area VIP)," in J. Paillard (ed.),* Brain and Space, *Oxford, Oxford University Press, 1991.*

fields of these cells are in striking correspondence across modalities, in terms of their location, size, shape, and in some cases, direction sensitivity. The following chapter includes further evidence, from humans with brain damage, of a supramodal representation of space in parietal cortex, and for its role in the attention system of the brain.

chapter eight

Hemispatial Neglect

8.1 Insights into spatial representation and attention from the neglect syndrome

In the previous chapter we concluded that posterior parietal cortex is responsible for constructing a stable and perceptually integrated world. The fact that objects seem to stay put as we dart our eyes about the scene, stimulating far-flung regions of our retinas, and the fact that the separately registered sights, sounds, and tactile feels of the world seem appropriately bound together, are both thanks to the parietal lobe. In this sense there is an analogy between the most general characterizations of temporal and parietal cortex in vision.

Recall that the function of the ventral visual system can be viewed as working backwards from the proximal retinal image of an object, with its distortions and occlusions, toward the distal object that gave rise to the image. Similarly, the function of the dorsal visual system can be viewed as working backwards from the multiple and shifting localizations of objects, as different transducer surfaces explore the scene, to the true layout of visible, audible, and touchable objects in the distal space. One important purpose served by this relatively stable and veridical representation of space is the ability to direct attention within early modality-specific regions on the basis of more abstract, memory-based representations of the external world.

How would the world appear without these contributions of our posterior parietal cortices? The study of patients with the neglect syndrome provides a partial answer. Such patients have much to teach us about the nature of spatial representation and attention in the human brain, and this chapter will review some of the central findings in this area.

8.2 A brief clinical and anatomical introduction to neglect

Hemispatial neglect is a fairly common neuropsychological impairment following posterior parietal damage, especially in the right hemisphere. Although subtle effects may pervade processing at all locations in space (e.g., Robertson, 1993; Samuelsson, Hjelmquist, Jensen, Ekholm, and Blomstrand, 1998), for most purposes the impairment affects the side of space contralateral to the brain lesion, hence the term "hemispatial." The term "neglect" itself is a fairly straightforward description of patients' behaviors. They neglect people, objects, and events in the contralesional hemifield, as well as neglecting the contralesional half of their own body.

The failure of contralesional stimuli to attract attention can be striking. Patients will search for a desired object, such as their reading glasses or a candy bar, over and over in the "good" hemispace, never once checking the other side. They will eat the food on one half of their plate and complain about the small portions, with half of their dinner still before them. If approached from the contralesional side, they will ignore a visitor, and fail to respond in conversation. Some patients have been observed to shave or apply make-up to just half of their face, or dress only one side of their body. They will even injure themselves by bumping into doorways or catching themselves in wheelchair wheels on their affected side. Clearly we cannot put ourselves in the shoes of a neglect patient simply by imagining what it would be like to be blind, deaf, and numb on one side of space. Hemianopia, for example, does not prevent people from visual exploration of the contralesional space. With an eye movement toward the contralesional space, the blindness is circumvented. The problem with neglect patients seems to be that, by their actions–and sometimes even by their words–there *is no* contralesional space. Perhaps this should not be surprising given our understanding of the function of parietal cortex: to construct a stable representation of external space in which the unstable inputs from multiple modalities can be integrated.

Common ways of assessing neglect

Neglect can be detected and its severity measured by a number of simple bedside tests. One of the quickest and most familiar is line bisection, in which a horizontal line of at least a few inches' length is placed directly in front of the patient, and he or she is asked to mark its midpoint. To the degree that the left side of the line is not perceived, the mark will be displaced to the right. Another paper and pencil test involving lines is the line cancellation test (Albert, 1973), in which the patient is asked to mark each one of a large number of lines scattered over a sheet of paper. Unlike a normal person, a patient with left neglect typically starts with the rightmost lines and works leftwards. As shown in figure 8.1, some lines on the left may never get marked. The copying of simple drawings is also commonly used. Figure 8.2 shows some typical copies made by patients with left neglect.

When neglect is mild, or in a related condition known as "extinction", perception of the contralesional stimulus is impeded only in the presence of competing ipsilesional stimuli. This phenomenon can be elicited clinically by having the patient fixate one's nose while detecting fingers wiggling in the left and right hemifields. Some patients can reliably detect a single wiggle on either side of space, but when the examiner wiggles fingers on both hands simultaneously, even when told both sides may wiggle at the same time, will report seeing motion only on the ipsilesional side.

Lesions causing neglect

By far the most common lesion associated with neglect is in the right inferior posterior parietal lobe. For example, Vallar and Perani (1986) superimposed the reconstructed lesions of 8 patients with severe left neglect, as shown in figure 8.3, and found a clear focus of overlap there. More superior parts of the posterior parietal lobe, including

Figure 8.1   The line cancellation performance of a patient with left neglect.
From K. M. Heilman et al., "Neglect: clinical and anatomic aspects," in T. E. Feinberg and M. J. Farah (eds) Behavioral Neurology and Neuropsychology, New York, McGraw-Hill, 1997.

regions frequently activated in PET studies of visual attention, tend not to cause neglect when damaged, but have been implicated in patients with pure extinction and in patients with disorders of visually-guided reaching. Thus the neuropathology of spatial and attentional disorders in humans offers hints regarding the division of labor among the various spatial and attentional functions of the parietal lobe, but the underlying basis of that division of labor has yet to be well worked out. The changes in functional neuroanatomy within this general region of the brain, going phylogenetically from monkey to man (refer to figure 7.6) prevent the animal research literature from cleanly resolving these ambiguities. Although it is generally assumed that monkey area 7 corresponds to human superior posterior parietal

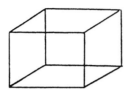 

COPY THIS CUBE IN THE SPACE BELOW   COPY THIS STAR IN THE SPACE BELOW

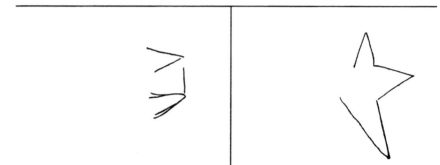

Figure 8.2   Two attempts to copy simple figures by a patient with left neglect.
From J. A. Ogden, Fractured Minds: A Case-Study Approach to Clinical Neuropsychology, *New York, Oxford University Press, 1996.*

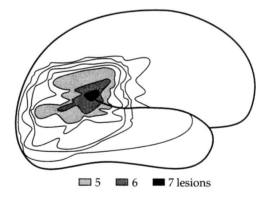

▢ 5   ▧ 6   ■ 7 lesions

Figure 8.3   Reconstructed lesions of eight patients with severe neglect, showing the location of maximal overlap in the inferior posterior parietal region.
From G. Vallar and D. Perani, "The anatomy of unilateral neglect after right hemisphere stroke lesions: a clinical CT scan correlation study in man," Neuropsychologia, 24, 1986, with permission of Elsevier Science.

regions, on the basis of functional similarities and patterns of connection to other areas, the inferior region implicated in neglect may have no homolog at all in the monkey brain (Milner, 1997).

Given that full-blown neglect does not occur after parietal lesions just a couple of inches superior to the hot spot shown in figure 8.3, it is surprising that much more distant lesion sites have been associated with neglect. Several subcortical areas, including posterior and medial thalamus and basal ganglia, have been implicated in clinical case studies of neglect, along with frontal cortex, more often in the right than in the left hemisphere (see Vallar, 1993, for a review). The finding of classic neglect in patients with such disparate lesions has led many authorities to the conclusion that the visual attention system of the brain is best conceptualized as a network. Among the well-known network models for attention based on data from human patients are those of Mesulam (1981), Heilman et al. (1993), and Posner, Inhoff, Friedrich, and Cohen (1987).

Mesulam's (1981) model is a network in that it assigns different functions to each of the relevant brain areas, which are known to be mutually interconnected and to receive inputs from the reticular formation. The functions attributed to these areas include the representation of external space (posterior parietal cortex), the representation of actions in space (premotor frontal cortex), and the representation of motivational valence (cingulate cortex). Heilman et al.'s (1993) network similarly distinguishes between perceptual and motor aspects of neglect by hypothesizing two circuits, one linking posterior parietal, posterior cingulate, and certain parts of the thalamus, and one linking premotor, anterior cingulate, other parts of the thalamus, and basal ganglia. These models are derived from a combination of general functional neuroanatomy background and specific clinical observations of neglect patients with different lesions. Posner et al.'s (1987) model assigns different components of his cognitive theory of attention, disengaging, moving, and engaging attention, to areas of the brain, specifically posterior parietal, midbrain, and pulvinar, respectively, on the basis of patients' detailed patterns of performance in reaction time tasks. The framework of Duncan and colleagues, discussed in the previous chapter, could be added to the list of network theories of attention as well. Indeed, it makes more serious explanatory use of some of the technical features of network computation, such competition and completion phenomena, than the other examples cited here. The various network models of neglect and attention are difficult to compare directly with one another, as they differ with regard to which psychological and anatomical data they are intended to explain. What they have in common is the explicit recognition that neglect may emerge as a result of interrupting many different components of a distributed network.

The asymmetry of lesions causing neglect has intrigued many researchers, with right-hemisphere cases outnumbering left-hemisphere cases by a large factor. Different studies have obtained different estimates of the factor, depending on the way in which neglect is assessed, the recency of subjects' brain damage, the inclusion of patients with severe language impairments, and the like. A good representative study is that of Gainotti (1968) who screened 110 unilaterally brain-damaged subjects with a systematic battery of tests, and found 30 who met his criteria for neglect. Of these, 23 had right hemisphere lesions and only 7 had lesions on the left. Furthermore, the severity of neglect in the left-hemisphere-damaged patients was less. Indeed, most cases of frank neglect for the right side of space have been associated with bilateral, rather than left-sided, lesions (e.g. Weintraub, Daffner, Ahern, Price, and Mesulam, 1996).

The correct explanation for the asymmetry is not obvious. The observation that, for example, speech is more disrupted after left than right hemisphere lesions can be explained by hypothesizing that the left hemisphere is specialized for speech. But the analogous hypothesis for neglect, that the right hemisphere is specialized for visual attention, does not account for a hemispatial impairment; it would simply predict an overall impairment of visual attention after right hemisphere damage. Subtler hypotheses have therefore been proposed. For example, Kinsbourne (1993) suggests that the two hemispheres direct attention through a fundamentally competitive process, with each hemisphere vying to shift attention in a contralateral direction and to inhibit the opposing attentional tendencies of the opposite hemisphere. He cites evidence from a variety of sources that this competition is not perfectly balanced in the normal intact brain, and that in fact the left hemisphere has the stronger influence on the normal allocation of attention. According to this model, damage to the right hemisphere further tips the balance in favor of the left hemisphere, leading to overt neglect of the left hemispace.

A.　　　　　　*B.*　　　　　　*C.*

Figure 8.4 A demonstration of the dissociability of local and global form information. (a) the stimulus to be copied: a big M made up of little Z's. (b) the copy of a right-hemisphere damaged patient, who was able to use local but not global information in copying. (c) the copy of a left-hemisphere damaged patient, showing the opposite pattern.
From D. C. Delis et al., "Hemispheric specialization of memory for visual hierarchical stimuli," Neuropsychologia, 24, 1986, with permission of Elsevier Science.

A very different account comes from Heilman and co-workers, who have proposed that the right hemisphere can direct attention to both sides of space, whereas the left hemisphere can direct attention only contralaterally, to the right hemifield (Heilman, Watson, and Valenstein, 1993). Thus after left-hemisphere damage, both hemifields are still attentionally "covered," whereas after right-hemisphere damage there is no cortical control of attention to the left hemifield. This hypothesis finds independent support in studies of normal subjects' brain activity, for example Corbetta *et al.*'s (1993) PET study, in which attention to either hemifield activated right parietal cortex whereas left parietal cortex was activated only when attention shifted to the right.

Yet a third and distinct account comes from Rafal (1997). He suggests that the attentional component of neglect is not asymmetrically represented in the brain, citing the lack of hemispheric asymmetry in the occurrence of pure extinction, and that the unique contribution of the right parietal lobe in neglect instead concerns the perception of global scene structure. Robertson and colleagues have shown that right temporo-parietal damage leads to an over-focusing on the local features of a visual display, and an inability to appreciate the more global layout (Robertson and Lamb, 1991). A simple but striking graphic example of the evidence supporting this claim is shown in figure 8.4. Rafal proposes that this bias towards the trees rather than the forest, in combination with an impairment of attention, accounts for the behaviors of the neglect syndrome and their association with right-hemisphere lesions.

Research on the anatomical bases of neglect provides an excellent example of synergism between clinical observation of patients and more controlled laboratory research. The foregoing review has barely scratched the surface of this large literature. Nevertheless, I will stop here and turn to a very different set of research issues concerning neglect.

8.3   Neglect as a window on spatial representation

As intensively as the anatomy of neglect has been studied, there is at least as large a literature on neglect that makes virtually no reference to brain anatomy at all. This is the literature on neglect as a window on the cognitive structures underlying spatial attention, particularly the representation of space.

The general approach of this research tradition is to draw inferences about the functional characteristics of the spatial attention system by using neglect as an experimental "manipulation." This manipulation dissects the representation of space into left and right halves, and thereby enables researchers to answer a variety of questions about the representation itself. For example: With respect to what frame(s) of reference are locations represented and left and right defined? Is visual space represented integrally with auditory space, such that losing the left side of one representation affects the left side of the other? What about tactile space? Is space represented as a raw bitmap of locations, such that left and right cleave apart in the same place regardless of the contents of the visual field, or does the structure of the objects in central vision affect the spatial representation and its fracture lines? Is the spatial layout of words represented separately from the spatial representation of nonword patterns?

Representation or attention?: a nonissue

Before reviewing the literature on these and related issues, let me raise – and then dismiss – one seemingly more fundamental issue at the outset. This is the issue of whether neglect is a disorder of representation or attention.

A stimulus may be neglected one moment and then noticed the next, particularly if the patient is forcefully encouraged to attend to it. This dynamic, changeable quality of neglect, and its (at least modest) susceptibility to instructions to pay attention, lead naturally to the conclusion that neglect is a disorder of attention. However, some authors have suggested that, in some or all cases of neglect, the problem lies with the representation of space rather than with spatial attention (e.g., Bisiach and Luzzatti, 1978; Pizzamiglio, Vallar, and Doricchi, 1997; Rizzolatti and Berti, 1993).

The most compelling evidence for a representational as opposed to attentional disorder comes from experiments in which patients with neglect visualize a familiar scene from memory. Bisiach and Luzzatti (1978) asked their patients to imagine standing in the Piazza del Duomo in Milan, a large public square that is well known to all Milanese, and to report what they saw in their mind's eye. The results are represented in figure 8.5. When the patients visualized the square from the perspective of someone standing at the northern end, in front of the cathedral, they mostly named landmarks on the western side of the square, those landmarks that would have been visible on the right side of their mental image. When asked to imagine the square from the southern end, the opposite vantage point, they then listed landmarks on the eastern side, the right side of the new image. This deservedly famous experiment shows that the patients had retained long-term memory knowledge of both sides of the square, yet when required to mentally represent the spatial layout of the square from any particular view, neglected the left side of that view.

There is no doubt that these patients had a problem with representing the left side of space. But this is not inconsistent with a problem in attending to the left side of space. Perhaps the intuition that this experiment supports a representational *as opposed to* attentional explanation comes from the feeling that attentional explanations must be limited to phenomena involving external stimuli. To my knowledge, no such restriction attaches to any current conception of attention. Furthermore, the evidence to be discussed in the following chapter suggests that many of the visual representations used for visual stimuli during perception are also recruited for mental imagery. This

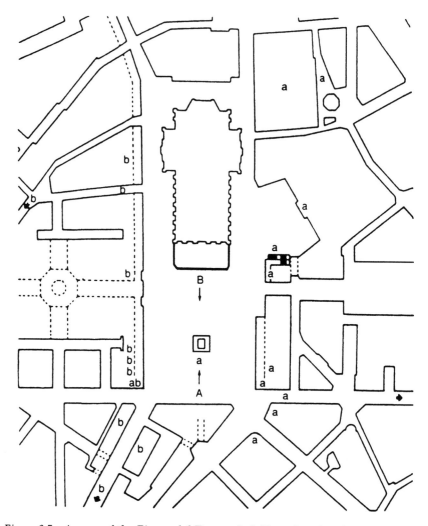

Figure 8.5   A map of the Piazza del Duomo in Milan, showing the two locations at which neglect patients were to imagine themselves standing, and the locations of the landmarks visualized from memory. When imagining the view facing the cathedral, from location A, patients named the landmarks indicated by a's; when imagining the piazza from the perspective B, they named the landmarks indicated by b's.

From M. J. Farah, "The neural bases of mental imagery," in M. S. Gazzaniga (ed.), The Cognitive Neurosciences, Cambridge, MA, MIT Press, 1995.

suggests a reinterpretation of Bisiach and Luzzatti's finding in terms of impaired attention to the left side of mental images. After all, once a representation is activated, it is hard to see why the original source of its activation should have any bearing on the process of attending to it. Conversely, just as an attentional explanation is perfectly compatible with neglect for imagined stimuli, a representational explanation is capable of explaining neglect in perceptual tasks. If the internal representations of stimuli are impaired, performance in perceptual tasks will suffer.

These considerations might seem to suggest that it is difficult to discriminate empirically between the representational and attentional theories of neglect. The problem with the representation versus attention issue is more fundamental than this. The two alternatives are not conceptually distinct. As far as I can tell, they are two complementary vocabularies for describing the same phenomenon, and intertranslation seems straightforward. If we remember that perception is simply a process of internally representing external stimuli, then what does a failure of attention do, other than prevent stimuli from being fully represented? Although the distinction between information-bearing structure and information-transforming process can be maintained in some artificially engineered systems, such as symbol-manipulating computers, our best models of neural information processing are lacking any such structure–process distinction. Long-term knowledge representation and the capacity for different kinds of processing are indivisibly instantiated in the patterns of synaptic connections among neurons. Active representation and ongoing process are indivisibly instantiated in the patterns of activation over neurons.

This line of thought can be carried even further, to question the distinction between internal representation and attention, on the one hand, and perception, on the other. The box-and-arrow tradition of thinking about the mind leads us to assume that attention must be a functionally or anatomically separate process or temporally distinct stage of processing. Yet this is not necessarily the most fruitful way to think about attention. Recall Desimone and Duncan's (1995) view of attention, discussed in the last chapter. According to them, attention is the result of competitive interactions among perceptual representations, which can be biased by higher level representations. There is no place in this theory to point at and label with the word "attention"

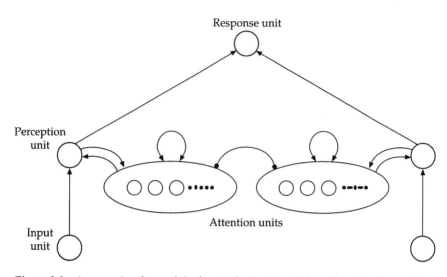

Figure 8.6   A very simple model of spatial attention. When the attention units are damaged asymmetrically, the model produces behavior similar to that of neglect patients: stimuli on the lesioned side are neglected, particularly when attention has first been drawn to the other side. When following the flow of activation through the network on a given trial, it is hard to see why we would reserve the term "representation" for the perception units and not for the attention units. Indeed, attention units could be viewed as another layer of perceptual representation.

From J. D. Cohen et al., "Mechanisms of spatial attention: the relation of macrostructure to miscrostructure in parietal neglect," Journal of Cognitive Neuroscience, 6, 1994.

separate from perception or representation. Instead, attention is a state of the whole system, which emerges under certain circumstances. The same can be said of the current representional content of the system at any moment. A simple connectionist model of attention gives a concrete illustration of this point, and supports the idea that neglect could be just as well described as a "perceptual" impairment as an "attentional" impairment.

The model, shown in figure 8.6, was intended to account for attentional effects in a lateralized simple reaction-time task, in the normal brain and after parietal damage (Cohen, Romero, Servan-Schreiber, and Farah, 1994). "Perception" units on each side of space feed activation forward to a higher layer of units, labelled "attention" units. The attention units for each side of space are competitive, mutually inhibiting each other (we did not model competition at earlier levels), and feed activation back to the perception units on their side of space. When the system is primed with a stimulus on one side, and activation reaches the attention units, the future responsivity of the system is changed in two key ways. First, the perception units on the stimulated side gain activation by a top-down route, thus decreasing the additional activation needed from an external stimulus to reach a given degree of activation. This represents the reaction-time benefit of a cue on the same side of space as the target. Second, the attention units on the unstimulated side become inhibited, thus increasing the additional activation needed from an external stimulus on that side for the perception units to reach a given degree of activation (as they are deprived of the top-down activation from the attention units). This represents the reaction-time cost from a cue on the wrong side of space. When the attention units are damaged unilaterally, the dynamics of the network change. The most pronounced change is seen if the intact side is stimulated first (the cue) and then the damaged side is stimulated (the target). In this case target detection is greatly prolonged. Such an extinction-like pattern of reaction times is commonly seen in unilateral parietal-damaged patients, and Posner and colleagues have interpreted this as an impaired "disengage" mechanism.

In the context of this exceedingly simple mechanism for explaining some spatial attentional effects in normal and brain-damaged subjects, we can ask: Is there a meaningful structural distinction between perception and attention? Although we followed convention in calling the earlier units "perception" units and the later units "attention," there is no reason for making this distinction. Both sets of units are really perception units, differing only in their connectional distance from the input; the label "attention" is better applied to the emergent phenonena of competition and priming in this perceptual network.

In sum, the phenomena of neglect provide a window on the perception *and/or* internal representation *and/or* attentional processing of spatial information in the human brain. In the remainder of the chapter I will review some of the key cognitive issues that have been illuminated by the study of neglect, which can equally well be framed in terms of the perception or representation of space or the spatial attention system.

In the last chapter I suggested that posterior parietal cortex earns its keep, as a component of the spatial attention system, in two main ways: Integrating spatial information from different modalities, and stabilizing that representation of space over eye movements. Humans with spatial attentional impairments after parietal damage provide support for both of these functions. In surveying the cognitive issues illuminated by neglect, I begin with these issues.

8.4 Modality-specificity

A desirable property of the spatial representations underlying attention would be supramodality. A sound coming from the bushes should attract not just auditory attention but also visual attention to the same location. The posterior parietal lobe receives projections from at least three modalities, visual, somatasensory, and auditory, and single unit recording studies have revealed neurons with bimodal receptive fields, co-indexed to the same locations in space (Duhamel, Colby, and Goldberg, 1992). What evidence do we have that the human parietal lobe houses a supramodal spatial representation? In the absence of imaging studies that address this issue, our main source of evidence is the neglect syndrome.

Neglect sometimes seems to affect more than one modality, but it is difficult to tease apart the contributions of vision, hearing, and touch in naturalistic observations of patients exploring their environment. The more controlled task of testing for extinction with double simultaneous stimulation affords a relatively clean assay for impairments in different modalities. Visual extinction can be tested clinically by finger wiggling or by the more precisely controlled onsets of shapes on either side of a computer screen. Auditory extinction can be tested by finger snaps or the softer sound of fingers being rubbed together near each ear, or by computer-controlled loudspeakers. Similarly, tactile extinction can be demonstrated by low-tech methods, such as tapping a patient with one's finger, and by potentially higher-tech means involving solenoid-driven robotic tappers.

DeRenzi, Gentilini, and Pattacini (1984) assessed the severity of auditory and visual extinction in a series of patients and found a relatively low correlation between them as assessed clinically. Vallar,

Rusconi, Bignamini, Germiani, and Perani (1994) tested their patients for tactile and visual extinction with similarly low-tech methods and reported finding dissociations in both directions: visual extinction without tactile, and tactile extinction without visual. At first glance these findings are not what one would predict given the hypothesis of a supramodal representation of space in the parietal lobe. However, they are not strictly incompatible with it, for several reasons. One easy "out," for someone wishing to preserve the supramodal hypothesis, is the weakness of the bedside testing methods used in these studies, which may not be sensitive enough to detect subtle extinction, or which may introduce variability that is mistaken for dissociations. A careful enumeration of the relevant alternative hypotheses being tested provides even more compelling reason to withhold judgment. Parietal cortex could house just one supramodal representation of space, or it could house several unimodal representations, or it could house both unimodal and supramodal representations. Furthermore, extinction could be caused by a lesion to any one or more of these representations, or by a lesion to one or more pathways from modality-specific cortices to these representations. If the distinction of theoretical interest is between hypotheses that do and do not contain a supramodal representation of space, then dissociations of the types reported here are not very informative. They could be the result of lesions affecting just the unimodal representations but sparing coexisting supramodal representations, or they could be the result of lesions disconnecting supramodal representations from earlier sensory cortices. In short, the finding of dissociations is ambiguous, and does not rule out the existence of a supramodal representation.

Of course, the finding of associations among extinction in different modalities is also ambiguous, for the well-known reason that neuropsychological associations are always regarded with skepticism: A single lesion could damage more than one functionally distinct system. We must therefore seek a different approach, something qualitatively different from either dissociations or associations between extinction in different modalities.

That different approach is suggested by the original rationale for expecting space representation to be supramodal, namely the need for cross-modality attentional effects–the rustle in the bushes that attracts our visual attention. Such effects, particularly if they happen quickly and automatically so that strategic factors can be ruled out, provide positive evidence for a supramodal spatial representation. If extinction is found between stimuli in different modalities after parietal damage, this provides positive evidence for a supramodal spatial representation in parietal cortex.

My colleagues and I tested the hypothesis that parietal cortex represents visual and auditory space integrally in an experiment involving the detection of visual targets preceded by either visual or auditory stimuli (Farah, Wong, Monheit, and Morrow, 1989). The visual targets were crosses that appeared in one of two boxes on either side of a computer screen. The preceding visual stimuli consisted of a brightening of one of the boxes and the preceding auditory stimuli consisted of a tone emanating from one of two loudspeakers placed on either side of the computer screen. Posner, Walker, Friedrich, and Rafal (1984) have shown that an ipsilesional stimulus can extinguish a later contralesional stimulus; the stimuli need not be simultaneous. We replicated their findings with visual stimuli and, of more interest for the present issue, found similar effects when the preceding stimulus was auditory. Neither visual nor auditory stimuli predicted the location of the target stimulus, making it unlikely that the cross-modal effects were the result of strategic shifts of attention, and the short time delay between preceding stimuli and targets (as little as 50 ms) further reduces this possibility. The finding that a tone on the right side of space interferes with the detection of a cross on the left in patients with right parietal damage implies that the damaged tissue was essential to the normal deployment of attention to an integrated representation of visual and auditory space.

Two studies with similar designs have assessed the representation of visual and somatasensory space in parietal cortex. Inhoff, Rafal, and Posner (1992) were unable to demonstrate cross-modal extinction between visual and tactile stimuli. Mattingley, Driver, Beschin, and Robertson (1997) critiqued some aspects of Inhoff *et al.*'s experimental methods, and carried out their own study in which all patients tested showed cross-modal extinction. They found that both ipsilesional tactile stimuli extinguished contralesional visual stimuli and ipsilesional visual stimuli extinguished contralesional tactile stimuli.

On balance, the spatial impairments of patients with parietal damage seem to affect perception supramodally. If extinction reflects the tendency of contralesional stimuli to lose in competition with ipsilesional stimuli, then the results described here imply that the competition is not limited to stimuli within the same modality. Instead, the representation within which the competition occurs encompasses visual, auditory, and tactile stimuli.

8.5   Frames of reference

Beyond retinotopy

As we saw in chapters 1 and 2, many of the computations of early and intermediate vision are well-served by the retinotopic format in which the nervous system initially receives visual information. But just as the problem of object recognition described in chapter 3 requires that we abandon retinotopy, so does the problem of attentional selection of objects in space. In order to co-index visual location representations with nonretinotopic representations of locations from hearing and touch for the supramodal representation just discussed, clearly some transformation is needed. For any vision chauvinist who thinks the proper transformation is to convert the auditory and tactile representations to a retinotopic frame of reference, consider that retinotopic representations will be unwieldy even for a purely visual spatial attention system, given the intimate relation between shifts of visual attention and eye movements.

Candidate frames of reference for the parietal lobe's representation of space include a multitude of nonretinotopic viewer-centered frames, such as head-centered and body- or trunk-centered, as well as entirely external frames centered on the environment itself or objects of interest within the environment. There is no reason to assume that the right answer will consist of just one frame. Given the many ways in which spatial information is likely to be used in the human brain, and given the major role of posterior parietal cortex in spatial representation, we should be prepared for an answer of the form "all of the above."

The earliest research to address this issue was carried out by Heilman and Valenstein (1979), who simply administered the line bisection task, described earlier, varying the location of the lines relative to the patients' trunks. Patients were free to move their head

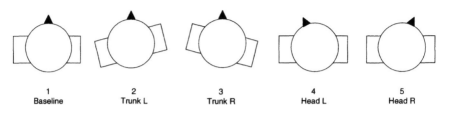

1	2	3	4	5
Baseline	Trunk L	Trunk R	Head L	Head R

Figure 8.7   Manipulations of patient position used to disentangle the contributions of two nonretinotopic frames of reference used in the allocation of spatial attention: the head-centered and trunk-centered frames.

and eyes, so that when the line was placed to the left or right of the patient, its location varied within a trunk-centered frame, but presumably not within a head-centered or retinotopic frame. The bisection asymmetry varied systematically with this manipulation of trunk-centered location, with the greatest rightward displacement of perceived midpoint when lines were placed to the patients' left. In other words, the "left" of left neglect is defined at least partly with respect to the viewer's trunk. Bisiach, Capitani, and Porta (1985) also found support for a trunk-centered frame of reference, using a tactile exploration task in which patients were asked to remove pegs from a pegboard hidden underneath a cloth. The array was placed either in front of, or to the right of, each patient's trunk, and the patient was asked either to keep their head and eyes straight ahead or diverted to the right. Neglect of the left side of the array was affected independently by both the position of the array relative to the trunk and relative to the line of head–eye gaze.

The possibility of a truly head-centered frame of reference, deconfounded from the retinotopic frame, was tested directly by Schindler and Kerkhoff (1997) with the conjunctions of eye, head, and trunk orientation shown in figure 8.7. Patients' line bisection and reading performance both indicated improved perception of the left side of fixation with either trunk or head orientation shifted left, consistent with attentional allocation relative to both.

It is easy to miss the grand implications of these findings, perhaps especially so for people familiar with neglect patients. Clinicians and patients' families know well the importance of standing to the patient's right and placing needed objects to the right in order to be noticed, even though patients are of course free to move their heads and eyes. It might therefore seem obvious, and hence trivial, that position relative to trunk and head affects the perception of neglect patients. But consider this finding in the context of the well-established principle of the crossed organization of perceptual systems, including vision. Inputs from the left ear, left body surface, and left hemiretina are projected to the right hemisphere, and vice versa. This general principle is violated in the experiments just described! Information coming through left and right hemiretinae was equivalent in all conditions. This means that the right parietal lobe is not merely representing the left side of space by passively receiving the contents of half of the retina, delivered to it through a fixed and well-known set of pathways. Instead, it is actively constructing a representation of space, combining retinal inputs with as yet unknown extraretinal inputs specifying the disposition of the head and body in space.

An even more impressive feat of parietal computation is the construction of an environment-centered frame of reference, independent of the entire body's disposition in the environment. Calvanio, Petrone, and Levine (1987) administered a visual search task to patients with neglect, in which the patients were to name all of the pictures scattered across the four quadrants of a large display. The key experimental manipulation was to test the patients in both an upright position or reclining on their left or right sides. When patients were sitting upright, they named more pictures on the right than on the left side of the display. When reclining, they named most pictures from the quadrant that was on both their personal right and the right of the environment, and the fewest from the quadrant that was on both their personal left and on the left of the environment. Performance on the remaining two quadrants was intermediate. This pattern of results is consistent with an impaired representation of the left relative to two independent frames of reference: one centered on the viewer, and one centered on the external environment. A similar result was obtained by Ladavas (1987), who measured simple reaction time to stimuli at different positions in the visual field while subjects either sat upright or tilted their heads to the side.

What information is used by the parietal lobe to locate the environmental frame of reference relative to the egocentric frames within which sensory stimuli are delivered to it? Although Ladavas (1987) conjectured that gravitational cues, transduced by the otolith system of the inner ear, provided the information, recent data suggest that the cues are likely to be purely visual. Karnath, Fetter, and Niemeier (1998) tracked the eye movements of neglect patients as they searched for a point of light in a darkened experimental chamber, while tilted at various angles. Deprived of visual input, the patients showed no environmental influence on their search asymmetries. This suggests that the environmental frame, within which the parietal lobe directs attention, is derived from visual cues such as the location of the floor, walls, and ceiling, and the disposition of furniture, experimenters, etc. Of course, the use of such visual cues requires some level of recognition of these objects, demonstrating an even greater computational complexity to the construction of the parietal lobe's representation of space.

Object-centered neglect?

The frame of reference is a fundamental way of characterizing any spatial representation, and once neuropsychologists realized that these frames could be decoupled by simple spatial manipulations of patient and stimulus display, experimental variations and permutations abounded. Much of the ensuing experimental work focused on the object-centered frame of reference. Recall from chapter 3 that an object-centered frame of reference represents locations relative to the intrinsic axes of an object. Any object that has a distinct top, bottom, front, back, left, and right provides a frame of reference for uniquely localizing points in space. Object-centered frames have been considered a desirable form of spatial representation for purposes of solving the problem of object recognition, as they automatically confer constancy over all spatial transformations of the object; the receiver is "on top of" the desk phone, in phone-centered coordinates, even if the phone is lying on its side on the desk.

Although it is not clear, computationally, what advantage there would be to representing space in object-centered coordinates for purposes of spatial attention, hints of object-centered neglect may be found in the drawings of some neglect patients. The copies shown in figure 8.8 illustrate an apparent form of object-based neglect. Information is included from both sides of space, but the left side of each

Figure 8.8   Examples of copying in which the left side of each object in a scene is neglected, including objects on the left. This is consistent with an object-centered neglect, but other interpretations are also possible.

From M. J. Farah and L. J. Buxbaum, "Object-based attention is visual neglect: conceptual and empirical distinctions," in P. Their and H. S. Karnath (eds), Parietal Lobe Contributions to Orientation in 3D Space, *Heidelberg, Springer-Verlag, 1997.*

individual object is omitted. Such observations appear, at first glance, to support the contention that visual processing in neglect may be disordered with respect to object-centered as well as viewer-centered and environment-centered frames of reference. This evidence is at best only suggestive, however. For example, neglect of the left sides of objects in 8.8 could reflect neglect in retinotopic coordinates if subjects make separate eye fixations on each object they copy. Copying a scene of any complexity requires multiple fixations as different parts of the scene are separately copied.

More direct tests of the hypothesis of object-centered neglect were therefore undertaken. My colleagues and I (Farah, Brunn, Wallace, Wong, and Carpenter, 1990) adapted the method of Calvanio *et al.* by rotating the display object as well as the patient. Calvanio *et al.*

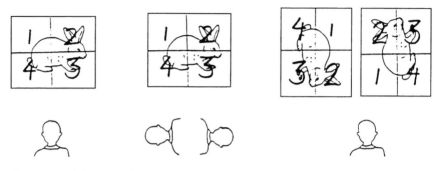

Figure 8.9   Schematic depiction of an experimental design that disentangles the object-centered and environment-centered frames in neglect.
From M. J. Farah and L. J. Buxbaum, "Object-based attention is visual neglect: conceptual and empirical distinctions," in P. Their and H. S. Karnath (eds), Parietal Lobe Contributions to Orientation in 3D Space, Heidelberg, Springer-Verlag.

had interpreted their finding of nonviewer-centered neglect as an environment-centered neglect, and Ladavas (1987) drew a similar conclusion from her results, suggesting that the cue to the disposition of the environment was specifically gravitational. We considered an alternative interpretation of these results in terms of object-centered neglect, where the experimental display is the object of interest. Our task involved presenting patients with scattered letters to read, super-imposed on pictures of objects, which were presented either upright or rotated by 90 degrees as shown in figure 8.9. We found evidence that attention was differentially allocated to the right sides of the viewer-centered and the environment-centered frames, but found no evidence for the use of an object-centered frame.

Behrmann and Moscovitch (1994) attempted a stronger test for the existence of an object-centered frame of reference for allocation of attention to space. They suggested that the objects used in our task did not affect distribution of attention because they were superfluous to the task. They redesigned the task so that drawings were the object of the search, not merely a background, by outlining the drawings of objects with different colors to be reported. Even under such condi-tions they failed to find neglect of the intrinsic left of the objects. They next considered the possibility that object-centered frames would only be used for objects such as asymmetric letters, whose identities depend on differences between the left and right. In this final experiment, patients did neglect the left sides of 90 degree-rotated asymmetric letters, consistent with object-centered neglect.

Another apparently positive finding of object-centered neglect comes from the reading errors of a neglect dyslexic studied by Caramazza and Hillis (1990a,b). Their patient made more errors on the intrinsic right than on the left sides of words, and this was true whether the words were printed normally or mirror-reversed or even printed vertically. That is, when the words were presented mirror-reversed, she neglected the letters on her left, and when they were presented vertically she neglected the bottom letters. Caramazza and Hillis interpreted these results as a demonstration that neglect may occur with respect to an orientation-invariant canonical representation of a word form.

Although the results of Behrmann and Moscovitch and Caramazza and Hillis are consistent with the use of an object-centered frame in neglect, a recent case study has led us to consider an alternative explanation of these results. According to several theorists (e.g., Jolicoeur, 1985; Tarr and Pinker, 1990), noncanonically oriented (e.g. tilted) objects may be recognized by mental rotation of the object to an upright position based on low-level properties of the object's shape, such as its axis of elongation. The rotated shape is subsequently matched to stored orientation-specific (e.g., upright) representations. If such mental rotation procedures occur prior to the processing stage at which neglect arises, then at least some cases of apparent object-centered neglect may not reflect neglect of the intrinsic left of the object. Instead, they could reflect neglect of the viewer- or environment-centered left of the object after it has been mentally rotated to its upright position. In other words, mental rotation procedures may allow viewer- or environment-centered neglect to masquerade as object-centered neglect.

Using the same color reporting procedure as Behrmann and Moscovitch (1994), we assessed whether this might be the case. We asked a subject with neglect to report colors outlining tilted asymmetric and symmetric objects and letters in two conditions (Buxbaum, Coslett, Montgomery, and Farah, 1996). In the first condition, he was asked to imagine that the tilted figures were upright and then name the colors. In the second condition, he was explicitly asked to refrain from mentally rotating the figures and instead simply to name the colors as he saw them. Only when he was explicitly asked to mentally rotate the figures did we find apparent object-centered neglect. When he simply viewed the tilted figures, and recognized them, but did not explicitly visualize them upright, he did not show object-centered neglect. In other words, apparently object-centered neglect occurred only when the left and right sides of the figures were mentally aligned with the viewer- and environment-centered left and right. The intrinsic characteristics of the objects (e.g., their symmetry) were irrelevant to this effect. This suggests that the neglect of the objects occurred with respect to the viewer- and/or environment-centered frames and not with respect to an orientation-invariant representation of the object.

It is possible that other cases of apparent object-centered neglect may be similarly attributable to viewer- or environment-centered neglect occurring after mental rotation. Indeed, the Caramazza and Hillis findings could be explained in this way, given Koriat and Norman's (1984) finding that normal subjects mentally transform misoriented words in order to read them. This possibility, coupled with our own failure to find object-centered neglect in symmetrical or asymmetrical objects or letters (except when mental rotation was explicitly used) leads me to doubt that object-centered frames of reference are used in allocating attention in neglect.

Distinguishing among different types of object effects in neglect

In addition to the issue of an object-centered reference frame for allocating spatial attention in neglect, there are a number of other interesting research issues involving objects and neglect. Unfortunately, these issues are easily confused with the issue of object-centered frames of reference, given the occurrence of terms like "object-centered" and "object-based" in connection with all of them. Laurel Buxbaum and I (Farah and Buxbaum, 1997) attempted to disentangle these two issues and then review the evidence relevant to each.

The issue most closely related, conceptually, to object-centered frames of reference concerns what Driver, Baylis, Goodrich, and Rafal (1994) have called "axis-based" neglect. Whereas full object-centered

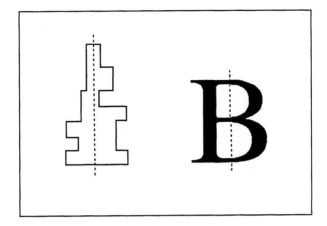

Figure 8.10 Two objects whose principal axes divide space into left and right halves.
From M. J. Farah and L. J. Buxbaum, "Object-based attention is visual neglect: conceptual and empirical distinctions," in P. Their and H. S. Karnath (eds), Parietal Lobe Contributions to Orientation in 3D Space, *Heidelberg, Springer-Verlag.*

neglect would require that an object's intrinsic left be neglected, regardless of its orientation with respect to the patient, in axis-based neglect the dividing line between the left and right – defined relative to the patient – is determined by an object's major axis. For example, in the left part of figure 8.10, taken from the work of Driver and Halligan (1991), the object defines a dividing line between the space to the left and right of its axis of elongation.

The way in which the object in figure 8.10 helps to define left versus right contrasts with the stronger sense of object-centered neglect discussed earlier, in which stored knowledge about which are the left and right sides of objects determines the distribution of attention. For example, one can say that the capital B in figure 8.10 has the straight line on the left and the loops on the right, where left and right refer to intrinsic sides of the object. The axis-based type of object-centered frame is parasitic on the viewer-centered frame for the assignment of left and right. This point can be appreciated by looking at figure 8.11, in which the shapes from figure 8.10 have been rotated 180 degress from upright. The axis-based left of the novel shape is still on the viewer's left, whereas the left of the B is now on the viewer's right.

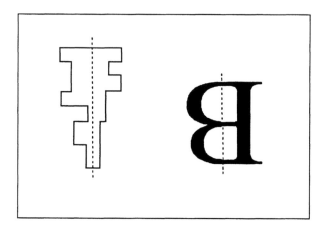

Figure 8.11   When the two objects from figure 8.10 are inverted, we can observe a difference in the way they define the left and right sides of space. The novel figure continues to provide a dividing line between left and right, but which side is which remains the same with respect to the viewer. In contrast, the letter B has an intrinsic left and right, providing both a dividing line and a left/right polarity, such that the B's left is now on the viewer's right and vice versa.

From M. J. Farah and L. J. Buxbaum, *"Object-based attention is visual neglect: conceptual and empirical distinctions," in P. Their and H. S. Karnath (eds),* Parietal Lobe Contributions to Orientation in 3D Space, *Heidelberg, Springer-Verlag.*

Driver and Halligan (1991) provided compelling evidence of axis-based neglect in a task requiring detection of differences between two elongated novel shapes in both upright and 45 degrees rotated orientations. In the rotated condition, portions of the left sides of the stimuli fell on the right side of viewer-centered and environment-centered space such that putative object-centered and viewer-centered frames were uncoupled. The subject was significantly less likely to detect left-sided as compared to right-sided differences between the shapes in both the upright and rotated conditions. Driver and Halligan suggested that these data supported the presence of object-centered neglect defined with respect to the left and right of the objects' principal axes.

Subsequently, Driver, Baylis, Goodrich, and Rafal (1994) demonstrated that when egocentric location as well as object shape and orientation are held constant, the neglected regions of objects may be

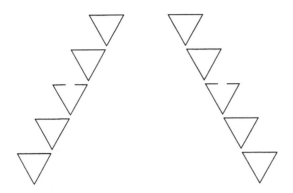

Figure 8.12 Context can determine the perceived principal axis. In this demonstration, identically located gaps on an equilateral triangle are neglected or not as a function of whether they fall to the left or right of the contextually implied axis.
From M. J. Farah and L. J. Buxbaum, "Object-based attention is visual neglect: conceptual and empirical distinctions," in P. Their and H. S. Karnath (eds), Parietal Lobe Contributions to Orientation in 3D Space, Heidelberg, *Springer-Verlag.*

modified by a *perceived* major axis. Patients with neglect viewed equilateral triangles which, while identical in all cases, were biased to appear to be pointing in one of two directions by manipulation of the array in which they were presented, as shown in figure 8.12. The relative location of a gap with respect to the perceived principal axis of the triangle was varied, while holding constant the gap's egocentric location. Subjects neglected more gaps to the left than right of the perceived major axis. In response to these data, Driver *et al.* (1994) suggested that the principal axes of objects may indeed be used to divide objects into two regions. Critically, since triangles do not have intrinsic lefts and rights, the neglected side of the axis is determined by the viewer's left.

Further evidence that can be interpreted in terms of axis-based neglect comes from the study of Behrmann and Tipper (1994) in which subjects with neglect were asked to respond to targets appearing on the ends of a barbell-shaped stimulus. In the condition of interest, the barbell rotated 180 degrees while the subjects watched, such that the left side of the barbell ended up on the right side of the subjects and vice versa. After the barbell stopped a target appeared on one end or the other. Response times to the targets in the moving condition were compared to those in a static condition in which the barbell remained stationary throughout the trial. Detection was faster for targets on subjects' lefts and slower for targets on their rights in the moving, relative to static, condition. This effect of the ends' original position was not found when the connecting bar was eliminated, and the display was perceived as two separate objects.

This type of object effect can also be characterized as axis-based, in the sense that the ends of the barbell were coded as left and right as a function of their original locations on either side of the barbell's vertical axis, relative to the viewer. It is certainly not the case that stored knowledge concerning the left and right sides of barbells determined the allocation of attention to the left and right sides of the display, analogous to the B in figure 8.11. Indeed, Mozer (1999) has simulated this type of object-based attentional effect in a simple neural network model with purely viewer-centered representations and attentional mechanisms. The movement of attention in his simulation depends jointly on endogenous influences, specifically the viewer-centered locations recently attended, and exogenous influences, specifically the viewer-centered locations currently stimulated. These two influences interact to drag attention all the way leftward in the rotating single object condition, but not without the crossbar's exogenous influence in the two object condition.

Studies of the perception of chimeric figures, that is, figures composed of the left and right halves of two different objects as shown in the top part of figure 8.13, provide another demonstration that objects can influence the distribution of attention in neglect, without necessarily imposing an object-centered frame of reference specifying the object's intrinsic left and right. Some subjects with neglect are more likely to report the left sides of chimeric figures when the chimeric "object" is split down the middle by a small gap (Buxbaum and Coslett, 1994; Young, Hellawell, and Welch, 1992). In other words, for certain patients, when the two halves of the chimeric are joined to make a single object, the left side of the object is neglected. Although there seems to be some contribution of stored object knowledge to this effect, as the effect is stronger when the two half-objects are semantically related, the object effects are still axis-based, rather than derived from a truly object-centered frame of reference, in that the object

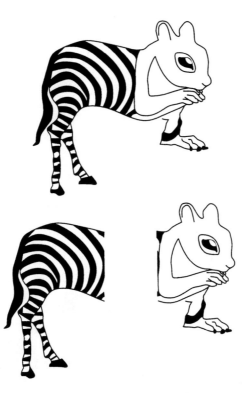

Figure 8.13 When mismatched halves of chimeric objects are joined to form a perceptual whole, the left side is more likely to be neglected, demonstrating another way in which objecthood affects the allocation of attention in neglect. *From M. J. Farah and L. J. Buxbaum, "Object-based attention is visual neglect: conceptual and empirical distinctions," in P. Their and H. S. Karnath (eds), Parietal Lobe Contributions to Orientation in 3D Space, Heidelberg, Springer-Verlag.*

supplies the axis only, and the determination of left and right is viewer- or environment-centered. This conclusion follows from the observation that when the chimerics are inverted, so that the object's intrinsic left is on the subject's right and vice versa, subjects with left neglect continue to neglect the half-object on their (viewer- or environment-centered) left.

A novel demonstration of this type of object-centered neglect was provided by Anjan Chatterjee (1994), who gave his patients cameras and had them photograph horizontal lines and objects. Chatterjee reasoned that object-centered neglect would lead patients to compose their pictures with the object displaced to the left of center, because they would underestimate the leftward extent to the object, whereas viewer-centered neglect would lead to an opposite displacement because patients would underestimate the left side of egocentric space. Both patterns were found, in different patients.

There is a very different sense in which neglect might be said to be object-based, which does not concern spatial frames of reference at all, but instead concerns the units of visual information that are perceived or neglected. Is the spatial representation that is damaged in neglect essentially a raw bitmap of locations, or is it carved into regions reflecting the structure of objects contained in the space? In order to answer this question, my colleagues and I examined the fine-grained pattern of neglect across the visual field when patients viewed meaningless blob objects (Farah, Wallace, and Vecera, 1993). We asked patients with neglect to name as many letters as they could from a scattered array which was superimposed on one of two kinds of backgrounds: large, elongated blobs that either straddled the left and right sides of space or were contained entirely within either the left or right side of space.

Although the blobs are not relevant to the task of reading the letters, they are perceived by at least some levels of the visual system, and the question is what, if any, effect do they have on the distribution of attention over the stimulus field? If the representation of space to which attention is allocated is parsed along the lines of objects, then there will be a tendency for entire blobs to be either attended or non-attended, in addition to the tendency for the right to be attended and the left to be non-attended. This leads to different predictions for performance in the two conditions. When the blobs extend from the right to the left hemifield, there should be more attention allocated to the left than when the blobs are each contained within one side. This is what was found: subjects named more letters on the left, and started their searches on the left, more often in the straddling blobs condition. The results of this experiment suggest that objects do affect the distribution of attention in neglect, and imply that visual attention is object-based as well as location-based.

Is the effect of objects on the structure of the parietal representation of space a purely "bottom-up" effect, determined by relatively low-level object properties such as size and shape, or does higher level memory knowledge play a role? To answer this question, we followed up on a phenomenon first observed by Sieroff and Posner (1988). They found that neglect patients are less likely to neglect the left half of a letter string if the string makes a word than if it makes a nonword. For example, patients are less likely to omit or misread the "t" in "table" than in "tifcl." One possible explanation for this phenomenon is in terms of the role of objects in spatial representation. If attention is not allocated to a bitmap representation of space, pixel by pixel, but is instead allocated to a representation that has been parsed into higher order units corresponding to objects, then the left sides of objects, including lexical "objects," should benefit. Of course, this would imply that the objects into which space is parsed can be defined by very abstract properties such as lexical status, as well as low-level physical features.

In order to test this interpretation of Sieroff *et al.*'s observation, and thereby determine whether pattern familiarity can be a determinant of objecthood for the visual attention system, we showed word and nonword letter strings printed with each letter a different color, and asked subjects to both read the letters and name the colors (Brunn and Farah, 1990). If there is a reallocation of attention to encompass entire objects, in this case lexical objects, then patients should be more accurate at naming the colors on the left sides of words than nonwords. This is what we found, providing further evidence that object-based selection affects the distribution of attention in neglect.

Further insight into the effects of object structure on the spatial allocation of attention comes from the work of Egly, Driver, and Rafal (1994). They used the stimulus display shown in figure 8.14, in which bars straddle either the upper and lower or left and right sides of the visual field. By cueing one end of one bar, and then presenting a target at a different location on the same or a different bar, they could hold spatial separation between the first and second stimulus constant and vary whether the extinction was purely a function of spatial location, with contralesional stimuli extinguished by ipsilesional stimuli, or whether there was additional competition from ipsilesional stimuli that were separate objects. Their subjects were both right and left parietal-damaged patients who showed extinction on pre-testing. They found that objects mattered, but only to the left parietal-damaged

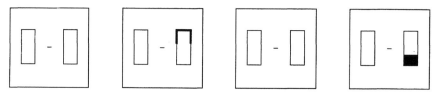

Figure 8.14   Sequence of stimulus displays in a typical trial from a cued simple reaction time experiment. Following fixation, one of four stimulus locations is cued, and following an additional delay, a stimulus is presented. The elongated boxes connecting pairs of stimulus locations allow the effects of spatial separation same versus different object to be disentangled.

From M. J. Farah and L. J. Buxbaum, "Object-based attention is visual neglect: conceptual and empirical distinctions," in P. Their and H. S. Karnath (eds), Parietal Lobe Contributions to Orientation in 3D Space, Heidelberg, Springer-Verlag.

patients. For right parietal patients, spatial location *per se* determined the severity of the extinction (measured as slowing in reaction time to contralesional targets when preceded by an ipsilesional cue). For the left parietal damaged patients, the severity of their extinction was a function of both spatial location and object structure; when the ipsilesional cue was part of a separate object, detection of the contralesional target was further slowed. A different way of expressing these results is that when the bars straddled the left and right sides of the visual field, there was less extinction of contralesional by ipsilesional stimuli, consistent with the findings described earlier with blobs and words. One discrepancy is that Egly *et al.* found this to be true for their left parietal-damaged patients only, whereas we found object effects with our right parietal-damaged patients. A difference in severity may explain this discrepancy: our patients had overt clinical neglect whereas theirs showed only extinction.

8.6   Modularity of spatial representations

Modularity, meaning the existence of multiple independent mental systems, is a cherished concept in neuropsychology. The most influential contributions of neuropsychology to the science of the mind have virtually all been demonstrations of modularity, by dissociation among abilities after brain damage. Mental systems that seemed unitary, such as learning or vision, have been shown to have surprisingly independent subsystems, such as explicit and implicit learning (e.g., Squire, 1992) or seeing what versus seeing where (e.g., Ungerleider and Mishkin, 1982).

Dissociations abound within the general syndrome of neglect, and have led to a variety of claims about the number and variety of different representations of space or spatial attentional systems. In some cases the dissociations point to modular divisions that seem sensible, or have some independent confirmation from the psychophysics or physiology lab. In other cases we end up with rather bizarre conclusions if we interpret the dissociations in the most straightforward way. Of course, the truth can be bizarre, and so it behooves us to examine these dissociations with an open mind, yet alert to alternative interpretations.

One general and often-replicated dissociation is between forms of neglect that primarily affect perception and forms that primarily affect action. Perceptual neglect has been the focus of the chapter thus far, partly because this book is about vision, and partly because perceptual neglect is more common. Nevertheless, a disinclination to respond motorically toward the affected side of space or with the affected side of the body often accompanies visual neglect and in some cases can be found in relatively pure form. In "motor neglect" there is a disinclination to move the contralesional side of the body. They may show normal strength if aroused by urgent pleas to raise their arm or squeeze a dynamometer, but left to their own devices appear hemiplegic. In "premotor neglect," also called "hemispatial hypokinesia," the impairment is not tied to the effector but rather the target of the action. Such patients show a disinclination to launch actions into the affected side of space. Under normal circumstances, it is difficult to tease apart perceptual neglect from premotor neglect, but several ingenious methods have been developed for this purpose.

For example, Coslett, Bowers, Fitzpatrick, Haws, and Heilman (1990) had patients bisect lines in the left and right hemispace while looking at the lines on a closed circuit TV, which could be moved independently into the right or left hemispace. Some patients' performance was entirely consistent with a perceptual neglect, in other words it was worse when the TV screen was in the left hemispace and was unaffected by the location of the actual line being bisected. Other patients showed the opposite pattern, performing worse when the line and their actions upon it were located to the left, independent of the side of visual feedback, consistent with premotor neglect. Other experimental approaches to the same issue have made use of mirrors (Tegner and Levander, 1991) and even pulleys (Bisiach, Geminiani, Berti, and Rusconi, 1990)!

Motor neglect and premotor neglect reveal the spatial organization of both the effectors and their action plans, and dissociations with perceptual neglect suggest a modularity among representations of effector, planned action, and perceived target of action. They also provide clues to the anatomical bases of these different representations. Although the case material is often messy, Vallar (1993) has summarized the general trends thus: Motor neglect may be found after a variety of lesions, cortical and subcortical, anterior and posterior. He suggests that premotor neglect is often, but not invariably, associated with right frontal lesions, and that perceptual neglect is most strongly associated with right inferior parietal lesions. However, these generalizations should be viewed as rules of thumb concerning the most florid manifestations of neglect. Careful testing of parietal-damaged patients has shown that their visual neglect is accompanied by slowed initiation of movements towards left-sided targets (Mattingley, Husain, Rorden, Kennard, and Driver, 1998).

An intriguing dissociation within perceptual neglect is between neglect for near and far space, sometimes framed in terms of "personal" or "peripersonal" space and "extrapersonal" space. The first hint of such a dissociation came from a large series of patients studied by Bisiach, Perani, Vallar, and Berti (1986), who measured the performance of 97 right-hemisphere damaged patients on two different tests of neglect: Reaching for the left hand with the right one, and canceling out scattered circles on a sheet of paper in front of them. Performance on the two tests was not highly correlated, due mainly to the greater incidence of neglect in the "far" circle canceling task relative to the "near" hand touching task. This result in itself is just as consistent with a single type of neglect measured by two tasks of unequal difficulty as with two distinct underlying forms of neglect. However, one patient showed neglect on the hand-touching task and not on the circle canceling task, consistent with truly distinct underlying forms of neglect. Unfortunately, scaling issues aside, the result is

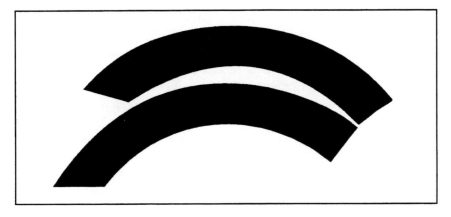

Figure 8.15   The Wundt–Jastrow illusion. The upper line will appear to be the longer one if the left side of the pair is neglected.
From L. Pizzamiglio et al., "Visual neglect for far and near extra-personal space in humans," Cortex, 25, 1989.

ambiguous with respect to the nature of the separable systems. Is the double dissociation observed in this study a dissociation between near and far space, or between a somatasensory representation of self and a visual representation of the external world? Either distinction would be of great theoretical interest, but the data themselves do not distinguish between the two.

Partly to resolve the ambiguity of Bisiach *et al.*'s (1986) finding, and partly motivated by the finding of Rizzolatti, Gentilucci, and Matelli (1985) that small lesions in monkey cortex can dissociate attention to near and far space, another large-scale study was undertaken. Pizzamiglio, Cappa, Vallar, Zoccolotti, Bottini, Ciurli, Guariglia, and Antonucci (1989) screened 28 patients for visual neglect of near and far space using a simple and well-controlled pair of tasks. The Wundt–Jastrow illusion, shown in figure 8.15, normally gives the impression that the lower line is longer than the upper line. When the left side is neglected (or when a normal person holds their hand over the left edge) the upper line appears longer. This simple figure therefore provides a quick test for neglect that can be administered to patients in either near or far space. Pizzamiglio and colleagues failed to find any clear dissociations between neglect for near and far space using this method.

Two later cases provided what appears to be an "existence proof" that selective neglect of near space is possible (Halligan and Marshall, 1991; Vuilleumier, Valenza, Mayer, Reverdin, and Landis, 1998). For purposes of understanding spatial representation in the human brain, the rarity of full dissociations makes them no less important. The likely size of the functional subdivisions of cortex is small relative to the typical lesions in neglect, and this predicts a high degree of association simply on the basis of coincident damage to the two areas. Halligan and Marshall (1991) reported a patient with pronounced neglect on a variety of tests in near space, including line bisection. Surprisingly, when asked to indicate the midpoint of a distant horizonal line (2.44 meters from the patient) using a light pen, he performed quite accurately. Similar results were obtained when the patient aimed darts at the midpoint of the lines.

In contrast, Vuilleumier and colleagues (1998) noticed that one of their patients showed neglect for far objects, for example failing to find doors on the left, but not for near objects, eating from both sides of her plate and reading a book without difficulty. They systematically assessed her ability to perceive the left and right sides of stimuli shown near and far, scaling the real size of their stimuli so that the visual angle subtended by them was the same in near and far conditions. Across a variety of tasks, including cancellation and counting tasks, line bisection, and word reading, the patient showed a pronounced neglect for far space and little or no neglect for near space. This patient's lesion was in the right temporal lobe, a lesion location not typically associated with neglect. In a group study of parietal-damaged neglect patients, Cowey, Small, and Ellis (1994) found a trend in the same direction: relatively more neglect for far space. Taken together, these dissociations support the idea that near, peripersonal space, roughly within arm's reach, is separately represented from far extrapersonal space. The different potential uses of information about near and far space, including the possibility of touching and grasping objects in near space, makes it plausible that this sector of space would be separately represented.

As already noted, "personal" space can refer to locations in the nearby "sphere of action" or to the spatial representation of the self, and the Bisiach *et al.* (1986) study did not clearly distinguish between the two. The dissociations observed in the later studies clearly concerned the first sense of personal space. A patient described by Guariglia and Antonucci (1992) showed a selective personal neglect in the second sense.

Guariglia and Antonucci's patient showed no visual extinction or neglect in near or far space when tested with an extensive battery of tasks, including paper and pencil tests such as line cancellation as well as the Wundt–Jastrow illusion shown in figure 8.15. He showed only mild tactile extinction (2 out of 10 trials). Yet his performance on a series of tasks involving localization of named, depicted, or touched body parts showed a severe impairment on the left side of his body, contrasting with good performance on the right. His localization errors were a mixture of mislocalizations to the right side, and nearby left-sided mislocalizations (e.g., substituting the back of the left hand for the left wrist). Perhaps more telling than any test score, the patient's wife complained that, 18 months after the onset of his neglect, her husband was still waking her in the middle of the night to help him find his left arm!

Another striking dissociation observed by Cecilia Guariglia and colleagues is neglect for mental imagery without visual perceptual neglect (Guariglia, Padovani, Pantano, and Pizzamiglio, 1993). Since Bisiach and Luzzatti's first demonstration of neglect for mental images, described earlier, other groups have replicated the phenomenon of parallel neglect for percepts and mental images (e.g., Meador, Loring, Bowers, and Heilman, 1987; Ogden, 1985). The patient studied by Guariglia *et al.* had a different problem. Following damage to his right frontal and anterior temporal cortex, he did not appear to have neglect at all, performing normally on a range of tests for visual neglect. His mental imagery abilities were also generally good, as evidenced by descriptions of the visual appearances of single objects. However, when asked to describe familiar city scenes from memory, he consistently omitted or mislocalized the landmarks that would appear on the left, and the same was true when asked to describe different views of a room from memory after being allowed to study and explore it in advance. Similar patients have been described more recently by Beschin, Cocchini, Della Sala, and Logie (1997) and Coslett (1997).

Of course, the spatial exploration of a mental image, which requires active mental effort to generate and maintain, is arguably more taxing than the exploration of a visually presented scene. Perhaps the dissociation in these patients can be explained by a mild general neglect, for which imagery tests provide a more sensitive test. Branch Coslett (1997) has pointed out the need for a double dissociation in neglect for images and percepts before any conclusions regarding modularity can be drawn. He reported a pair of patients who demonstrated just such a double dissociation within a common set of tests for perceptual and imaginal neglect. Like Guariglia *et al.*'s and Beschin *et al.*'s cases, his first case performed normally on a variety of standard tests for neglect, including a sensitive reaction-time task. However, when asked to describe the contents of familiar rooms from different perspectives, or the landmarks she would pass walking first from her house to a friend's and then from the friend's house to hers, she consistently omitted the objects that would be visible on the left. In contrast, Coslett's second case showed substantial neglect on the same tests of visual perception, but performed well, and with no left–right asymmetry, on the tests of imagery. A similar case was encountered by Bartolomeo, D'Erme, and Gianotti (1994), who screened patients for both perceptual and imaginal neglect and found one who, though he initially neglected both mental images and percepts, eventually showed perceptual neglect only.

The dissociations discussed so far among different forms of neglect suggest that spatial representation may have a modular internal structure, with modules devoted to action or motor planning, near and far space, the spatial representation of the body, and imagined versus perceived space. In all of these cases, the content of the hypothesized module is information that is explicitly spatial. This is self-evident for near and far space, and for the body part localization tasks used by Guariglia and Antonucci (1992). It is equally true that the motor programs underlying our actions must ultimately be encoded in spatial terms. Finally, the tasks used to show imaginal neglect test knowledge of spatial layouts. The patient of Guariglia and colleagues (1993) had no trouble describing both the left and right sides of single objects; the impairment was confined to mental images of familiar spaces, and in all cases of imaginal neglect the critical tests involve visualizing whole views or scenes from memory.

Several other neglect dissociations do not fit this sensible rule. For example, Young, de Haan, Newcombe, and Hay (1990) have described

Figure 8.16 Drawings of faces and a car made by a patient with face-specific left neglect.
From A. W. Young et al., "Facial neglect," Neuropsychologia, 28, 1990, with permission of Elsevier Science.

a patient with neglect for faces and nothing else. This man came to the authors with the complaint that faces looked different. The authors began their investigation by asking him to draw some faces, as well as other complex symmetrical stimuli. Examples of the results are shown in figure 8.16. Although the patient had a fairly high level of drawing skill, the left sides of the faces are distorted and slightly disorganized. In contrast, the car is detailed, well organized, and symmetrical. In a series of tests with faces and other objects divided in half along their vertical midline, the patient performed well at recognizing the right halves of faces, and both halves of other objects, but made significantly more errors with the left sides of faces. This was true whether the face was upright or inverted. Of particular interest, given the issue of object-centered neglect discussed earlier, when the faces were inverted the impairment was for half faces presented on the patient's left side, not for the intrinsic left half of the face. The most straightforward interpretation of these data, and the interpretation endorsed by the authors, is in terms of "face-specific attentional mechanisms." Making an analogy with dissociations among visual, auditory, tactile, and personal neglect, the authors suggest that there is a separate system of spatial attention and/or spatial representation required for face perception, and that this system is disrupted in their patient. Let us scrutinize this analogy. Different perceptual modalities, such as visual and auditory, do have distinct representations within the nervous system, as well as participating in supramodal representations. Furthermore, at least some information in these modalities is spatially organized, within a retinotopic or head-centered frame of reference. Faces, too, are separately represented within the nervous system, as discussed in chapter 5. And faces, like any pattern, also have a spatial organization relative to the viewer. At first glance, then, the analogy seems natural. However, the level of representation at which faces are represented separately from other objects, and the level of representation at which the locations of their different parts are represented in a spatial array relative to the viewer, are different. Relatively early visual representations of faces, and other patterns as well, have components that can be localized in terms of left and right with respect to the viewer, but there is no evidence that face representation is segregated from object representation within these representations. It is only the higher level representations of faces and objects that show segregation, and these are in nonretinotopic areas, with large bilateral receptive fields. It is therefore difficult to understand how a patient could have an impairment with both spatial selectivity (viewer-centered left impaired) and object category selectivity (faces impaired).

Face-specific neglect is not the only form of neglect that poses this paradox. Word reading, number reading, and writing all involve representations that may well be segregated from more general pattern processing at certain levels of representation (as discussed in chapter 6), but those levels are presumably not levels at which the representations explicitly encode spatial layout relative to the viewer. Nevertheless, there are well-documented reports of several cases of selective neglect for recognizing printed words (Bisiach, Vallar, Perani, Papagno, and Berti, 1986; Costello and Warrington, 1987; Cubelli, Nichelli, Bonito, De Tanti, and Inzaghi, 1991; Katz and Sevush, 1989; Riddoch, Humphreys, Luckhurst, Burroughs, and Bateman, 1995), as well as single cases of neglect for number reading (Cohen and Dehaene, 1991) and for writing (Baxter and Warrington, 1983). Does this imply that we have separate modules for the spatial representation of, or spatial attention to, faces, words, numbers, and the motor plans involved in writing? At least one writer has surveyed the literature and drawn this very conclusion (Umilta, 1995).

Anything is possible, but in these cases it seems worthwhile considering alternative interpretations. One possible alternative is suggested by research on a very different and seemingly unrelated topic, optic aphasia. Patients with optic aphasia have difficulty naming visually presented stimuli, but remain able to name stimuli through other modalities (tactile, auditory) and remain able to indicate their recognition of stimuli nonverbally. This profile of impaired and preserved abilities seems paradoxical for the same kind of reason as the domain-specific neglects: Modality is clearly an important organizing principle within our nervous system, so vision-specific impairments in general can be understood, and likewise naming is well-known to be a separable ability from other ways of indicating recognition. These organizing principles are depicted in the box and arrow diagram of figure 8.17. The paradox of optic aphasia is that the brain systems within which linguistic and nonlinguistic responses are segregated (upper boxes of figure 8.17) are not the brain systems within which different input modalities are segregated (lower boxes of figure 8.17). In short, modality of input clearly determines the nature of input processing, but there is no reason to think that linguistic output is processed by different systems as a function of which input system "historically" delivered the information to prelinguistic semantic representations.

Sitton, Mozer, and Farah (in press) have proposed an explanation of optic aphasia that may also explain the highly selective forms of neglect reviewed here. When the model shown in figure 8.17 is implemented as a highly interactive neural network, partial damage to two pathways, the vision-to-semantics pathway and the semantics-to-naming pathway, the effects are synergistic, impairing the mapping from vision to names far more than other input–output mappings.

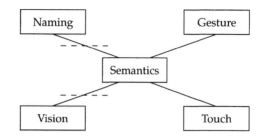

Figure 8.17   An example of a parsimonious way of explaining neuropsychological impairments that combine selectivity along pairs of dimensions associated with different subsystems. A modality-specific naming impairment might seem to imply a lexical-semantic system used exclusively by visual inputs, but can be explained by the model shown here after lesions in the visual input pathway and the verbal output pathway, in conjunction with some processing assumptions described in the text. Similarly, a material-specific spatial attention impairment need not imply material-specific spatial attention systems, but rather lesions to material-specific representation and spatial attention.

This is because the interactivity of such networks creates attractor states, which can "clean up" slightly noisy or damaged representations by pulling them back into attractors, provided the representations do not fall too far from the correct attractor state. But past a certain degree of damage, the input is likely to fall within the range of influence of a different and incorrect attractor. A task that requires traversing just one partially damaged pathway can make use of the cleanup abilities of the rest of the processing path, whereas a task that requires traversing two partially damaged pathways cannot, and errors rise disproportionately.

It is possible that the same general type of explanation might apply to the highly specific neglects. An impairment in early spatial attention could synergize with higher level impairments in face representation, word representation, number representation, or graphemic output representation, which are known to be separately lesionable. I grant that an explanation featuring two separate lesions is less parsimonious than an explanation featuring only one. But this loss of parsimony is outweighed, in my view, by the parsimony we gain in eliminating face-specific, word-specific, number-specific, and writing-specific systems of spatial representation or attention from our theories. Furthermore, the rarity of these highly selective neglects is consistent with a need for two lesions.

The most challenging data to explain without recourse to multiple modules comes from patients who show neglect for one side of words, and for the other side of nonword stimuli. The first detailed report of this rather astonishing condition came from Costello and Warrington (1987). Their patient failed to copy figures on the right side of the page, and bisected lines to the left of center, both consistent with right neglect. Yet his errors in word reading were virtually all on the left, for example reading *make* as "cake" or *cap* as "soap." In subsequent years a number of similar patients have been described (Cubelli, Nichelli, Bonito, De Tanti, and Inzaghi, 1991; Katz and Sevush, 1989; Riddoch, Humphreys, Luckhurst, Burroughs, and Bateman, 1995).

A single general-purpose system of spatial representation and attention can be maintained in the face of these cases, too, again by hypothesizing two lesions. Riddoch *et al.* (1995) have pointed out that damage to both hemispheres could reduce the overall spatial attentional capacity of the system, leaving it susceptible to the rightward or leftward biasing influences of tasks that activate the left or right hemisphere. Thus, they explain right neglect on nonreading tasks by hypothesizing that the right hemisphere is activated by the visuospatial scanning requirements of these tasks, causing an attentional bias in favor of the left side of space. Left neglect when reading can be explained by the known tendency of verbal tasks to activate the left hemisphere, in turn biasing attention to the right. This hypothesis accords well with the fact that in all cases in which neglect dyslexia affects a different side of space from neglect in nonreading tasks, the neglect dyslexia is on the right.

I suggest an even simpler version of this hypothesis: The distribution of attention is bilaterally reduced, but more so on the right, resulting in right neglect as the default, and only when the left hemisphere is activated by the focal, verbal processing of word reading does the balance of attention shift. This avoids the need to hypothesize an active rightward shift of cerebral activation in order for the more generally present neglect of the right to be manifest. The known neuropathology is consistent with this idea. The larger lesion, or the only known lesion, in these cases is in the left hemisphere (Costello and Warrington, 1987; Cubelli *et al.*, 1991; Katz and Sevush, 1989; Riddoch *et al.*, 1995).

Modularity in moderation

As every neuropsychologist knows, the phenomena of neglect are fascinating to the most jaded undergraduate dozing in a lecture hall or the most non-academic relative at Thanksgiving dinner. The fascination goes beyond the entertainment value of the phenomena. The research reviewed in this chapter shows the many ways in which neglect can inform our theories of human spatial cognition.

Some of the phenomena of neglect confirm or refine our theories of space representation derived from other sources, or teach us something new that nevertheless fits with our general thinking about brain organization. It makes sense that visual attention would be allocated to supramodal spatial representations, and to representations encoded relative to the more stable body-centered and environment-centered frames of reference. It also makes sense that visual percepts and motor plans would be encoded within distinct systems of spatial representation. The idea that spatial relations among body parts are represented separately from spatial relations of other objects is an interesting one, which is not especially obvious from other sources of evidence but can be accommodated within our evolving understanding of space representation without undue strain. The same is true of the idea that near and far space have separate representations.

Other aspects of neglect, when taken at face value, challenge our most basic background beliefs. Do we really have separate spatial representation and attention systems for words, numbers, and faces? A number of well-documented cases are consistent with this extravagantly modular cognitive architecture. But they are no more than consistent. Alternative interpretations are possible, and are in need of more attention and systematic empirical testing.

The "splitters" of neuropsychology often accuse the "lumpers" of mindlessly accepting the longstanding and broad categories of clinical taxonomy, instead of looking at the within-category variability more carefully and with an eye toward theories of the underlying cognitive componentry. In the light of the observations on premotor versus visual neglect and personal versus extrapersonal neglect, it is clear that neglect is not a single entity, and some so-called "fractionation" is certainly called for. But to reify every dissociation as a new taxonomic entity, proving the existence of a new module in the cognitive architecture, is mindless in its own way. Indeed more, rather than less, theoretical sophistication is called for when we have to think about the effects of lesions in complex, interactive systems. In so doing, we often find that highly specific behavioral impairments can emerge as a result of interactions among lesioned and intact components of a more general nature, rather than reflecting in a direct way the loss of one highly specialized modular component (Farah, 1994).

chapter nine

Mental Imagery

9.1 Perception versus cognition

The idea that a line can be drawn between perception and cognition is encouraged by our language, which labels them with different words: *perceiving, seeing, detecting, recognizing,* versus *thinking, recalling, surmising,* and so on. It is also entrenched in the academic approach to these issues, with Psychology majors offered separate courses on Perception and Cognitive Psychology, and professors affiliating themselves with such organizations as the Association for Research on Vision and Ophthalmology (commonly called ARVO) or the Cognitive Science Society, which have minimally overlapping memberships. Epistemologically, there is plenty of motivation for separating perception and cognition. It allows us to believe that, as subjective and generally fallible as our thinking might be, our observations of the world are potentially objective and untainted by our expectations and beliefs. Alas, what we know about the neural information processing underlying perception suggests that this separation is untenable.

A more realistic view is that we process stimuli through a large number of different types of representation, and that these representations form a continuum that stretches from a more perceptual end to a more cognitive end. The previous eight chapters of this book describe a segment of that continuum.

The perception–cognition continuum

By what criteria would a representation be placed near one end or the other of this continuum? I suggest that the following two criteria capture most people's intuitions fairly well.

The first criterion concerns the determinants of the representational "vocabulary," that is, the range of representations available for activation. The vocabulary can be innately determined or dependent on learning. At the periphery, the available representations are largely hardwired. The three different wavelength ranges represented by the three different types of cones, for example, are presumably innate. Of course, all gene expression depends to some extent on interactions with the environment. For present purposes the relevant criterion is that whatever learning must occur depends minimally on the psychologically meaningful content of experience. The determinants of ocular dominance for representations in primary visual cortex, for example, include visual experience, but whether each eye is seeing landscapes or faces does not matter.

In contrast, toward the more cognitive end of the continuum the representational vocabulary is more dependent on experience; the development of a full vocabulary of representation requires experience with both landscapes and faces. Indeed, these representations require extensive postnatal experience with exemplars of the right categories to develop. This is illustrated by the embarrassing situation in which we confuse two students in a big lecture class who are members of the same racial minority. The reason is that our inferotemporal vocabulary of face representations is less extensive for facial types of which we have seen fewer exemplars. Perhaps the strongest evidence of experience-shaped inferotemporal representations comes from the "wordform" area activated in neuroimaging studies. Recall that the visual association cortex of the left hemisphere contains tissue that orthographically distinguishes legal and illegal strings of letters.

The other criterion by which visual representations can be said to be more or less "cognitive" concerns the determinants of the moment-to-moment activity within the relatively fixed vocabulary of representations. At peripheral levels, what is being represented at time t is largely determined by what stimulated the retina some number of milliseconds before. The activity of more cognitive representations becomes harder to predict knowing just the retinal image. As we saw in chapter 7, attention modulates the effects of retinal stimulation, with effects detectable as early as primary visual cortex and robust in the higher level visual areas.

Mental imagery is another example of a nonretinal determinant of activity. Indeed, whereas attention mainly *modulates* activity of retinal origin, I will argue that imagery activates visual representations quite independently of retinal input. (Note that I am using the word "visual" to describe what is being represented, rather than its immediate origin.) The evidence to be reviewed in this chapter suggests that most of the visual representations described in this book, with the possible exception of chapter 1, can be activated endogenously by the mental intention to form a visual image. In this sense, representations only a few synapses away from the eye are "cognitive." So, if one wants to maintain a categorical perception–cognition distinction, one must exclude most of occipital cortex from perception!

9.2   Mental imagery: definitions and issues

What color are the stars on the American flag? To answer this question, it is very likely that you called up a mental image of the flag in your "mind's eye," and "saw" that the stars are white. It is this process of visualizing objects, people, and scenes from memory that is the topic of this chapter. I will not discuss mental manipulations of spatial images such as mental rotation here.

Early pioneers of imagery research in cognitive psychology devised many elegant and ingenious experimental paradigms to demonstrate the distinction between imagery and verbal thought, and to characterize imagery in objective information-processing terms (e.g., Kosslyn, 1980; Paivio, 1971; Shepard, 1978). Starting in the late 1970s, two related issues concerning imagery came into focus. The first was whether mental imagery involved some of the same representations normally used during visual perception, or whether imagery involved only more abstract, postperceptual representations. This issue was discussed most explicitly by Finke (e.g., 1980) and Shepard (e.g., 1978). The second issue was whether mental images had an array-like format (e.g., retinotopic), or whether they were propositional (symbolic or language-like) in format. The research of Kosslyn was aimed at addressing this issue (e.g., Kosslyn, 1980). The two issues are conceptually distinct, although they are in fact closely related, given that much of visual representation is array-like.

9.3 Cognitive neuroscience prehistory: the imagery debate

Although these issues are straightforwardly empirical in nature, they proved difficult to settle using the experimental methods of cognitive psychology. The classic image scanning experiments of Kosslyn (e.g., Kosslyn, Ball, and Reiser, 1978) will be used to illustrate this point. Kosslyn and associates instructed subjects to focus their attention on one part of an image, and then move it, continuously and as quickly as possible, to some other part of the image. The time taken to scan between the two locations was directly proportional to their metric separation, just as if subjects were scanning across a perceived stimulus. This finding follows naturally from the view that images share representations with visual percepts, and that these representations have a spatial format.

Not all psychologists agreed with this interpretation, and controversy ensued. The relation between imagery and visual perception, particularly array-format visual representations, became the focus of the so-called imagery debate. This debate consisted of numerous iterations of clever cognitive psychology experiments showing visual, array-format properties of mental images, each time countered by alternative explanations in terms of nonvisual representations. Two types of alternative explanation were particularly difficult to dispel, and motivated me to turn to neuroscience for more decisive evidence (Farah, 1988).

Tacit knowledge

Pylyshyn (1973, 1981) was the most influential critic of imagery research in the 1970s and 1980s. According to his view of the cognitive architecture, cognition is a symbolic form of information processing, distinct from perceptual processing. As discussed earlier, mental imagery poses a problem for any theory that categorically separates perception and cognition. Pylyshyn was therefore obligated to account for mental imagery in terms of symbolic, postperceptual processes. He did so by applying a sweeping reinterpretation to all of the data in cognitive psychology that had initially seemed to support the use of visual, array-format representations during imagery.

Pylyshyn suggested that subjects in imagery experiments take their task to be simulating the use of visual representations, using symbolic, nonvisual representations. He further suggested that subjects have tacit knowledge of the functioning of their visual systems, which enables them to carry out the appropriate simulation. For example, in an image scanning experiment subjects interpret the task as, in effect, pretending they are scanning a real visual display. They know that further distances take longer to scan, and so they produce scanning times that are proportional to imagined distance.

The tacit knowledge account can, in principle, explain any of the results initially taken to support visual, array-format representations in imagery. Although tacit knowledge accounts of imagery experiments vary in their plausibility, they nevertheless had their adherents.

Experimenter expectancy effects

Intons-Peterson (1983) suggested that subjects in imagery experiments may be responding to experimenter expectancies. She carried out experiments showing that at least certain aspects of the data in imagery experiments were susceptible to the experimenter's preconceptions about likely experimental outcomes. For example, she showed that subjects' average image scanning times depended on what the research assistants running the experiments expected the overall speed to be. Intons-Peterson proposed that many, if not all, of the results in cognitive psychology that seemed to support a visual, array-format nature for mental imagery might instead reflect the experimenter's beliefs to that effect. Like the tacit knowledge account, this alternative account cannot in principle be ruled out for any of the existing data from mental imagery experiments.

An impasse

In 1978, John Anderson argued that data from cognitive psychology experiments could never, in principle, determine the nature of internal mental representations. He used the imagery debate as an illustration for this depressing conclusion. In the simplest terms, the problem is that cognitive psychology data is limited to input–output pairings, and there will always be numerous different possible mechanisms that could intervene between stimulus and response and produce any given set of pairings. The same behavioral data that are consistent with visual, array-format properties for imagery representation are also consistent with different mechanisms operating on symbolic representations. Anderson was careful to point out that this problem was limited to input–output data of the kind collected by cognitive psychologists, and that if we could augment that type of data with more direct information about the neural states intervening between input and output, we could test hypotheses more decisively.

This is essentially what I set out to do when I surveyed the neuroscience literature on imagery in 1988. My goal was to show that the methods of neuroscience could specifically rule out the tacit knowledge and experimenter expectancy accounts, and provide decisive evidence for the visual nature of mental images, including the involvement of early occipital representations (Farah, 1988). In the following two sections I provide an updated review of that literature.

9.4   Imaging imagery: brain activity while normal subjects visualize from memory

SPECT studies

The earliest neuroimaging studies of imagery were done with single photon emission computed tomography (SPECT). Roland and Friberg (1985) examined patterns of regional bloodflow while subjects performed three different cognitive tasks, one of which was to visualize a walk through a familiar neighborhood, making alternate left and right turns. In this task, unlike the other tasks, bloodflow indicated activation of the posterior regions of the brain, including visual cortices of the parietal and temporal lobes. These results are therefore consistent with the general hypothesis that mental imagery is a function of visual cortical areas, but failed to support the more specific hypothesis of early, occipital involvement.

Georg Goldenberg and his colleagues performed a series of blood-flow studies of mental imagery using SPECT. They inferred which brain areas were activated by mental imagery using impressive experimental designs in which the imagery task was closely matched with control tasks involving many of the same processing demands except for the mental imagery *per se* (e.g., Goldenberg, Podreka, Steiner, and Willmes, 1987; Goldenberg, Podreka, Steiner, Willmes, Suess, and Deecke, 1989; Goldenberg, Podreka, Uhl, Steiner, Willmes, and Deecke, 1989; Goldenberg, Podreka, Steiner, Franzen, and Deecke, 1991; Goldenberg, Steiner, Podreka, and Deecke, 1992). For example, one imagery task was the memorization of word lists using an imagery mnemonic, and its control task was memorization without imagery (Goldenberg *et al.*, 1987). Another task involved answering questions of equal difficulty, which either required mental imagery (e.g., "What is darker green, grass or a pine tree?") or did not (e.g., "Is the Categorical Imperative an ancient grammatical form?" Goldenberg *et al.*, 1989a). In all of these studies, visual imagery was found to be associated with occipital and temporal activation. It is possible that the greater parietal involvement observed by Roland and colleagues (Roland and Friberg, 1985; Roland *et al.*, 1987) is related to the need to represent spatial aspects of the environment in their mental walk task.

Another SPECT study whose design is helpful in isolating mental imagery-related brain activity was carried out by Charlot, Tzourio, Zilbovicius, Mazoyer, and Denis (1992). Their subjects generated and scanned images, as in the classic cognitive psychology image scanning paradigm, and also found activation of visual association cortex, including occipital cortex.

ERP studies

Event-related potentials (ERPs) can also be used to address the question of whether visual mental imagery has a visual locus in the brain. Although this method affords only fairly crude localization, compared to bloodflow-based imaging methods, its excellent temporal resolution can be useful in localizing imagery within the visual system. It also had the advantage, much appreciated by my colleagues and I in the mid-eighties, of being readily available at a time when facilities for SPECT and PET were few and access was difficult. In one study, we used ERPs to map out, in space and in time, the interaction between mental imagery and concurrent visual perception (Farah, Peronnet, Gonon, and Giard, 1988) We compared the visual ERP to brief, threshold H's and T's when subjects were imaging the same letter as presented or a different letter. We reasoned that if imagery has a systematic effect on the visual ERP to a stimulus, there must be some brain locus at which they interact. If imagery has a content-specific effect on the ERP – that is, if imaging an *H* affects the ERP to *H*s more than the ERP to *T*s, and if imaging a *T* affects the ERP to *T*s more than the ERP to *H*s – then that interaction must be taking place at some brain locus where the differences between *H*s and *T*s is preserved, that is, at a representational locus. Imagery had a content-specific effect on the ERP to a visual stimulus early in stimulus processing, within the first 200 ms. This implies that imagery involves visual cortical representations that are normally activated in early visual perception. The effect was tightly synchronized in time with the N1 component of the visual ERP, which originates in occipital association cortex. Thus the temporal dimension of the ERP provides evidence of a relatively early extrastriate locus for imagery in the visual system. Interpolated maps of the scalp-recorded ERPs were also consistent with this conclusion. Figure 9.1 shows the scalp distribution of the content-specific imagery effect at its maximum.

In a second series of studies, Farah, Peronnet, Weisberg, and Monheit (1989) took a very different approach to localizing imagery in the brain using ERP methods. Rather than observing the interaction between imagery and concurrent perception, we simply asked subjects to generate a mental image from memory, in response to a visually presented word. By subtracting the ERP to the same words when no imagery instructions were given from the ERP when subjects were imaging, we obtained a relatively pure measure of the brain electrical activity that is synchronized with the generation of a mental image. Again, we constructed maps of the scalp distribution of the ERP imagery effect, in order to determine whether the maxima lay over

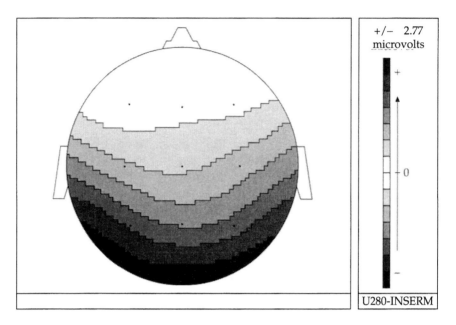

Figure 9.1   Scalp distribution of the effect of imagery on perception. The
occipital and posterior temporal maximum, and its synchronization with the
visual N1, are consistent with the existence of shared representations for
imagery and perception in modality-specific visual cortex.

*From M. J. Farah et al., "Electrophysiological evidence for a shared representational medium for
visual images and percepts," Journal of Experimental Psychology: General, 117, 1988;
copyright 1988 by the American Psychological Association; reprinted with permission.*

modality-specific visual perceptual areas. Despite the very different
experimental paradigm, we found a highly similar scalp distribution
to the previous experiment, as shown in figure 9.2a. When the experiment was repeated using auditory word presentation, the same visual
scalp topography was obtained, as can be seen in figure 9.2b. Control
experiments showed that the imagery effects in these experiments
were not due to the cognitive effort expended by subjects when imaging (as opposed to imagery *per se*), or to eye movements.

Farah and Peronnet (1989) reported two studies in which subjects
who rated their imagery as relatively vivid showed a larger occipital
ERP imagery effect when generating images than subjects who claimed
to be relatively poor imagers. This result, which we then replicated
under slightly different conditions, suggests that some people are

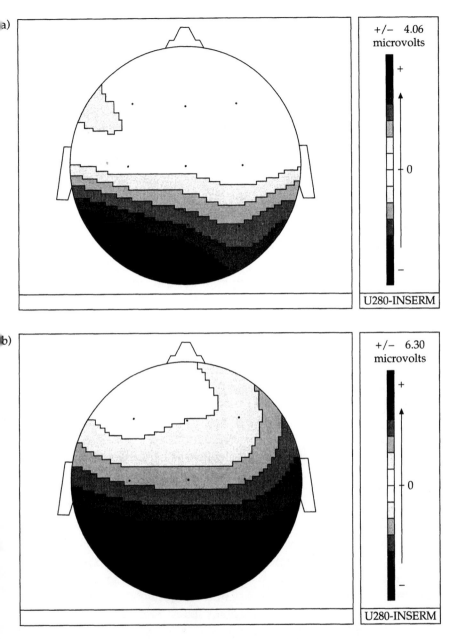

Figure 9.2   Scalp distribution of endogenous ERP associated with the
generation of a visual image from memory, triggered by (a) a visual
or (b) an auditory cue.
From M. J. Farah and F. Peronnet, "Event-related potentials in the study of mental imagery,"
Journal of Psychophysiology, 3, 1989.

more able to efferently activate their visual systems than others, and that such people experience especially vivid imagery. In sum, when operationalized in terms of interactions with perceptual processing, or with straightforward instructions to generate images, or by individual differences in imagery, imagery was consistently associated with occipital scalp distributions.

Uhl, Goldenberg, Lang, Lindinger, Steiner, and Deecke (1990) used scalp-recorded DC shifts to localize brain activity during imagery for colors, faces, and maps. Following transient positive deflections of the kind observed by Farah *et al.* (1989), a sustained negative shift was observed over occipital, parietal, and temporal regions of the scalp. Consistent with the different roles of the two cortical visual systems, the effect was maximum over parietal regions during map imagery, and maximum over occipital and temporal regions during face and color imagery.

PET and fMRI studies

With the advent of positron emission tomography (PET) and functional magnetic resonance imaging (fMRI), the spatial localization of cognitive neuroimaging improved greatly, and researchers soon applied these techniques to experiments on imagery. An early study by Roland, Eriksson, Stone-Elander, and Widen (1987) repeated their mental walk task with PET and again found only higher order visual association cortices activated. In subsequent years Roland and colleagues conducted a number of simple experiments intended to map the neural substrates of imagery, without observing reliable occipital activation (Roland and Gulyas, 1994).

Kosslyn, Alpert, Thompson, Malijkovic, Weise, Chabris, Hamilton, Rauch, and Buonanno (1993) also used PET to localize imagery, and obtained results more consistent with the preponderance of neuroimaging studies so far reviewed. In the first two of their experiments, subjects viewed grids in which block letters were either present or to be imagined, and judged whether an "x" occupying one cell of the grid fell on or off the letter. Comparisons between imagery and relevant baseline conditions showed activation of many brain areas, including occipital visual cortex. In a third experiment, subjects generated either large or small images of letters of the alphabet with eyes closed, and Kosslyn *et al.* directly compared the two imagery conditions. They found that the large images activated relatively more anterior parts of visual cortex than the small ones, consistent with the known mapping of the visual field onto primary visual cortex. A later study by the same group also found that occipital patterns of activation varied according to image size in a way that is consistent with the anatomy of primary visual cortex (Kosslyn, Thompson, Kim, and Alpert, 1995). Other PET studies of imagery have agreed with these studies insofar as occipital cortex was activated, but have disagreed as to whether primary visual cortex is involved (e.g., Mellet, Tzourio, Denis, and Mazoyer, 1995; Mellet, Tzourio, Crivello, Joliot, Denis, and Mazoyer, 1996).

Recently, functional magnetic resonance imaging (fMRI) has allowed researchers to obtain bloodflow-based images of function with good temporal as well as spatial resolution. The earliest study to exploit these qualities for the study of mental imagery was reported by Le Bihan, Turner, Zeffiro, Cuenod, Jezzard, and Bonnerot (1993) who measured brain activity in primary visual cortex as subjects alternately viewed flashing patterns and imagined them. The results shown for one subject in figure 9.3 provide a striking demonstration of the involvement of primary visual cortex in mental imagery as well as in perception.

D'Esposito, Detre, Aguirre, Stallcup, Alsop, Tippett, and Farah (1997) measured regional activity throughout the brain with fMRI while subjects performed the image generation task used by Farah *et al.* (1989) with ERPs: either passively listening to words or generating mental images of the words' referents. We found temporo-occipital activation, extending further into occipital cortex for some subjects than for others, but in no case reaching primary visual cortex.

Perhaps not surprisingly, there are differences in the conclusions that can be drawn from the studies reviewed here, which varied in their imaging techniques and cognitive tasks. Nevertheless, some generalizations can be made. In almost every study, mental imagery activates modality-specific visual cortical areas, including spatially mapped regions of occipital association cortex. The broader theoretical implications of this conclusion for the imagery debate will be discussed after the evidence from brain-damaged patients has been reviewed.

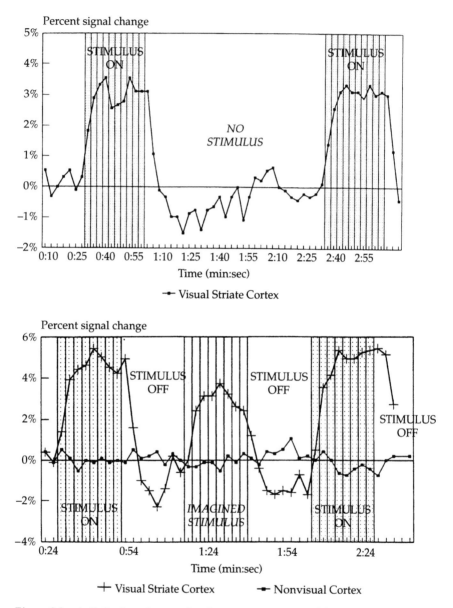

Figure 9.3   Activity in primary visual cortex, as measured by fMRI, as a function of visual stimulation and imagined visual stimulation.

From M. J. Farah, "The neural bases of mental imagery," in M. S. Gazzaniga (ed.), The Cognitive Neurosciences, Cambridge, MA, MIT Press, 1995.

9.5 Mental imagery in patients with damage to the cortical visual system

The most straightforward and parsimonious conclusion from the data reviewed so far is that mental imagery is a function of cortical visual representations. However, a diehard follower of Pylyshyn might resist this conclusion by suggesting that the visual area activation in these cases is epiphenomenal, that is, a spillover from true imagery activity elsewhere in the brain or in some other way a nonfunctional correlate. One way to test this possibility is to assess mental imagery in patients with focal cortical visual system damage. If the visual representations implicated by the functional neuroimaging studies are involved in imagery only epiphenomenally, there should be no effect of their loss on mental imagery ability. In contrast, if these visual representations are serving two purposes in the human brain, supporting both perception and mental imagery, then we should find that patients' perceptual impairments are paralleled by corresponding impairments in mental imagery.

One of the best-known examples of parallel impairment in perception and imagery was already discussed in the previous chapter. Bisiach and Luzzatti's (1978) seminal finding, illustrated in figure 8.5, was that patients with left visual neglect also neglect the left sides of their mental images. This implies that imagery and perception share neural substrates at the level of parietal spatial-attentional processes.

The earliest experimental study to find parallel impairments in perception and imagery was reported by DeRenzi and Spinnler (1967). They assessed various color-related abilities in a large group of unilaterally brain-damaged patients and found an association between impairment on color vision tasks, such as the Ishihara test of color blindness, and on color imagery tasks, such as verbally reporting the colors of common objects from memory. Beauvois and Saillant (1985) provided a complementary approach to the topic of color perception and imagery impairments, studying one patient in enormous detail. This patient had a visual–verbal disconnection syndrome, such that she performed well on purely visual color tasks (e.g., matching color samples) and purely verbal color tasks (e.g., answering questions such as "What color is associated with envy?") but could not perform tasks in which a visual representation of color had to be associated with a verbal label (e.g., color naming). When the patient's color imagery was tested purely visually, by selecting the color sample that represents the color of an object depicted in black and white, she did well. However, when the equivalent problems were posed verbally (e.g., "What color is a peach?") she did poorly. In other words, mental images interacted with other visual and verbal task components as if they were visual representations. De Vreese (1991) reported two cases of color imagery impairment, one of whom had left occipital damage and displayed the same type of visual–verbal disconnection as the patient just described, and the other of whom had bilateral occipital damage and parallel color perception and color imagery impairments.

Levine, Warach, and Farah (1985) studied the roles of the two cortical visual systems, discussed in chapter 2, in mental imagery. Our first case had visual disorientation following bilateral parieto-occipital damage. The second case was patient L.H., described in chapter 5, who had prosopagnosia and some degree of visual agnosia following bilateral inferior temporal damage. We found that the preserved and impaired aspects of visual imagery paralleled the patients' visual abilities: Case 1 could neither localize visual stimuli in space nor accurately describe the locations of familiar objects or landmarks from memory. However, he was good at both perceiving object identity from appearance and describing object appearance from memory. Case 2 was impaired at perceiving object identity from appearance and describing object appearance from memory, but was good at localizing visual stimuli and at describing their locations from memory. Although mental imagery had not been the focus of previous case studies of agnosia and visual disorientation, we found that the same pattern was discernible in numerous case studies already in the literature (Farah, 1984; Levine *et al.*, 1985).

We later carried out more detailed testing on the second patient (Farah, Hammond, Levine, and Calvanio, 1988) . We adapted a large set of experimental paradigms from the cognitive psychology literature that had been used originally to argue for either the visual nature of imagery (i.e. the "picture in the head" imagery mentioned in the first paragraph) or for its more abstract spatial nature. Our contention was that both forms of mental imagery exist, contrary to much of the research in cognitive psychology aimed at deciding which of the two characterizations of imagery was correct. On the basis of the previous study, we conjectured that cognitive psychology's so-called visual imagery tasks would be failed by the patient with the damaged ventral temporo-occipital system, whereas cognitive psychology's so-called spatial imagery tasks would pose no problem for him because of his intact dorsal parieto-occipital system.

The visual imagery tasks included imagining animals and reporting whether they had long or short tails, imagining common objects and reporting their colors, and imagining triads of states within the USA and reporting which two are most similar in outline shape. The spatial imagery tasks included such mental image transformations as mental rotation, scanning and size scaling, and imagining triads of shapes and reporting which two are closest to one another. As shown in figure 9.4, the patient was impaired relative to control subjects at the visual pattern–color imagery tasks, but entirely normal at the spatial imagery tasks.

Although the foregoing studies implicate modality-specific visual representations in imagery, they are either ambiguous as to the level of visual representation involved, or they implicate relatively high-level representation in the temporal and parietal lobes. My colleagues and I were therefore particularly interested in studying the effects of a surgical lesion confined to occipital cortex on mental imagery (Farah, Soso, and Dasheiff, 1992). If imagery consists of activating relatively early representations in the visual system, at the level of the occipital lobe, then it should be impossible to form images in regions of the visual field that are blind due to occipital lobe destruction. This predicts that a patient with homonymous hemianopia should have a smaller maximum image size, or visual angle of the mind's eye. The maximum image size can be estimated using a method developed by Kosslyn (1978), in which subjects imagine walking towards objects of different sizes and report the distance at which the image just fills their mind's eye's visual field and is about to "overflow." The trigonometric relation between the distance, object size, and visual angle can then be used to solve for the visual angle.

We were fortunate to encounter a high-functioning, college-educated young woman who could perform the rather demanding task of introspecting on the distance of imagined objects at "overflow." In addition, she could serve as her own control because we

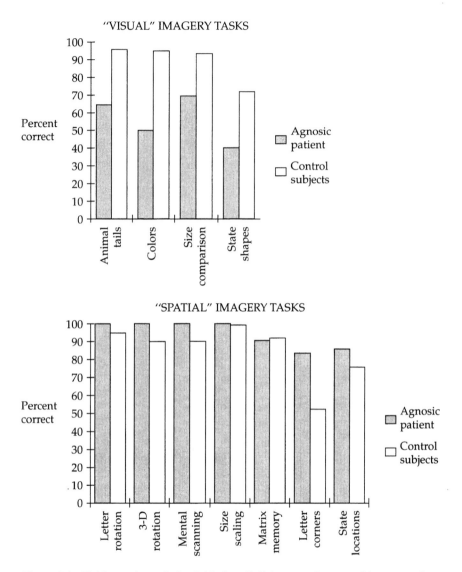

Figure 9.4   Evidence for a "what"/"where" dichotomy in mental imagery. An agnosic patient performed poorly on tests of imagery for visual appearance (upper panel) but did as well as control subjects on spatial imagery tasks.
From M. J. Farah, "The neural bases of mental imagery," in M. S. Gazzaniga (ed.), The Cognitive Neurosciences, *Cambridge, MA, MIT Press, 1995.*

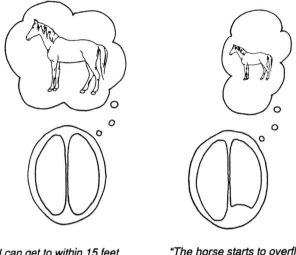

"I can get to within 15 feet
of the horse in my imagination
before it starts to overflow"

"The horse starts to overflow
at an imagined distance of
about 35 feet"

Figure 9.5   Demonstration of a reduction in the mind's eye's field after
occipital lobectomy.
*From M. J. Farah, "The neural bases of mental imagery," in M. S. Gazzaniga (ed.), The
Cognitive Neurosciences, Cambridge, MA, MIT Press, 1995.*

encountered her before she underwent unilateral occipital lobe resection for treatment of epilepsy. We found that the size of her largest possible image was reduced after surgery, as represented in figure 9.5. Furthermore, by measuring maximal image size in the vertical and horizontal dimensions separately, we found that only the horizontal dimension of her imagery field was significantly reduced. These results provide strong evidence for the use of occipital visual representations during imagery.

Discrepant findings: perceptual impairments with preserved imagery

Although the results from brain-damaged patients are generally consistent with the hypothesis that mental imagery involves representations within the visual system proper, including relatively early representations in the occipital lobe known to be spatial in format, there are discrepant findings as well. Goldenberg, Mulbacher, and Nowack (1995) described a case of cortical blindness following bilateral occipital lobe lesions who performed well on some, but not all, imagery tasks, with the suggestion that occipital cortex may not be necessary for mental imagery. This patient did, however, retain some small islands of intact occipital cortex, and eventually recovered vision in the sectors of the visual field corresponding to the preserved cortex, raising the question of whether this occipital cortex was also subserving her mental imagery.

More clear-cut cases of perceptual impairment with preserved imagery involve patients with neglect and agnosia. As discussed in the previous chapter, patients with left neglect may sometimes retain the ability to represent the left sides of mental images. The apperceptive agnosic patient, D.F., studied intensively by Milner, Goodale, and their colleagues and mentioned in chapter 2, performs well on imagery tasks despite a perceptual impairment so severe that squares and circles cannot reliably be distinguished. Behrmann, Moscovitch, and Winocur (1994) and Bartolomeo, Bachoud-Levi, de Gelder, Denes, Dalla Barba, Brugieres and Degos (1998) describe associative agnosic patients who demonstrate good visual mental imagery abilities.

On the face of things, these observations conflict with the hypothesis that imagery and visual perception share representations. Of course, if we accept the alternative hypothesis, that imagery does not share representations with perception, then the evidence reviewed earlier of parallel impairments in imagery and perception is equally confounding. The data from neuroimaging experiments in normal subjects also conflicts with this hypothesis. Is there some way to accommodate both the associations and the dissociations between imagery and perception?

It is hard for me to see how the hypothesis of distinct and non-overlapping representations for imagery and perception could be amended to accommodate the numerous findings of parallel impairments and the large literature showing visual area activation in normal subjects during imagery. In contrast, I can see at least a few ways that the hypothesis of shared representations could be made to accommodate the discrepant findings reviewed above. The occasional failure to observe early visual area activation in neuroimaging experiments is, of course, a null result and might signify nothing more than an insensitive experiment. What about the discrepant patient data?

One possibility that must always be raised in neuropsychology when confronting a surprising dissociation is a disconnection syndrome. Geschwind (1965) reintroduced disconnection syndromes into neuropsychology as parsimonious explanations of dissociations that would otherwise require more complex or unpalatable models of brain organization. Recall his explanation of pure alexia from chapter 6. Rather than hypothesize a specific brain center for visual language, which strikes many people as implausible, pure alexia could simply reflect a disconnection between general vision and general language. By the same token, it is possible that there are general visual representations common to imagery and perception, and that these representions can be disconnected from afferent perceptual inputs. This would lead to preserved visual imagery with perceptual impairments such as agnosia or neglect. In the light of this possibility, it is interesting to note that the MRI of Bartolomeo *et al.*'s (1998) agnosic shows predominantly white-matter damage, undercutting intact visual association cortex (see their fig. 1).

A related possibility concerns damage to relatively early levels of cortical visual processing. Assume the damaged representations are among those shared by imagery and perception, not purely perceptual afferents, and consider the impact of interrupting processing at this stage: When the flow of processing is bottom-up or afferent, as in perception, the impact will be large because the majority of visual representations cannot be accessed. In contrast, when the flow of processing is top-down or efferent, as in imagery, the impact will be smaller, because only a minority of the representations normally activated in imagery are unavailable. This possibility seems relevant in cases with evidence of early damage, such as apperceptive agnosia or the associative agnosic of Behrmann *et al.* (1994), whose perceptual impairment was evident on such low-level visual tasks as segmenting overlapping figures.

A final possibility, which may interact with the previous one, concerns individual differences in imagery ability. Given that people differ in how fully they engage their early visual representations when generating mental images (Farah and Peronnet, 1989), some people's mental imagery ability may be more susceptible to early visual system damage than others. The same hypothetical lesion in visual association cortex might interfere with one person's imagery, whereas an individual whose imagery was confined to higher levels of association cortex might be unaffected.

To conclude, in most (but not all) cases of selective visual impairments following damage to the cortical visual system, patients manifest qualitatively similar impairments in mental imagery and perception. Spatial attention impairments for the left side of the visual scene also affect the left side of mental images. Central impairments of color perception tend to co-occur with impairments of color imagery. Higher order impairments of visual–spatial orientation sparing visual object recognition, and the converse, are associated with impairments of spatial imagery sparing imagery for object appearance, and the converse. Finally, hemianopia resulting from surgical removal of one occipital lobe is associated with a corresponding loss of half the mind's eye's visual field.

A case study in the relevance of neuroscience to cognitive science

The intractable nature of the imagery debate in the 1980s made it essential to find alternative sources of evidence on the issue. My own interest in cognitive neuroscience can be traced to the realization, as a graduate student in the early 1980s, that neuroimaging and lesion data were immune to the alternative explanations that plagued the cognitive psychology approach to the debate. I promptly shifted my thesis research from psychophysical studies of imagery–perception interaction to the neuropsychology of mental imagery, and went about surveying the literature on impairments of mental imagery. Bloodflow-based neuroimaging had yet to be harnessed for basic cognitive research in those days, but luckily I found the superb group of ERP researchers in Lyon with whom to collaborate. With the rough spatial localization and excellent temporal resolution of ERP, we were able to demonstrate a probable occipital locus for mental imagery. This conclusion found converging support from the concurrent studies of Goldenberg and others using SPECT, as well as later replications and extensions with PET and fMRI and the complementary contributions of patient-based research. By the 1990s, cognitive psychologists were moving on to other issues, and few persisted in arguing against the visual nature of mental images.

Let us take a closer look at the way in which the neuroimaging and lesion data were more decisive than the traditional data of cognitive psychology. A tacit knowledge account of the electrophysiological and bloodflow data, implicating the use of cortical visual areas during visual imagery activity, would need to include the following two assumptions: (a) that subjects know what parts of their brains are normally active during vision and (b) that subjects can voluntarily alter their brain electrical activity, or modulate or increase regional bloodflow to specific areas of their brains. It is clear that most subjects do not consciously know which brain areas are involved in vision, but what about the possibility of tacit knowledge? Tacit knowledge of the neural localization of visual processing would be impossible to acquire: Whereas one could conceive of mechanisms by which a subject might acquire tacit knowledge of many subtle functional properties of his or her visual system (by observing aftereffects, illusions, the relative difficulty of seeing different stimuli, etc.), there are no conceivable mechanisms by which a subject could gain tacit knowledge of the neuroanatomical locations of visual processing. The second assumption is also difficult to accept; whereas subjects can learn through biofeedback techniques to modulate EEG spectra, for example, untrained subjects cannot voluntarily change features of their EEG.

How would the tacit knowledge account explain functional parallels observed between perceptual and imaginal deficits after brain damage? As with normal subjects, the assumption would be made that the patients take their task to be behaving as if they were actually seeing the to-be-imagined stimuli. But this answer does not entirely constrain a prediction, because we do not know whether patients who know they have visual deficits would behave as if they were seeing with normal visual systems (i.e., using their tacit knowledge of normal vision) or with their defective visual systems (i.e., using their more recently acquired tacit knowledge of their impaired vision). An independent basis for deciding between these two predictions comes from studies of subjects who were peripherally (as opposed to cortically) blinded late in life. These subjects perform essentially normally on visual imagery tasks (Hollins, 1985). In terms of a tacit knowledge account of performance in imagery tasks, this implies that patients with visual deficits will interpret imagery tasks as demanding the simulation of intact visual processes. This leads to the prediction that patients with acquired visual disorders of cerebral origin should continue to perform normally in imagery experiments, a prediction which is clearly disproved by the available evidence.

Even if it is assumed that, unlike the patients with peripheral visual disorders, the patients with central visual disorders make the strategic decision to tailor their imagery task performance to match their own, defective, perceptual performance, several problems remain for the tacit knowledge account. First, whereas normal subjects in imagery tasks would be modulating subtle properties of their responses (such as response latency), to simulate visual processes patients would be feigning an inability to perform certain imagery tasks. It is somewhat implausible that patients would persist in failing easy tasks when they could be giving correct responses. Second, studies of malingering patients, who do intentionally perform poorly on neuropsychological tests, have shown that statistical naiveté leads them to perform significantly worse than chance (Lezak, 1983), which is not the case with the patients in the studies reviewed earlier. A final difficulty with the tacit knowledge account is specific to the findings on visual neglect in imagery: Many patients with visual neglect deny that they have any visual difficulty, and the two patients in Bisiach and Luzzatti's (1978) study were both unaware of their neglect. Nevertheless, and contrary to the tacit knowledge hypothesis, these patients demonstrated parallel deficits in their imagery performance.

Could experimenter expectancy have produced some or all of the neuropsychological evidence reviewed here? In the case of the observed parallels between perceptual and imaginal deficits this possibility certainly exists, but it is less likely than in the corresponding cognitive literature because of the wide range of investigators, whose work spans several decades before the imagery debate. Nonetheless, the effects of experimenter expectancy on this data cannot strictly be ruled out. In contrast, the EEG, ERP, and bloodflow findings represent psychophysiological measures that would be impossible to "shape" by the normal mechanisms of experimenter expectancy in psychological research. Unless the two assumptions needed for a tacit knowledge account of these findings are granted, namely, that subjects know where their visual processing areas are and have the ability to tailor their EEG, ERP, and bloodflow accordingly, there is no way that instructions given prior to the recording of EEG, ERP, or bloodflow could produce the results actually obtained in these studies. For most of the studies, communication from the experimenters during the recording sessions could not affect the results through a biofeedback mechanism either: In the ERP studies, for example, subjects were isolated from the experimenters during data collection.

9.6   Mental image generation

Generating a mental image can be thought of as, roughly speaking, running the process of perception backwards. In perception, retinotopically formatted representations activate a sequence of more central representations, culminating in relatively abstract and non-retinotopic inferotemporal and parietal representations. In imagery, the information about appearance and location in these latter representations is used to activate the earlier retinotopic representations, in a direction of information flow that cognitive psychologists call "top-down." Whether the image generation process can trigger activity all the way down into primary visual cortex remains controversial, but at least some evidence supports this idea directly (see figure 9.3).

An important difference between bottom-up perception and top-down image generation concerns the automaticity of the processes involved. One cannot see a familiar object and fail to recognize it. But we often think about familiar objects without inexorably calling to mind a visual mental image. This suggests that the activation of retinotopic cortical regions from memory requires the intervention of a separate, attention-demanding process, needed for imagery but not for visual perception and object recognition. This is the process of image generation.

Two issues about mental image generation have been the focus of research in cognitive neuroscience: The status of image generation as a separate component of the cognitive architecture, and hemispheric specialization for image generation.

A dedicated image generation process?

Not every cognitive ability is the product of a distinct mental process, dedicated just to that ability. A ludicrous example may help to make this point: We have the ability to name green objects, but there is no green-object-naming system. Although the ability to generate a mental image seems distinct from the most closely related abilities, visual perception, and recall of non-imaginal information, how can we determine whether there is a system or process specific for image generation? Neuropsychological dissociations are informative here.

An early review of the neurological literature on imagery impairments revealed a set of cases consistent with a selective impairment in image generation, in that perception and recall of non-imaginal information were grossly intact (Farah, 1984). In subsequent years, a small number of additional cases of selectively impaired imagery have been studied, with improved experimental control over the cognitive and perceptual processes of interest (e.g., Farah, Levine, and Calvanio, 1988; Goldenberg, 1992; Grossi, Orsini, and Modafferi, 1986; Riddoch, 1991). In addition, similar but weaker dissociations have been found in subgroups of patients in group studies of mental imagery (Bowers, Blonder, Feinberg, and Heilman, 1991; Goldenberg, 1989; Goldenberg and Artner, 1991; Stangalino, Semenza, and Mondini, 1995). On the face of things, the preservation of perceptual abilities in the context of impaired imagery is consistent with the existence of a distinct image generation process.

For example, in our study of case R.M., Farah *et al.* (1988) administered a sentence verification task developed by Eddy and Glass (1981). Half of the sentences required the use of visual imagery to verify (e.g., "A grapefruit is larger than a cantaloupe"), and half did not (e.g., "The US government functions under a two-party system"). Eddy and Glass had shown that normal subjects find the two sets of questions equally difficult (as did right-hemisphere damaged control subjects tested by Farah *et al.*), and that performance on the imagery questions was selectively impaired by visual interference, thus validating them as imagery questions. R.M. showed a selective deficit for imagery on this validated task: He performed virtually perfectly on the non-imagery questions, and performed significantly worse on the imagery questions.

R.M.'s object recognition and perceptual abilities were also tested, to rule out the possibility that his imagery impairment resulted from damage to structures shared by imagery and perception. R.M. was not agnosic, and passed a stringent test of object recognition designed to assess long-term visual memory of the same items he was asked to image. In this test, R.M. was asked to select the correct drawing of an object from a pair. For example, a fish was either the correct shape or peanut-shaped. He performed this test perfectly. The corresponding imagery test involved either drawing the same objects, or completing a drawing of objects (e.g., adding the feet to a duck) from memory. He was able to copy the correct drawings and completions. Nevertheless, he performed poorly at drawing from memory and refused to finish this portion of the task. Finally, R.M. was tested on imagery for the colors of objects, along with perception of color and long-term visual memory knowledge of the colors of objects. In the imagery condition, a black and white drawing of a characteristically-colored object (e.g., a cactus) was presented along with three colored pencils, and R.M. had to choose the correct pencil. To assess color perception and long-term memory for object colors, three colored versions of each drawing were presented and R.M. has to recognize which drawing was correctly colored. Although he did not perform perfectly on the color perception control condition, he did significantly better in this condition than in the imagery condition, with the same objects and colors.

The pattern of preserved and impaired abilities in R.M. is consistent with an impairment of mental image generation, in that he performs poorly when image generation is required, but performs normally in a similar task that is equally difficult but does not require imagery, and in tasks that test the ability to perceive and recognize the same items that could not be imagined. The existence of patients with selective impairments in image generation is consistent with the hypothesis that image generation is a distinct component in the cognitive architecture of the mind and brain.

Goldenberg (1992; Goldenberg and Artner, 1991) proposed an alternative interpretation of cases such as R.M., according to which they have a subtle impairment of long-term visual memory knowledge. He thus calls into question the neuropsychological support for a distinct image generation process. According to Goldenberg, there is a distinction between the kinds of visual knowledge required to recognize an object, which might include the object's global form, and the kinds of visual knowledge required to create a mental image of the object, which might include small details and surface properties such as color and texture. If the latter type of knowledge was impaired by brain damage, a patient could retain the ability to recognize objects while suffering an imagery impairment.

Support for Goldenberg's interpretation comes from two studies. The first was a group study by Goldenberg and Artner (1991) comparing left and right posterior cerebral artery stroke patients and non-brain-damaged control patients in a set of tasks requiring image generation and visual recognition memory for subtle features of objects' appearances. An example of an imagery question was to verify the sentence "The ears of a bear are rounded." An example of the corresponding visual memory item was a choice between a picture of a bear with rounded ears, and a picture of a bear with pointed ears. As predicted by Goldenberg and Artner on the basis of previous research (to be reviewed in the next section), the left PCA group performed worst on the imagery tasks. However, this group also performed worst on the visual memory tasks, and in fact their impairment relative to those of the other groups was statistically stronger in the visual memory condition. This suggested to Goldenberg and Artner that the depressed imagery scores of the left PCA patients were the result of subtly impaired long-term visual memory, rather than a mild image generation deficit. A single case study of a more severe imagery impairment by Goldenberg (1992) confirmed this general pattern. The patient K.Qu. complained spontaneously of an inability to visualize objects from memory, and performed poorly on a variety of imagery tests. Although he was not agnosic, he also performed poorly at visual memory discriminations of the kind developed by Goldenberg and Artner.

If Goldenberg's interpretation of imagery impairments is correct, then none of the previous cases of apparent image generation deficit really prove the existence of a distinct image generation process. The poor performance of his patients on subtle tests of visual memory would appear to implicate a visual memory deficit, rather than an image generation deficit. However, it is possible that the normal way people perform such subtle tests of visual memory is to generate an image of the depicted object in order to determine whether, for example, the bear with rounded ears or the bear with pointed ears is correct. When less subtle discriminations are required, as in the testing with R.M., as well as in some additional testing reported with K.Qu., there is a dissociation observed between imagery and visual memory recognition. For example, K.Qu. could correctly reject experimenter's copies of his own inaccurate drawings of objects from memory.

The difficulty of resolving this issue may go beyond the practical problem of creating visual discrimination tests that are equated with imagery tests for difficulty but free of contamination by imagery. Perhaps our tendency to generate images when trying to distinguish the correct appearance of stimuli should be viewed not as a source of contamination in recognition tests, but as a reflection of the interactive nature of normal perception and the coexistence of bottom-up and top-down perceptual processes. When we must perceive subtle differences between a visual stimulus and our memory of that stimulus, part and parcel of the perceptual process may be image generation. If so, we should not expect to be able to dissociate image generation and stringent tests of object recognition.

We thus arrive at a *rapprochement* between the view that image generation is a distinct component and the view that image generation is accomplished with the same visual representations and processes that are used in visual recognition. Imagery may not involve any processes that are not, at times, also involved in perception. However, perception is not always a passive, bottom-up process. Under certain circumstances perception may require an active top-down mechanism, which could be called attention or imagery. The identification of image generation with a form of attention is not a new idea (Neisser, 1976; Ryle, 1949). Indeed, when I compared the effects of passive perception, attention, and imagery on visual signal detection, I found that imagery and attention had similar effects, distinct from passive perception (Farah, 1989).

Hemispheric specialization for image generation

The localization of mental image generation has been a controversial topic, particularly the question of whether the left hemisphere is specialized for this process. Pop psychologists still refer to the right hemisphere as the seat of imagination, to be cultivated and cherished in our overly left-hemispheric world. The first researchers to test the right-hemisphere hypothesis were Ehrlichman and Barrett (1983), who surveyed the neuropsychology literature and pointed out that there was no direct evidence for this hypothesis.

In an early analysis of published case reports of mental imagery impairment, I distinguished among different components of imagery and noted a trend for left posterior damage when image generation was impaired (Farah, 1984). Closer scrutiny of these and additional cases led David Levine, Ron Calvanio, and myself to suggest that the left temporo-occipital area is critical (Farah *et al.*, 1988).

More recent reviews have considered the hypothesis of left-hemisphere specialization for mental image generation, and come to a range of different conclusions. Sergent and Corballis (1990) argued against the hypothesis of left hemisphere specialization for image generation, concluding that "in spite of recent claims that the left hemisphere is specialized for the generation of visual mental images, an examination of the relevant data and experimental procedures provides little support for this view, and suggests that both hemispheres simultaneously and conjointly contribute to this process" (p. 98). Her conclusions followed persuasively from her reading of the literature, although one could take issue with this reading at a number of points. For example, our case study of patient R.M., whose performance on tests of image generation, object recognition, and color perception were described in the previous section, was discounted on the grounds that his object recognition and color perception were not tested.

Tippett (1992) arrived at a less extreme conclusion, declaring that "what is striking in this area is the pervasiveness of findings (especially with brain-damaged patients) that seem to implicate the left hemisphere in the image generation process" (p. 429), and concluded that "support is found for the involvement of the left hemisphere, although many researchers claim that the posterior regions of both hemispheres contribute to image generation" (p. 415). Trojano and Grossi (1994) reviewed the case report literature on mental imagery defects with and without accompanying visual recognition impairments. Of the latter type of imagery defect, corresponding to the hypothesized image generation defect, they conclude that "mental imagery relies on dissociable processes which are localized in left hemisphere posterior areas" (p. 213).

Given that the available literature reviews come to a rather wide range of different conclusions, I will summarize the empirical findings themselves in the next three sections.

Image generation deficits in brain-damaged patients

If a patient has impaired imagery with grossly intact perception and recognition, the most straightforward interpretation is that they have lost the component of the mental imagery system not shared with perception, namely, image generation. The initial review of the case study literature showed a mixture of bilateral and dominant hemisphere damage in cases fitting the behavioral profile of loss of image generation (Farah, 1984), a pattern consistent with a left hemisphere critical lesion site. Although these cases were of variable quality from the point of view of anatomical precision and behavioral analysis, whatever inaccuracies might be present would be unlikely to bias the set towards implicating a left-hemisphere locus for image generation. Certainly no one at that point, least of all myself, had predicted left-hemisphere specialization for image generation. I had merely stumbled over an empirical trend in these early cases. This trend suggested the working hypothesis of left-hemisphere specialization, which I and others then tested with new data.

The more recently studied cases of image generation impairment have uniformly sustained damage to the left temporo-occipital region (Farah *et al.*, 1988; Goldenberg, 1992; Grossi *et al.*, 1986; Riddoch, 1990). Several group studies of mental imagery in brain-damaged patients have been reported, and some of them allow for inferences concerning the localization of mental image generation. Goldenberg (1989) tested 74 unilaterally brain-damaged patients on a variety of imagery tasks. No patient or patient group performed consistently poorly on all tests of image generation, suggesting that there were no cases of full-blown image generation deficit in the sample. There was one clear association between lesion and image generation task performance highlighted by Goldenberg. This was the association between left temporo-occipital lesions and the inability to benefit from imagery mnemonics in a verbal memory task. None of the four left temporo-occipital damaged patients tested benefited from instructions to use imagery, whereas the one right temporo-occipital damaged patient did benefit.

Goldenberg's later group study was specifically focused on patients with damage to the temporal and occipital areas (Goldenberg and Artner, 1991). As mentioned earlier in connection with this study, the patients with left-sided lesions showed the greatest imagery impairment.

Bowers, Blonder, Feinberg, and Heilman (1991) assessed imagery for objects and for facial expressions in unilaterally brain-damaged patients, and found that those with right hemisphere damage did worse answering facial expression imagery questions (e.g., "Imagine you are looking at the face of someone who is very frightened. Do the eyes look twinkly?"), whereas those with left hemisphere damage did worse answering object imagery questions (e.g. "Is the date on a penny towards the top or the bottom?"). Perception of facial expressions was also tested, and the right-hemisphere damaged group was also impaired on this task, implying that this group's imagery impairment was secondary to a loss of knowledge about facial expression, rather than a problem with image generation *per se*. Note that the subjects in this study had unilateral lesions anywhere within the hemisphere, and most were anterior and dorsal to the temporo-occipital region that other studies suggest is critical for image generation. One right-hemisphere damaged patient performed poorly on just the facial expression imagery task, which the authors interpreted as a loss of facial expression image generation ability. Two patients performed poorly on both types of imagery task and were normal at perception of facial expression, which the authors interpreted as a general loss of image generation ability, and both were left-hemisphere damaged.

Most recently, Stangalino, Semenza, and Modini (1995) reported the results of a large study of unilaterally brain-damaged patients, specifically designed to isolate and assess the image generation process *per se*. Using a variety of verbal and constructional tests of imagery, along with control tasks to evaluate non-imagery components of the imagery tasks, they tested 70 patients and identified 19 whose performance fit the profile of impaired image generation. Fifteen of these individuals had unilateral left-hemisphere lesions, affecting the posterior left hemisphere in all but one case. The remaining four subjects had right posterior lesions. This study provides another strong indication that the posterior left hemisphere plays a special role in image generation.

The evidence from brain-damaged patients suggests that when an impairment in image generation is found, the patient will likely have a posterior left hemisphere lesion. The reverse implication is not true: Lesions of the left temporo-occipital region (the most likely critical site within the left hemisphere) do not invariably result in obvious image generation impairments, although group studies have documented a reliable depression in the performance of image generation tasks with lesions in this region (Goldenberg, 1989; Goldenberg and Artner, 1991). This is consistent with a range of degrees of hemispheric specialization for image generation in the normal population, analogous to De Renzi's claim about hemispheric specialization for face recognition discussed in chapter 5 (De Renzi, Perani, Carlisimo, Silveri, and Fazio, 1994). For individuals at the extreme of specialization, a unilateral left hemisphere lesion will disrupt image generation ability. Other individuals may have more bilaterally represented image generation ability, such that a left hemisphere lesion will not entirely obliterate the ability.

Laterality experiments in normal subjects and split-brain patients

In the days before functional neuroimaging, laterality experiments provided the primary means of studying hemispheric specialization in the normal brain. Typically stimuli were projected briefly to one side or the other of visual fixation, resulting in the initial arrival of the stimulus representation in the contralateral hemisphere, with the ipsilateral hemisphere receiving the information only after callosal transmission. The time delay and presumed degradation associated with an additional synaptic transmission were assumed to put the contralateral hemisphere in a better position to process the stimulus than the ipsilateral hemisphere, and indeed many findings are consistent with this. Many language tasks, for example, are performed better when the stimulus is presented in the right visual field and is therefore received more directly by the left hemisphere. Another type of laterality manipulation is lateralized interference, whereby unilateral motor activity disrupts contralateral hemispheric processing more than ipsilateral. Whereas the effects of laterality manipulations in normal subjects are small and often frustratingly hard to replicate, the same manipulations yield huge effects in patients whose hemispheres have been surgically disconnected by cutting the corpus callosum. These so-called split-brain patients are epileptics whose disease could not be managed with medication alone, and therefore underwent this surgery to limit the spread of epileptic activity between the hemispheres. If one assumes that split-brain patients have normal hemispheres, and that their only abnormality is the callosotomy, then they seem to be an ideal subject population for answering questions about hemispheric specialization. Unfortunately, this is invariably a wrong assumption. They have a grave neurological disease, which generally begins in the childhood years during which hemispheric specialization is developing. Indeed, the variability of results from one split-brain patient to another (see Gazzaniga, 1983) is consistent with some degree of abnormal hemispheric specialization in this population. For this reason, we should generalize from any given split-brain patient to the normal population with extreme caution.

The earliest laterality experiment involving image generation was carried out by Cohen (1975) many years before hemispheric specialization for this process became a subject of controversy. Her task came from the classic work of Cooper and Shepard (1973) on the mental rotation of letters. When subjects must decide as quickly as possible whether a letter has been printed normally or mirror-reversed, and that letter is tilted, their average response times are directly proportional to the degree of tilt. This has been interpreted as evidence for a continuous, analog "mental rotation" process whereby the perceptual representation of the tilted letter is returned to the upright orientation in order to be judged normal or mirror-reversed. There is one condition under which subjects do not show the mental rotation response time pattern in this task: when they are cued in advance of the stimulus presentation with both the letter and the orientation. This is because they are able to generate an image of the normal letter at that orientation in advance, which can then be compared directly to the stimulus when it appears. Cohen's innovation was to present the stimuli to the left and right of fixation, enabling her to infer which hemisphere was superior at image rotation (with no advance cue) and which hemisphere was superior at image generation (with the advance cue). She remarked that the result of the image generation condition was a surprising one, specifically, that the left hemisphere seemed better able to generate and use the mental image for performing the task.

In subsequent years a number of experiments have been carried out testing hemispheric specialization for image generation using lateralized stimulus presentations with normal subjects. Readers who would like a detailed accounting of the individual experiments and their findings can find this in my 1995 review article. I believe it is fair to summarize the literature by saying that some experiments support left hemisphere superiority, some support right, and some find no hemispheric differences, although the left hemisphere findings have a slight edge in numbers when fully detailed images are required.

Laterality experiments using more novel methods have also been applied to the issue of mental image generation. For example, Lempert (1987, 1989) measured interference with hand-tapping. Her subjects listened to sentences while tapping as quickly as possible with either the left or the right hand. In two experiments the use of imagery was manipulated by instructions to image the sentence or simply rehearse it silently, and in another by the nature of the sentences (e.g. "The giant chased the jogger" evokes imagery, whereas "The mood suited the moment" does not). Imagery use was validated by better recall for imaged than non-imaged sentences. With the exception of the male subjects in one experiment, who also did not show a recall advantage with imagery, the imagery conditions in all three experiments were associated with greater right- than left-handed tapping decrement, borderline significant in one experiment and significant in two, implicating left-hemisphere dominance in the imagery conditions.

Shuren, Greer, and Heilman (1996) asked 50 right-handed subjects to generate an image of just half of an object and then to report which half they imaged. Subjects were more likely to image an object's right half, and this tendency was strongest in subjects who were most strongly right-handed (and hence presumably have the most extreme hemispheric specialization). They reasoned that, because the right hemispace is represented by the left hemisphere, this result is consistent with left hemisphere specialization for image generation.

Four split-brain subjects have been studied with image generation tasks. In a preliminary study of case J.W., Farah, Gazzaniga, Holtzman, and Kosslyn (1985) assessed the ability of J.W.'s two hemispheres to perform a simple image generation task and control tasks designed to require all of the same processing components except for image generation. The task was to decide whether the lower-case version of an upper-case letter extended above or below the line (e.g., "b," "y") or did not (e.g., "r"). The control tasks were to find the correct lower-case form in a visual array when shown an upper-case letter, and to make the extending/non-extending decision about visually presented lower-case forms. Whereas both hemispheres performed the control tasks well, only the left hemisphere could perform the imagery task; the right hemisphere performed at chance. A subsequent study by Kosslyn, Holtzman, Farah, and Gazzaniga (1985) found the same pattern of performance with J.W. in a task in which lower-case letters were the cue and upper-case letters had to be classified on the basis of whether they contained any curved line segments (e.g., "S", "B") or did not (e.g., "N"). In addition, J.W. was tested on three other imagery tasks: Deciding whether animals' ears protruded above the top of the head or did not, deciding whether an object was larger or smaller than a goat, and deciding whether an object was taller than it was wide or wider than it was tall. The "ears" task was performed well by J.W.'s left hemisphere and poorly by his right; the other two tasks were performed well by both hemispheres. The authors pointed out that the taller/wider and size comparison tasks could be performed without fully detailed images.

Kosslyn *et al.* (1985) also tested case V.P. on the straight versus curved letter task, and initially found the same pattern of performance with her as with J.W. After experience with the task, however, she began to perform well when stimuli were projected to her right hemisphere. (J.W.'s pattern of performance was stable until he was induced to imagine *writing* the letters, at which point right-hemisphere trials were also performed well.) Kosslyn *et al.* cautioned that results from V.P. should not be generalized to the normal brain, as this subject can also access speech from the right hemisphere.

Corballis and Sergent (1988) tested case L.B. on image generation and as well as mental rotation tasks. In the straight versus curved letter task, both hemispheres performed above chance, with the left hemisphere performing more accurately though more slowly. In a second task of image generation involving visualizing a clock face and judging the angle formed by the hands for a given digitally presented time, the right hemisphere performed at chance whereas the left was correct two-thirds of the time. In a follow-up study of L.B.'s performance of the letter imagery task, Sergent and Corballis (1990) found equal performance for L.B.'s two hemispheres.

Finally, a patient with an apparent stroke affecting the posterior half of the corpus callosum was tested by Blanc-Garin, Faure, and Sabio (1993) on the letter imagery task and on a size comparison task similar to those of Kosslyn *et al.*'s (1985) split-brain study. Initially, there was an absolute superiority of the left hemisphere for the letter imagery task and for the size comparsion task, with the right hemisphere performing at chance. However, as with case V.P., experience led to an improvement on right-hemisphere trials, although the left remained relatively better. With the size comparison task, a similar pattern emerged, although the hemispheres performed equivalently when the to-be-imaged object was presented pictorially.

The findings from split-brain patients are variable, and not generally stable over time for a given patient. In all cases so far tested, there has been an initial left hemisphere superiority for image generation. However, the left hemisphere advantage may diminish or even disappear with task experience, depending upon the patient and task.

Localizing image generation with functional imaging

A more direct way of studying hemispheric specialization in normal subjects is with electrical and hemodynamic measures of regional brain activity. In this section we will revisit the functional neuroimaging studies reviewed earlier, specifically those which contrast an image generation task with a suitable control task. A more comprehensive review of asymmetries in neuroimaging studies of mental imagery can be found in Farah (1995).

Beginning as before with SPECT, several of the studies by Goldenberg and his colleagues have designs that make them useful for localizing the process of image generation. For example, in the study described earlier comparing questions that require imagery to answer and questions that do not, there was a significant focus of activity in the left inferior occipital-temporal region associated with image generation. In most of the studies by this group cited earlier there was either significant activation of this area (Goldenberg *et al.*, 1989, 1991, 1992) or activation that was, in the authors' words, "salient" in some subjects, but too variable from subject to subject to reach significance (Goldenberg *et al.*, 1987, 1991).

Turning to the ERP studies, the most relevant design is that of Farah *et al.* (1989), who compared brain activity while subjects either viewed or listened to words, and while subjects viewed or listened to words and then generated images of them. There was a significant asymmetry favoring the left hemisphere recorded over the temporo-occipital regions of the scalp.

Among PET studies, two of Kosslyn *et al.*'s (1993) experiments involve what they describe as generating images from long-term visual memory as opposed to what they term "attentional imagery." Although one of these experiments was aimed at comparing activation patterns for large and small images, and thus did not include a no-imagery baseline to allow inferences about image generation *per se*, Experiment 2 showed greater activity in left temporal and occipital association areas. Our own recent fMRI study of imagery, comparing image generation cued by auditory words to passive hearing of auditory words (D'Esposito *et al.*, 1997) also found a significant left temporo-occipital focus.

Conclusions about hemispheric specialization

The foregoing data do not fit well with the hypothesis that image generation is a perfectly bilateral function of the brain, let alone a unilateral right hemisphere function. But neither do they support the hypothesis of complete and extreme left hemisphere specialization, analogous to the nature of hemispheric specialization for speech. Indeed, if most of us were exclusively left-lateralized for image generation, one would expect virtually all patients with damage to the left temporo-occipital region to have image generation deficits. As Goldenberg and Artner (1991) showed, left posterior cerebral artery strokes do in general depress imagery performance, but there were apparently no striking cases of loss of imagery among their group of 19 such subjects, and Stangalino *et al.* (1995) found that only some of their left posterior-damaged subjects displayed clear-cut image generation deficits.

The most promising hypothesis is that the left hemisphere is specialized for image generation in the sense analogous to right-hemisphere specialization for face perception. Consider what is known of hemispheric specialization for face perception. Face perception appears to be more efficiently carried out by the right hemisphere, as measured by lateralized studies in normal subjects and split-brain patients (e.g., Geffen, Bradshaw, and Wallace, 1971; Levy, Trevarthan, and Sperry, 1972), although depending upon task and stimulus variables this pattern can be reversed (Sergent, 1982). Imaging studies have shown a preponderance of right-sided visual system activity during face perception (e.g. Horwitz, Grady, Haxby, Shapiro, Rapaport, Ungerleider, and Mishkin, 1992; Sergent, Ohta, and MacDonald, 1992), although some have not (e.g., Grusser and Landis, 1991). Unilaterally damaged patients who lose the ability to recognize faces invariably have right hemisphere lesions, but most cases have bilateral damage (Farah, 1990). These observations are all consistent with the hypothesis of DeRenzi and colleagues (De Renzi, *et al.*, 1994), discussed in chapter 5, that the right hemisphere is specialized for face recognition, but the degree of specialization varies within the population, with most individuals having some capability for face recognition within the left hemisphere. A similar hypothesis, with hemispheres reversed, seems to be appropriate here: The left hemisphere plays the dominant role in image generation for most people, and in the most extremely lateralized individuals it plays the exclusive role in image generation, such that unilateral left hemisphere damage can abolish image generation ability in these individuals.

chapter ten

Visual Awareness

10.1 Conscious awareness as a topic for empirical research

I suspect that most people who enter the field of cognitive neuroscience are motivated by the mind–body problem. We want to know how conscious mind can emerge from matter. Of course, this is not exactly a question ready to be translated into an experimental design, and so most of us end up carving out a research program that relates some aspect of cognition to some aspect of brain function, but leaves the most quintessentially mental phenomenon of consciousness out of the equation. In recent years, however, an increasing number of researchers have included consciousness among the aspects of cognition they study. Much of this work concerns consciousness of visual perception, also called visual awareness. In the final chapter of this book, I will review what we currently know about the neural basis of visual awareness.

Research on visual awareness has been made possible by the occurrence of dissociations in some brain-damaged patients between vision and awareness of vision. Evidence of preserved visual perception with impaired visual awareness has now been documented in six different syndromes, in which at least some patients seem to perceive much more than they are aware of. For anyone interested in studying empirically the mechanisms of awareness, this pattern of dissociation is a dream come true: By comparing the brain function of a person with intact vision but impaired visual awareness to the brain function of a normal person, with intact vision and intact visual awareness, we should be able to isolate the neural mechanisms of awareness *per se*.

Patients with ostensibly good perception and impaired awareness allow us, in effect, to use a subtraction method to identify brain mechanisms of awareness: Brain-function-of-normal-people minus brain-function-of-people-missing-awareness equals brain-mechanisms-of-awareness. There is no doubt that this is an ambitious undertaking. But is it also a foolish undertaking, or does it at least make sense in principle?

If by "consciousness" or "awareness" of visual information we mean something like "having the information accessible to control systems, verbal output, and so forth" then I assume no one would object. In this sense, robots can be visually aware, and there are no deep problems associated with identifying the programs or wiring pattern that enables the robot to be aware in this sense. But there is something about the idea of conscious awareness that most of us would not attribute to robots, at least current-day robots, which has sometimes been described in terms of "qualia" (Block, 1980), "p-consciousness" for phenomenal consciousness (Block, 1992), or "what it feels like" to be a bat or a person (Nagel, 1974). Philosophers are divided on whether it makes sense to identify this sense of consciousness with physical brain mechanisms. I tend to find whoever I am reading on the subject persuasive, and so until I come to a better understanding of the issue I will err on the side of conservatism in the following way: I will speak of the neural correlates of awareness, reserving judgment about whether they are correlated with but distinct from awareness or whether they actually just *are* awareness at a neural level, in the way that mean kinetic energy just *is* temperature on a molecular scale (see Churchland, 1998).

The theoretical claims about visual awareness and the brain are at least as numerous as the empirical phenomena they are meant to explain. Therefore, I will begin by laying out a general framework for theorizing about the neural correlates of visual awareness, within which the different claims can be grouped into general categories and related to one another. I will then review representative findings in each of the six syndromes, and their theoretical interpretations *vis-à-vis* the neural correlates of visual awareness. In the final section I will attempt an integration across the six syndromes, with the goal of generalizing about vision, awareness, and the brain.

10.2   Neural correlates of conscious awareness: types of accounts

Claims about conscious awareness in neuroscience are claims about the aspects of brain function that correlate with conscious awareness. I have grouped the different claims concerning the relevant aspects of brain function into three categories (Farah, 1994). Like almost any attempt to reduce many things to a few things, this system of categories does not do perfect justice to all of the relevant claims. Nevertheless, it does bring out some fundamental similarities and differences among the claims, which I believe are just as important as the details of each, though less often discussed.

Consciousness as the privileged role of particular brain systems

The most straightforward account of the relation between consciousness and the brain is to conceive of particular brain systems as mediating conscious awareness. The great grandfather of this type of account is Descartes' theory of mind–body interaction through the pineal gland. Patterns of brain activity impinging on the pineal gland, unlike patterns of activity in other parts of the brain, were consciously experienced. The most direct and influential descendant of this tradition is the DICE model of Schacter, McAndrews, and Moscovitch (1988), shown in figure 10.1. Although Schacter *et al.* do not propose a localization for the Conscious Awareness System (CAS), the account does suppose that there is some brain system or systems, the CAS, separate from the brain systems concerned with perception, cognition, and action, whose activity is necessary only for conscious experience. Within this framework, vision without awareness can be explained very simply in terms of a disconnection between visual systems and the CAS.

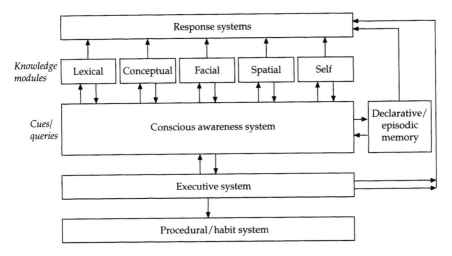

Figure 10.1   The DICE model of brain systems underlying perception, memory, and conscious awareness.

From D. L. Schacter et al., "Access to consciousness: dissociations between implicit and explicit knowledge in neuropsychological syndromes," in L. Weiskrantz (ed.), Thought without Language, Oxford, Oxford University Press, 1988.

The brain systems that play a privileged role in mediating conscious awareness could also carry out other functions as well. For example, Gazzaniga (1988) attributes many of the differences between what one would call conscious and unconscious behavior to the involvement of left-hemisphere interpretive mechanisms, closely related to speech. Thus, unconscious perception could be explained as the failure of a perceptual representation to access critical areas of the left hemisphere. For brevity, this first class of accounts will be referred to as *privileged role* accounts, because according to them, only certain systems play a role in mediating conscious awareness.

Consciousness as a state of integration among distinct brain systems

In contrast to the first type of approach, the next two types attempt to explain the relations between conscious and unconscious information processing in terms of the dynamic states of brain systems, rather than in terms of the enduring roles of particular brain systems themselves. Kinsbourne's (1988) "integrated field theory" is a good example of an approach that emphasizes integration as the underlying basis of conscious awareness. According to Kinsbourne, conscious awareness is a brain state in which the various modality-specific perceptions, recollections, current actions, and action plans are mutually consistent. Normally, the interactions among these disparate brain systems automatically bring the ensemble into an integrated state, continually updated to reflect the current information available in all parts of the brain. However, anatomical disconnection can prevent integration, as in split-brain patients who may have two separate awarenesses, or damage to one system may weaken its influence on the global brain state, thus preventing it from updating the contents of awareness, as when neglect patients are unaware of stimuli in the neglected hemifield. Thus, vision without awareness can be explained either by disconnection of or damage to the visual system, preventing it from participating in the integrated patterns of activity over the rest of the brain.

Related accounts have been proposed by Crick and Koch (1990) and by Damasio (1990). Crick and Koch specifically focus on the issue of visual awareness, and equate the phenomenon of visual awareness with the binding together of the different, separately represented visual properties of a stimulus (e.g., color, shape, depth, motion) into a single integrated percept. They draw heavily on the ideas of Singer and colleagues (e.g., Singer and Gray, 1995), discussed in chapter 2, concerning synchronized oscillations in visual cortex. According to Crick and Koch, synchronization across visual areas could enable both binding and conscious awareness of stimuli. Damasio has proposed a similar identification of binding with conscious awareness, within and beyond the visual system. The type of binding he discusses operates across different modality-specific representations of an object as well as within each modality-specific system, and is mediated by specific brain areas that he calls "convergence zones." In the remainder of the chapter, accounts of this second type will be referred to as *integration* accounts.

Consciousness as a graded property of neural information processing

Information representation in neural networks is not "all or none," such that a stimulus must either be represented within the visual system or not. Rather, it may be partially represented, as a result of either impoverished input or damage to the network itself. The third view of the relation between brain mechanisms and conscious awareness is based on the observation that, in normal and in brain-damaged subjects, there is a correlation between the "quality" of the perceptual representation and the likelihood of conscious awareness. Experiments on subliminal perception in normal subjects invariably dissociate perception and awareness by using very brief, masked stimulus presentations, by dividing attention, or by embedding the stimulus to be perceived in a high level of noise. In other words, to reduce the likelihood of conscious awareness in normal subjects, one must use experimental manipulations known to degrade the quality of the perceptual representation. Similarly, one could argue that in many if not all of the neuropsychological syndromes in which visual perception has been dissociated from conscious awareness, patients' visual performance reflects a degree of impairment in visual perception *per se*, not merely the stripping away of conscious experience from a normal percept (e.g., Farah, Monheit, and Wallace, 1991; Farah, O'Reilly, and Vecera, 1993). Consciousness may be associated only with the higher-quality end of the continuum of degrees of representation. This type of account will hereafter be referred to as a *quality of representation* account.

It is worth noting that these different types of explanation are not necessarily mutually exclusive. For example, if specific "convergence zones" were needed to enable the activity of widespread regions to become integrated, then there would be a sense in which the first type of explanation and the second were both correct. Alternatively, if a representation in one part of the brain were degraded, it would be less able to participate in an integrated state with other parts of the brain, in which case both the second and third types of explanation would be correct. Nevertheless, many of the explanations to be reviewed in the remainder of this chapter were intended to exemplify one of these categories, and the proposed three-category framework helps make clear the relations among the different explanations to be considered, even in the hybrid cases just mentioned.

10.3   Blindsight

Patients with damage to primary visual cortex may show a surprising degree of preserved perception for stimuli presented in regions of the visual field formerly represented by the damaged cortex. The first documentation of this phenomenon was made by Poppel, Held, and Frost (1973), who found that patients with large scotomata could move their eyes to the location of a light flash presented in the scotomatous region of their visual field. Although the eye movements were not highly accurate, they were more accurate than would be expected by chance, and perhaps most remarkable, were not accompanied by any conscious visual experience according to patients' reports.

Representative findings

Shortly after Poppel *et al.*'s initial report, Weiskrantz and his colleagues undertook extensive and rigorous investigations of vision in hemianopic fields, which they termed "blindsight" (e.g., Weiskrantz, Warrington, Sanders, and Marshall, 1974; Weiskrantz, 1986). They were able to demonstrate a much greater degree of preserved visual function in some of their subjects than in Poppel *et al.*'s initial series. Case D.B., in particular, was the subject of many investigations in which the abilities to point to stimulus locations, to detect movement, to discriminate the orientation of lines and gratings, and to discriminate shapes such as *X*s and *O*s were found to be remarkably preserved.

Over subsequent years, a number of different patients with blindsight have been studied in different laboratories (see Stoerig and Cowey, 1997, for a review). The pattern of preserved and impaired abilities has been found to vary considerably from case to case. Detection and localization of light, and detection of motion are invariably preserved to some degree. In addition, many patients can discriminate orientation, shape, direction of movement, and flicker. Color vision mechanisms also appear to be preserved in some cases (Brent, Kennard, and Ruddock, 1994).

In addition to explicit tests of visual abilities, such as multiple choice questions about the "unseen" stimulus, a wealth of additional information about blindsight comes from indirect measures of the visual capabilities in the blind field. For example, Marzi, Tassinari, Aglioti, and Lutzemberger (1986) showed that subjects with blindsight, like normal subjects, respond more quickly in a simple reaction time task when there are two stimuli instead of one, and that this is true even when the second stimulus falls in the blind field. This is an indirect test because the subject is not asked to judge the presence of a stimulus in the blind field. Rafal, Smith, Krantz, Cohen, and Brennan (1990) studied the effects of a second stimulus in the blind field on the speed with which hemianopic subjects could make a saccade to a stimulus in their normal field. With their task, a second stimulus was found to inhibit the saccade. Like the facilitation of manual reaction time found by Marzi *et al.*, this inhibition shows that the stimulus was perceived, in that it influenced performance. Significantly, Rafal *et al.* found this effect only when the second stimulus was presented to the temporal half of the retina, that is, to the half of the retina that projects to the superior colliculus. The projections from the retina to the cortical visual system are symmetrical, with equal connectivity between each hemiretina and the LGN.

Marcel (1998) used an indirect method to demonstrate the most spectacular blindsight capability of all in two patients he tested, namely word reading. Words such as "money" or "river," presented in the patients' blind hemifields, were said to bias their interpretation of subsequently presented ambiguous words, such as "bank."

Blindsight is the one instance of a perception–awareness dissociation that has been studied with animal models as well as with human patients. Although most of the animal research has been aimed at documenting preserved performance in different visual tasks after striate cortical removal, one recent study tackles the question of awareness *per se* after such surgery. Cowey and Stoerig (1997) taught monkeys to perform tasks that were as close as possible to stating what they saw, without verbalization. The tasks were to report the number of stimuli they perceived, or the presence versus absence of a single stimulus, by different manual responses. After unilateral removal of primary visual cortex, these monkeys retained the ability to reach for stimuli in the affected hemifield, thus demonstrating preserved vision. However, the monkeys responded in the number and detection tasks as if stimuli presented in the affected hemifield were not present, in effect reporting that they did not see such stimuli.

Awareness of perception

Just as the particular set of visual abilities, and level of performance, varies from patient to patient, so does the nature of patients' subjective report. Some subjects claim to be guessing on the basis of no sense whatsoever. In other studies, patients report some "feeling" that guides their responses, but the feeling is not described as specifically visual in nature. For example, patients will state that they felt the onset of a stimulus, or felt it to be in a certain location. Shape discriminations between circles and crosses are made on the basis of "jagged" versus "smooth" feelings, which are nevertheless not subjectively visual. Some subjects may occasionally report specifically visual sensations, such as "dark shadows," particularly for very intense or salient stimuli.

Explanations of blindsight

The mechanism of blindsight has been a controversial topic. Some researchers have argued that the phenomenon is mediated, directly or indirectly, by residual functioning of primary visual cortex, and should therefore be considered an artifact. Even for researchers who reject the artifact explanation, the mechanism of blindsight has not been settled decisively, and there remain at least two different types of account.

The idea that blindsight is not truly vision in the absence of striate cortex, but is rather vision mediated by remaining striate cortex, has been proposed in various forms. Campion, Latto, and Smith (1983) alleged that striate cortex is involved either indirectly, by light from the scotomatous region of the visual field reflecting off other surfaces into regions of the visual field represented by intact primary visual cortex, or directly, by residual functioning of lesioned areas of primary visual cortex. The latter idea is an example of a quality of representation account. Fendrich, Wessinger, and Gazzaniga (1992) have also argued that preserved islands of striate cortex, which could escape detection by normal methods of measuring scotomata, enable blindsight performance. These accounts are plausible in general outline, but fail to account for psychophysical and neuroimaging data from a variety of different labs. As an example of the problematic psychophysical data, it is difficult to see how scattered light would enable case D.B. to perceive black figures on a bright background, nor how this account could explain the qualitative differences in his performance within his natural blindspot and his aquired blind region. Residual functioning of spared cortex is clearly not a possibility for hemidecorticate subjects, and yet they, too, show a wide range of blindsight abilities. In addition, neuroimaging methods have been used to test for activity in primary visual cortex during visual stimulation in individuals with blindsight, and have failed to detect any (Barbur, Watson, Frackowiak, and Zeki, 1993; Stoerig, Kleinschmidt, and Frahm, 1998). Finally, recall the results of Rafal *et al.* (1990) on inhibition of saccades by stimuli presented to the blind field. This result has the important property of demonstrating subcortical mediation of blindsight by a positive finding, namely nasal-temporal asymmetries, rather than by the always ambiguous null result concerning primary visual cortex involvement.

If blindsight is not mediated by primary visual cortex, then what neural systems are involved? Initially, the answer was thought to be the subcortical visual system, discussed in chapter 1, consisting of projections from the retina to the superior colliculus, and on to the pulvinar and cortical visual areas. This is an instance of a privileged role account, in that both cortical and subcortical visual systems are hypothesized to mediate various types of visual information processing, but the mediation of visual awareness is taken to be the privileged role of the cortical visual system. There is evidence in favor of the subcortical mediation hypothesis for at least some blindsight abilities. The close functional similarities between the known specializations of the subcortical visual system and many of the preserved abilities in blindsight, such as detection and localization of onsets and moving stimuli (e.g., Schiller and Koerner, 1971), constitutes one source of evidence. In addition, the nasal-temporal asymmetries found in Rafal *et al.*'s (1990) study are indicative of the collicular mediation.

Cowey and Stoerig (1989) have suggested that the cortical visual system, too, mediates blindsight. They marshalled evidence, from their own experiments and other research, of a population of cells in the LGN that project directly to extrastriate visual cortex, and which could therefore bring stimulus information into such areas as V4 and MT in the absence of primary visual cortex. This type of mechanism fits most naturally with the quality of representation hypotheses. According to this account, many of the same visual association areas are engaged in blindsight as in normal vision. What distinguishes normal vision and visual performance without awareness is that in the latter only a subset of the normal inputs arrive in extrastriate visual cortex. The remaining inputs are both fewer in number, and lacking whatever type of processing is normally accomplished in primary visual cortex. Consciousness awareness may only occur when these areas are operating on more complete and more fully processed visual representations.

Evidence for this hypothesis is still preliminary. In addition to the demonstration of anatomical connections between the LGN and the extrastriate visual areas, their functional significance in blindsight is hinted at by a comparison between the blindsight abilities of patients with circumscribed striate lesions and with damage to visual association areas as well. The latter group is made up of patients who have undergone hemidecortication, the removal of an entire hemisphere. Stoerig and Cowey (1997) review the findings from a number of studies that are reasonably consistent with the generalization that the ability to make explicit judgments of properties such as motion and color depends on intact visual association cortex.

In sum, blindsight is not the result of degraded normal vision, if "normal" is taken to mean relying on primary visual cortex. It is also clearly not a single homogeneous phenomenon: At the level of preserved visual abilities, subjective experience, and neural mechanisms, there is apparently much variation from subject to subject. An important research goal in this area is to establish correspondences among these three levels of individual difference, as a means of characterizing the functional and experiential roles of different components of the visual system. In the meantime, we can discern two main types of mechanism that may account for the dissociations between visual abilities and conscious awareness in blindsight: Subcortical visual mechanisms, and direct projections from the LGN to extrastriate areas.

10.4 Preserved vision for action in apperceptive agnosia

Recall from chapter 2 that patients with apperceptive agnosia have a profound impairment in shape perception, failing to discriminate squares from circles or Xs from Os, despite good perception of local visual qualities such as brightness and color. In one such patient, researchers have documented a surprising degree of preserved vision when the response involves acting upon an object rather than making a conscious judgment about it.

Representative findings

Patient D.F. is in many ways a typical apperceptive agnosic. Indeed, like the young soldier described in chapter 2, D.F. also suffered carbon monoxide poisoning while in the shower. The earliest clue that D.F. had some degree of preserved form processing came from observations of her reaching behavior. Whereas she could not accurately describe or compare the sizes, shapes, and orientations of objects, her motoric interactions with the world seemed normal, including shaping her hand to the proper grip size while reaching to grasp a door knob or a pencil. Milner, Goodale, and colleagues (Milner, Perrett, Johnston, Benson, Jordan, Heeley, Bettucci, Mortara, Mutani, Terazzi, and Davidson, 1991; Goodale, Milner, Jakobson, and Carey, 1991; Milner and Goodale, 1995) formalized this observation in a series of ingenious tests, for example comparing D.F.'s hand motions when asked to put a card through a slot, with the slot at different orientations, and when asked to describe the angle of the slot or to turn a second slot to match the angle of the first. Figure 10.2 shows the difference in accuracy between the two ways of accessing her perception of orientation, by conscious judgment or matching, and by action. The former is variable and inaccurate; the latter flawless.

An interesting boundary condition on this dissociation was demonstrated by Goodale, Jakobson, Milner, Perrett, Benson, and Heitanen (1994), who repeated the slot experiment with a T-shaped opening. D.F. was unable to insert T-shaped blocks into the opening, suggesting that the preserved vision for action does not extend to full-blown shape perception.

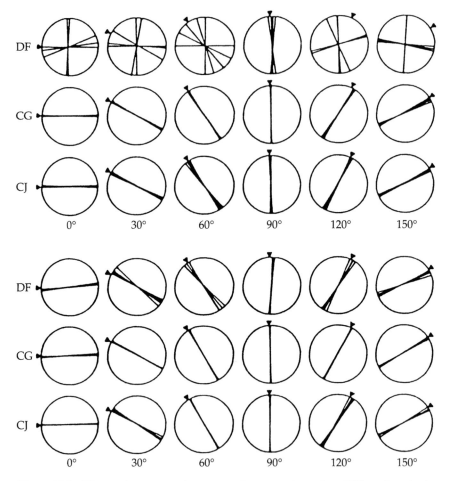

Figure 10.2   The performance of apperceptive agnosic patient D.F. and control subjects at explicit judgments of slot orientation (top) and at manipulating a card to fit through slots of the same orientations (bottom), demonstrating preserved orientation perception for the guidance of action.
From M. A. Goodale and D. A. Milner, "Separate visual pathways for perception and action," Trends in Neurosciences, *15(1), 1992, with permission from Elsevier Science.*

Awareness of perception

The researchers studying D.F. have not included much in their written reports concerning D.F.'s subjective visual experiences. The most pertinent statement I can find is from Milner (1997) to the effect that

"D.F. has no explicit knowledge (i.e., awareness) of the shapes and sizes that she is able to grasp" (p. 1252).

Explanation of implicit shape perception

Milner and Goodale propose an anatomical disconnection between early visual representation and higher level representations of object appearance in the ventral stream, discussed in chapter 2. This is responsible for D.F.'s failure on explicit judgments of shape, size, and orientation, but allows the dorsal visual stream to compute at least some of these properties for purposes of action programming. Although the diffuse nature of damage from carbon monoxide makes anatomical claims inherently uncertain in cases like this, an MRI showed the greatest damage in this case to ventral visual association cortex, consistent with Milner and Goodale's claim. This explanation is an example of a privileged role account, because both dorsal and ventral streams are hypothesized to be capable of representing size and orientation, but only the ventral representations support conscious awareness of those characteristics.

10.5 Implicit object recognition in associative visual agnosia

To review the criteria for associative agnosia discussed in chapter 4, object recognition is impaired despite adequate elementary perceptual abilities and general intellectual functioning. Higher level perception of objects may appear to be preserved as well, although more careful testing reveals characteristic problems in representing complex shape, and this presumably underlies the object recognition impairment. In a small number of cases of associative visual agnosia, patients have been shown to retain some implicit recognition of objects which, by standard testing methods, they cannot recognize.

Representative findings

The earliest observation of implicit object recognition in associative agnosia was reported by Taylor and Warrington (1971), who noted

Figure 10.3   A picture association task on which an associative agnosic performed moderately well, despite her inability to assess her own recognition of the object to be associated.
From M. J. Farah and T. E. Feinberg, "Perception and Awareness," in T. E. Feinberg and M. J. Farah (eds), Behavioral Neurology and Neuropsychology, *New York, McGraw-Hill, 1997.*

that a severely agnosic patient was able to turn misoriented pictures to their upright orientation, despite being unable to recognize them, and to sort unrecognized pictures into semantic categories. Todd Feinberg and colleagues carried out a detailed examination of a similar patient (Feinberg, Dyckes-Berke, Miner, and Roane, 1995). Despite a severe impairment in naming, describing, or pantomiming the use of visually presented objects, their patient performed well above chance in multiple choice tests such as the one shown in figure 10.3. The patient's task was to look first at the top picture, then find the picture most related to it in the bottom row. The number of choices was varied, which influenced the difficulty of the task. Feinberg and colleagues also asked the patient both to assess her knowledge of the top picture before choosing a picture from the bottom row, and to assess her accuracy after having chosen. The two judgments provide direct measures of her awareness of perception, and will therefore be discussed in the following section. Of interest here is that despite her profound agnosia, when the choice set was limited to a relatively small number of pictures the patient performed above chance, and furthermore, the smaller the choice set the better the performance.

Awareness of perception

Like all associative visual agnosics, this patient denied recognizing most stimuli; consistent with this, her assessment of her recognition, prior to performing the multiple choice task, was a poor predictor of her accuracy. In other words, she was unaware of her perception. In contrast, once she had chosen a picture in the multiple choice task, she had some basis for assessing her accuracy. Even on trials for which she had rated herself as entirely unable to recognize the picture at the outset, once she had made a choice she was able to assess its accuracy to some degree, stating she was sure of her response on almost 80 percent of the trials on which she was correct compared to only 25 percent of the trials in which she was not.

Explanation of implicit object recognition

Feinberg and colleagues argue that the patient's reasonably good awareness of her accuracy is not consistent with two separate systems, one for awareness and one for recognition, as hypothesized in the DICE model, for example. They point to several aspects of the case that favor the hypothesis of degraded object representations, underlying both recognition and awareness: the above-chance performance with multiple choices, the dependence of the multiple choice performance on the number of choices, and the correlation between the patient's judgments of her own knowledge and of her performance with her performance accuracy. The idea that degraded object representations can support performance and self-assessment of accuracy in sufficiently constrained tasks, but can support neither in open-ended tasks, is an example of a quality of representation account.

10.6 Covert recognition of faces in prosopagnosia

The evidence reviewed in chapter 5 suggests that prosopagnosia is a distinct disorder from object agnosia, in which face recognition is disproportionately impaired. In some cases of prosopagnosia there is a dramatic dissociation between the loss of face recognition ability as measured by standard tests of face recognition and patients' own introspections, and the apparent preservation of face recognition when tested by certain indirect tests.

Representative findings

The literature on covert recognition in prosopagnosia is large, dating back to the early 1980s and involving researchers from a number of different labs who were quickly drawn in by this remarkable phenomenon. Only a small sample of the relevant findings can be summarized here. One of the most widely used methods of demonstrating preserved face recognition in prosopagnosia is by the paired-associate face–name relearning task, in which patients are taught to associate the facial photographs of famous people with the names of famous people. For some prosopagnosics, fewer learning trials are required when the pairing of names and faces is correct than when incorrect (e.g., Robert Redford's face with the name "Harrison Ford"). De Haan, Young, and Newcombe (1987a) showed this pattern of performance held even when the stimulus faces were selected from among those that the patient had been unable to identify in a pre-experiment stimulus screening test.

Evidence of covert recognition has also come from reaction time tasks in which the familiarity or identity of faces are found to influence processing time. In a visual identity matching task with simultaneously presented pairs of faces, de Haan, Young, and Newcombe (1987a) found that a prosopagnosic patient was faster at matching pairs of previously familiar faces than unfamiliar faces, as is true of normal subjects. In contrast, he was unable to name any of the previously familiar faces.

In another RT study, de Haan, Young, and Newcombe (1987a, b) found evidence that photographs of faces could evoke covert semantic knowledge of the depicted person, despite the inability of the prosopagnosic patient to report such information about the person when tested overtly. Their task was to categorize a printed name as belonging to an actor or a politician as quickly as possible. On some trials an irrelevant (i.e., to be ignored) photograph of an actor's or politician's face was simultaneously presented. Normal subjects are slower to categorize the names when the faces come from a different occupation category relative to a no-photograph baseline. Even though their prosopagnosic patient was severely impaired at categorizing the faces overtly as belonging to actors or politicians, he showed the same pattern of interference from different-category faces.

Awareness of perception

Prosopagnosic patients who manifest covert recognition appear to lack the subjective experience of recognition, at least for many of the faces for which they show covert recognition. Note that these patients may occasionally recognize a face overtly, that is, assign it the correct name and express a degree of confidence that they know who the person is. However, this happens rarely, and the dissociation between covert recognition and awareness of recognition holds for many faces that they fail to identify and for which they report no sense of familiarity.

Explanations of covert face recognition

There are several competing explanations for covert recognition prosopagnosia. The oldest is that the face recognition system is intact in these patients, but has been prevented from conveying information to other brain mechanisms necessary for conscious awareness. An explicit statement of this view comes from de Haan, Bauer, and Greve (1992), who proposed the model shown in figure 10.4. According to their model, the face-specific visual and mnemonic processing of a face (carried out within the "Face processing module") proceeds normally in covert recognition, but the results of this process cannot access the "Conscious awareness system" because of a lesion at location number 1. This account clearly falls into the privileged role category, in that it entails a specific brain system needed for conscious awareness, separate from the brain systems needed to carry out perception and cognition.

Another type of explanation was put forth by Bauer (1984), who suggested that there may be two neural systems capable of face recognition, only one of which is associated with conscious awareness. According to Bauer, the ventral visual areas damaged in prosopagnosic patients are the location of normal conscious face recognition. But the

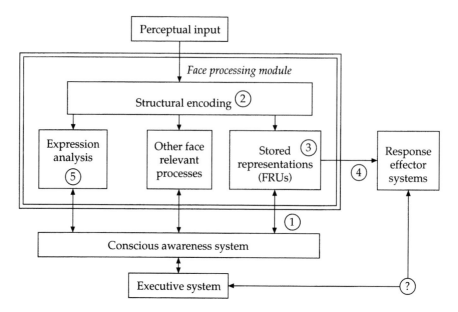

Figure 10.4   Model of face recognition with lesion site no. 1 as the hypothesized locus of disconnection between visual face processing and conscious awareness in a theory of covert face recognition.

From R. M. Bauer, "Autonomic recognition of names and faces in prosopagnosia: a neuropsychological application of the guilty knowledge text," Neuropsychologia, 22, 1984, with permission from Elsevier Science.

dorsal visual areas are hypothesized to be capable of face recognition as well, although they do not mediate conscious recognition but, instead, affective responses to faces. Covert recognition is explained as the isolated functioning of the dorsal face system. This account also fits into the general category of consciousness as a privileged property of particular brain systems. It is analogous to theorizing about the subcortical visual system in blindsight, in that two systems are postulated, which carry out related but distinct visual functions, and only one of which is endowed with conscious awareness.

Tranel and Damasio (1988) interpret covert recognition as the normal activation of visual face representations, which is prevented by the patients' lesions from activating representations in other areas of the brain, such as representations of the people's voices in auditory areas, affective valences in limbic areas, names in language areas, and

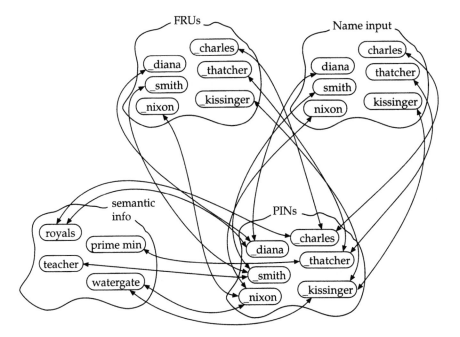

Figure 10.5 Another model of covert recognition featuring intact visual face processing disconnected from other parts of the system by a lesion interrupting the connections between the face recognition units (FRUs) and personal identity nodes (PINs).

so on. This interpretation is therefore of the second type described earlier, in that it requires an integration of active representations across different brain areas in order for conscious awareness to occur; we cannot be consciously aware of an isolated, modality-specific representation. This idea was recently embodied in a computer simulation of semantic priming effects, in which covert recognition was modeled as a partial disconnection separating intact visual recognition units from the rest of the system, as shown in figure 10.5 (Burton, Young, Bruce, Johnston, and Ellis, 1991).

The last account of the mechanism by which overt and covert recognition are dissociated is that covert recognition reflects the residual processing capabilities of a damaged, but not obliterated, visual face recognition system. Randy O'Reilly, Shaun Vecera, and I have argued that lower quality visual information processing is needed to support performance in tests of covert recognition (e.g., to show savings in relearning, and the various RT facilitation and interference effects) relative to the quality of information processing needed to support normal overt recognition performance (e.g., naming a face, sorting faces into those of actors and politicians: Farah *et al.*, 1993; see also O'Reilly and Farah, 1999). This account falls into the third category reviewed earlier, in that the difference between face recognition with and without conscious awareness is the quality of representations activated by the face.

What evidence is available to distinguish among these hypotheses? In general, prosopagnosics are impaired in their perception of faces, although this impairment may be subtle enough to require chronometric measures to detect (Farah, 1990). To take an example from the body of research under discussion, the prosopagnosic studied by de Haan *et al.* was both slower and considerably less accurate than normal subjects in the face matching task. This is not what one would expect assuming that the underlying impairment in prosopagnosia occurs downstream from visual face recognition processes. However, this assumption is central to all of the explanations reviewed so far, with the exception of the dual-route account of Bauer (1984) and our degraded systems hypothesis. Of course, brain-damaged patients often have deficits in more than one functional system, so it is in principle possible that problems with face matching are distinct from prosopagnosia.

If covert recognition reflects the normal functioning of a preserved face recognition system, then in addition to normal face perception, we should also find normal levels of covert recognition, as opposed to merely partial preservation of recognition. The issue here is analogous to the issue in amnesia research of whether nondeclarative memory measures such as priming are truly normal in amnesic patients. Much research has been devoted to answering this question, and the finding that such patients are normal in at least some measures of nondeclarative memory has played an important role in theorizing about the functional organization of memory (e.g., see Squire, 1992). Unfortunately, the data needed to test the analogous prediction for prosopagnosics are not available. In some cases, data from normal subjects would be impossible to obtain, as when famous faces and names are re-taught with either the correct or incorrect pairings.

In other cases, the problem of comparing effect sizes on different absolute measures arises. In both accuracy and reaction time paradigms, covert recognition is measured by differences between the dependent measures in two conditions (e.g., familiar and unfamiliar faces). Unfortunately, patients' accuracies are generally lower than normal subjects' and their RTs are longer (de Haan *et al.*, 1987). It is difficult to know how to assess the relative sizes of differences when the base measures are different. For example, is an effect corresponding to a 200 ms difference between RTs on the order of 2 seconds bigger than, comparable to, or smaller than an effect corresponding to a 100 ms difference between RTs of less than a second?

The study that comes closest to allowing a direct comparison of covert recognition in patients and normal subjects is the priming experiment of Young, Hellawell, and de Haan (1988). Recall that they found equivalent effects of priming name classification for their prosopagnosic patient with either photographs or names of semantically related people. Of course, this fact alone does not imply that the face-mediated priming was normal, as face-mediated priming in this task might normally be larger than name-mediated priming. Young *et al.* devised an ingenious way to address this problem. They refer back to an earlier experiment, reported in the same article, in which normal subjects were tested with both face primes and name primes. The normal subjects also showed equivalent amounts of priming in the two conditions. Unfortunately, the earlier experiment differed in several ways from the latter, which could conceivably shift the relative sizes of the face-mediated and name-mediated priming effects: normal subjects in the earlier experiment performed only 30 trials each, whereas the prosopagnosic patient performed 240 trials, items were never repeated in the earlier experiment, whereas they were in the later one, the type of prime was varied between subjects in the earlier experiment, whereas the patient received both types, different faces and names were used in the two experiments, and the primes were presented for about half as long in the earlier experiment as in the later one. Ideally, to answer the question of whether this prosopagnosic patient shows normal priming from faces, a group of normal control subjects should be run through the same experiment as the patient. Finally, as if empirical progress in this area is not difficult enough, there is an inherent ambiguity in one of the possible outcomes to such an experiment. Just as the finding of normal perception would disconfirm a quality of representation account but the finding of impaired perception is not decisive against the privileged role and integration accounts, so a finding of subnormal levels of covert recognition would disconfirm the privileged role and integration accounts but the finding of normal covert recognition would not be decisive against the quality of representation account. This is because the covert measures might have lower "ceilings" than overt measures of recognition, that is, they might work equally well with intact or partly degraded representations. Parametric study of the relations between covert and overt performance in normal subjects would determine whether this is true.

In sum, most of the current explanations of covert recognition assume both normal face perception and normal covert recognition in prosopagnosics, but neither assumption is empirically supported at present. When tested rigorously, face perception is not normal. However, this result should not be taken as decisive evidence against this class of hypotheses, because the perceptual impairments could be due to functionally distinct lesions from those causing the prosopagnosia. As to the question of whether covert recognition is truly normal, appropriate tests have not yet been carried out. When and if they are, a finding of impaired covert recognition would be immediately interpretable, but a finding of normal covert recognition would require further scaling studies with normal subjects to determine whether the normalcy is due to a ceiling effect.

Bauer's (1984) dual-route version of a privileged role explanation has not been subject to any direct tests. Its most distinctive prediction concerns the difference between face recognition for enabling appropriate affective responses and face recognition for other purposes. Consistent with this prediction is Greve and Bauer's (1990) finding that a prosopagnosic patient rated previously seen faces as more likeable, just as normal subjects tend to do. However, most findings of covert recognition have little to do with affective responses, instead engaging implicit knowledge of names or occupations, and this seems inconsistent with the dual-route hypothesis.

Turning to the quality of representation account of covert recognition, is there any independent evidence that a degraded, but not obliterated, face recognition system would lead to a dissociation between overt and covert recognition? In one study, Wallace and Farah (1992) showed that savings in face–name relearning can be obtained with

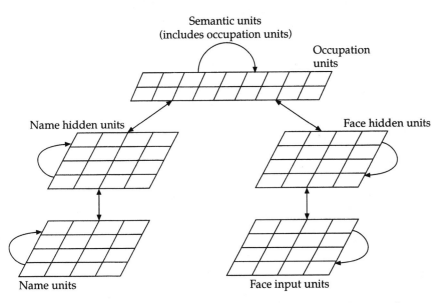

Figure 10.6   A model of covert recognition according to which the overt/covert dissociation emerges from the functioning of a damaged, but not obliterated, visual face recognition system.

From M. J. Farah et al., "Dissociated overt and covert recognition as an emergent property of a lesioned neural network," Psychological Review, 100, 1993; copyright 1993 by the American Psychological Association; reprinted with permission.

normal subjects who are trained on a set of face–name associations and then allowed for forget these associations over a six-month interval. Presumably normal forgetting does not involve the diverting of intact information from conscious awareness, but rather the degradation of representations (albeit in a different way from prosopagnosia).

Probably the strongest evidence for this view, however, is computational. Farah, *et al.* (1993) trained a neural network, shown in figure 10.6, to associate "face" patterns with "semantic" patterns, and to associate these, in turn, with "name" patterns. We found that, at levels of damage to the face representations that led to poor or even chance performance in overt tasks, the network showed all of the behavioral covert recognition effects reviewed above: It relearned correct associations faster than novel ones, it completed the visual analysis of familiar faces faster than unfamiliar, and it showed priming and interference from the faces on judgments about names. Figure 10.7 shows representative results. More recently, O'Reilly and

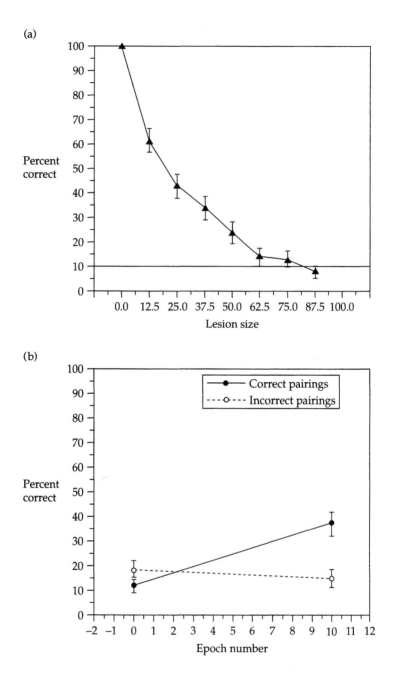

(a)

Percent correct

Lesion size

(b)

Percent correct

Correct pairings
Incorrect pairings

Epoch number

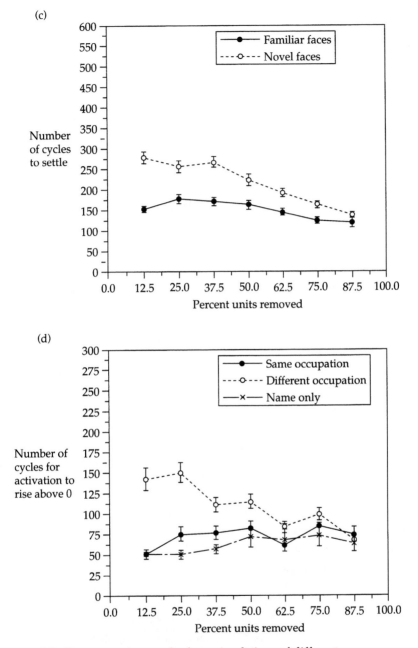

Figure 10.7 Representative results from simulations of different demonstrations of covert recognition using the model shown in figure 10.6.

From M. J. Farah et al., "Dissociated overt and covert recognition as an emergent property of a lesioned neural network," Psychological Review, 100, 1993; copyright 1993 by the American Psychological Association; reprinted with permission.

Farah (1999) simulated several more covert recognition tasks with the same basic model.

Why should a damaged neural network support performance in this range of covert tasks when overt recognition is poor or even at chance? The answer lies in the nature of information representation and processing in distributed, interactive networks. Recall from chapter 2 that representations in such networks consist of a pattern of activation over a set of units or neurons. These units are highly interconnected, and the extent to which the activation of one unit causes an increase or decrease in the activation of a neighboring unit depends on the "weight" of the connection between them. For the network to learn that a certain face representation goes with a certain name representation, the weights among units in the network are adjusted so that presentation of either the face pattern in the face units or the name pattern in the name units causes the corresponding other pattern to become activated. Upon presentation of the input pattern, all of the units connected with the input units will begin to change their activation in accordance with the activation value of the units to which they are connected and the weights on the connections. As activation propagates through the network, a stable pattern of activation eventually results, determined jointly by the input activation and the pattern of weights among the units of the network.

Our account of covert face recognition is based on the following key idea: The set of the weights in a network that cannot correctly associate patterns because it has never been trained (or has been trained on a different set of patterns) is different in an important way from the set of weights in a network that cannot correctly associate patterns because it has been trained on those patterns and then damaged. The first set of weights is random with respect to the associations in question, whereas the second is a subset of the necessary weights. Even if it is an inadequate subset for performing the association, it is not random; it has, "embedded" in it, some degree of knowledge of the associations. Hinton and colleagues (Hinton and Sejnowski, 1986; Hinton and Plaut, 1987) have shown that such embedded knowledge can be demonstrated when the network relearns, suggesting the findings of savings in relearning face–name associations may be explained in this way. In general, consideration of the kinds of tests used to measure covert recognition suggest that the covert measures would be sensitive to this embedded knowledge. The most obvious example is that a damaged network would be expected to relearn associations that it originally knew faster than novel associations because of the nonrandom starting weights. Less obvious, but confirmed by our simulations, the network would settle faster when given previously learned inputs than novel inputs, even though the pattern into which it settles is not correct, because the residual weights come from a set designed to create a stable pattern from that input. Finally, to the extent that the weights continue to activate partial and subthreshold patterns over the nondamaged units in association with the input, then these resultant patterns could prime (i.e., contribute activation towards) the activation of patterns by intact routes.

The general implication of these ideas is that as a neural network is increasingly damaged, there will be a window of damage in which overt associations between patterns (e.g., faces and names) would be extremely poor while the kinds of performance measures tapped by the covert tasks might remain at high levels.

In conclusion, all three types of explanation outlined earlier have been advanced to account for covert recognition in prosopagnosia. Many of the explanations would appear to run aground on evidence of perceptual impairment in prosopagnosia, as they maintain that the locus of impairment is postperceptual. However, the perceptual impairments could conceivably be distinct but associated impairments. The quality of representation explanation seems preferable in that it accounts for these perceptual impairments, as well as accounting for performance in the whole range of covert recognition tasks. However, not everyone agrees with this (see Young and Burton, 1999, for a dissenting opinion).

10.7 Unconscious perception in neglect and extinction

The behavior of patients with neglect and extinction suggests that they do not perceive neglected and extinguished stimuli. However, there is some evidence that, here too, considerable information about neglected and extinguished stimuli may be perceived by some patients.

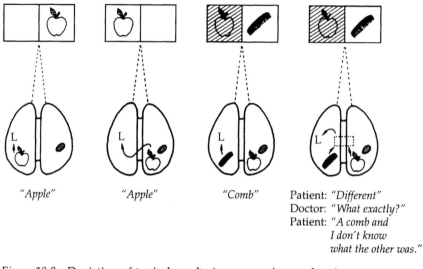

Figure 10.8   Depiction of typical results in an experiment showing a dissociation between impaired naming and preserved same/different matching of left-sided objects by patients with extinction.
From B. T. Volpe et al., "Information processing of visual stimuli in an 'extinguished' field," Nature, 282, 1979; copyright 1979 Macmillan Magazines Ltd.

As with covert recognition in prosopagnosia, this information is generally only detectable using indirect tests.

Representative findings

The first suggestion that patients with extinction may see more of the extinguished stimulus than is apparent from their conscious verbal report came from Volpe, LeDoux, and Gazzaniga (1979). They presented four right parietal-damaged extinction patients with pairs of visual stimuli, including drawings of common objects and three-letter words, one in each hemifield. On each trial, subjects were required to perform two types of task: First, to state whether the two stimuli shown were the same or different, and second, to name the stimuli. Figure 10.8 shows the stimuli and results from a typical trial. As would be expected, the subjects did poorly at overtly identifying the stimuli on the left. Two subjects failed to name any of the left stimuli correctly, and the other two named less than 50 percent. In view of this, their performance on the same/different matching task was surprising: Even though this task also requires perception of the left stimulus, subjects achieved between 88 and 100 percent correct. The same dissociation between identification of the left stimulus and cross-field same/different matching has also been obtained with parietal-damaged neglect patients, whose attentional impairment is so severe that contralesional stimuli may fail to be identified even in the absence of a simultaneously occurring ipsilesional stimulus (Karnath and Hartje, 1987; Karnath, 1988).

Unfortunately, it seems possible that the dissociation between naming and same/different matching could be explained by the differing demands these tasks make on the patient's damaged visual system. Consider the example of the comb and apple, shown in figure 10.8. If only partial stimulus information were picked up on the left, for example, the perception that there is something roundish and light-colored, this would be sufficient to enable fairly accurate same/different judgments. However, there are so many roundish, light-colored objects in the world, this partial perception would be of no help in naming the stimulus on the left. My colleagues and I performed two experiments to test the hypothesis that the differential amounts of stimulus information required for same/different matching and overt identification is what causes the dissociation between them (Farah, Monheit, and Wallace, 1991). First, we degraded the left side of the display with a translucent mask and repeated the Volpe *et al.* experiment with normal subjects. This manipulation was not intended as a simulation of extinction, but rather as a test of our hypothesis concerning the quality of visual information needed in the two kinds of task. Merely depriving normal subjects of some information from the left stimulus produced the same dissociation in normal subjects observed by Volpe *et al.* in patients with extinction.

Second, we repeated the Volpe *et al.* paradigm with extinction patients in its original form, and replicated the original finding, and also in an altered form, in which the overt identification task was administered in a forced-choice format. The purpose of this alteration was to enable us to equate the same/different trials and identification trials for the amount of information needed from the left stimulus. We did this by yoking trials from the two conditions, such that if there was a same/different trial with a triangle and a square, there was an identification trial in which one of these stimuli was presented on the left and the subject was asked "Did you see a triangle or a square?" When same/different matching and identification were equated for their demands on the quality of the subjects' representations of the left stimuli, the dissociation vanished. We concluded that the tasks of same/different matching and identification differ significantly in their demands on the quality of visual representation. This implies that the results of Volpe *et al.* are consistent with extinction affecting perception *per se*, and do not require us to conclude that perception is normal and only postperceptual access to conscious awareness is impaired by extinction. Specifically, our results suggest that extinction results in low-quality representations of stimuli, which support performance in matching tasks more adequately than in naming tasks.

This neat conclusion was challenged recently by Verfaellie, Milberg, McGlinchy-Berroth, and Grande (1995), who equated the same/different matching and the identification tasks in the same way we had, and found evidence of two subtypes of patient. One type performed above chance on the identification of the contralesional stimulus, and equivalently with the ostensibly implicit same/different matching task, thus replicating our findings. The other type had more severe neglect and performed at chance in identifying the contralesional stimulus. These patients did show a *bona fide* dissociation, performing significantly better on the same/different matching task.

Verfaellie's study was also designed to address a question originally raised by Berti, Allport, Driver, Dienese, Oxbury, and Oxbury (1992), namely whether the representation of the extinguished contralesional stimulus is limited to partial visual information or also includes semantic information. Berti and colleagues had varied the similarity relations among the left and right stimuli, including pictures that were visually similar but semantically distinct or semantically similar but visually distinct. The Verfaellie group adopted this design as well, and although they critiqued Berti's methods of data analysis, their conclusions were compatible: It took patients longer to respond "different" when the two pictures bore either a visual or a semantic similarity to each other, implying that both types of information had been at least partly extracted from the contralesional stimulus.

Further evidence of semantic encoding of neglected stimuli comes from studies of semantic priming. When a semantically related word or picture accompanies a target word, that word is recognized more quickly. Ladavas, Paladini, and Cubelli (1993) presented a neglect patient with priming words on the neglected side of fixation and letter strings for a lexical decision task on the right. They also assessed the patient's ability to perform various tasks with the left-sided priming words, such as reading them aloud and classifying them by semantic category. Despite chance performance in a number of these tasks testing explicit perception of the contralesional words, the patient's lexical decision latencies to words on the right were significantly primed as a function of the semantic content of the words on the left. Similar findings have been reported by McGlinchey-Berroth, Milberg, Verfaellie, Alexander, and Kilduff (1993).

Perhaps the best known, if now controversial, evidence of implicit perception in neglect comes from Marshall and Halligan's (1988) observation of one patient's strange but systematic behavior with one pair of drawings. They repeatedly showed her two versions of a house, one with flames shooting out of the left side and one without. She evinced a consistent preference for a picture of a normal house over the burning one, despite her inability to say how (or even whether) the two stimuli differed. This pattern of performance is consistent with a fairly high degree of understanding of material presented in the neglected hemifield, without that understanding being accessible to conscious verbal report.

Bisiach and Rusconi (1990) tested four different patients with burning and nonburning houses, and other similar pairs of drawings, but failed to replicate the Marshall and Halligan result. Often patients displayed no consistent preference. Perhaps more revealingly, when patients did have a preference, it was not necessarily in the normal, rational direction. For example, the only patients who showed a preference with the house stimuli preferred the burning house! Bisiach and Rusconi queried their subjects as to the reasons for their preferences, and found that the reasons fell into two categories: Real but minor differences on the right sides of the stimulus materials, and confabulated differences, such as alleged differences in the layouts of the houses or the numbers of rooms. These confabulations are not uninteresting, as they suggest that patients with neglect may detect differences on the left that they cannot describe verbally, instead evoking confabulations. However, the results of Bisiach and Rusconi do suggest that Marshall and Halligan's case was probably responding either to some minor difference on the right side of the stimulus pair, or to some dimly perceived difference on the left, rather than to the unconscious realization that one of the houses was on fire and would therefore be a dangerous place to live.

Awareness of perception

Patients with neglect and extinction generally report no awareness of neglected stimuli. One measure of this is their tendency to remark on the silliness or absurdity of answering questions about stimuli on the left, or choosing between a pair of stimuli identical except for a feature on the left (e.g., Marshall and Halligan, 1989; Volpe *et al.*, 1979). Such tasks would indeed seem silly if one were not aware of a stimulus on the left, or of the difference between the paired stimuli. It should be noted, however, that the ways in which awareness of perception was formally operationalized in these studies was not to ask the subjects whether or not they detected a stimulus. Rather, the most common means was verbal identification of the stimulus. This was used in the studies of same/different matching ability, and in the studies of letter perception within word and nonword letter strings. Although Volpe *et al.* stated that their subjects sometimes denied seeing any stimulus at all on the left, no systematic data is reported on detection; they contrasted same/different matching performance only with naming. Other tasks intended to assess conscious awareness of stimulus identity included the reading and categorization tasks of Ladavas *et al.* (1993), and the same/different judgment of Marshall and Halligan. In contrast to the research reviewed earlier on covert recognition in prosopagnosia, research on unconscious perception in neglect and extinction has not drawn a clear and principled line between those tasks that require overt conscious awareness of perception and those tasks considered to be indirect tests of unconscious perception. The fact that same/different matching was considered an indirect test of unconscious perception by Volpe *et al.*, and a test of overt conscious perception by Marshall and Halligan, is symptomatic of this problem.

Explanations of perceptual dissociations in patients with neglect and extinction

The earliest and most straightforward interpretation of the dissociation between perception and awareness in patients with neglect and/or extinction was offered by Volpe *et al.* They suggested that extinction in their subjects consisted of "a breakdown in the flow of information between conscious and non-conscious mental systems. The stimulus comparison task in our study appears to have been carried out at a post-perceptual, pre-verbal level, with only the resultant comparison entering consciousness." This account clearly falls into the privileged property category. Although the authors are not very explicit on the point, it appears from the quote just excerpted and from another reference to "some level of neuronal processing which allows for verbal description, if not conscious awareness," that the system required for consciousness is the language system (cf. Gazzaniga, 1988).

An alternative interpretation of the kinds of dissociations reviewed here has been offered by Kinsbourne (1988). Rather than viewing consciousness as a property of some neural systems and not others, he considers it a state of integration among different neural systems. According to this view, neglect does not divert percepts from conscious awareness by somehow preventing their transmission to another system that is required for consciousness. Rather, it weakens or degrades the representation of the stimulus, such that the representation does not have sufficient influence over the other, concurrent, patterns of activity in the brain to create a new global brain state into which the stimulus representation is integrated. A related interpretation seems to be advocated by Bisiach (e.g., 1992). He rejects the notion of a single central locus of consciousness, which he identifies with Cartesianism and the homunculus, and calls our attention to the possibility of numerous parallel mechanisms linking stimuli and responses.

The dissociations reviewed above can also be explained by a quality of representation account. According to this type of account, extinction and neglect result in poor quality perceptual representations, which supply input, albeit degraded input, to higher levels of semantic processing. This is not really very different from Kinsbourne's integration account, in that both emphasize the degradation of perception and consequent weakening of the influence of neglected and extinguished percepts on other parts of the system. The accounts differ in emphasis in that the integration account stresses the lessening of influence on the rest of the system, whereas the quality of representation account stresses the existence of the residual influence.

One might ask how a degraded perceptual representation, postulated by both the integration and quality of representation accounts, could support semantic priming and produce other evidence of semantic processing of neglected stimuli. The answer is that the visual system need not have completed its processing of a stimulus and have derived a high quality representation in order for it to pass some information on to semantic levels of processing. One source of evidence for this is the literature on subthreshold semantic priming with normal subjects. Marcel (1983) and others have shown that subliminal tachistoscopic presentations of words can prime judgments about subsequent supraliminal words. Limiting the exposure duration of a word and following it with a mask clearly interferes with the perceptual processing of the word. Therefore, we should not infer that if a word or picture can semantically prime subsequent stimulus processing, that it must have been perceived normally.

A mechanistic explanation of how poor quality perceptual representations could produce priming at semantic levels is suggested by the covert face recognition model of Farah *et al.* (1993), already discussed. In our model the locus of damage was visual, and the quality of the visual representations was such that multiple choice naming was poor or at chance. However, the model showed semantic priming. This was because the patterns of activation reaching semantic levels of representation contained partial, noisy, and subthreshold information about the semantic identity of the stimulus. The resultant pattern in semantics would, on average, be more consistent with the semantics of that stimulus, or a semantically related stimulus, than with an unrelated stimulus, and hence tended to have a net facilatatory effect on the semantic representation of identical or related stimuli, relative to unrelated stimuli. However, because much of this priming effect was caused by subthresold activation in the semantics units, the semantic representations engendered by the poor quality visual input were not, themselves, able to activate response representations such as names. This suggests a reason why indirect tests may be more sensitive to the residual capabilities of damaged systems: Such tests generally require that residual knowledge affect the processing of a probe stimulus within the perceptual and semantic layers, as opposed to requiring that knowledge to be propagated through additional levels of representation for an overt response. The model of Farah *et al.* is sufficiently simple and generic that it is equally relevant to priming in neglect as in prosopagnosia.

Verfaellie and colleagues' (1995) finding of a true dissociation in the severest cases of neglect between overt identification performance and same/different matching provides more of a challenge to accounts based on degraded perceptual processing. As these authors point out, this would seem to implicate a qualitative rather than quantitative difference between the modes of perception needed for the two kinds of tasks. However, the difference need not be in conscious awareness *per se*. These same authors point out that their overt identification task required the maintenance of a memory trace, whereas the same/different matching task could be performed on the stimuli the instant they appeared. Neglect has been shown experimentally to impair stimulus memory (Heilman, Watson, & Shulman, 1974; Samuels, Butters, & Goodglass, 1971), and it is a commonplace clinical observation that signs of neglect may be subtle when a patient copies the Rey complex figure, while a flagrantly asymmetrical construction may be produced just minutes later (e.g., Lezak, 1983).

In sum, we find ourselves in roughly the same position with respect to explanations of unconscious perception in neglect and extinction as we did with explanations of covert face recognition. The current body of empirical knowledge is of great interest and utility in establishing certain important qualitative conclusions: That patients can be unable to report the identity of a neglected or extinguished stimulus, but still manifest a fair degree of perceptual and even semantic knowledge about it. Yet these results are ambiguous with respect to the mechanisms by which neglect and extinction have these effects. The hypothesis that neglect and extinction spare perceptual and semantic processing, and affect only subsequent processing by some other system that plays a privileged role in mediating conscious awareness, seems inconsistent with the finding that perception is not normal in neglect and extinction (Farah *et al.*, 1991). Demonstrations of semantic processing in neglect and extinction have not provided the kind of careful quantitation of effect sizes needed to determine whether semantic processing is normal, or merely partially preserved. Thus, there is no decisive evidence in favor of the privileged role account, and a small amount of evidence against it. The integration account of Kinsbourne and our idea of quality of representation are essentially the same in this context, as integration is hypothesized to fail because of weak and degraded perceptual representations. Although the findings of semantic processing of neglected stimuli might at first seem to disconfirm both, in fact there is empirical and computational evidence that degraded perceptual representations can partially activate appropriate semantic representations.

10.8   Implicit reading in pure alexia

As we saw in chapter 6, patients with pure alexia are impaired at reading, despite being able to write normally and understand spoken words. It has generally been assumed that patients' oral reading abilities reflect their reading comprehension abilities, and indeed the everyday behavior and clinical test performance of pure alexics suggests that they cannot understand words that they fail to decipher by letter-by-letter reading.

This belief was first called into question by Landis, Regard, and Serrat (1980), in a case study of a patient recovering from surgery for a left occipital tumor. The patient was a pure alexic, and when tested within a week of the surgery, was unable to read words that were flashed for only 30 ms in a tachistoscope. However, he was able to point to objects in the room whose names had been presented in this manner. Unfortunately, he was tested with relatively few words on that day, and when re-tested a week later, had lost his ability to point to the words' referents, even though his explicit reading performance had improved.

Representative findings

Subsequent studies have examined the implicit reading of pure alexics more thoroughly. Patterson and Kay (1984) reported several unsuccessful attempts to elicit evidence of comprehension of briefly presented unread words in their pure alexic subjects. Shortly thereafter, Grossi, Fragassi, Orsini, De Falco, and Sepe (1984) presented evidence of disproportionately preserved picture–word matching in one case of pure alexia, and Shallice and Saffran (1986) carried out a comprehensive investigation of implicit word recognition and comprehension in another pure alexic. Shallice and Saffran's subject was able to perform lexical decision with relatively high accuracy on letter strings that were presented for two seconds, which was too quickly for him to reliably identify the words explicitly. The subject was best at recognizing high frequency words, and the closer the resemblance between nonwords and words, the harder it was for him to reject the nonwords. For high frequency words, he was able to classify 90 percent as words, and false alarmed to only 38 percent of the pseudo-words derived from the high frequency words by changing one or two letters. An interesting exception to his generally good lexical decision ability was that he was unable to discriminate appropriately and inappropriately affixed words, for example calling *applaudly* a word. Shallice and Saffran also demonstrated that their subject was able to make reasonably accurate semantic categorizations of words presented too briefly to be read. For example, he correctly classified 94 percent of unread place names as in or out of Europe, 93 percent of unread people's names as authors or politicians, and 87 percent of unread concrete nouns as living or nonliving.

Coslett and Saffran (1989) replicated and extended these findings with four new cases of pure alexia. Like Shallice and Saffran (1986), they found effects of word frequency on lexical decision, and an insensitivity to affixes. They also found better lexical decison performance for concrete and imageable words, and for content words, in general, relative to functors. In a subsequent study, Saffran and Coslett (1998) report that they tested one of their subjects on rhyme/nonrhyme judgments with written words, and found that he performed at chance. Perhaps their most striking finding is that their subjects performed the implicit reading tasks more accurately with extremely brief exposures of the words, such as 250 ms, than with exposures of 2 seconds. They interpret this in terms of the different strategies needed for implicit and explicit reading. Explicit letter-by-letter reading is incompatible with the strategy needed for implicit reading. Coslett and

Saffran were able to foil subjects' attempts at letter-by-letter reading by using extremely short exposure durations, and thereby enabled the alternative strategy to be expressed. This is consistent with Landis *et al.*'s original case study, in which implicit reading was lost as explicit reading improved. It also suggests a reason why Patterson and Kay may not have detected any preserved implicit reading in their subjects: In attempting to maximize the chances of eliciting implicit reading in their subjects, they used words that were most likely to be recognized explicitly, that is, very short words and words that had been successfully read explicitly.

Awareness of perception

Although patients' reports of their subjective experiences are not reported in great detail in most cases, there is a suggestion of some variability among cases. Whereas Landis *et al.* and Coslett and Saffran's subjects generally complained of not even being able to see the stimuli clearly when they were manifesting implicit reading, Shallice and Saffran's case was able to give rather detailed descriptions of how he performed the lexical decision and semantic categorization tasks. For lexical decision, he described "a process of looking at the whole length of the word and finding a combination of letters that can't be right, or looking at the whole word and seeing that it looked sensible." For semantic categorization, he reported getting a "first impression" of each word, and, with a particular category in mind, deciding whether he "feels the first flash is right." I spent some time studying an implicit reader with Karen Klein, and with the help of Coslett and Saffran replicated all of their findings with him, with one exception: He did not need tachisticopic presentations in order to read implicitly; he displayed his abilities under conditions with no time limitation. He was also quite aware of the information he gleaned during implicit reading and was reasonably confident of his responses.

From this very small and sketchy empirical base I will tentatively suggest that, for pure alexics who are able to abandon the letter-by-letter strategy and manifest implicit reading at relatively long exposure durations, there is no dissociation between the information that has been processed in implicit reading and awareness of having processed that information. The striking dissociation in these cases is between knowing the specific word presented and knowing its lexical status and semantic category. However, this dissociation does not have any direct implications for the relation between word perception and awareness thereof. Only when exposure durations must be extremely short, for subjects who would otherwise persist in letter-by-letter reading, do subjects manifest knowledge in their implicit reading performance that they, themselves, are not aware of possessing. Under these circumstances, however, the dissociation between performance and awareness may be attributable to the same mechanisms as subthreshold perception in normal subjects, with thresholds being higher for brain-damaged subjects.

Explanations of implicit reading

Because it is not clear whether implicit reading necessarily involves a dissociation between subjects' experience of reading and their performance, it is equally unclear whether the types of explanations discussed above are really relevant. Nevertheless, for the sake of completeness, I will review the proposals that have been put forth by researchers studying implicit reading.

Recall from chapter 6 that several accounts of pure alexia exist, and that they have in common some hypothesized capacity which is necessary for reading and which is either damaged or disconnected from early visual representations of words. The capacity in question has been hypothesized to be language in general, word form knowledge in particular, or the ability to rapidly encode multiple visual shapes, perhaps letters in particular, and in all cases is assumed to be localized to the left hemisphere. The different accounts of implicit reading can be differentiated from one another with respect to the role played by these left hemisphere mechanisms.

The DICE model has been applied to implicit reading, and suggests that implicit reading is simply normal reading, drawing as usual upon the critical left hemisphere-mediated processing, deprived of access to other systems necessary for conscious awareness (Schacter *et al.*, 1988). This is an example of a privileged role account.

Implicit reading has also been explained by a quality of representation account. Shallice and Saffran (1986) suggested that "lexical decision above chance but well below normal levels; recognition of morphemes but insensitivity to the appropriateness of their combination; limited access to semantic information [and] the failure to identify the stimulus explicitly, could conceivably be explained in terms of decreased levels of activation within the system that normally subserves explicit identification."

Finally, Shallice and Saffran also discuss the possibility that implicit reading reflects the operation of right hemisphere reading mechanisms, a view that Coslett and Saffran (1989) have also endorsed. This constitutes a different type of privileged role account, according to which the normal left-hemisphere component of the reading system is uniquely endowed with the ability to mediate conscious awareness of reading (if the account is to be applied to awareness) and with the more fine-grained semantic distinctions and syntactic and morphological capabilities found to be lacking in implicit reading.

How does the available evidence adjudicate among these alternatives? The DICE model does not provide an explanation of the peculiarities of implicit reading with regard to part of speech, morphology, and concreteness, and so on, and is therefore not a very satisfactory account of the phenomenon. In contrast, the right hemisphere hypothesis seems particularly well-suited to explaining these findings. On the basis of independent evidence with split-brain patients and with normal subjects, the right hemisphere appears to be better at reading high frequency and concrete words, and to be ignorant of morphology (see e.g., Baynes, 1990, for a review). The right hemisphere is also believed to be deficient at deriving phonology from print, consistent with inability of one of Coslett and Saffran's subjects to make rhyme judgments on pairs of printed words, which Klein and I also observed with our implicit reader. Finally, Coslett and Monsul (1994) used transcranial magnetic stimulation (TMS) with one alexic patient to find out which hemisphere was mediating his residual reading ability. Only right hemisphere TMS interfered with the patient's reading, providing a very direct demonstration of that hemisphere's role. However, the relevance of this case to implicit reading is limited as the patient was only stimulated while engaging in the explicit reading of words aloud.

It is not clear exactly how well the hypothesis of a degraded reading system accounts for these phenomena. On the basis of general properties of neural network models, one might well expect higher frequency words to be better preserved, on the basis of more initial learning. One might also predict greater preservation of concrete and imageable words, especially with the assumption that such words have more associated semantic attributes (e.g., Plaut and Shallice, 1993). On these points, the quality of representation approach does well in accounting for some of the features of implicit reading. In contrast, the more regular mapping between orthography and phonology, relative to the mapping between orthography and semantics, would seem to predict the relative preservation of phonological judgments relative to semantic ones, just the opposite of what is observed, on grounds similar to the prediction concerning frequency effects: To the extent that sets of similar looking words have similar sounding pronunciations, the learning accomplished for each one will also generalize towards the others. Finally, the finding that shorter exposure durations lead to better implicit reading in at least some patients is awkward for a quality of representation account.

In sum, there is a good deal of relatively fine-grained information about implicit reading, concerning the effects of different stimulus properties, instructions, and tasks, and these enable us to evaluate the different explanations of the phenomenon that have been put forward. Pending some counter-intuitive results concerning the modes of failure in damaged reading networks, the available evidence seems most consistent with right-hemisphere mediation of implicit reading. However, dissociated awareness is not an essential aspect of implicit reading, and the mechanism of implicit reading is therefore not necessarily relevant to the neural bases of visual awareness.

10.9 General conclusions

What generalizations can be drawn about the six syndromes reviewed here? And more importantly, what general conclusions follow from them for the neural correlates of visual awareness?

In six neuropsychological syndromes, visual awareness and visual perception appear to be dissociable. It is tempting to consider the six dissociations as replications, at different levels of visual processing, of the same basic phenomenon. On closer examination, however, both the sense in which visual awareness can be said to be impaired, and the criteria by which visual perception can be said to be preserved, differ across the syndromes. This heterogeneity is not, in my view, reason to discount some or all of the the syndromes as irrelevant. With the possible exception of implicit reading, all seem to be showing us something about the way perception and awareness can come unglued. We must simply be aware of the differences among these dissociations at a descriptive, empirical level if we are eventually to make sense of them in terms of the likely underlying neural mechanisms.

Visual awareness has been operationalized in different ways. The literature on blindsight contains the richest information about patients' introspective self-reports, and includes three ways in which visual awareness can be said to be absent or impaired. In some instances, patients claim that they are guessing on the basis of no subjective experience whatsoever, with resulting very low confidence. In other instances, they say that they are answering based on an experience, but not one that they would classify as "visual." Very occasionally a specifically visual experience is reported.

The agnosic patients studied differ in their degree of confidence in perceptions, which is presumably a measure of their subjective awareness of having perceived. The apperceptive agnosic patient reports no awareness of the sizes and orientations that her visuomotor system deals with so accurately, whereas the associative agnosic does retain some feeling of knowing, and this feeling is strongest, crucially, for items on which her implicit recognition performance is better. Prosopagnosics typically report no sense of familiarity when they view a face and have low confidence in their identifications, and some demonstrations of covert face recognition have used only faces for which the patient earlier demonstrated no overt recognition.

In neglect and extinction, the perception–awareness dissociation is sometimes framed in terms of the patients' unawareness of having seen anything at all. However, the only systematically collected data concerns their ability to make various explicit judgments about the stimuli. Finally, in implicit reading, the dissociation that holds for all patients is between the ability to report a specific word and the ability to make judgments about the lexicality and semantic category of the word, not the dissociation between word perception and awareness of that perception. For two cases, at least, subjects report being aware of the information they are using to make these judgments, and confident of their answers. In sum, the six syndromes comprise a heterogeneous group from the point of view of awareness.

The six syndromes also appear to be heterogeneous in terms of the way in which preserved vision is operationalized and the scope and degree of preservation. Consider the way in which the aware–unaware distinction is operationalized. Matching tasks were used with an apperceptive agnosic and a neglect patient to operationalize aware vision, and with extinction patients to operationalize preserved vision without awareness. There appears to be no principled basis for deciding when a task requires visual awareness, and thus no uniformity across syndromes in the way vision without awareness is measured.

Consider also the scope of preserved vision in the syndromes. In apperceptive agnosia, it comprises only a small fraction of the abilities impaired in conscious vision (size and orientation, but not shape). In implicit reading, many but not all properties of words are recognized. Specifically, implicit readers appear to be blind to the morphological and phonological properties of words. The limits of implicit or covert recognition in the associative object agnosia and prosopagnosia are less clearly delineated, but they appear to comprise a much fuller range of recognition abilities (implicit access to semantic information from objects and faces, and even name information from faces).

The degree of preservation of vision without awareness also varies and, surprisingly, not in a way correlated with the scope. For example, although the apperceptive agnosic shows preservation of only a narrow range of the abilities compromised at the level of aware vision in her syndrome, her performance within that range is normal. In contrast, the associative object agnosic was merely above chance in her ability to pair semantically related objects, but nowhere near normal. At this point we do not know whether the priming and other implicit perception effects in neglect and prosopagnosia are truly normal or merely present to some degree.

Neural correlates of visual awareness

If the phenomena themselves are heterogeneous, then it is unlikely that a single mechanism will be responsible for the vision–awareness dissociation in each case. In fact, all three of the general types of hypotheses concerning the neural correlates of awareness seem to have their place in explaining one syndrome or another. There is evidence from blindsight for a priviledged role for the cortical visual system, as opposed to the subcortical, in visual awareness. Similarly, observations in one case of apperceptive agnosia implicate the ventral pathway of the cortical visual system as playing a privileged role. Other aspects of blindsight, as well as associative object agnosia, prosopagnosia, extinction, and neglect are generally consistent with an explanation in terms of either degraded quality of representation or disrupted integration caused by that degradation. Although the phenomenon of implicit reading *per se* is probably not directly relevant to awareness, as some implicit readers are aware, a quality of representation account probably explains the lack of awareness for patients whose implicit reading can only be demonstrated with tachistoscopically presented words.

What general conclusions emerge from this heterogeneous set of phenomena concerning the neural correlates of visual awareness? The six syndromes together support a hybrid account. According to this hybrid, some but not all visual system representations are accompanied by awareness, but even those representations that do normally play a privileged role in awareness will not if they are degraded. Thus, awareness is denied to both a normally functioning superior colliculus or dorsal visuomotor pathway, and to damaged cortical areas. Of course, this hybrid of the privileged role and quality of representation accounts also includes a form of integration account, too, because the conditions under which poor quality representations fail to reach awareness are the conditions under which they fail to influence the more global state of the brain.

As a grand conclusion, this might seem like the height of wishy-washiness, or worse. Didn't Karl Popper tell us that science progresses through disconfirmation of hypotheses, and aren't I saying that all of the hypotheses seem to fit the data? To this I have three answers. First, we have in effect ruled out some hypotheses. After reviewing the extensive literature on perception–awareness dissociations, we failed to find any support for the existence of a dedicated conscious awareness system. Similarly, there is no clear evidence for separate convergence zones whose only function is to integrate information for conscious awareness. The only reason for hypothesizing such systems in the first place, over and above the systems responsible for perception itself, was the impression that awareness could be selectively impaired without any accompanying perceptual impairment. Scrutiny of the literature suggests that such a truly isolated impairment in perceptual awareness has yet to be reported, and the dissociations that are found can be explained more simply without separate systems for awareness or convergence. Although this is not quite the same as finding evidence inconsistent with these hypotheses, it does deprive them of the only motivation for proposing them in the first place.

Second, not all scientific insight consists of lopping branches off a decision tree. The identification of the quality of representation account with some versions of the integration account is a form of progress. The greatest strength of the quality of representation account is its obvious and direct relation to the manipulations that rise to perception–awareness dissociations, namely brain damage or tachistoscopic presentation to normal subjects. The greatest strength of the integration account is its obvious and direct relation to the fundamentally unitary nature of awareness. Learning that degradation of representations affects their ability to become integrated into the global state of a simple neural network simulation thereby links the key empirical facts to the key phenomenological fact by way of an explicit mechanism.

Finally, when asking how the brain accomplishes some function, it may be unrealistic to expect that the set of alternative hypotheses will always be reducible to a single right answer. Throughout this book we have seen numerous examples where this expectation seemed wrong. Are object and spatial vision segregated into separate streams, or do they interact and share resources? Are the visual representations underlying object recognition local or distributed? Are they viewer-centered or object-centered? Are they subdivided for visual tasks as specific as face recognition and reading, or are systems individuated by more formal criteria such as geometric properties of the stimuli? In each case a simple answer of "the former" or "the latter" would have made our scientific lives easier, but in each case the reality appears to be more complex. Returning to the neural correlates of conscious awareness, we should not expect the reality here to be substantially simpler!

References

Adelson, E. H. and Bergen, J. (1991). The plenoptic function and the elements of early vision. In M. S. Landy and J. A. Movshon (eds), *Computational Models of Visual Processing*. Cambridge, MA: MIT Press.

Adler, A. (1944). Disintegration and restoration of optic recognition in visual agnosia: Analysis of a case. *Archives of Neurology and Psychiatry*, 51, 243–59.

Aine, C. J. and Harter, M. R. (1984). Event-related potentials to Stroop stimuli: Color and word processing. *Annals of the New York Academy of Sciences*, 425, 152–3.

Albert, M. C. (1973). A simple test of visual neglect. *Neurology*, 23, 658–64.

Albright, T. (1984). Direction and orientation selectivity of neurons in visual area MT of the macaque. *Journal of Neurophysiology*, 52, 1106–130.

Allison, T., McCarthy, G., Nobre, A. C., Puce, A. and Belger, A. (1994). Human extrastriate visual cortex and the perception of faces, words, numbers, and colors. *Cerebral Cortex*, 5, 544–54.

Allport, A. (1989). Visual attention. In M. I. Posner (ed.), *Foundations of Cognitive Science*. Cambridge, MA: MIT Press.

Anderson, J. R. (1978). Arguments concerning representation for mental imagery. *Psychological Review*, 85, 249–77.

Andersen, R. A. (1989). Visual and eye movement functions of the posterior parietal cortex. *Annual Review of Neuroscience*, 12, 377–403.

Andersen, R. A., Essick, G. K. and Siegel, R. M. (1985). Encoding of spatial location by posterior parietal neurons. *Science*, 230, 456–8.

Arguin, M. and Bub, D. N. (1993). Single character processing in a case of pure alexia. *Neuropsychologia*, 31, 435–58.

Bartolomeo, P., Bachoud-Levi, A. C., De Gelder, B., Denes, G., Dalla Barba, G., Brugieres, P. and Degos, J. D. (1998). Multiple-domain dissociation between impaired visual perception and preserved mental imagery in a patient with bilateral extrastriate lesions. *Neuropsychologia*, 36(3), 239–49.

Bartolomeo, P., D'Erme, P. and Gainotti, G. (1994). The relationship between visuospatial and representational neglect. *Neurology*, 44, 1710–14.

Bauer, R. M. (1984). Autonomic recognition of names and faces in prosopagnosia: A neuropsychological application of the guilty knowledge test. *Neuropsychologia*, 22, 457–69.

Baxter, D. M. and Warrington, E. K. (1983). Neglect dysgraphia. *Journal of Neurology, Neurosurgery and Psychiatry*, 46, 1073–8.

Bay, E. (1953). Disturbances of visual perception and their examination. *Brain*, 76, 515–30.

Baylis, G. C., Rolls, E. T. and Leonard, C. M. (1985). Selectivity between faces in the responses of a population of neurons in the cortex in the superior temporal sulcus of the monkey. *Brain Research*, 342, 91–102.

Baylis, G. C., Rolls, E. T. and Leonard, C. M. (1987). Functional subdivisions of the temporal lobe neocortex. *Journal of Neuroscience*, 7, 330–42.

Baynes, K. (1990). Language and reading in the right hemisphere: Highways or byways of the brain? *Journal of Cognitive Neuroscience*, 2, 159–79.

Baynes, K., Holtzman, J. D. and Volpe, B. T. (1986). Components of visual attention: Alterations in response pattern to visual stimuli following parietal lobe infarction. *Brain*, 109, 99–114.

Beauvois, M. F. and Saillant, B. (1985). Optic aphasia for colours and colour agnosia: A distinction between visual and visuo-verbal impairments in the processing of colours. *Cognitive Neuropsychology*, 2, 1–48.

Behrmann, M., Black, S. E. and Bub, D. (1990). The evolution of letter-by-letter reading. *Brain and Language*, 39, 405–27.

Behrmann, M., Black, S. E. and Bub, D. (1990). The evolution of pure alexia: A longitudinal study of recovery. *Brain and Language*, 39, 405–27.

Behrmann, M. and Moscovitch, M. (1994). Object-centered neglect in patients with unilateral neglect: Effects of left-right coordinates of objects. *Journal of Cognitive Neuroscience*, 6, 1–16.

Behrmann, M., Moscovitch, M. and Winocur, G. (1994). Intact visual imagery and impaired visual perception in a patient with visual agnosia. *Journal of Experimental Psychology: Human Perception and Performance*, 20, 1068–87.

Behrmann, M. and Shallice, T. (1995). Pure alexia: An orthographic not spatial deficit. *Cognitive Neuropsychology*, 12, 409–27.

Behrmann, M. and Shallice, T. (in press). Pure alexia: A nonspatial visual disorder affecting letter activation. *Cognitive Neuropsychology*.

Bender, M. B. and Feldman, M. (1972). The so-called visual agnosias. *Brain*, 95, 173–86.

Benson, D. F. and Greenberg, J. P. (1969). Visual form agnosia. *Archives of Neurology*, 20, 82–9.

Benton, A. L., Hamsher, K., Varney, N. R. and Spreen, O. (1983). *Contributions to Neuropsychological Assessment*. New York: Oxford University Press.

Berti, A., Allport, A., Driver, J., Deneis, Z., Oxbury, J. and Oxbury, S. (1992). Levels of processing for visual stimuli in an extinguished field. *Neuropsychologia*, 30, 403–15.

Beschin, N., Cocchini, G., Sala, S. D. and Logie, R. H. (1997). What the eyes perceive, the brain ignores: A case of pure unilateral representational neglect. *Cortex*, 33, 3–26.

Biederman, I. (1987). Recognition-by-components: A theory of human image understanding. *Psychological Review*, 94, 115–47.

Bisiach, E. (1992). Understanding consciousness: Clues from unilateral neglect and related disorders. In A. D. Milner and M. D. Rugg (eds), *The Neuropsychology of Consciousness*. San Diego: Academic Press.

Bisiach, E., Capitani, E. and Porta, E. (1985). Two basic properties of space representation in the brain: Evidence from unilateral neglect. *Journal of Neurology, Neurosurgery, and Psychiatry*, 48, 141–4.

Bisiach, E., Geminiani, G., Berti, A. and Rusconi, M. L. (1990). Perceptual and premotor factors of unilateral neglect. *Neurology*, 40, 1278–81.

Bisiach, E. and Luzzatti, C. (1978). Unilateral neglect of representational space. *Cortex*, 14, 129–33.

Bisiach, E., Perani, D., Vallar, G. and Berti, A. (1986). Unilateral neglect: Personal and extra-personal. *Neuropsychologia*, 24, 759–67.

Bisiach, E. and Rusconi, L. L. (1990). Break-down of perceptual awareness in unilateral neglect. *Cortex*, 26, 643–9.

Blanc-Garin, J., Faure, S. and Sabrio, P. (1993). Right hemisphere performance and competence in processing mental images, in a case of partial interhemispheric disconnection. *Brain and Cognition*, 22, 118–33.

Block, N. (1978). Troubles with functionalism. In C. W. Savage (ed.), *Minnesota Studies in the Philosophy of Science*, vol. 9. Minneapolis: University of Minnesota Press, 261–325.

Block, N. (1995). On a confusion about a function of consciousness. *Behavioral and Brain Sciences*, 18, 227–87.

Blum, J. S., Chow, K. L. and Pribram, K. H. (1950). A behavioral analysis of the organization of the pareito-temporo-preoccipital cortex. *Journal of Comparative Neurology*, 93, 53–100.

Bowers, D., Blonder, L. X., Feinberg, T. and Heilman, K. M. (1991). Differential impact of right and left hemisphere lesions on facial emotion and object imagery. *Brain*, 114, 2593–609.

Brent, P. J., Kennard, C. and Ruddock, K. H. (1994). Residual colour vision in a human hemianope: spectral responses and colour discrimination. *Proceedings of the Royal Society of London, Series B: Biological Sciences*, 256, 219–25.

Britten, K. H., Shadlen, M. N., Newsome, W. T. and Movshon, J. A. (1992). The analysis of visual motion: A comparison of neuronal and psychophysical performance. *Journal of Neuroscience*, 12, 4745–65.

Brown, J. W. (1972). *Aphasia, Apraxia and Agnosia: Clinical and Theoretical Aspects*. Springfield, IL: Charles C. Thomas.

Bruce, V. (1988). *Recognizing Faces*. Hove: Erlbaum.

Brunn, J. L. and Farah, M. J. (1991). The relation between spatial attention and reading: Evidence from the neglect syndrome. *Cognitive Neuropsychology*, 8, 59–75.

Bub, D. N., Arguin, M. and Lecours, A. R. (1993). Jules Dejerine and his interpretation of pure alexia. *Brain and Language*, 45, 531–59.

Bub, D. N., Black, S. and Howell, J. (1989). Word recognition and orthographic context effects in a letter-by-letter reader. *Brain and Language*, 36, 357–76.

Burke, W. and Cole, A. M. (1978). Extra-retinal influences on the lateral geniculate nucleus. *Review of Physiology, Biochemistry, and Pharmacology*, 80, 105–66.

Burton, A. M., Young, A. W., Bruce, V., Johnston, R. A. and Ellis, A. W. (1991). Understanding covert recognition. *Cognition*, 39, 129–66.

Bushnell, M. C., Goldberg, M. E. and Robinson, D. L. (1981). Behavioral enhancement of visual responses in monkey cerebral cortex. I. Modulation in posterior parietal cortex related to selective visual attention. *Journal of Neurophysiology*, 46, 755–72.

Butter, C. M. (1968). The effect of discrimination training on pattern equivalence in monkeys with infero-temporal and lateral striate lesions. *Neuropsychologia*, 6, 27–40.

Butter, C. M., Mishkin, M. and Rosvold, H. E. (1965). Stimulus generalization in monkeys with infero-temporal lesions and lateral occipital lesions. In D. J. Mostofsky (ed.), *Stimulus Generalization*. Palo Alto: Stanford University Press.

Buxbaum, L. J. and Coslett, H. B. (1994). Neglect of chimeric figures: Two halves are better than a whole. *Neuropsychologia*, 32, 275–88.

Buxbaum, L. J., Coslett, H. B., Montgomery, M. and Farah, M. J. (1996). Mental rotation may underlie apparent object-based neglect. *Neuropsychologia*, 34, 113–26.

Calvanio, R., Petrone, P. N. and Levine, D. N. (1987). Left visual spatial neglect is both environment-centered and body-centered. *Neurology*, 37, 1179–83.

Campbell, R., Heywood, C. A., Cowey, A., Regard, M. and Landis, T. (1990). Sensitivity to eye gaze in prosopagnosic patients and monkeys with superior temporal sulcus ablation. *Neuropsychologia*, 28, 1123–42.

Campion, J., Latto, R. and Smith, Y. M. (1983). Is blindsight an effect of scattered light, spared cortex, and near-threshold vision? *The Behavioral and Brain Sciences*, 3, 423–47.

Caramazza, A. and Hillis, A. E. (1990a). Spatial representation of words in the brain implied by studies of a unilateral neglect patient. *Nature*, 346, 267–9.

Caramazza, A. and Hillis, A. E. (1990b). Where do semantic errors come from? *Cortex*, 26, 95–122.

Charlot, V., Tzourio, N., Zilbovicius, M., Mazoyer, B. and Denis, M. (1992). Different mental imagery abilities result in different regional cerebral blood flow activation patterns during cognitive tasks. *Neuropsychologia*, 30, 565–80.

Chatterjee, A. (1994). Picturing unilateral spatial neglect: viewer versus object centred reference frames. *Journal of Neurology, Neurosurgery and Psychiatry*, 57, 1236–40.

Chelazzi, L., Miller, E. K., Duncan, J. and Desimone, R. (1993). A neural basis for visual search in inferior temporal cortex. *Nature*, 363, 345–7.

Churchland, P. S. (1988). What should we expect from a theory of consciousness? *Advances in Neurology, 77*, 19–30; discussion, 30ff.

Clark, V. P. and Hillyard, S. A. (1996). Spatial selective attention affects early extrastriate but not striate components of the visual evoked potential. *Journal of Cognitive Neuroscience, 8*, 387–402.

Clarke, S., Lindemann, A., Maeder, P., Borruat, F. X. and Assal, G. (1997). Face recognition and postero-inferior hemispheric lesions. *Neuropsychologia, 35*, 1555–63.

Clarke, S. and Miklossy, J. (1990). Occipital cortex in man. Organization of callosal connections, related myelo- and cytoarchitecture, and putative boundaries of functional visual areas. *Journal of Computational Neurology, 298*, 188–214.

Cohen, G. (1975). Hemispheric differences in the utilization of advance information. In P. M. A. Rabbit and S. Dornic (eds), *Attention and Performance, Vol. 5*. New York: Academic Press.

Cohen, J. D., Romero, R. D., Servan-Schreiber, D. and Farah, M. J. (1994). Mechanisms of spatial attention: The relation of macrostructure to microstructure in parietal neglect. *Journal of Cognitive Neuroscience, 6*, 377–87.

Cohen, L. and Dehaene, S. (1991). Neglect dyslexia for numbers? A case report. *Cognitive Neuropsychology, 8*, 39–58.

Coltheart, M. (1985). Cognitive neuropsychology and the study of reading. In M. I. Marin (ed.), *Attention and Performance XI*. London: Erlbaum Associates, 3–37.

Coltheart, M. (1996). Phonological dyslexia: Past and future issues. *Cognitive Neuropsychology, 13*, 749–62.

Connor, C. E., Preddie, D. C., Gallant, J. L. and Van Essen, D. C. (1997). Spatial attention effects in macaque area V4. *The Journal of Neuroscience, 17*, 3201–14.

Cooper, L. A. and Shepard, R. N. (1973). Chronometric studies of the rotation of mental images. In W. G. Chase (ed.), *Visual Information Processing*. New York: Academic Press.

Corballis, M. C. (1988). Recognition of disoriented shapes. *Psychological Review, 95*, 115–23.

Corballis, M. C. and Sergent, J. (1988). Imagery in a commissurotomized patient. *Neuropsychologia, 26*, 13–26.

Corballis, M. C., Zbrodoff, N. J., Shetzer, L. I. and Butler, P. B. (1978). Decisions about identity and orientation of rotated letters and digits. *Memory and Cognition, 6*, 98–107.

Corbetta, M. (1998). Frontoparietal cortical networks for directing attention and the eye to visual locations: identical, independent, or overlapping neural systems? *Proceedings of the National Academy of Sciences of the United States of America, 95*, 831–8.

Corbetta, M., Miezin, F. M., Dobmeyer, S., Shulman, G. L. and Petersen, S. E. (1990). Attentional modulation of neural processing of shape, color, and velocity in humans. *Science, 248*, 1556–9.

Corbetta, M., Miezin, R. M., Dobmeyer, S., Shulman, G. L. and Petersen, S. E. (1991). Selective and divided attention during visual discriminations of shape, color, and speed: Functional anatomy by positron emission tomography. *Journal of Neuroscience*, 11, 2382–402.

Corbetta, M., Miezin, F. M., Shulman, G. L. and Petersen, S. E. (1993). A PET study of visuospatial attention. *Journal of Neuroscience*, 13, 1202–26.

Corbetta, M., Shulman, G. L., Miezin, F. M. and Petersen, S. E. (1995). Superior parietal cortex activation during spatial attention shifts and visual feature conjunction. *Science*, 270, 802–5.

Coslett, H. B. (1997). Neglect in vision and visual imagery: A double dissociation. *Brain*, 120, 1163–71.

Coslett, H. B., Bowers, D., Fitzpatrick, E., Haws, B. and Heilman, K. M. (1990). Directional hypokinesia and hemispatial inattention in neglect. *Brain*, 113, 475–86.

Coslett, H. B. and Monsul, N. (1994). Reading with the right hemisphere: Evidence from transcranial magnetic stimulation. *Brain and Language*, 46, 198–211.

Coslett, H. B. and Saffran, E. M. (1989). Evidence for preserved reading in pure alexia. *Brain*, 112, 327–59.

Costello, A. L. and Warrington, E. K. (1987). The dissociation of visuospatial neglect and neglect dyslexia. *Journal of Neurology, Neurosurgery and Psychiatry*, 50, 1110–16.

Cowey, A. and Marcar, V. L. (1992). The effect of motion perception of removing cortical visual area MT in the macaque: I. Motion discrimination using simple dots. *European Journal of Neuroscience*, 4, 1219–27.

Cowey, A., Small, M. and Ellis, S. (1994). Left visuo-spatial neglect can be worse in far than in near space. *Neuropsychologia*, 32, 1059–66.

Cowey, A. and Stoerig, P. (1989). Projection patterns of surviving neurons in the dorsal lateral geniculate nucleus following discrete lesions of striate cortex: Implications for residual vision. *Experiemntal Brain Research*, 75, 631–8.

Cowey, A. and Stoerig, P. (1997). Visual detection in monkeys with blindsight. *Neuropsychologia*, 35, 929–39.

Crick, F. (1984). Function of the thalamic reticular complex: The searchlight hypothesis. *Proceedings of the National Academy of Sciences of the United States of America*, 81, 4586–4590.

Crick, F. and Koch, C. (1990). Function of the thalamic reticular complex: The searchlight hypothesis. *Seminars in the Neurosciences*, 2, 263–75.

Cubelli, R., Nichelli, P., Bonito, V., De Tanti, A. and Inzaghi, M. G. (1991). Different patterns of dissociation in unilateral neglect. *Brain and Cognition*, 15, 139–59.

D'Esposito, M., Detre, J. A., Aguire, G. K., Alsop, D. C., Tippett, L. J. and Farah, M. J. (1997). A functional MRI study of mental image generation. *Neuropsychologia*, 35, 725–30.

Damasio, A. R. (1990). Synchronous activation in multiple cortical regions: A mechanism for recall. *Seminars in the Neurosciences*, 2.

Damasio, A. R. and Damasio, H. (1983). The anatomic basis of pure alexia. *Neurology*, 33, 1573–83.

Damasio, A. R., Damasio, H. and Van Hoesen, G. W. (1982). Prosopagnosia: Anatomic basis and behavioral mechanisms. *Neurology*, 32, 331–41.

Damasio, A. R., Yamada, T., Damasio, H., Corbett, J. and McKee, J. (1980). Central achromatopsia: Behavioral, anatomic, and physiologic aspects. *Neurology*, 30, 1064–71.

Davidoff, J. and Wilson, B. (1985). A case of visual agnosia showing a disorder of pre-semantic visual classification. *Cortex*, 21, 121–34.

De Haan, E. H., Bauer, R. M. and Greve, K. W. (1992). Behavioral and physiological evidence for covert face recognition in a prosopagnosic patient. *Cortex*, 28, 77–95.

De Haan, E. H., Young, A. W., and Newcombe, F. (1987a). Face Recognition without awareness. *Cognitive Neuropsychology*, 4, 385–415.

De Renzi, E., Faglioni, P. and Scotti, G. (1970). Hemispheric contribution to exploration of space through the visual and tactile modality. *Cortex*, 6, 191–203.

De Renzi, E., Gentilini, M. and Pattacini, F. (1984). Auditory extinction following hemisphere damage. *Neuropsychologia*, 22, 733–44.

De Renzi, E. and Lucchelli, F. (1993). The fuzzy boundaries of apperceptive agnosia. *Cortex*, 29, 187–215.

De Renzi, E., Perani, D., Carlesimo, G. A., Silveri, M. C. and Fazio, F. (1994). Propopagnosia can be associated with damage confined to the right hemisphere – An MRI and PET study and a review of the literature. *Neuropsychologia*, 32, 893–902.

De Renzi, E. and Spinnler, H. (1967). Impaired performance on color tasks in patients with hemispheric lesions. *Cortex*, 3, 194–217.

De Vreese, L. P. (1988). Category-specific vs. modality-specific aphasia for colors. *International Journal of Neuroscience*, 45, 195–206.

De Vreese, L. P. (1991). Two systems for color naming defects. *Neuropsychologia*, 29, 1–18.

Déjerine, J. (1892). Contribution à l'étude anatomo-pathologique et clinique des différentes variétés de cécité verbale. *Comptes Rendus Hebdomadaires de Séances et Mémoires de la Société de Biologie, Ninth Series*, 4, 61–90.

Desimone, R. (1991). Face-selective cells in the temporal cortex of monkeys. *Journal of Cognitive Neuroscience*, 3.

Desimone, R., Albright, T. D., Gross, C. D. and Bruce, C. (1984). Stimulus-selective properties of inferior temporal neurons in the macaque. *Journal of Neuroscience*, 4, 2051–62.

Desimone, R. and Duncan, J. (1995). Neural mechanisms of selective visual attention. *Annual Review of Neuroscience*, 18, 193–222.

Desimone, R. and Gross, C. G. (1979). Visual areas in the temporal cortex of the macaque. *Brain Research*, 178, 363–80.

Desimone, R. and Schein, S. (1987). Visual properties of neurons in area V4 of the macaque: Sensitivity to stimulus form. *Journal of Neurophysiology*, 57, 835–68.

Desimone, R., Schein, S. J., Moran, J. and Underleider, L. G. (1985). Contour, color and shape analysis beyond the striate cortex. *Vision Research*, 25, 441–52.

D'Esposito, M., Detre, J. A., Aguirre, G. K., Stallcup, M., Alsop, D. C., Tippet, L. J., and Farah, M. J. (1997). A functional MRI study of mental image generation. *Neuropsychologia*, 35, 725–30.

di Pellegrino, G. and Wise, S. P. (1993a). Primate frontal cortex: Visuospatial vs. visuomotor activity, premotor vs. prefrontal cortex. *Journal of Neuroscience*, 13, 1227–43.

di Pellegrino, G. and Wise, S. P. (1993b). Effects of attention on visuomotor activity in the premotor and prefrontal cortex of a primate. *Somatosen and Motor Research*, 10, 245–62.

Diamond, R. and Carey, S. (1986). Why faces are and are not special: an effect of expertise. *Journal of Experimental Psychology: General*, 115, 107–17.

Dowling, J. E. (1987). *The Retina: An Approachable Part of the Brain*. Cambridge: Harvard University Press.

Driver, J., Baylis, G. C., Goodrich, S. and Rafal, R. D. (1994). Axis-based neglect of visual shapes. *Neuropsychologia*, 32, 1353–65.

Driver, J. and Halligan, P. W. (1991). Can visual neglect operate in object-centered coordinates? An affirmative single-case study. *Cognitive Neuropsychology*, 8, 475–96.

Driver, J. and Tipper, S. P. (1989). On the nonselectivity of "selective" seeing: Contrasts between interference and priming in selective attention. *Journal of Experimental Psychology: Human Perception and Performance*, 15, 304–14.

Duhamel, J. R., Colby, C. L. and Goldberg, M. E. (1992). The updating of the representation of visual space in parietal cortex by intended eye movements. *Science*, 255, 90–2.

Duncan, J. (1984). Selective attention and the organization of visual information. *Journal of Experimental Psychology: General*, 113, 501–17.

Duncan, J. (1996). Coordinated brain systems in selective perception and action. In T. Inui and J. L. McClelland (eds), *Attention and Performance, XVI*. Cambridge, MA: MIT Press.

Eddy, P. and Glass, A. (1981). Reading and listening to high and low imagery sentences. *Journal of Verbal Learning and Verbal Behavior*, 20, 333–45.

Edelman, S. and Bulthoff, H. H. (1991). Generalization of object recognition in human vision across stimulus transformations and deformations. In Y. A. Feldman and A. Bruckstein (eds), *Artificial Intelligence and Computer Vision*. North Holland: Elsevier Science.

Efron, R. (1968). What is perception? *Boston Studies in Philosophy of Science*, 4, 137–73.

Egly, R., Driver, J. and Rafal, R. (1994). Shifting visual attention between objects and locations: Evidence from normal and parietal lesion subjects. *Journal of Experimental Psychology: General*, 123, 161–77.

Ehrlichman, H. and Barrett, J. (1983). Right hemispheric specialization for mental imagery: A review of the evidence. *Brain and Cognition*, 2, 55–76.

Eimer, M. (1997). An event-related potential (ERP) study of transient and sustained visual attention to color and form. *Biological Psychology*, 44, 143–60.

Ekstrom, R., French, J. W. and Harman, H. H. (1976). *Manual for Kit of Factor-Referenced Cognitive Tests*. Princeton, NJ: Educational Testing Service.

Ellis, W. D. (1938). *A Sourcebook of Gestalt Psychology*. New York: Harcourt Brace.

Eriksen, C. W. and Hoffman, J. E. (1973). The extent of processing of noise elements during selecting encoding from visual displays. *Perception and Psychophysics*, 12, 201–4.

Farah, M. J. (1984). The neurological basis of mental imagery: A componential analysis. *Cognition*, 18, 245–72.

Farah, M. J. (1988). Is visual imagery really visual? Overlooked evidence from neuropsychology. *Psychological Review*, 95, 307–17.

Farah, M. J. (1989). Mental imagery and the brain. In J. W. Brown (ed.), *The Neuropsychology of Visual Perception*. Hillsdale, NJ: Erlbaum Associates.

Farah, M. J. (1990). *Visual Agnosia: Disorders of Object Recognition and What They Tell Us About Normal Vision*. Cambridge, MA: MIT Press/Bradford Books.

Farah, M. J. (1991). Patterns of co-occurrence among the associative agnosias: Implications for visual object representation. *Cognitive Neuropsychology*, 8, 1–19.

Farah, M. J. (1994). Visual perception and visual awareness after brain damage: A tutorial review. In M. Moscovitch and C. Umilta (eds), *Conscious and Unconscious Information Processing: Attention and Performance XV*. Cambridge: MIT Press, 37–76.

Farah, M. J. (1995). Current issues in the neuropsychology of mental image generation. *Neuropsychologia*, 33, 1445–71.

Farah, M. J. (1996). Is face recognition special? Evidence from neuropsychology. *Behavioral Brain Research*, 76, 181–9.

Farah, M. J. and Aguirre, G. K. (1999). Imaging visual recognition: PET and fMRI studies of functional anatomy of human visual recognition. *Trends in Cognitive Sciences*, 3, 179–85.

Farah, M. J., Brunn, J. L., Wong, A. B., Wallace, M. and Carpenter, P. A. (1990). Frames of reference for allocating attention to space: Evidence from the neglect syndrome. *Neuropsychologia*, 28, 335–47.

Farah, M. J. and Buxbaum, L. J. (1997). Object-based attention in visual neglect: Conceptual and empirical distinctions. In H. O. Karnath and P. Thier (eds), *Parietal Lobe Contributions to Orientation in 3D Space*. New York: Springer-Verlag.

Farah, M. J., Gazzaniga, M. S., Holtzman, J. D. and Kosslyn, S. M. (1985). A left hemisphere basis for visual mental imagery? *Neuropsychologia*, 23, 115–18.

Farah, M. J. and Grossman, M. (1997). Semantic Memory Impairment. In T. E. Feinberg and M. J. Farah (eds), *Behavioral Neurology and Neuropsychology*. New York: McGraw-Hill.

Farah, M. J., Hammond, K. L., Levine, D. N., and Calvanio, R. (1988). Visual and spatial mental imagery: Dissociable systems of representation. *Cognitive Psychology*, 20, 439–62.

Farah, M. J., Klein, K. L. and Levinson, K. L. (1995). Face perception and within-category discrimination in prosopagnosia. *Neuropsychologia*, 33, 661–74.

Farah, M. J. and Hammond, K. H. (1988). Mental rotation and orientation-invariant object recognition: Dissociable processes. *Cognition*, 29, 29–46.

Farah, M. J., Hammond, K. L., Levine, D. N. and Calvanio, R. (1988). Visual and spatial mental imagery: Dissociable systems of representation. *Cognitive Psychology*, 20, 439–62.

Farah, M. J., Hammond, K. H., Mehta, Z. and Ratcliff, G. (1989). Category-specificity and modality-specificity in semantic memory. *Neuropsychologia*, 27, 193–200.

Farah, M. J., Levine, D. N. and Calvanio, R. (1988). A case study of mental imagery deficit. *Brain and Cognition*, 8, 147–64.

Farah, M. J., Levinson, K. L. and Klein, K. L. (1995). Face perception and within-category discrimination in prosopagnosia. *Neuropsychologia*, 33, 661–74.

Farah, M. J. and McClelland, J. L. (1991). A computational model of semantic memory impairment: Modality-specificity and emergent category-specificity. *Journal of Experimental Psychology: General*, 120, 339–57.

Farah, M. J., Monheit, M. A. and Wallace, M. A. (1991). Unconscious perception of extinguished visual stimuli: Reassessing the evidence. *Neuropsychologia*, 29, 949–58.

Farah, M. J., O'Reilly, R. C. and Vecera, S. P. (1993). Dissociated overt and covert recognition as an emergent property of a lesioned neural network. *Psychological Review*, 100, 571–88.

Farah, M. J. and Peronnet, F. (1989). Event-related potentials in the study of mental imagery. *Journal of Psychophysiology*, 3, 99–109.

Farah, M. J., Peronnet, F., Gonon, M. A. and Giard, M. H. (1988). Electrophysiological evidence for a shared representational medium for visual images and percepts. *Journal of Experimental Psychology: General*, 117, 248–57.

Farah, M. J., Peronnet, F., Weisberg, L. L. and Monheit, M. A. (1989). Brain activity underlying mental imagery: Event-related potentials during image generation. *Journal of Cognitive Neuroscience*, 1, 302–16.

Farah, M. J., Rochlin, R. and Klein, K. L. (1994). Orientation invariance and geometric primitives in shape recognition. *Cognitive Science*, 13, 325–44.

Farah, M. J., Soso, M. J. and Dasheiff, R. M. (1992). The visual angle of the mind's eye before and after unilateral occipital lobectomy. *Journal of Experimental Psychology: Human Perception and Performance*, 18, 241–6.

Farah, M. J., Stowe, R. M. and Levinson, K. L. (1996). Phonological dyslexia: Loss of a reading-specific component of the cognitive architecture? *Cognitive Neuropsychology*, 13, 849–68.

Farah, M. J., Tanaka, J. R. and Drain, H. M. (1995). What causes the face inversion effect? *Journal of Experimental Psychology: Human Perception and Performance*, 21, 628–34.

Farah, M. J. and Wallace, M. A. (1991). Pure alexia as a visual impairment: A reconsideration. *Cognitive Neuropsychology*, 8, 313–34.

Farah, M. J. and Wallace, M. A. (1992). Semantically-bounded anomia: Implications for the neural implementation of naming. *Neuropsychologia*, 30, 609–21.

Farah, M. J., Wallace, M. A. and Vecera, S. P. (1993). What and Where in Visual Attention: Evidence from the Neglect Syndrome. In I. H. Robertson and J. C.

Marshall (eds), *Unilateral Neglect: Clinical and Experimental Studies*. Hove: Lawrence Erlbaum Associates.

Farah, M. J., Wilson, K. D., Drain, H. M. and Tanaka, J. R. (1995). The inverted inversion effect in prosopagnosia: Evidence for mandatory, face-specific perceptual mechanisms. *Vision Research*, 35, 2089–93.

Farah, M. J., Wilson, K. D., Drain, M. and Tanaka, J. N. (1998). What is special about face perception? *Psychological Review*, 105, 482–98.

Farah, M. J., Wong, A. B., Monheit, M. A. and Morrow, L. A. (1989). Parietal lobe mechanisms of spatial attention: Modality-specific or supramodal? *Neuropsychologia*, 27, 461–70.

Feinberg, T. E., Schindler, R. J., Ochoa, E., Kwan, P. C. and Farah, M. J. (1994). Associative visual agnosia and alexia without prosopagnosia. *Cortex*, 30, 395–411.

Fendrich, R., Wessinger, C. M. and Gazzaniga, M. S. (1992). Residual vision in a scotoma: Implications for blindsight. *Science*, 258, 1489–91.

Ferrera, V. P., Nealey, T. A. and Maunsell, J. H. R. (1992). Mixed parvocelluar and magnocellular geniculate signals in visual area V4. *Nature*, 358, 756–8.

Ferrera, V. P., Nealey, T. A. and Maunsell, J. H. R. (1994). Responses in macaque visual area V4 following inactivation of the parvocellular and magnocellular LGN pathways. *Journal of Neuroscience*, 14, 2080–8.

Finke, R. A. (1980). Levels of equivalence in imagery and perception. *Psychological Review*, 87, 113–32.

Fodor, J. A. (1983). *The Modularity of Mind*. Cambridge, MA: MIT Press.

Foldiak, P. (1991). Learning invariance from transformation sequences. *Neural Computation*, 3, 194–200.

Friedman, R. B. and Alexander, M. P. (1984). Pictures, images, and pure alexia: A case study. *Cognitive Neuropsychology*, 1, 9–23.

Fuster, J. M. (1973). Unit activity in prefrontal cortex during delayed-response performance: neuronal correlates of transient memory. *Journal of Neurophysiology*, 36, 61–78.

Fuster, J. M. and Jervey, J. P. (1982). Neuronal firing in the inferotemporal cortex of the monkey in a visual memory task. *Journal of Neuroscience*, 2, 361–75.

Gainotti, G. (1968). Les manifestations de négligence et d'inattention pour l'hémispace. *Cortex*, 4, 64–91.

Gandhi, S. P., Heeger, D. J., and Boynton, G. M. (1999). Spatial attention affects brain activity in human primary visual cortex. *Proceedings of the National Academy of Sciences, USA*, 96, 3314–19.

Gauthier, I. Anderson, A. W., Tarr, M. J., Skudlarski, P. and Gore, J. C. (1997). Levels of categorization in visual recognition studied using functional magnetic resonance imaging. *Current Biology*, 7, 645–51.

Gauthier, I. and Tarr, M. J. (1997). Becoming a "Greeble" expert: Exploring mechanisms for face recognition. *Vision Research*, 37, 1673–82.

Gauthier, I., Williams, P., Tarr, M. J. and Tanaka, J. (1998). Training "Greeble" experts: A framework for studying expert object recognition processes. *Vision Research*, 38, 2401–28.

Gazzaniga, M. S. (1983). Right hemisphere language following brain bisection. A 20 year perspective. *American Psychologist*, 38, 525–37.

Gazzaniga, M. S. (1988). Brain modularity: Towards a philosphy of conscious experience. In A. J. Marcel and E. Bisiach (eds), *Consciousness in Contemporary Science*. Oxford: Clarendon Press.

Geffen, G., Bradshaw, J. and Wallace, G. (1971). Interhemispheric effects on reaction time to verbal and nonverbal visual stimuli. *Journal of Experimental Psychology*, 87, 415–22.

Gelb, A. and Goldstein, K. (1918). Analysis of a case of figural blindness. *Neurology and Psychology*, 41, 1–143.

Geschwind, N. (1965). Disconnexion syndromes in animals and man. Part II. *Brain*, 88, 584–644.

Gilbert, C. D. (1992). Horizontal integration and cortical dynamics. *Neuron*, 9, 1–13.

Gnadt, J. W. and Andersen, R. A. (1988). Memory related motor planning activity in posterior parietal cortex of macaque. *Experimental Brain Research*, 70, 216–20.

Goldenberg, G. (1989). The ability of patients with brain damage to generate mental visual images. *Brain*, 112, 305–25.

Goldenberg, G. (1992). Loss of visual imagery and loss of visual knowledge – A case study. *Neuropsychologia*, 30, 1081–99.

Goldenberg, G. and Artner, C. (1991). Visual imagery and knowledge about the visual appearance of objects in patients with posterior cerebral artery lesions. *Brain and Cognition*, 15, 160–86.

Goldenberg, G., Podreka, I., Steiner, M., Franzen, P. and Deecke, L. (1991). Contributions of occipital and temporal brain regions to visual and acoustic imagery-aspect study. *Neuropsychologia*, 29, 695–702.

Goldenberg, G., Podreka, I., Steiner, M. and Willmes, K. (1987). Patterns of regional cerebral blood flow related to memorizing of high and low imagery words: An emission computer tomography study. *Neuropsychologia*, 25, 473–85.

Goldenberg, G., Podreka, I., Steiner, M., Willmes, K., Suess, E. and Deecke, L. (1989). Regional cerebral blood flow patterns in visual imagery. *Neuropsychologia*, 27, 641–64.

Goldenberg, G., Podreka, I., Uhl, F., Steiner, M., Willmes, K. and Deecke, L. (1989). Cerebral correlates of imagining colours, faces and a map – I. Spect of regional cerebral blood flow. *Neuropsychologia*, 27, 1315–28.

Goldenberg, G., Steiner, M., Podreka, I. and Deecke, L. (1992). Regional cerebral blood flow patterns related to verification of low- and high-imagery sentences. *Neuropsychologia*, 30, 581–6.

Goldman-Rakic, P. S. (1987). Circuitry of primate prefrontal cortex and regulation of behavior by representational memory. In F. Plum (ed.), *Handbook of Physiology: Nervous System Vol. V: Higher Functions of the Brain*. Bethesda, MD: American Psychological.

Goldman-Rakic, P. W. (1988). Topography of cognition: Parallel distributed networks in primate association cortex. *Annual Review of Neuroscience*, 11, 137–56.

Goodale, M. A., Milner, A. D., Jakobson, L. S. and Carey, D. P. (1991). A neurological dissociation between perceiving objects and grasping them. *Nature*, 349, 154–6.

Goodglass, H., Wingfield, A., Hyde, M. R. and Theurkauf, J. C. (1986). Category-specific dissociations in naming and recognition by aphasic patients. *Cortex*, 22, 87–102.

Gray, C. M., Konig, P., Engel, A. K. and Singer, W. (1989). Oscillatory responses in cat visual cortex exhibit inter-columnar synchronization which reflects global stimulus properties. *Nature*, 338, 334–7.

Greenblatt, S. H. (1983). Localization of lesions in alexia. In A. Kertesz (ed.), *Localization in Neuropsychology*. New York: Academic Press.

Groh, J. M., Seidemann, E. and Newsome, W. T. (1996). Neurophysiology: Neural fingerprints of visual attention. *Current Biology*, 6, 1406–9.

Gross, C. G. (1978). Inferior temporal lesions do not impair discrimination of rotated patterns in monkeys. *Journal of Comparative and Physiological Psychology*, 92, 1095–109.

Gross, C. G., Bender, D. B. and Rocha-Miranda, C. E. (1969). Visual receptive fields of neurons in inferotemporal cortex of the monkey. *Science*, 166, 1303–6.

Gross, C. G. and Mishkin, M. (1977). The neural basis of stimulus equivalence across retinal translation. In S. Harnard, R. W. Doty, L. Goldstein, J. Jaynes, and G. Krauthamer (eds), *Lateralization in the Nervous System*. New York: Academic Press.

Gross, C. G., Rocha-Miranda, C. E. and Bender, D. B. (1972). Visual properties of neurons in inferotemporal cortex of the macaque. *Journal of Neurophysiology*, 35, 96–111.

Gross, C. G., Schiller, P. H., Wells, C. and Gerstein, G. L. (1967). Single unit activity in temporal association cortex of the monkey. *Journal of Neurophysiology*, 30, 833–43.

Gross, C. G. and Sergent, J. (1992). Face recognition. *Current Opinion in Neurobiology*, 2, 156–61.

Grossi, D., Fragassi, N. A., Orsini, A., De Falco, F. A. and Sepe, O. (1984). Residual reading capability in a patient with alexia without agraphia. *Brain and Language*, 23, 337–48.

Grossi, D., Orsini, A. and Modafferi, A. (1986). Visuoimaginal constructional apraxia: On a case of selective deficit of imagery. *Brain and Cognition*, 5, 255–67.

Grusser, O. and Landis, T. (1991). *Visual Agnosia*. Boca Raton: CRC Press.

Guariglia, C. and Antonucci, G. (1992). Personal and extrapersonal space: a case of neglect dissociation. *Neuropsychologia*, 30, 1001–9.

Guariglia, C., Padovani, A., Pantano, P. and Pizzamiglio, L. (1993). Unilateral neglect restricted to visual imagery [see comments]. *Nature*, 364, 235–7.

Gulyas, B. and Roland, P. E. (1994). Processing and analysis of form, colour and binocular disparity in the human brain: Functional anatomy by positron emission tomography. *European Journal of Neuroscience*, 6, 1811–28.

Halligan, P. W. and Marshall, J. C. (1991). Recovery and regression in visuospatial neglect: A case study of learning in line bisection. *Brain Injury*, 5, 23–31.

Hart, J., Berndt, R. S. and Caramazza, A. (1985). Category-specific naming deficit following cerebral infarction. *Nature*, 316, 439–40.

Hasselmo, M. E., Rolls, E. T. and Baylis, G. C. (1989). The role of expression and identity in the face-selective responses of neurons in the temporal visual cortex of the monkey. *Behavioural Brain Research*, 32, 203–18.

Hasselmo, M. E., Rolls, E. T., Baylis, G. C. and Nalwa, V. (1989). Object-centered encoding by face-selective neurons in the cortex in the superior temporal sulcus of the monkey. *Experimental Brain Research*, 75, 417–29.

Heilman, K. M. and Valenstein, E. (1979). Mechanisms underlying hemispatial neglect. *Annals of Neurology*, 5, 166–70.

Heilman, K. M., Watson, R. T. and Valenstein, E. (1993). Neglect and related disorders. In K. M. Heilman and E. Valenstein (eds), *Clinical Neuropsychology*. Oxford: Oxford University Press.

Heinze, H. J., Mangun, G. R., Burchert, W., Hinrichs, H., Scholz, M., Munte, T. F., Gos, A., Scherg, M., Johannes, S., Hundeshagen, H., Gazzaniga, M. and Hillyard, S. A. (1994). Combined spatial and temporal imaging of brain activity during visual selective attention in humans. *Nature*, 372, 543–6.

Heywood, C. A. and Cowey, A. (1987). On the role of cortical area V4 in the discrimination of hue and pattern in macaque monkeys. *Journal of Neuroscience*, 7, 2601–17.

Heywood, C. A. and Cowey, A. (1992). The role of face-cell area in the discrimination and recognition of faces by monkeys. *Philosophical Transactions of the Royal Society of London, Series B: Biological Sciences*, 335, 31–8.

Heywood, C. and Cowey, A. (1993). Colour and face perception in man and monkey: the missing link. In B. Gulyas, D. Ottoson, and P. Roland (eds), *Functional Organisation of the Human Visual Cortex*. Oxford: Pergamon Press.

Hillyard, S. A. (1993). Electrical and magnetic brain recordings: Contributions to cognitive neuroscience. *Current Opinion in Neurobiology*, 3, 217–24.

Hillyard, S. A. and Anllo-Vento, L. (1998). Event-related brain potentials in the study of visual selective attention. *Proceedings of the National Academy of Sciences of the United States of America*, 95, 781–7.

Hillyard, S. A. and Picton, T. W. (1978). On and off components in the auditory evoked potential. *Perception & Psychophysics*, 24, 391–8.

Hillyard, S. A., Vogel, E. K. and Luck, S. J. (1998). Sensory gain control (amplification) as a mechanism of selective attention: electrophysiological and neuroimaging evidence. *Philosophical Transactions of the Royal Society of London – Series B: Biological Sciences*, 353, 1257–70.

Hinton, G. E., McClelland, J. L. and Rumelhart, D. E. (1986). Distributed Representations. In D. E. Rumelhart and J. L. McClelland (eds), *Parallel Distributed Processing: Explorations in the Microstructure of Cognition*. Cambridge, MA: MIT Press.

Hinton, G. E. and Sejnowski, T. J. (1986). Learning and relearning in Boltzmann machines. In D. E. Rumelhart and J. L. McClelland (eds), *Parallel Distributed Processing: Explorations in the Microstructure of Cognition*. Cambridge, MA: MIT Press.

Hinton, G. E. and Shallice, T. (1991). Lesioning an attractor network: Investigations of acquired dyslexia. *Psychological Review*, 98, 74–95.

Hodges, J. R., Patterson, K., Oxbury, S. and Funnell, E. (1992). Semantic dementia. *Brain*, 115, 1783–806.

Hoffman, J. E. and Nelson, B. (1981). Spatial selectivity in visual search. *Perception and Psychophysics*, 30, 283–90.

Hollins, M. (1985). Styles of mental imagery in blind adults. *Neuropsychologia*, 23, 561–6.

Holmes, E. J. and Gross, C. G. (1984). Stimulus equivalence after inferior temporal lesions in monkeys. *Behavioral Neuroscience*, 98, 898–901.

Holmes, G. (1918). Disturbances of visual orientation. *British Journal of Ophthalmology*, 2, 449–68 and 506–18.

Howard, D., Patterson, K., Wise, R., Brown, W. D., Friston, K., Weiller, C. and Frackowiak, R. (1992). The cortical localization of the lexicons: Positron emission tomography evidence. *Brain*, 115, 1769–82.

Hubel, D. H. (1988). *Eye, Brain, and Vision*. New York: W. H. Freeman and Company.

Hubel, D. H. and Livingstone, M. S. (1987). Segregation of form, color, and stereopsis in primate area 18. *Journal of Neuroscience*, 7, 3378–415.

Hubel, D. H. and Wiesel, T. N. (1962). Receptive fields, binocular interaction, and functional architecture in the cat's visual cortex. *Journal of Physiology*, 160, 106–54.

Humphrey, N. K. and Weiskrantz, L. (1969). Size constancy in monkeys with inferotemporal lesions. *Quarterly Journal of Experimental Psychology*, 21, 225–38.

Humphreys, G. W. and Riddoch, M. J. (1987). *To See but Not to See: A Case Study of Visual Agnosia*. Hillsdale, NJ: Lawrence Erlbaum Associates.

Inhoff, A. W., Rafal, R. D. and Posner, M. J. (1992). Bimodal extinction without cross-modal extinction. *Journal of Neurology, Neurosurgery and Psychiatry*, 55, 36–9.

Intons-Peterson, M. J. (1983). Imagery paradigms: How vulnerable are they to experimenters' expectations? *Journal of Experimental Psychology: Human Perception and Performance*, 9, 394–412.

Iversen, S. D. and Weiskrantz, L. (1967). Perception of redundant cues by monkeys with inferotemporal lesions. *Nature, London*, 214, 241–3.

Iwai, E. (1985). Neuropsychological basis of pattern vision in macaque monkeys. *Vision Research*, 25, 425–39.

Johnson, M. H. (1997). *Developmental Cognitive Neuroscience*. Cambridge, Mass.: Blackwell Publishers.

Johnson, M. H., Dziurawiec, S., Ellis, H. D. and Morton, J. (1991). Newborns' preferential tracking of face-like stimuli and its subsequent decline. *Cognition*, 40, 1–19.

Johnston, J. C. and McClelland, J. C. (1980). Experimental tests of a hierarchical model of word identification. *Journal of Verbal Learning and Verbal Behavior*, 19, 503–24.

Jolicoeur, P. (1985). The time to name disoriented natural objects. *Memory and Cognition,* 13, 289–303.

Jonides, J. and Gleitman, H. (1972). A conceptual category effect in visual search. *Perception & Psychophysics,* 12, 457–60.

Kanwisher, N., Chun, M. M., McDermott, J. and Ledden, P. J. (1996). Functional imaging of human visual recognition. *Cognitive Brain Research,* 5, 55–67.

Kanwisher, N., McDermott, J. and Chun, M. M. (1997). The fusiform face area: a module in human extrastriate cortex specialized for face perception. *Journal of Neuroscience,* 17, 4302–11.

Kanwisher, N., Woods, R., Iacoboni, M. and Mazziotta, J. (1997). A locus in human extrastriate cortex for visual shape analysis. *Journal of Cognitive Neuroscience,* 9, 133–42.

Karnath, H. O. (1988). Deficits of attention in acute and recovered visual hemineglect. *Neuropsychologia,* 26, 27–43.

Karnath, H. O., Fetter, M. and Niemeier, M. (1998). Disentangling gravitational, environmental, and egocentric reference frames in spatial neglect. *Journal of Cognitive Neuroscience,* 10, 680–90.

Karnath, H. O. and Hartje, W. (1987). Residual information processing in the neglected visual half-field. *Journal of Neurology,* 234, 180–4.

Kastner, S., De Weerd, P., Desimone, R. and Ungerleider, L. G. (1998). Mechanisms of directed attention in the human extrastriate cortex as revealed by functional MRI. *Science,* 282, 108–11.

Katz, R. B. and Sevush, S. (1989). Positional dyslexia. *Brain and Language,* 37, 266–89.

Kay, J. and Hanley, R. (1991). Simultaneous form perception and serial letter recognition in a case of letter-by-letter reading. *Cognitive Neuropsychology,* 8, 249–73.

Kinsbourne, M. (1988). Integrated field theory of consciousness. In A. J. Marcel and E. Bisiach (eds), *Consciousness in Contemporary Science.* Oxford: Clarendon Press.

Kinsbourne, M. (1993). Orientational bias model of unilateral neglect: Evidence from attentional gradients within hemispace. In I. H. Robertson and J. C. Marshall (eds), *Unilateral Neglect: Clinical and Experimental Studies* Hillsdale, NJ: Lawrence Erlbaum.

Kinsbourne, M. and Warrington, E. K. (1962). A variety of reading disability associated with right hemisphere lesions. *Journal of Neurology, Neurosurgery, and Psychiatry,* 25, 339–44.

Kinsbourne, M. and Warrington, E. K. (1964). Observations on color agnosia. *Journal of Neurology, Neurosurgery, and Psychiatry,* 27, 296–9.

Kluver, H. and Bucy, P. C. (1937). Psychic blindness and other symptoms following bilateral temporal lobectomy in rhesus monkeys. *American Journal of Physiology,* 119, 352–3.

Koenderink, J. J. and van Doorn, A. J. (1979). The internal representation of solid shape with respect to vision. *Biological Cybernetics,* 32, 211–16.

Koriat, A. and Norman, J. (1984). What is rotated in mental rotation? *Journal of Experimental Psychology: Learning, Memory and Cognition,* 10, 421–34.

352 *References*

Kosslyn, S. M. (1978). Measuring the visual angle of the mind's eye. *Cognitive Psychology*, 10, 356–89.

Kosslyn, S. M. (1980). *Image and Mind*. Cambridge, MA: Harvard University Press.

Kosslyn, S. M. (1996). *Image and Brain: The Resolution of the Imagery Debate*. Cambridge, MA: MIT Press.

Kosslyn, S. M., Alpert, N. M., Thompson, W. L., Maljkovic, V., Weise, S., Chabris, C. F., Hamilton, S. E., Rauch, S. L. and F. S., B. (1993). Visual mental imagery activates topographically organized visual cortex: PET investigations. *Journal of Cognitive Neuroscience*, 5, 263–87.

Kosslyn, S. M., Ball, T. M. and Reiser, B. J. (1978). Visual images preserve metric spatial information: Evidence from studies of image scanning. *Journal of Experimental Psychology: Human Perception and Performance*, 4, 47–60.

Kosslyn, S. M., Holtzman, J. D., Farah, M. J. and Gazzaniga, M. S. (1985). A computational analysis of mental image generation: Evidence from functional dissociations in split-brain patients. *Journal of Experimental Psychology: General*, 114, 311–41.

Kosslyn, S. M., Thompson, W. L., Kim, I. J. and Alpert, N. M. (1995). Topographical representations of mental images in primary visual cortex. *Nature*, 378, 496–8.

Kurbat, M. A. and Farah, M. J. (1998). Is the category-specific deficit for living things really spurious? *Journal of Cognitive Neuroscience*, 10, 355–61.

LaBerge, D. and Buchsbaum, M. S. (1990). Positron emission tomographic measurements of pulvinar activity during an attention task. *Journal of Neuroscience*, 10, 613–19.

Ladavas, E. (1987). Is the hemispatial deficit produced by right parietal lobe damage associated with retinal or gravitational coordinates? *Brain*, 110, 167–80.

Land, E. H. (1977). The retinex theory of color vision. *Scientific American*, 237, 108–28.

Land, E. H., Hubel, D. H., Livingstone, M. S., Perry, S. H. and Burns, M. M. (1983). Colour-generating interactions across the corpus callosum. *Nature*, 303, 616–18.

Landis, T., Graves, R., Benson, F. and Hebben, N. (1982). Visual recognition through kinaesthetic mediation. *Psychological Medicine*, 12, 515–31.

Landis, T., Regard, M. and Serrat, A. (1980). Iconic reading in a case of alexia without agraphia caused by brain tumor: A tachistoscopic study. *Brain and Language*, 11, 45–53.

Lange, J. (1936). Agrosien und Apraxien. In O. Bunke and O. Foerster (ed.), *Handbuch der Neurologie*. Berlin: Springer-Verlag.

Lawler, K. A. and Cowey, A. (1987). On the role of posterior parietal and prefrontal cortex in visuo-spatial perception and attention. *Experimental Brain Research*, 65, 695–8.

Le Bihan, D., Turner, R., Zeffiro, T. A., Cuenod, C. A., Jezzard, P. and Bonnerot, V. (1993). Activation of human primary visual cortex during visual recall:

A magnetic resonance imaging study. *Proceedings of the National Academy of Sciences of the United States of America*, 90, 11802–5.

Lecas, J. (1995). Prefrontal neurones sensitive to increased visual attention in the monkey. *NeuroReport*, 7, 305–9.

Lehky, S. R. and Sejnowski, T. J. (1988). Network model of shape-from-shading: Neural function arises from both receptive and projective fields. *Nature*, 333, 452–4.

Lempert, H. (1987). Effect of imaging sentences on concurrent unimanual performance. *Neuropsychologia*, 25, 835–9.

Lempert, H. (1989). Effect of imaging versus silently rehearsing sentences on concurrent unimanual tapping: A follow-up. *Neuropsychologia*, 27, 575–9.

Lettvin, J. Y., Maturana, R. R., McCulloch, W. S., and Pitts, W. H. (1959). What the frog's eye tells the frog's brain. *Proceedings of the Institute of Radio Engineering*, 47, 1940–51.

Levine, D. N. (1978). Prosopagnosia and visual object agnosia: A behavioral study. *Neuropsychologia*, 5, 341–65.

Levine, D. N. and Calvanio, R. (1978). A study of the visual defect in verbal alexia-simultanagonosia. *Brain*, 101, 65–81.

Levine, D. and Calvanio, R. (1989). Prosopagnosia: A defect in visual configural processing. *Brain and Cognition*, 10, 149–70.

Levine, D. N., Warach, J. and Farah, M. J. (1985). Two visual systems in mental imagery: Dissociation of What and Where in imagery disorders due to bilateral posterior cerebral lesions. *Neurology*, 35, 1010–18.

Levy, J., Trevarthen, C. and Sperry, R. (1972). Reception of bilateral chimeric figures following hemispheric deconnexion. *Brain*, 95, 61–78.

Lezak, M. (1983). *Neuropsychological Assessment* (2nd ed.). New York: Oxford University Press.

Linsker, R. (1986). From basic network principles to neural architecture: Emergence of orientation-selective cells. *Proceedings of the National Academy of Sciences*, 83, 8390–4.

Lissauer, H. (1890). Ein fall von seelenblindheit nebst einem Beitrage zur Theori derselben. *Archiv fur Psychiatrie und Nervenkrankheiten*, 21, 222–70.

Livingstone, M. S. and Hubel, D. H. (1988). Segregation of form, color, movement, and depth: Anatomy, physiology, and perception. *Science*, 240, 740–9.

Livingstone, M. S., Rosen, G. D., Drislane, F. W. and Galaburda, A. M. (1991). Physiological and anatomical evidence for a magnocellular defect in developmental dyslexia [published erratum appears in Proc Natl Acad Sci USA 1993 Mar 15; 90(6): 2556]. *Proceedings of the National Academy of Sciences of the United States of America*, 88, 7943–7.

Logothetis, N. K., Pauls, J., Bulthoff, H. H. and Poggio, T. (1994). View-dependent object recognition by monkeys. *Current Biology*, 4, 401–14.

Logothetis, N. K., Pauls, J. and Poggio, T. (1995). Shape representation in the inferior temporal cortex of monkeys. *Current Biology*, 5, 552–63.

Lovett, M. (1997). Developmental Reading Disorders. In T. E. Feinberg and M. J. Farah (eds), *Behavioral Neurology and Neuropsychology*. New York: McGraw-Hill.

Luck, S. J., Chelazzi, L., Hillyard, S. A. and Desimone, R. (1997). Neural mechanisms of spatial selective attention in areas V1, V2, and V4 of macaque visual cortex. *Journal of Neurophysiology*, 77, 24–42.

Luck, S. J., Fan, S. and Hillyard, S. A. (1993). Attention-related modulation of sensory-evoked brain activity in a visual search task. *Journal of Cognitive Neuroscience*, 5, 188–95.

Luck, S. J., Hillyard, S. A., Mouloua, M., Woldorff, M. G., Clark, V. P. and Hawkins, H. L. (1994). Effects of spatial cueing on luminance detectability: Psychophysical and electrophysiological evidence for early selection. *Journal of Experimental Psychology: Human Percepton and Performance*, 20, 887–904.

Lueck, C. J., Zeki, S., Friston, K. J., Deiber, M. P., Cope, P., Cunningham, V. J., Lammertsma, A. A., Kennard, C. and Frackowiak, R. S. (1989). The colour centre in the cerebral cortex of man. *Nature*, 340, 386–9.

Luzzatti, C. and Davidoff, J. (1994). Impaired retrieval of object-colour knowledge with preserved colour naming. *Neuropsychologia*, 32, 933–50.

Maffei, L. and Fiorentini, A. (1972). Retinogeniculate convergence and analysis of contrast. *Journal of Neurophysiology*, 35, 65–72.

Mangun, G. R., Buonocore, M. H., Girelli, M. and Jha, A. P. (1998). ERP and fMRI measures of visual spatial selective attention. *Human Brain Mapping*, 6, 383–9.

Mangun, G. R. and Hillyard, S. A. (1995). Attention: Mechanisms and models. In M. D. Rugg and M. G. H. Coles (eds), *Electrophysiology of Mind: Event-Related Potentials and Cognition*. Oxford: Oxford University Press, 40–85.

Marcel, A. J. (1983). Conscious and unconscious perception: Experiments on visual masking and word recognition. *Cognitive Psychology*, 15, 197–237.

Marr, D. (1982). *Vision*. San Francisco: Freeman.

Marr, D. and Nishihara, H. K. (1978). Representation and recognition of the spatial organization of three-dimensional shapes. *Proceedings of the Royal Society of London – Series B: Biological Sciences*, B200, 269–94.

Marshall, J. C. and Halligan, P. W. (1988). Blindsight and insight in visuo-spatial neglect. *Nature*, 336, 766–7.

Martin, A. and Fedio, P. (1983). Word production and comprehension in Alzheimer's Disease: The breakdown of semantic knowledge. *Brain and Language*, 19, 124–41.

Martinez, A., Anllo-Vento, L., Sereno, M. I., Frank, L. R., Buxton, R. B., Dubowitz, D. J., Wong, E. C., Hinrichs, H., Heinze, H. J., and Hillyard, S. A. (1999). Involvement of striate and extrastriate visual cortical areas in spatial attention. *Nature Neuroscience*, 2, 364–9.

Marzi, C. A., Tassinari, C., Aglioti, S. and Lutzemberger, L. (1986). Spatial summation across the vertical meridian in hemianopics: A test of blindsight. *Neuropsychologia*, 24, 749–58.

Mattingley, J. B., Driver, J., Beschin, N. and Robertson, I. H. (1997). Attentional competition between modalities: Extinction between touch and vision after right hemisphere damage. *Neuropsychologia*, 35, 867–80.

Maunsell, J. H. R., Nealey, T. A. and DePriest, D. D. (1990). Magnocellular and parvocellular contributions to responses in the middle temporal visual area (MT) of the macaque monkey. *Journal of Neuroscience*, 10, 3323–34.

McCarthy, G., Puce, A., Gore, J. C. and Allison, T. (1997). Face-specific processing in human fusiform gyrus. *Journal of Cognitive Neuroscience*, 9, 605–10.

McClelland, J. L. and Rumelhart, D. E. (1981). An interactive activation model of context effects in letter perception: Part 1. An account of basic findings. *Psychological Review*, 88, 345–407.

McGlinchey-Berroth, R., Milberg, W. P., Verfaellie, M., Alexander, M. and Kilduff, P. T. (1993). Semantic processing in the neglected visual field: Evidence from a lexical decision task. *Cognitive Neuropsychology*, 10, 79–108.

McMullen, P. A. and Farah, M. J. (1991). Object-centered representations in the recognition of naturalistic line drawings. *Psychological Science*, 2, 275–7.

McNeil, J. E. and Warrington, E. K. (1993). Prosopagnosia: A face-specific disorder. *Quarterly Journal of Experimental Psychology: Human Experimental Psychology*, 46A, 1–10.

Meador, K. J., Loring, D. W., Bowers, D. and Heilman, K. M. (1987). Remote memory and neglect syndrome. *Neurology*, 37, 522–6.

Meadows, J. C. (1974). The anatomical basis of prosopagnosia. *Journal of Neurology, Neurosurgery, and Psychiatry*, 37, 489–501.

Mellet, E., Tzourio, N., Denis, M. and Mazoyer, B. (1995). A Positron Emission Tomography study of visual and mental spatial exploration. *Journal of Cognitive Neuroscience*, 7, 433–45.

Mellet, E., Tzourio, N., Crivello, F., Joliot, M., Denis, M. and Mazoyer, B. (1996). Functional anatomy of spatial mental imagery generated from verbal instructions. *Journal of Neuroscience*, 16, 6504–12.

Merigan, W. H., Bryne, C. E. and Maunsell, J. H. R. (1991). Does primate motion perception depend on the magnocellular pathway? *Journal of Neuroscience*, 11, 3422–9.

Merigan, W. H. and Maunsell, J. H. R. (1993). How parallel are the primate visual pathways? *Annual Review of Neuroscience*, 16, 369–402.

Merzenich, M. M. (1987). Dynamic neocortical processes and the origins of higher brain functions. In J. P. Changeux and M. Konishi (eds), *Neural and Molecular Bases of Learning*. Chichester, England: John Wiley and Sons.

Mesulam, M. M. (1981). A cortical network for directed attention and unilateral neglect. *Annals of Neurology*, 10, 309–25.

Miller, K. D., Keller, J. B. and Stryker, M. P. (1989). Ocular dominance column development: Analysis and simulation. *Science*, 245, 605–15.

Milner, A. D. (1997). Vision without knowledge. *Philosophical Transactions of the Royal Society of London – Series B: Biological Sciences*, 352, 1249–56.

Milner, A. D. and Goodale, M. A. (eds) (1995). *The Visual Brain in Action*. Oxford: Oxford Science Publications.

Milner, A. D., Perrett, D. I., Johnston, R. S., Benson, P. J., Jordan, T. R., Heeley, D. W., Bettucci, D., Mortara, F., Mutani, R., Terrazzi, E. and Davidson, D. L. W. (1991). Perception and action in visual form agnosia. *Brain*, 114, 405–28.

Mishkin, M. (1954). Visual discrimination performance following partial ablations of the temporal lobe: II. Ventral surface vs. hippocampus. *Journal of Comparative and Physiological Psychology*, 47, 187–93.

Mishkin, M. (1966). Visual mechanisms beyond the striate cortex. In R. Russel (ed.), *Frontiers in Physiological Psychology*. New York: Academic Press.

Mishkin, M. and Pribram, K. H. (1954). Visual discrimination performance following partial ablations of the temporal lobe: I. ventral vs. lateral. *Journal of Comparative and Physiological Psychology*, 47, 14–20.

Mishkin, M., Ungerleider, L. G. and Macko, K. A. (1983). Object vision and spatial vision: Two cortical pathways. *Trends in Neurosciences*, 6, 414–17.

Miyashita, Y., Date, A. and Okuno, H. (1993). Configurational encoding of complex visual forms by single neurons of monkey temporal cortex. *Neuropsychologia*, 31, 1119–31.

Moran, J. and Desimone, R. (1985). Selective attention gates visual processing in extrastriate cortex. *Science*, 229, 782–4.

Moscovitch, M., Winocur, G. and Behrmann, M. (1997). What is special about face recognition? Nineteen experiments on a person with visual object agnosia and dyslexia but normal face recognition. *Journal of Cognitive Neuroscience*, 9, 555–604.

Motter, B. C. (1993). Focal attention produces spatially selective processing in visual cortical areas V1, V2, and V4 in the presence of competing stimuli. *Journal of Neurophysiology*, 70, 909–19.

Movshon, J. A., Adelson, E. H., Gizzi, M. S. and Newsome, W. T. (1985). The analysis of moving visual patterns. In C. Chagas, R. Gattass, and C. Gross (eds), *Pattern Recognition Mechanisms*. New York: Springer-Verlag.

Mozer, M. C. (submitted). Frames of reference in unilateral neglect and visual perception: A Computational perspective.

Nagel. T. (1974). What is it like to be a bat? *Philosophical Review*, 83, 435–50.

Nealey, T. A. and Maunsell, J. H. R. (1994). Magnocellular and parvocellular contributions to the responses of neurons in macaque striate cortex. *Journal of Neuroscience*, 14, 2069–79.

Neisser, U. (1976). *Cognition and Reality*. San Francisco: Freeman.

Newcombe, F. and Russell, W. (1969). Dissociated visual perceptual and spatial deficits in focal lesions of the right hemisphere. *Journal of Neurology, Neurosurgery, and Psychiatry*, 32, 73–81.

Newsome, W. T. and Pare, E. B. (1988). A selective impairment of motion perception following lesions of the middle temporal visual area (MT). *Journal of Neuroscience*, 8, 2201–11.

Newsome, W. T., Shadlen, M. N., Zohary, E., Britten, K. H. and Movshon, J. A. (1995). Visual motion: Linking neuronal activity to psychophysical performance. In M. S. Gazzaniga (ed.), *The Cognitive Neurosciences*. Cambridge, MA: MIT Press.

Nobre, A. C., Sebestyen, G. N., Gitelman, D. R., Mesulam, M. M., Frackowiak, R. S. J. and Frith, C. D. (1997). Functional localization of the system for visuospatial attention using positron emission tomography. *Brain*, 120, 515–33.

O'Reilly, R. C. and Farah, M. J. (1999). Simulation and explanation in neuropsychology and beyond. *Cognitive Neuropsychology*, 16, 1–48.

Ogden, J. A. (1985). Contralesional neglect of constructed visual images in right and left brain-damaged patients. *Neuropsychologia*, 23, 273–7.

Paivio, A. (1971). *Imagery and Verbal Processes*. New York: Holt, Rinehart, and Winston.

Pallis, C. A. (1955). Impaired identification of faces and places with agnosia for colors. *Journal of Neurology, Neurosurgery and Psychiatry*, 18, 218–24.

Pashler, H. (1998). *Attention*. East Sussex, UK: Psychology Press.

Patterson, K. E. and Hodges, J. (1992). Deterioration of word meaning: Implications for reading. *Neuropsychologia*, 30, 1025–40.

Patterson, K. E. and Kay, J. (1982). Letter-by-letter reading: Psychological descriptions of a neurological syndrome. Quarterly *Journal of Experimental Psychology: Human Experimental Psychology*, 34A, 411–41.

Pentland, A. P. (1986). Perceptual organization and the representation of natural form. *Artificial Intelligence*, 28, 293–331.

Perrett, D. I., Mistlin, A. J. and Chitty, A. J. (1987). Visual neurones responsive to faces. *Trends in Neuroscience*, 10, 358–64.

Perrett, D. I., Oram, M. W., Harries, M. H., Bevan, R., Hietanen, J. K., Benson, P. J. and Thomas, S. (1991). Viewer-centred and object-centred coding of heads in the macaque temporal cortex. *Experimental Brain Research*, 86, 159–73.

Perrett, D. I., Smith, P. A., Potter, D. D., Mistlin, A. J., Head, A. S., Milner, A. D. and Jeeves, M. A. (1985). Visual cells in the temporal cortex sensitive to face view and gaze direction. *Proceedings of the Royal Society of London, Series B*, 223, 293–317.

Petersen, S. E., Fox, P. T., Snyder, A. Z. and Raichle, M. E. (1990). Activation of extrastriate and frontal cortical areas by visual words and word-like stimuli. *Science*, 249, 1041–4.

Pizzamiglio, L., Cappa, S., Vallar, G., Zoccolotti, P., Bottini, G., Ciurli, P., Guariglia, C. and Antonucci, G. (1989). Visual neglect for far and near extra-personal space in humans. *Cortex*, 24, 471–7.

Pizzamiglio, L., Vallar, G. and Doricchi, F. (1997). Gravitational inputs modulate visuospatial neglect. *Experimental Brain Research*, 117, 341–5.

Plaut, D. C. and Farah, M. J. (1990). Visual object representation: Interpreting neurophysiological data within a computational framework. *Journal of Cognitive Neuroscience*, 2, 320–43.

Pohl, W. (1973). Dissociation of spatial discrimination deficits following frontal and parietal lesions in monkeys. *Journal of Comparative and Physiological Psychology*, 82, 227–39.

Polk, T. A. and Farah, M. J. (1995a). Brain localization for arbitrary stimulus categories: A simple account based on Hebbian learning. *Proceedings of the National Academy of Sciences*, 92, 12370–3.

Polk, T. A. and Farah, M. J. (1995b). Late experience alters vision. *Nature*, 376, 648–9.

Polk, T. A. and Farah, M. J. (1997). A simple co-occurence account for the development of abstract letter identities. *Neural Computation*, 9, 1277–89.

Polk, T. A. and Farah, M. J. (1998). The neural development and organization of letter recognition: Evidence from functional neuroimaging, computational modeling, and behavioral studies. *Proceedings of the National Academy of Sciences*, 95, 847–52.

Poppel, E., Held, R. and Frost, D. (1973). Letter: Residual visual function after brain wounds involving the central visual pathways in man. *Nature*, 243, 295–6.

Posner, M. I. (1980). Orienting of attention. *Quarterly Journal of Experimental Psychology*, 32, 3–25.

Posner, M. I., Inhoff, A. W., Freidrich, F. J. and Cohen, A. (1987). Isolating attentional systems: A cognitive-anatomical analysis. *Psychobiology*, 15, 107–21.

Posner, M. I. and Presti, D. (1987). Selective attention and cognitive control. *Trends in Neurosciences*, 10, 13–17.

Posner, M. I., Walker, J. A., Friedrich, F. J. and Rafal, R. D. (1984). Effects of parietal lobe injury on covert orienting of visual attention. *Journal of Neuroscience*, 4, 1863–74.

Potzl, O. (1928). *Die Aphasielehre vom Standpunkte der Kliniscen Psychitrie*. Leipzig: FranzDeudicte.

Pribram, K. H. (1954). Toward a science of neuropsychology: Method and data. In R. A. Patton (ed.), *Current Trends in Psychology and the Behavioral Sciences*. Pittsburgh: University of Pittsburgh Press.

Price, C. J., Wise, R. J. F., Watson, J. B. G., Patterson, K., Howard, D. and Frackowiak, R. S. J. (1994). Brain activity during reading: The effects of exposure duration and task. *Brain*, 117, 1255–69.

Pylyshyn, Z. W. (1973). What the mind's eye tells the mind's brain: A critique of mental imagery. *Psychological Bulletin*, 80, 1–24.

Pylyshyn, Z. W. (1981). The imagery debate: Analogue media versus tacit knowledge. *Psychological Review*, 88, 16–45.

Rafal, R. (1997). Hemispatial neglect: Cognitive neuropsychological aspects. In T. E. Feinberg and M. J. Farah (eds), *Behavioral Neurology and Neuropsychology*. New York: McGraw-Hill.

Rafal, R., Smith, J., Krantz, J., Cohen, A. and Brennan, C. (1990). Extrageniculate vision in hemianopic humans: Saccade inhibition by signals in the blind field. *Science*, 250, 118–21.

Rapp, B. C. and Caramazza, A. (1991). Spatially determined deficits in letter and word processing. *Cognitive Neuropsychology*, 8, 275–311.

Ratcliff, G. and Newcombe, F. (1982). Object recognition: Some deductions from the clinical evidence. In A. W. Ellis (ed.), *Normality and Pathology in Cognitive Functions*. New York: Academic Press.

Reicher, G. M. (1969). Perceptual recognition as a function of meaningfulness of stimulus material. *Journal of Experimental Psychology*, 81, 275–80.

Reid, R. C. (1999). Vision. In M. J. Zigmond, F. E. Bloom, S. C. Landis, J. L. Roberts, and L. R. Squire (eds), *Fundamental Neuroscience*. San Diego: Academic Press.

Reuter-Lorenz, P. A. and Brunn, J. L. (1990). A prelexical basis for letter-by-letter reading: A case study. *Cognitive Neuropsychology*, 7, 1–20.

Rhodes, G., Carey, S., Byatt, G. and Proffitt, F. (1998). Coding spatial variations in faces and simple shapes: a test of two models. *Vision Research*, 38, 2307–21.

Richmond, B. J. and Sato, T. (1987). Enhancement of inferior temporal neurons during visual discrimination. *Journal of Neurophysiology*, 58, 1292.

Riddoch, M. J. (ed.) (1991). Special issue of *Cognitive Neuropsychology* "Neglect and the peripheral dyslexias: Part 2", Vol. 8.

Riddoch, M. J. and Humphreys, G. W. (1987). A case of integrative visual agnosia. *Brain*, 110, 1431–62.

Riddoch, M. J., Humphreys, G. W., Luckhurst, L., Burroughs, E. and Bateman, A. (1995). Paradoxical neglect: Spatial representations, hemisphere-specific activation, and spatial cueing. *Cognitive Neuropsychology*, 12, 569–604.

Rizzolatti, G. and Berti, A. (1993). Neural mechanisms of spatial neglect. In I. H. Robertson and J. C. Marshall (eds), *Uniltaral Neglect: Clinical and Experimental Studies*. Hillsdale, NJ: Lawrence Erlbaum Publishers.

Rizzolatti, G., Gentilucci, M. and Matelli, M. (1985). Selective spatial attention: One center, one circuit, or many circuits? In M. Posner and O. Marin (eds), *Attention and Performance X*. Hillsdale, NJ: Lawrence Erlbaum Associates.

Robertson, L. C. and Lamb, M. R. (1991). Neuropsychological contributions to theories of part/whole organization. *Cognitive Psychology*, 23, 299–330.

Robertson, I. H. (1993). The relationship between lateralised and non-lateralised attentional deficits in unilateral neglect. In I. H. Robertson and J. C. Marshall (eds), *Unilateral Neglect: Clinical and Experimental Studies*. Hillsdale, NJ: Lawrence Erlbaum Publishers.

Rock, I. and DiVita, J. (1987). A case of viewer-centered object perception. *Cognitive Psychology*, 19, 280–93.

Rock, I., DiVita, J. and Barbeito, R. (1981). The effect on form perception of change of orientation in the third dimension. *Journal of Experimental Psychology: Human Perception and Performance*, 7, 719–32.

Roland, P. E., Eriksson, L., Stone-Elander, S. and Widen, L. (1987). Does mental activity change the oxidative metabolism of the brain? *The Journal of Neuroscience*, 7, 2373–89.

Roland, P. E. and Friberg, L. (1985). Localization of cortical areas activated by thinking. *Journal of Neurophysiology*, 53, 1219–43.

Roland, P. E. and Gulyas, B. (1994). Visual imagery and visual representation. *Trends in Neurosciences*, 17, 281–7; 294–7.

Rolls, E. T., Judge, S. J. and Sanghera, M. K. (1977). Activity of neurons in the inferotemporal cortex of the alert monkey. *Brain Research*, 130, 229–38.

Rosch, E., Mervis, C. B., Gray, W., Johnson, D., and Boyes-Braem, P. (1976). Basic Objects in natural categories. *Cognitive Psychology*, 8, 382–429.

Rosen, A. C., Rao, S. M., Caffarra, P., Scaglioni, A., Bobholz, J. A., Woodley, S. J., Hammeke, T. A., Cunningham, J. M., Prieto, T. E., and Binder, J. R. (1999). Neural basis of endogenous and exogenous spatial orienting: A functional MRI study. *Journal of Cognitive Neuroscience*, 11, 135–52.

Rubens, A. B. and Benson, D. F. (1971). Associative visual agnosia. *Archives of Neurology*, 24, 305–16.

Ryle, G. (1949). *The Concept of Mind*. London: Hutchison and Co., Ltd.

Sacks, O. and Wasserman, R. (1987). The case of the colorblind painter. *New York Review of Books*, 25–34.

Saffran, E. M. and Coslett, H. B. (1998). Implicit vs. letter-by-letter reading in pure alexia: A tale of two systems. *Cognitive Neuropsychology*, 15, 141–65.

Saffran, E. M. and Schwartz, M. F. (1994). Of cabbages and things: Semantic memory from a neurological perspective. In C. Umilta and M. Moscovitch (eds), *Conscious and Nonconscious Information Processing: Attention and Performance XV*. Cambridge, MA: MIT Press.

Salzman, C. D., Murasugi, C. M., Britten, K. H. and Newsome, W. T. (1992). Microstimulation in visual area MT: Effects on direction discrimination performance. *Journal of Neuroscience*, 12, 2331–55.

Samuelsson, H., Hjelmquist, E. K., Jensen, C., Ekholm, S. and Blomstrand, C. (1998). Nonlateralized attentional deficits: an important component behind persisting visuospatial neglect? *Journal of Clinical and Experimental Neuropsychology*, 20, 73–88.

Sary, G., Vogel, R. and Orban, G. (1993). Cue-invariant shape selectivity of Macaque inferior temporal neurons. *Science*, 260, 995–7.

Sato, T. (1988). Effects of attention and stimulus interaction on visual responses of inferior temporal neurons in macaque. *Journal of Neurophysiology*, 60, 344–64.

Sato, T., Kawamura, T. and Iwai, E. (1980). Responsiveness of inferotemporal single units to visual pattern stimuli in monkeys performing discrimination. *Experimental Brain Research*, 38, 313–19.

Schacter, D. L., McAndrews, M. P. and Moscovitch, M. (1988). Access to consciousness: Dissociations between implicit and explicit knowledge in neuropsychological syndromes. In L. Weiskrantz (ed.), *Thought Without Language*. Oxford: Oxford University Press.

Schein, S. J. and Desimone, R. (1990). Spectral properties of V4 neurons in the macaque. *Journal of Neuroscience*, 10, 3369–89.

Schiller, P. H. (1993). The effects of V4 and middle temporal (MT) area lesions on visual performance in the rhesus monkey. *Visual Neuroscience*, 10, 717–46.

Schiller, P. H. and Koerner, F. (1971). Discharge characteristics of single units in superior colliculus of the alert rhesus monkey. *Journal of Neurophysiology*, 34, 920–36.

Schiller, P. H. and Logothetis, N. K. (1990). The color-opponent and broadband channels of the primate visual system. *Trends in Neurosciences*, 13, 392–8.

Schindler, I. and Kerkhoff, G. (1997). Head and trunk orientation modulate visual neglect. *Neuroreport*, 8, 2681–5.

Schneider, G. E. (1969). Two visual systems: Brain mechanisms for localization and discrimination are dissociated by tectal and cortical lesions. *Science*, 163, 895–902.

Schneider, W. and Shiffrin, R. M. (1977). Controlled and automatic human information processing: I. Detection, search and attention. *Psychological Review*, 84, 1–66.

Seacord, L., Gross, C. G. and Mishkin, M. (1979). Role of inferior temporal cortex in interhemispheric transfer. *Brain Research*, 167, 259–72.

Sekuler, E. B. and Behrmann, M. (1996). Perceptual cues in pure alexia. *Cognitive Neuropsychology*, 13, 941–74.

Sereno, A. B. and Maunsell, J. H. (1998). Shape selectivity in primate lateral intraparietal cortex [see comments]. *Nature*, 395, 500–3.

Sergent, J. (1982). About face: Left-hemisphere involvement in processing physiognomies. *Journal of Experimental Psychology: Human Perception and Performance*, 8, 1–14.

Sergent, J. (1990). The neuropsychology of visual image generation: Data, method, and theory. *Brain and Cognition*, 13, 98–129.

Sergent, J. and Corballis, M. C. (1990). Generation of multipart images in the disconnected cerebral hemispheres. *Bulletin of the Psychonomic Society*, 28, 309–11.

Sergent, J., Ohta, S. and MacDonald, B. (1992). Functional neuroanatomy of face and object processing. *Brain*, 115, 15–36.

Shallice, T. (1984). More functionally isolable subsystems but fewer "modules"? *Cognition*, 17, 243–52.

Shallice, T. and Saffran, E. (1986). Lexical processing in the absence of explicit word identification: Evidence from a letter-by-letter reader. *Cognitive Neuropsychology*, 3, 429–58.

Shapley, R. (1995). Parallel neural pathways and visual function. In M. S. Gazzaniga (ed.), *The Cognitive Neurosciences*. Cambridge, MA: MIT Press.

Shepard, R. N. (1978). The mental image. *American Psychologist*, 33, 125–37.

Sheth, B. R., Sharma, J., Rao, S. C., and Sur, M. (1996). Orientation maps of subjective contours in visual cortex. *Science*, 274, 2110–15.

Shulman, G. L., Corbetta, M., Buckner, R. L., Raichle, M. E., Fiez, J. A., Miezin, F. M., and Petersen, S. E. (1997). Top-down modulation of early sensory cortex. *Cerebral Cortex*, 7, 193–206.

Shulman, G. L., Remington, R. W. and McLean, J. P. (1979). Moving attention through visual space. *Journal of Experimental Psychology: Human Perception and Performance*, 5, 522–6.

Shuren, J. E., Greer, D. and Heilman, K. M. (1996). The use of hemi-imagery for studying brain asymmetries in image generation. *Neuropsychologia*, 34(6), 491–2.

Shuttleworth, E. C., Syring, V. and Allen, N. (1982). Further observations on the nature of prosopagnosia. *Brain and Cognition*, 1, 307–22.

Sieroff, E. and Posner, M. I. (1988). Cueing spatial attention during processing of words and letters strings in normals. *Cognitive Neuropsychology*, 5, 451–72.

Singer, W. (1999). Time as coding space? *Current Opinion in Neurobiology*, 9, 189–94.

Singer, W. and Gray, C. M. (1995). Visual feature integration and the temporal correlation hypothesis. *Annual Review of Neuroscience*, 18, 555–86.

Sitton, M., Mozer, M. C. and Farah, M. J. (in press). Superadditive effects of multiple lesions in a connectionist architecture: Implications for the neuropsychology of optic aphasia.

Somers, D. C., Dale, A. M., Seiffert, A. E. and Tootell, R. B. (1999). Functional MRI reveals spatially specific attentional modulation in human primary visual cortex. *Proceedings of the National Academy of Sciences of the United States of America*, 96, 1663–8.

Spillmann, L. and Werner, J. S. (1996). Long-range interactions in visual perception. *Trends in Neurosciences*, 19, 428–34.

Spitzer, H., Desimone, R. and Moran, J. (1988). Increased attention enhances both behavioral and neuronal performance. *Science*, 240, 338–40.

Squire, L. (1992). Memory and the hippocampus: A synthesis of findings from rats, monkeys and humans. *Psychological Review*, 99, 195–231.

Stangalino, C., Semenza, C. and Mondoni, S. (1995). Generating visual mental images: Deficit after brain damage. *Neuropsychologia*, 33, 1473–83.

Sternberg, S. (1969). The discovery of processing stages: Extensions of Donders' method. *Acta Psychologica*, 30, 276–315.

Stoerig, P. and Cowey, A. (1990). Wavelength sensitivity in blindsight. *Nature*, 342, 916–18.

Stoerig, P. and Cowey, A. (1997). Blindsight in man and monkey. *Brain*, 120, 535–59.

Stoerig, P., Kleinschmidt, A. and Frahm, J. (1998). No visual responses in denervated V1: high-resolution functional magnetic resonance imaging of a blindsight patient. *Neuroreport*, 9, 21–5.

Tanaka, J. W. and Farah, M. J. (1991). Second-order relational properties and the inversion effect: Testing a theory of face perception. *Perception and Psychophysics*, 50, 367–72.

Tanaka, J. W. and Farah, M. J. (1993). Parts and wholes in face recognition. *Quarterly Journal of Experimental Psychology: Human Experimental Psychology*, 46A, 225–45.

Tanaka, J. W. and Sengco, J. A. (1997). Features and their configuration in face recognition. *Memory and Cognition*, 25, 583–92.

Tanaka, J. W. and Taylor, M. (1991). Object categories and expertise: Is the basic level in the eye of the beholder? *Cognitive Psychology*, 23, 457–82.

Tanaka, K. (1996). Inferotemporal cortex and object vision. *Annual Review of Neuroscience*, 19, 109–39.

Tanaka, K., Saito, H. A., Fukada, Y. and Moriya, M. (1991). Coding visual images of objects in the inferotemporal cortex of the macaque monkey. *Journal of Neurophysiology*, 66, 170–89.

Tarr, M. J. (1995). Rotating objects to recognize them: A case study on the role of viewpoint dependency in the recognition of three-dimensional shapes. *Psychological Bulletin and Review*, 2, 55–82.

Tarr, M. J. and Pinker, S. (1989). Mental rotation and orientation dependence in shape recognition. *Cognitive Psychology*, 21, 233–82.

Tarr, M. J. and Pinker, S. (1990). When does human object recognition use a viewer-centered reference frame? *Psychological Science*, 1, 253–6.

Taylor, A. M. and Warrington, E. K. (1971). Visual agnosia: A single case report. *Cortex*, 7, 152–61.

Teuber, H. L. (1968). Alteration of perception and memory in man. In L. Weiskrantz (ed.), *Analysis of Behavioral Change*. New York: Harper and Row.

Thompson-Schill, S. L., Aguirre, G. K., D'Esposito, M. and Farah, M. J. (in press). A neural basis for category and modality specificity of semantic knowledge. *Neuropsychologia*.

Tipper, S. P. (1985). The negative priming effect: Inhibitory effects of ignored primes. *Quarterly Journal of Experimental Psychology*, 37A, 571–90.

Tippett, L. J. (1992). The generation of visual images: A review of neuropsychological research and theory. *Psychological Bulletin*, 112, 415–32.

Tippett, L. J. and Farah, M. J. (1994). A computational model of naming in Alzheimer's Disease: Unitary or multiple impairments? *Neuropsychology*, 8, 3–13.

Tippett, L. J., Miller, L. and Farah, M. J. (in press). Prosopamnesia: A selective new learning impairment for faces.

Tootell, R. B., Silverman, M. S., Switkes, E. and Valois, R. L. (1982). Deoxyglucose analysis of retinotopic organization in primate striate cortex. *Science*, 218, 902–4.

Tovee, M. J. and Rolls, E. T. (1992). Oscillatory activity is not evident in the primate temporal visual cortex with static stimuli. *NeuroReport*, 3, 369–72.

Tranel, D. (1997). Disorders of color processing (Perception, imagery, recognition, and naming). In T. E. Feinberg and M. J. Farah (ed.), *Behavioral Neurology and Neuropsychology*. New York: McGraw-Hill.

Tranel, D. and Damasio, A. R. (1988). Non-conscious face recognition in patients with face agnosia. *Behavioural Brain Research*, 30, 235–49.

Treisman, A. and Gelade, G. (1980). A feature-integration theory of attention. *Cognitive Psychology*, 12, 97–136.

Treue, S. and Maunsell, J. H. R. (1996). Attentional modulation of visual motion processing in cortical areas MT and MST. *Nature*, 382, 539–41.

Trojano, L. and Grossi, D. (1994). A critical review of mental imagery defects. *Brain and Cognition*, 24, 213–43.

Uhl, F., Goldenberg, G., Lang, W., Lindinger, G., Steiner, M. and Deecke, L. (1990). Cerebral correlates of imagining colours, faces and a map – II. Negative cortical DC potentials. *Neuropsychologia*, 28, 81–93.

Ullman, S. (1989). Aligning pictorial descriptions: An approach to object recognition. *Cognition*, 32, 193–254.

Umilta, C. (1995). Domain-specific forms of neglect. *Journal of Clinical and Experimental Neuropsychology*, 17, 209–19.

Ungerleider, L. G. and Mishkin, M. (1982). Two cortical visual systems. In D. J. Ingle, M. A. Goodale, and R. J. W. Mansfield (eds), *Analysis of Visual Behavior*. Cambridge, MA: MIT Press.

Valentine, T. (1988). Upside-down faces: A review of the effect of inversion upon face recognition. *British Journal of Psychology*, 79, 471–91.

Vallar, G. (1993). The anatomical basis of spatial hemineglect in humans. In I. H. Robertson and J. C. Marshall (eds), *Unilateral Neglect: Clinical and Experimental Studies*. Hillsdale, NJ: Lawrence Erlbaum Publishers.

Vallar, G. and Perani, D. (1986). The anatomy of unilateral neglect after right hemisphere stroke lesions: A clinical CT scan correlation study in man. *Neuropsychologia*, 24, 609–22.

Vallar, G., Rusconi, M. L., Bignamini, L., Geminiani, G. and Perani, D. (1994). Anatomical correlates of visual and tactile extinction in humans: a clinical CT scan study. *Journal of Neurology, Neurosurgery and Psychiatry*, 57, 464–70.

Vandenberghe, R., Dupont, P., De Bruyn, B., Bormans, G., Michiels, J., Mortelmans, L. and Orban, G. A. (1996). The influence of stimulus location on the brain activation pattern in detection and orientation discrimination: A PET study of visual attention. *Brain*, 119, 1263–76.

Vecera, S. P. and Farah, M. J. (1994). Does visual attention select objects or locations? *Journal of Experimental Psychology: General*, 123, 146–60.

Vecera, S. P. and Farah, M. J. (1997). Is image segmentation a bottom-up or interactive process? *Perception and Psychophysics*, 59, 1280–96.

Vidyasagar, T. R. (1998). Gating of neuronal responses in macaque primary visual cortex by an attentional spotlight. *Neuroreport*, 9, 1947–52.

Volpe, B. T., LeDoux, J. E. and Gazzangia, M. S. (1979). Information processing of visual stimuli in an extinguished visual field. *Nature*, 282, 722–4.

von der Heydt, R. (1995). Form analysis in visual cortex. In M. S. Gazzaniga (ed.), *The Cognitive Neurosciences*. Cambridge, MA: MIT Press.

von der Heydt, R., Peterhans, E. and Baumgartner, G. (1984). Illusory contours and cortical neuron responses. *Science*, 224, 1260–2.

von der Malsburg, C. (1985). Nervous structures with dynamical links. *Ber. Bunsenges. Phys. Chem.*, 89, 703–10.

Vuilleumier, P., Valenza, N., Mayer, E., Reverdin, A. and Landis, T. (1998). Near and far visual space in unilateral neglect. *Annals of Neurology*, 43, 406–10.

Wallace, M. A. and Farah, M. J. (1992). Savings in relearning face-name associations as evidence for covert recognition in prosopagnosia. *Journal of Cognitive Neuroscience*, 4, 150–4.

Wallis, G. and Rolls, E. T. (1997). Invariant face and object recognition in the visual system. *Progress in Neurobiology*, 51, 167–94.

Waltz, D. (1975). Understanding of line drawings and scenes with shadows. In P. Winston (ed.), *The Psychology of Computer Vision*. New York: McGraw-Hill.

Wapner, W., Judd, T. and Gardner, H. (1978). Visual agnosia in an artist. *Cortex*, 14, 343–64.

Warrington, E. K. (1985). Agnosia: The impairment of object recognition. In P. J. Vinken, G. W. Bruyn, and H. L. Klawans (eds), *Handbook of Clinical Neurology*. Amsterdam: Elsevier.

Warrington, E. K. and James, M. (1988). Visual apperceptive agnosia: A clinico-anatomical study of three cases. *Cortex*, 24, 13–32.

Warrington, E. K. and Shallice, T. (1980). Word-form dyslexia. *Brain*, 103, 99–112.

Warrington, E. K. and Shallice, T. (1984). Category specific semantic impairments. *Brain*, 107, 829–54.

Warrington, E. K. and Taylor, A. M. (1973). The contribution of the right parietal lobe to object recognition. *Cortex*, 9, 152–64.

Watanabe, T., Sasaki, Y., Miyauchi, S., Putz, B., Fujimaki, N., Nielsen, M., Takino, R. and Miyakawa, S. (1998). Attention-regulated activity in human primary visual cortex. *Journal of Neurophysiology*, 79, 2218–21.

Weintraub, S., Daffner, K. R., Ahern, G. L., Price, B. H. and Mesulam, M. M. (1996). Right sided hemispatial neglect and bilateral cerebral lesions. *Journal of Neurology, Neurosurgery and Psychiatry*, 60, 342–4.

Weiskrantz, L. (1986). *Blindsight: A Case Study and Implications*. Oxford: Oxford University Press.

Weiskrantz, L. (1990). Outlooks for blindsight: Explicit methodologies for implicit processes. *Proceedings of the Royal Society of London – Series B: Biological Sciences*, B239, 247–78.

Weiskrantz, L. and Saunders, R. C. (1984). Impairments of visual object transforms in monkeys. *Brain*, 107, 1033–72.

Weiskrantz, L., Warrington, E. K., Sanders, M. D. and Marshall, J. (1974). Visual capacity in the hemianopic visual field following a restricted occipital ablation. *Brain*, 97, 709–28.

Wheeler, D. D. (1970). Processes in word recognition. *Cognitive Psychology*, 1, 59–85.

Wolfe, J. M. (1998). Visual search. In H. Pashler (ed.), *Attention*. East Sussex, UK: Psychology Press.

Wong-Riley, M. (1979). Changes in the visual system of monocularly sutured or enucleated cats demonstrated with cytochrome oxidase histochemistry. *Brain Research*, 171, 11–28.

Wurtz, R. H. and Goldberg, M. E. (1972). The primate superior colliculus and the shift of visual attention. *Investigative Ophthalmology*, 11, 441–50.

Yamadori, A. (1980). Right unilateral dyscopia of letters in alexia without agraphia. *Neurology*, 30, 991–4.

Yamane, S., Kaji, S. and Kawano, K. (1988). What facial features activate face neurons in the inferotemporal corte of the monkey? *Experimental Brain Research*, 73, 209–14.

Young, A. W. and Burton, A. M. (1999). Simulating face recognition: Implications for modelling cognition. *Cognitive Neuropsychology*, 16, 49–72.

Young, A. W., de Haan, E. H., Newcombe, F. and Hay, D. C. (1990). Facial neglect. *Neuropsychologia*, 28, 391–415.

Young, A. W., Hellawell, D. and De Haan, E. H. F. (1988). Cross-domain semantic priming in normal subjects and a prosopagnosic patient. *Quarterly Journal of Experimental Psychology: Human Experimental Psychology*, 40A, 561–80.

Young, A. W., Hellawell, D. J. and Welch, J. (1992). Neglect and visual recognition. *Brain*, 115, 51–71.

Young, M. P. and Yamane, S. (1992). Sparse population coding of faces in the inferotemporal cortex. *Science*, 256, 1327–31.

Zeki, S. (1983). Colour coding in the cerebral cortex: The reaction of cells in monkey visual cortex to wavelengths and colours. *Neuroscience*, 9, 741–56.

Zeki, S. (1990). A century of cerebral achromatopsia. *Brain*, 113, 1721–77.

Zeki, S. (1993). *A Vision of the Brain*. Oxford: Blackwell Scientific Publications.

Zeki, S., Watson, J. D. G., Lueck, C. J., Friston, K., Kennard, C. and Frackowiak, R. S. (1991). A direct demonstration of functional specialization in human visual cortex. *Journal of Neuroscience*, 11, 641–9.

Zihl, J., von Cramon, D., Mai, N. and Schmid, C. H. (1991). Disturbance of movement vision after bilateral posterior brain damage. *Brain*, 114, 2235–52.

Zihl, J., von Cramon, D. and Mai, N. (1983). Selective disturbance of movement vision after bilateral brain damage. *Brain*, 106, 313–40.

Zipser, D. and Andersen, R. (1988). Back propagation programmed network that simulates response properties of a subset of posterior parietal neurons. *Nature*, 331, 679–84.

Subject Index

Author Index